THE FOURTH AGE OF

The Fourth Amendment is facing a crisis. New and emerging surveillance technologies allow government agents to track us wherever we go, to monitor our activities online and offline, and to gather massive amounts of information relating to our financial transactions, communications, and social contacts. In addition, traditional policing methods like stop and frisk have grown out of control, subjecting hundreds of thousands of innocent citizens to routine searches and seizures. In this work, David Gray uncovers the original meaning of the Fourth Amendment to reveal how its historical guarantees of collective security against threats of "unreasonable searches and seizures" can provide concrete solutions to the current crisis. This important work should be read by anyone concerned with the ongoing viability of one of our most important constitutional rights in an age of increasing government surveillance.

DAVID GRAY is a professor at the University of Maryland, Francis King Carey School of Law, where he teaches criminal law, criminal procedure, evidence, international criminal law, and jurisprudence. He has published dozens of articles in leading law reviews and is the coeditor of the *Cambridge Handbook of Surveillance Law*. Before his academic career, Professor Gray served as a judicial clerk and practiced white-collar criminal law at a leading law firm in Washington, DC.

THE FOURTH AMENDMENT IN AN AGE OF SURVEILLANCE

DAVID GRAY

University of Maryland School of Law

CAMBRIDGE
UNIVERSITY PRESS

CAMBRIDGE
UNIVERSITY PRESS

University Printing House, Cambridge CB2 8BS, United Kingdom

One Liberty Plaza, 20th Floor, New York, NY 10006, USA

477 Williamstown Road, Port Melbourne, VIC 3207, Australia

314-321, 3rd Floor, Plot 3, Splendor Forum, Jasola District Centre, New Delhi-110025, India

79 Anson Road, #06-04/06, Singapore 079906

Cambridge University Press is part of the University of Cambridge.

It furthers the University's mission by disseminating knowledge in the pursuit of education, learning and research at the highest international levels of excellence.

www.cambridge.org
Information on this title: www.cambridge.org/9781107133235
DOI: 10.1017/9781316459607

© David Gray 2017

This publication is in copyright. Subject to statutory exception and to the provisions of relevant collective licensing agreements, no reproduction of any part may take place without the written permission of Cambridge University Press.

First published 2017

A catalogue record for this publication is available from the British Library

Library of Congress Cataloging in Publication data
Names: Gray, David C., author.
Title: The Fourth Amendment in an age of surveillance / David Gray.
Description: New York : Cambridge University Press, 2017. | Includes bibliographical references and index.
Identifiers: LCCN 2017007123 | ISBN 9781107133235 (hardback)
Subjects: LCSH: Searches and seizures – United States. | United States. Constitution. 4th Amendment. | Electronic surveillance – United States. | BISAC: LAW / General.
Classification: LCC KF9630 .G67 2017 | DDC 345.73/0522–dc23
LC record available at https://lccn.loc.gov/2017007123

ISBN 978-1-107-13323-5 Hardback
ISBN 978-1-107-58978-0 Paperback

Cambridge University Press has no responsibility for the persistence or accuracy of URLs for external or third-party internet websites referred to in this publication, and does not guarantee that any content on such websites is, or will remain, accurate or appropriate.

For Stéphanie and Luc

CONTENTS

Acknowledgments   *page* viii
Table of Cases   x

Introduction: The Dangers of Surveillance   1
1 Our Age of Surveillance   23
2 The Fourth Amendment in the Twentieth Century   68
3 Some Competing Proposals   104
4 Fourth Amendment Remedies as Rights   134
5 Constitutional Remedies   190
6 The Fourth Amendment in an Age of Surveillance   249
Conclusion: Our Fourth Amendment Utopia   295

Index   301

ACKNOWLEDGMENTS

I am in debt to many people who contributed to this project in ways large and small. Although that list includes more people than I could hope to list here, a few deserve special attention:

I am forever grateful to Chris Anderson, Kiel Brennan-Marquez, Danielle Keats Citron, Stéphanie Gaillard, Caryl Gray, John Hecklinger, and Kevin Reger, all of whom read this manuscript with a careful eye.

At a critical stage, Judge Stephen Smith led a discussion of the work in this book at the Privacy Law Scholars Conference in Washington, DC.

Ronald Allen, Miriam Baer, Jack Balkin, Kevin Bankston, Steve Bellovin, Marc Blitz, Richard Boldt, Thomas Clancy, Julie Cohen, Thomas Crocker, Jennifer Daskal, Joshua Fairfield, Andrew Ferguson, Susan Freiwald, Barry Friedman, Brandon Garrett, Mark Graber, John Grant, James Grimmelmann, Michael Hayden, Deborah Hellman, Stephen Henderson, Leslie Henry, David Hoffman, Margaret Hu, Renée Hutchins, Orin Kerr, Jennifer Laurin, Arnold Loewy, Richard McAdams, Richard Myers, Brian Owsley, Frank Pasquale, Neil Richards, Laurent Sacharoff, Paul Schwartz, Christopher Slobogin, Peter Swire, David Super, Michael Van Alstine, Stephen Vladeck, and Russell Weaver provided insightful feedback on this project at different points along the way.

I am also in debt to those who commented on this work during presentations at Yale, Georgetown, Northwestern, and George Mason Universities, the Southeastern Association of Law Schools, The Law and Society Association, the Computers, Freedom, and Privacy Conference, the University of Maryland, New England Law School, Washington & Lee University, Texas Tech University, Elon University, the University of Bologna, the University of North Carolina, and the University of Georgia.

Susan McCarty and Michael Tennison spent countless hours cleaning up the manuscript and endnotes.

Frank Lancaster kept me afloat.

The W.P. Carey Foundation provided crucial financial support.

Deans Donald Tobin, Barbara Gontrum, and Maxwell Stearns at the University of Maryland, Francis King Carey School of Law, were supportive at every step along the way.

Matt Gallaway and Kristina Deusch at Cambridge were extremely patient and supportive and Allan Alphonse at Integra combed out every nit.

Luc Grayard took timely naps. Stéphanie Gaillard was always willing to listen as I talked things through.

Finally, I would like to thank my students. Their questions, challenges, and passion are a constant source of energy and inspiration.

TABLE OF CASES

Agnello v. United States
Berger v. New York
Boyd v. United States
Brown v. Mississippi
California Bankers Association v. Schulz
Carroll v. United States
Clapper v. Amnesty International
Davis v. United States
Devenpeck v. Alford
Elkins v. United States
Entick v. Carrington
Floyd v. City of New York
Go-Bart Importing Company v. United States
Goldman v. United States
Handschu v. Special Services Division
Huckle v. Money
Hudson v. Michigan
Katz v. United States
Kyllo v. United States
Mapp v. Ohio
Minnesota v. Carter
Miranda v. Arizona
Monell v. Department of Social Services of the City of New York
Money v. Leach
Olmstead v. United States
Palmieri v. Lynch
Paxton's Case
Rawlings v. Kentucky
Riley v. California
Silverthorne Lumber Company v. United States

Smith v. Maryland
State v. Andrews
Terry v. Ohio
United States v. Hoffa
United States v. Janis
United States v. Johnson
United States v. Jones
United States v. Karo
United States v. Knotts
United States v. Lefkowitz
United States v. Maynard
United States v. Miller
United States v. Payner
United States v. White
Virginia v. Moore
Weeks v. United States
Whren v. United States
Wilkes v. Wood
Wolf v. Colorado

INTRODUCTION

The Dangers of Surveillance

Pick your favorite fictional dystopia. Perhaps it's a movie, like *Terminator, Minority Report, The Hunger Games*, or the *Matrix* films. Perhaps it's Oceana from George Orwell's *1984*, Mordor from J.R.R. Tolkien's *Lord of the Rings* trilogy, The World State from Aldous Huxley's *Brave New World*, or the America foretold in Ray Bradbury's *Fahrenheit 451*. Chances are that your dystopia features a hegemon, whether an authoritarian ruler or omnipotent technology, who uses surveillance as a means to dominate and control. In Orwell's *1984*, Big Brother controlled the minds and souls of the citizens of Oceana by monitoring them through a network of two-way telescreens. In the *Lord of the Rings*, Sauron and his all-seeing eye "strove with great power to pierce all shadows of cloud, and earth, and flesh, and to see you: to pin you under its deadly gaze, naked, immovable."[1] Regardless of the particulars, these fictional accounts share an apocalyptic vision of the world where freedom of thought and action is imperiled by the unremitting stare of authority.

Life imitates art. We therefore find oppressive surveillance as a common feature of real-life dystopias. Take the German Democratic Republic during the Cold War. For the better part of four decades, the Ministerium für Staatssicherheit, known colloquially as the Stasi, projected power in the East German state through a vast network of citizen informants, whose information about neighbors, colleagues, and family members was used to compile dossiers on millions of citizens. Hardly unique behind the Iron Curtain, most Soviet Bloc countries had parallel state security agencies, such as the Committee for State Security (KGB) in the Soviet Union and the State Security Service of Yugoslavia. Like the Stasi, these notorious agencies pursued social control by subjecting their citizens to programs of broad and invasive surveillance. Pervasive surveillance has also been at the center of real-life dystopias closer to home, such as during the heyday of Senator Joseph McCarthy and the Red Scare, when domestic intelligence agencies developed extended

1

networks of informants and pursued "loyalty risks" by surreptitiously infiltrating political organizations and labor unions.

By the 1970s, domestic intelligence and law enforcement agencies had added technologies like wiretaps and remote listening devices to their surveillance toolkits. Fueled by the oppositional logic[2] of the Cold War, claims of executive necessity, and assertions of national security imperatives, the Department of Defense (DOD), the Central Intelligence Agency (CIA), and the National Security Agency (NSA), among others, dramatically expanded their surveillance capacities and programs.

The dangers posed by these new abilities became a serious public concern in the wake of the Watergate scandal. As part of broader reform efforts, the Senate Select Committee to Study Governmental Operations with Respect to Intelligence Activities conducted extensive investigations of domestic and foreign surveillance programs. This committee, which is often referred to as the "Church Committee" after its chairman Senator Frank Church, described some of what it found in a 1976 report:

> Too many people have been spied upon by too many Government agencies and to[o] much information has [been] collected. The Government has often undertaken the secret surveillance of citizens on the basis of their political beliefs, even when those beliefs posed no threat of violence or illegal acts on behalf of a hostile foreign power. The Government, operating primarily through secret informants, but also using other intrusive techniques such as wiretaps, microphone "bugs," surreptitious mail opening, and break-ins, has swept in vast amounts of information about the personal lives, views, and associations of American citizens. Investigations of groups deemed potentially dangerous – and even of groups suspected of associating with potentially dangerous organizations- – have continued for decades, despite the fact that those groups did not engage in unlawful activity. Groups and individuals have been harassed and disrupted because of their political views and their lifestyles. Investigations have been based upon vague standards whose breadth made excessive collection inevitable. Unsavory and vicious tactics have been employed – including anonymous attempts to break up marriages, disrupt meetings, ostracize persons from their professions, and provoke target groups into rivalries that might result in deaths. Intelligence agencies have served the political and personal objectives of presidents and other high officials. While the agencies often committed excesses in response to pressure from high officials in the Executive branch and Congress, they also occasionally initiated improper activities and then concealed them from officials whom they had a duty to inform. Governmental officials – including those whose

principal duty is to enforce the law – have violated or ignored the law over long periods of time and have advocated and defended their right to break the law.[3]

The surveillance state predicted in Orwell's *1984* had made an early arrival.

The Church Committee ultimately concluded "that intelligence activities ha[d] undermined the constitutional rights of citizens and that they ha[d] done so primarily because checks and balances designed by the framers of the Constitution to assure accountability ha[d] not been applied."[4] In an effort to restore those rights, Congress passed, and President Jimmy Carter signed, a series of measures designed to bring executive agencies involved in intelligence gathering "back within the constitutional scheme"[5] by banning some programs and subjecting others to more regular and rigorous legislative and judicial review. The centerpiece of these efforts was the Foreign Intelligence Surveillance Act (FISA), which established the Foreign Intelligence Surveillance Court. Among other reforms, FISA set strict limits on the surveillance of American citizens, established means of congressional oversight, and required agencies to secure prior approval from courts before engaging in electronic surveillance inside the United States or against US citizens.

Although the Church Committee reforms were incomplete, their work pulled us back from a precipice. In the wake of the Committee's investigations, Congress was more wary of "the drift toward 'Big Brother government' " in an era where "the technological capability of Government relentlessly increases" and the "potential for abuse is awesome."[6] In subsequent years, Congress worked to stem the tide by passing measures such as the Electronic Communications Privacy Act as part of a continuing effort to protect citizens and their rights by limiting the deployment and use of new surveillance technologies. Those efforts hit their zenith in 2003 when Congress defunded the Department of Defense's Information Awareness Office and its infamous Terrorism Information Awareness program (TIA), often referred to as the Total Information Awareness program.

Boasting a revealing insignia featuring an all-seeing eye casting its gaze over the Earth from atop a pyramid, the Information Awareness Office aspired to gather, consolidate, and analyze data from a wide variety of sources, including consumer transactions, banking records, electronic mail, telephone calls, public databases, and travel manifests. Amidst public criticism, then Secretary of Defense Donald Rumsfeld convened an ad hoc committee of experts to examine the Office and its programs. That committee issued a report in 2004 that was reminiscent of the Church Committee Report.[7] Unfortunately, the report's recommendations did little to control surveillance practices.

During the decade after the defunding of TIA, reporters and activists issued regular warnings that intelligence agencies, law enforcement, and their private contractors had continued undaunted in their efforts to dramatically expand government surveillance capacities under the auspices of the War on Terror. But those warnings fell on deaf ears. Many people simply discounted them as the paranoid delusions of a tinfoil hat-wearing fringe or reassured themselves with the slavish tropes of national security or naïve assumptions of personal immunity ("I'm not doing anything wrong, so they wouldn't be watching me!"). All that changed in the spring of 2013.

In June 2013, the *Guardian* and the *Washington Post* started publishing a series of stories on classified government documents and court orders showing just how far we have come down the road to a surveillance state. These documents, which had been leaked by a former NSA contractor named Edward Snowden, showed that federal agencies had been gathering and storing metadata associated with domestic phone calls, infiltrating private server networks operated by service providers like Google and Yahoo to obtain the contents of users' files and communications, directly accessing internet data at key communications chokepoints, and gathering vast amounts of the digital exhaust generated by our financial transactions, personal devices, and online activities. Separate from the Snowden revelations, investigative reporters have shown that government agencies are storing data on a massive scale. For example, the NSA has built several facilities capable of storing zettabytes and yottabytes of information – enough space to store years' worth of the data and voice communications generated by everyone in the United States.

Parallel to the buildup of surveillance capacities documented in the Snowden papers, there has been an explosion of tracking technologies that exploit our personal devices, including cellular phones. Among the most notorious of these are cell site simulators – sometimes referred to as "Stingrays" – which impersonate the cellular base stations that form the backbone of provider networks. In a purely indiscriminate manner, these devices can gather information from every cellular phone within their ranges of operation – often hundreds or thousands of phones at a time.

Using cell site simulators, law enforcement officers can learn the unique identification numbers associated with each of these phones, their locations, and basic information about communications and callers. These devices also have the capacity to gather the contents of cellular communications, including phone calls, text messages, and internet activities. Cell site simulators have become so common in the last ten years that it is virtually certain that everyone who has a cellular device has been subjected to surveillance by a cell site simulator. For readers who live in urban areas, near high-security facilities like airports, or in neighborhoods designated as "high crime," being surveilled by a cell site simulator is a routine fact of life.

The twenty-first century explosion in government surveillance has not all been about technology. We have also seen a rapid expansion in more direct, physical, and visceral forms of government surveillance. Foremost among these has been the rapid rise in "stops and frisks" and car stops, particularly in urban areas. Stops and frisks entail the seizure of a person – the stop – and a pat down of his outer clothing and personal items in search of weapons – the frisk. Although licensed by the Supreme Court in 1968 as a means for law enforcement officers to respond to "rapidly unfolding and often dangerous situations on city streets,"[8] stops and frisks have since become a routinized means of projecting state power. As a result, the numbers of stops and frisks conducted by law enforcement officers grew exponentially through the first decade of the twenty-first century to the point that being stopped and frisked became a feature of daily life for many citizens, and particularly for members of minority groups or residents of neighborhoods targeted by local police departments.

The ultimate goal of all these efforts seems to be complete, pervasive surveillance of everywhere we go in virtual and physical space, everything we do, everything we say, and everything we think. This is not to suggest that particular agents are acting with nefarious intent or that there is an evil mastermind behind our burgeoning surveillance state. To the contrary, the main motives for expanding government surveillance powers can be traced to the War on Terror or the War on Drugs.[9] Individually and together, these perpetual conflicts have put intelligence and law enforcement agencies in a state of constant emergency and crisis – not dissimilar to the endless wars waged by Oceana in Orwell's *1984*. This is hardly a new dynamic. As a prominent eighteenth-century social critic recounted, governments and their agents are "fond of doctrines of reason of state, and state necessity, and the impossibility of providing for great emergencies and extraordinary cases, without a discretionary power in the crown to proceed sometimes by uncommon methods not agreeable to the known forms of law."[10] Last century, the Church Committee reached a similar conclusion, reporting that "In time[s] of crisis, the Government will exercise its power to conduct domestic intelligence activities to the fullest extent."[11] As the Committee also pointed out, surveillance programs generate their own inertia. They therefore have a "tendency ... to expand beyond their initial scope" and "naturally generate ever-increasing demands for new data."[12] "And once intelligence has been collected, there are strong pressures to use it against the target."[13]

The recent explosion in surveillance technologies and the rapid expansion of domestic surveillance programs mark the beginnings of a twenty-first-century age of surveillance in the United States. As a consequence, in a recent ranking compiled by Privacy International comparing surveillance practices and privacy protections among nations, the United States landed at the very bottom, earning the designation "endemic surveillance society" along with Thailand, Taiwan, Singapore, Russia, China, Malaysia, and the United Kingdom.[14] This low standing is more than just embarrassing. It imperils our liberty as individuals and disturbs the basic foundations of our democratic society. To see why, it is important to have a sense of the critical place of privacy in our personal lives and our democracy.

Privacy is a complicated concept, and therefore resists reduction to a concise definition. Most accounts of privacy are tied to the ability to maintain boundaries and to limit access to the self.[15] A "Private" sign on a door marks a boundary. It signals that someone, perhaps the owner or tenant, has asserted her right to control access to that space. There is a shared understanding that no one should enter that room without permission.[16] Entering without permission would constitute a violation of privacy. In the face of such a violation, the owner would be right to feel a sense of violation. Similarly, if someone says "I need some privacy," then that person has asserted his right to control access to himself. We know that we should leave him be, absent permission or good and substantial reasons to invade his repose. Privacy in our thoughts, our activities, our relationships, and our personal information can be discussed in the same way. When we say "That's private!" we are asserting a right to limit access to information and to ourselves.

Importantly, privacy is content neutral and context dependent. Nothing is inherently private or not private. Places, things, activities, and relationships are only private or not private to the extent that they lie on one side of a guarded boundary. Neither is there a necessary link between privacy and what is sensitive, embarrassing, or even illegal. In fact, much of what we regard as private is perfectly ordinary. Privacy is, instead, about agency, status, and relationships. A claim of privacy is an act of will that entails assertions of personhood, dignity, and entitlement. It also orients self and others within a broader social constellation populated by spouses, parents, children, family, friends, acquaintances, and strangers. More fundamentally, then, privacy is about power. It is about the power to define ourselves.[17] It is about the power to negotiate and protect space "free from the demands and burdens of social interaction."[18] It is about the power to exclude. And it is about the power "to control what information about oneself is known to others and for what purposes that information is used."[19]

Although the rules governing privacy and norms regarding what can and cannot reasonably be maintained as private vary quite widely, privacy itself is universally human. Even in the most highly concentrated of cultural settings, people seek privacy. In a complementary fashion, there are social norms in every society that preserve space for individual privacy. For example, as political scientist and sociologist Barrington Moore, Jr., reports, the Inuit, who often live in close and constant proximity in relatively tiny spaces during long northern winters, reserve separate spaces for guests and intimates inside their igloo homes.[20] Within the space reserved for family members, individuals maintain both physical and social privacy in their personal sleeping spaces.[21] Even though there are no walls marking off these personal spaces, social norms protect peoples' privilege to exclude others, to withdraw, and to be left alone.

The universality of privacy reflects a basic existential reality of human existence. We are, after all, individuals separated from society by the inherent impenetrability of our own minds and bodies, but, at the same time, we are social animals, who are always already embedded in communities and cultures. Privacy describes our efforts to negotiate between these two, finding space to define for ourselves who we are, what we value, what we want to achieve, and what constitutes the good life. Privacy is therefore necessary to projects of ethical development. It provides us with the means and opportunity to withdraw from others in order to find and define ourselves without either negating the critical role of society and social engagement in those same projects or forgetting the blunt fact that we are social creatures who simply would not exist without society, culture, and language. In this sense, privacy claims provide us with "a set of circuit breakers for shedding social overload"[22] while always allowing that "privacy can be extinguished by a need for dependence that comes from awareness of [our fundamental] helplessness and isolation."[23] We deploy these circuit breakers in large and small ways every day when we don a pair of earphones on the subway, decline a call, or close the doors of our homes.

Viewed through this existential lens, privacy has critical positive value for individuals. In fact, privacy is a necessary condition of personhood. Absent privacy, we would lose all sense of individuality and agency, becoming much like the Borg from *Star Trek* or the vacuous citizens of the World State in Huxley's *Brave New World*. Privacy also secures space for us to develop and explore. As Professor Neil Richards has argued, privacy is a condition of intellectual freedom that allows for the possibility of free thought and expression.[24] As Professor Julie Cohen points out, privacy also provides space "to develop critical perspectives on the world around [us]."[25] In this sense, Cohen continues, "privacy is one of the resources that situated subjects require to flourish."[26]

Privacy has important social value as well. By preserving space for personal exploration and development, privacy provides the conditions necessary for creativity and innovation. Absent privacy, society would simply replicate the same endless stream of banality. There would be no creativity or progress. Privacy is also necessary to projects of democratic self-governance. Absent privacy, and the opportunities for ethical self-development and critical reflection it provides, citizens would lose the capacity to engage effectively in civil society and politics. There would be no contest of ideas, much less the process of persuasion and consensus-building that defines democratic societies. Political life would instead mean nothing more than parroting received truths, much like the citizens in Orwell's Oceana. It is therefore no accident that Winston Smith, Orwell's protagonist in *1984*, first starts to experience new thoughts and freedom of consciousness when he finds privacy outside the view of the telescreens to write in a journal and to have unmonitored conversations – not to mention sex – with his mistress.

By contrast, the absence of privacy is associated with psychological degradation and authoritarian control. The standard trope deployed to prove this point is the Panopticon proposed by eighteenth-century philosopher and social critic Jeremy Bentham as a "new mode of obtaining power of mind over mind."[27]

Bentham's Panopticon is an architectural concept that he promoted as an ideal design for prisons, reformatories, poor houses, hospitals, asylums, and even factories and offices – wherever the institutional goal is to control behavior and normalize character. The Panopticon features individual cells arrayed in a circle around a central "inspector's lodge."[28] Prisoners, patients, or workers occupy the cells. The central position houses an authority figure, such as a guard, nurse, teacher, or manager. Arranged thusly, Bentham tells us, "the persons to be inspected are under the eyes of the persons who should inspect them."[29] The panoptic "Ideal," according to Bentham, is achieved when subjects are under surveillance "during every instant."[30] If this is impossible, however, Bentham recommends arranging the structure to ensure that "at every instant, seeing reason to believe as much, and not being able to satisfy himself to the contrary, he should *conceive* himself to be [subject to inspection]."[31] Bentham suggests that this can be accomplished by using blinds or other means to hide the interior of the inspector's lodge from the occupants of the cells.[32] As a result, those in the cells would be constantly visible to any inspector, but subjects housed in the cells would never know whether they are actually being watched at any particular moment. This, according to Bentham, is the "essence" of the plan: "the centrality of the inspector's situation, combined with the well-known and most effectual contrivances for *seeing without being seen*."[33] In this way, one inspector can exercise effective control over an almost unlimited number of subjects by maintaining for each of them the very real possibility that he is, or very well may well be, under active surveillance, and therefore subject to judgment and potential discipline.

In his famous account of the Panopticon, philosopher and historian Michel Foucault explained how Bentham's arrangement could not only control behavior but change character and personality.[34] According to Foucault, by subjecting someone to "a state of conscious and permanent visibility," panoptic surveillance causes subjects to internalize the norms and expectations that they perceive as providing the standards by which they are judged by their observer. Because, by design, they do not know precisely who is watching, or whether anyone is watching at all, subjects in a Panopticon live in a state of constant anxiety that what they do, or even what they think, may expose them to ill-judgment and even disciplinary action. They therefore err constantly in the direction of what they presume are the most innocuous, mainstream, and acceptable thoughts and actions. In this way, Foucault concludes,

"The Panopticon is a marvelous machine which, whatever use one may wish to put it to, produces homogenous effects of power."[35] In this way, panoptic surveillance can replace violence as a means of social control, "So it is not necessary to use force to constrain the convict to good behaviour, the madman to calm, the worker to work, the schoolboy to application, the patient to the observation of the regulations."[36] Simply letting them believe that they are under constant surveillance is enough to do the trick.

Bentham's basic insight should be familiar. For example, you may have driven past a driverless police cruiser parked to face oncoming traffic or a sign that uses radar to determine your speed of travel, which it then displays beside a sign showing the speed limit. Both techniques demonstrably reduce speeding and accidents simply by presenting drivers with the possibility that they are being watched. Each Christmas, parents also deploy the threat of surveillance as a means to discourage their children from misbehaving, some by introducing an "Elf on the Shelf" into their homes, and others by simply singing about good old Saint Nicholas. After all:

> He knows when you're sleeping.
> He knows when you're awake.
> He knows when you've been bad or good.
> So be good for goodness sake.[37]

For Bentham, the Panopticon was a shining jewel of progress. In a world where public institutions were squalid and exercises of state power often brutal, the prospect of achieving social goals through remote, nonviolent applications of power in the context of clean and orderly institutions seemed miraculously attractive. In the context of contemporary conversations about government surveillance, the Panopticon provides the standard dystopic image of life in a surveillance state. It certainly helps us to understand the potential threats of contemporary surveillance to personal liberty and democratic society.

As the image of the Panopticon reveals, programs of broad and indiscriminate government surveillance threaten to subject all of us to constant scrutiny by government agents. Perhaps more insidiously, the existence of these programs leaves each of us to wonder whether we are, or very well may be, subject to government surveillance wherever we go and whatever we do. The consequence is a dramatic expansion of state power and the ability of governments to project that power into the far peripheries of our lives. These surveillance programs also threaten the conditions necessary to preserve individual agency by denying us the ability to negotiate boundaries between what is public and what is private.[38] That is because, in effect, if not in reality, nothing is private in a surveillance state. There is no place to go in the real world or in virtual worlds where we can be certain that we are not being watched, evaluated, and judged by one or more government agencies.

To allow government surveillance programs to expand to panoptic proportions would have dramatic and deleterious effects on each of us and all of us.[39] It would be a source of considerable daily stress[40] that might very well harm our perceptions of personal control and our abilities to perform daily tasks.[41] Faced with the prospect of being constantly watched, we would be far less likely to engage in the kinds of intellectual experiments and expressive explorations that are central to processes of personal development and feed the wells of creativity and innovation that allow our society to grow and adapt.[42] This is not merely a matter of speculation. In a recent study, economists Alex Marthews and Catherine Tucker showed that the Snowden revelations had an immediate effect on internet search activity, leading to a significant drop in Google inquiries involving terms that might be seen as risqué, transgressive, politically charged, or embarrassing.[43] New threats of surveillance have also suppressed journalists, undermining our ability to engage in critical projects of self-government.[44] More directly, the prospect of living in a surveillance state would upend the presumption of self-governance[45] because, as Justice Sonia Sotomayor has pointed out, "Awareness that the Government may be watching chills associational and expressive freedoms ... [and] may alter the relationship between citizen and government in a way that is inimical to democratic society."[46] That is because panoptic surveillance undermines trust between citizens and governments,[47] harming perceptions of legitimacy and authority.[48] It can also have dramatic, long-term effects on economic activity, leading to depressed growth, less innovation, and reduced diversification as compared to states that value privacy rights.[49]

For some readers, these concerns may seem overblown. A common refrain is that "If you are not doing anything wrong, then you should not care who is watching." In a similar vein, some maintain that, if our lives are uninteresting, then government authorities will not bother to watch. Others assert that they just do not care whether the government is watching what they make for breakfast. Although claims along these lines have been common currency in public conversations about government surveillance programs, they do not survive serious examination.

First of all, being innocent or boring does not necessarily protect you from the harms of surveillance. Take, for example, governments' use of data surveillance technologies to construct watch lists such as the notorious "No-Fly" list. As Professor Jeffrey Kahn has shown, these lists are shockingly inaccurate and virtually immune to correction.[50] They routinely target people based on bad information, causing perfectly innocent and, yes, boring people – we're talking of nuns and senators here – to be denied the right to travel, access to credit, and the ability to work. For these innocent victims, modern surveillance technologies are far from benign. That any of us might at any moment find our lives similarly shattered is certainly reason for pause.

Puffery aside, it's also probably not true that boring and law-abiding folks don't care if the government is watching. This is a point made quite elegantly by a comic that ran in a recent edition of the New Yorker.[51] It depicts a man and a woman in bed. There are two surveillance cameras installed above their headboard, both of which are trained down on them as they settle in for the night. As the woman lies awake, apparently unable to relax under the cameras' gaze, the man offers this reassurance: "If you are not planning to break the law, why should you care?"

Imagine that all the walls in your house were replaced with uncovered windows, thus rendering your entire home and everything you did inside visible to your neighbors and anyone walking on the sidewalk, driving along the road, or flying overhead. Imagine further that all interior spaces in the house were continuously illuminated. Would living in that constant state of exposure affect your conduct? Your basic sense of comfort and security? Your ease in the banalities of everyday life? Your willingness to experiment and try new things, whether it is an intimate act or a risky yoga pose? Upon honest reflection, would anyone choose life in this kind of glass house over life behind the private confines of opaque walls and curtains?

Imagine that a rotating squad of police officers, psychologists, religious leaders, and, on occasion, your mother stationed themselves around your glass house twenty-four hours a day. Now ask yourself the same questions.

Shifting the terms of the mind experiment a bit more, imagine that, instead of glass walls, your house was constructed of one-way glass such that anyone standing outside could see everything going on inside, but you could not see outside to know whether anyone is actually watching. Would this change any of your answers? Might it actually be more disconcerting than living in the glass house?

Finally, imagine that, instead of glass walls, your house was wired with cameras that linked to a central viewing station where the streams would be monitored by law enforcement agents. Would living in such an environment be just as free, comfortable, and desirable as life in a home without all the cameras?[52]

We could spin out variations on this basic theme long into the night, but the straightforward point is this: nobody would choose to live in conditions of panoptic surveillance, and for good reason. Whether one's private life is banal or exciting, mainstream or transgressive, and whether or not domestic activities are cause for pride or embarrassment, they are private. When they are no longer private, something critical is lost. That loss is all the more harmful if it is imposed on us against our wills. That is because violations of privacy entail denials of autonomy, freedom, choice, and control. They inflict deep dignitary harms. It is quite right, then, that we feel a sense of violation upon finding that someone has read our diary, rummaged through our bedside table, disclosed a secret, or shared an intimate picture on the Internet. After all, privacy is often about respect.

Although brief, this discussion is sufficient to at least cast some doubt on claims that we should not be concerned about government surveillance either because we are not engaged in illegal activities or because most of what we do is not particularly interesting. In doing so, I have of course appealed to your instincts on the assumption that we share some basic sensibilities regarding privacy and its value. One might worry that these instincts are outmoded; that they reflect twentieth-century thinking; and that millennials and future generations, who will grow up in an era of social media and expanding government surveillance capacities, just do not care about privacy. As proof of this proposition, one might point to instances when some young person has shared what we regard as very intimate details with thousands of her "friends" on Facebook or followers on Twitter. If this is the new norm, then might it be true that privacy is an artifact of the past? If it is, then it seems we should not make too much fuss over the looming threat of a surveillance state.

These kinds of arguments misconstrue the nature of privacy. It is no doubt true that people have different views on what is and is not private. Those differences of opinion manifest within generational groups as much as between them, however. Some people just share way too much. But no matter how notorious their acts of oversharing may be, they do not represent the views of society as a whole. It is also true that social media provides forums for people who like to share a lot more with a lot more people. That some people avail themselves of these opportunities does not mean that privacy is dead, however. It does not even prove that those who are into sharing do not care about privacy. Quite to the contrary, it proves that privacy is not about stable or universal categories that dictate what is and what is not private. It instead reinforces the fact that privacy is about individuals' and groups' power to negotiate boundaries.

Everyone values privacy. Different people just draw different boundaries. That is true even of millennials. In study after study, researchers have found that, although people in the 16- to 25-year-old demographic tend to be more active in social media than older generations, they nevertheless value privacy as much, or even more, than their elders.[53] The gap between perception and reality here is in part a function of different views on the nature of social media. Many people think of social media as purely public spaces. But millennials who participate in social media tend to treat them as highly negotiable. They therefore develop and deploy strategies that allow them to participate in social media while maintaining zones of privacy and trust. Participants in social media also develop and internalize social norms governing access and sharing. Ethnographer danah boyd has done stunning work among this tribe, documenting how millennials exercise agency by controlling boundaries and limiting access in the contexts of both their online and offline interactions.[54] Her work shows that, when these strategies fail, or when norms are violated, her millennial informants suffer in the very same ways those of us from older generations might suffer upon discovering that someone has read a diary or that a trusted friend has disclosed an intimate secret.

* * * * * * * * * *

We are living in an age of surveillance marked by an explosion in surveillance technologies and a rapid expansion of surveillance programs. Despite the dangers posed to our individual liberty and democratic society, there have been few serious legislative efforts to impose real restraints. We have not seen a Church Committee for the twenty-first century. To the contrary, our burgeoning twenty-first-century surveillance state has met predominately with legislative acquiescence. The best hope to curtail the expansion of our surveillance state might therefore seem to be the courts, whose solemn constitutional duty it is to constrain the political branches' inevitable expansions of state power. In particular, we might invest hope in protections afforded by the Fourth Amendment, which provides that

> The right of the people to be secure in their persons, houses, papers, and effects, against unreasonable searches and seizures, shall not be violated, and no Warrants shall issue, but upon probable cause, supported by Oath or affirmation, and particularly describing the place to be searched, and the persons or things to be seized.

Unfortunately, three long-standing doctrines – the "public observation doctrine," the "third-party doctrine," and rules governing Fourth Amendment "standing" – appear to put most contemporary surveillance initiatives beyond the reach of Fourth Amendment review and regulation. To bring the Fourth Amendment to bear in our age of surveillance will therefore require a revolution in Fourth Amendment doctrine. Fortunately, the moment seems to be ripe for just such an event.

In a case called *United States v. Jones*, decided in 2012,[55] at least five justices on the United States Supreme Court indicated their willingness to consider revolutionary changes in Fourth Amendment law. In that case, law enforcement officers attached a GPS-enabled tracking device to Antoine Jones's car because they suspected his involvement in a narcotics conspiracy. They used that device to track his movements for twenty-eight days, gathering thousands of pages of data in the process. On appeal, Jones argued that law enforcement violated his Fourth Amendment rights, first by installing, and then by monitoring the tracking device. Writing for a five-justice majority, Justice Antonin Scalia resolved the case on narrow grounds, holding that the physical intrusion required to install the device, no matter how brief or minor, violated Jones's Fourth Amendment rights. Justice Scalia avoided the much more difficult question: whether using the device also raised Fourth Amendment concerns.

Although Justice Scalia's majority opinion in *Jones* was important in its own right, the real front-page stories came from two concurring opinions, one written by Justice Samuel Alito and the other by Justice Sonia Sotomayor. In his concurring opinion, which was joined by Justices Ruth Bader Ginsburg, Stephen Breyer, and Elena Kagan, Justice Alito contended that law enforcement officers violated Jones's Fourth Amendment rights when they tracked his movements over a long period of time, gathering a large amount of data in the process. In making this argument, Justice Alito seemed to propose a novel "quantitative" theory of Fourth Amendment privacy. "Under this approach," Justice Alito wrote, "relatively short-term monitoring of a person's movements on public streets accords with expectations of privacy that our society has recognized as reasonable. But the use of longer term GPS monitoring in investigations of most offenses impinges on [reasonable] expectations of privacy."[56] "For such offenses," he continued, "society's expectation has been that law enforcement agents and others would not – and indeed, in the main, simply could not secretly monitor and catalogue every single movement of an individual's car."[57]

In a separate concurring opinion, Justice Sotomayor indicated her broad agreement with Justice Alito's quantitative approach. She went further, however, arguing that expanding governmental access to personal information threatens the balance of power between the government and the governed in ways that threaten the very foundations of our democratic society.[58] In light of these dangers, she suggested that the Court may need to revisit the third party and the public observation doctrines in order to set some limits on our burgeoning surveillance state.

Although the concurring opinions in *Jones* were long on aspirations, they were short on details. They did not explain where we can find the historical or doctrinal foundations for a quantitative approach to the Fourth Amendment. They failed to describe in any detail how a quantitative approach would work in practice. Those omissions are perfectly understandable given the way the Court works. The justices can only address the questions presented by the cases that come before them. They are not in the business of building elaborate theories or speculating about the future. By contrast, that is precisely what law professors, philosophers, and political scientists do for a living. It should therefore come as no surprise that *Jones* has sparked a lively conversation among academics about the future of the Fourth Amendment. This book adds to these debates by explaining how the Fourth Amendment can have a prominent role in twenty-first-century discussions of privacy, technology, and surveillance.

As we will see in this book, the Fourth Amendment "erects a wall between a free society and overzealous police action" and in the process protects us from the "tyranny of the police state."[59] It is concerned in particular with means and methods capable of facilitating programs of broad and indiscriminate search and seizure. That is because these are the kinds of programs that threaten "the right of the people to be secure ... against unreasonable searches and seizures." In order to vindicate these concerns, the Fourth Amendment guarantees a collective right to constitutional remedies that limit the discretionary authority of government agents to deploy and use these means and methods and hold them accountable for their conduct. By both limiting access and ensuring accountability, these remedial measures allow all of us and each of us to live relatively free from fear that we will be subjected to unreasonable searches or seizures. The task for the Court in our age of surveillance is to fashion new Fourth Amendment remedies to meet twenty-first-century challenges.

Chapter 1 sets the stage by exploring in detail some of the means and methods that are poised to define our age of surveillance. This chapter will discuss both the role of modern technologies in expanding governmental surveillance programs and the explosive growth of more traditional methods like stop and frisk. Absent some sources of restraint, Chapter 1 concludes that we are facing the prospect of life in a surveillance state where we will be subjected to the kind of constant, invasive observation that characterized Bentham's Panopticon.

Chapter 2 asks how we got here. Most people reading the Fourth Amendment would assume that it protects us from the kinds of broad, indiscriminate, and pervasive surveillance that are characteristic of a surveillance state. Unfortunately, as Chapter 2 explains, twentieth-century developments in Fourth Amendment doctrine have left us with few protections against the means, methods, and programs discussed in Chapter 1. Although a majority of justices on the Supreme Court indicated their willingness to revisit those doctrines in the *Jones* case, the Court has yet to chart a course for the Fourth Amendment in our age of surveillance. This has left the field open for policymakers, scholars, and others to suggest possible directions. A number of prominent academics, lawyers, and judges have answered that invitation. Chapter 3 summarizes and critically assesses the most important of their proposals. It ultimately concludes that the most promising way forward is to focus on limiting the discretionary authority of government agents to deploy and use means and methods of search and seizure that are capable of facilitating programs of broad and indiscriminate search and seizure.

Chapter 4 advances a novel Fourth Amendment theory that supports the proposal advanced in Chapter 3. The theory is grounded in a careful reading of the text of the Fourth Amendment that takes seriously its historical context. These efforts reveal that the Fourth Amendment establishes a collective right to prospective remedies that are sufficient to guarantee that each of us and all of us can live free from fear of unreasonable searches and seizures. The principal goal of these remedies is to limit the discretion of government agents to deploy and use means and methods capable of facilitating programs of broad and indiscriminate search and seizure. By limiting that discretion, Chapter 4 concludes that the Fourth Amendment can guarantee that most people, most of the time, will be secure against threats of unreasonable search and seizure.

Although the theory advanced in Chapter 4 is novel, Chapter 5 shows that it is nevertheless well grounded in Fourth Amendment doctrine. This is not the first time we have faced a monumental threat to our collective right to be secure against unreasonable searches and seizures. In the late nineteenth and early twentieth centuries, we faced a similar crisis. The source of the threat then was the birth and expansion of professional, paramilitary police forces, which did not exist in the United States when the Fourth Amendment was ratified. The Supreme Court responded to this crisis by elaborating several prospective constitutional remedies that were designed to restore the security of the people. Foremost among these were the warrant requirement, the exclusionary rule, and the *Miranda* prophylaxis – those warnings officers must always recite so that arrestees know they have the right to remain silent and the right to an attorney. By retracing the Court's reasoning in the cases where it formulated and adopted these remedial measures, Chapter 5 distills a basic set of criteria that courts can apply when considering potential remedies in our age of surveillance.

Chapter 6 applies the lessons learned in Chapters 4 and 5 to the means and methods discussed in Chapter 1. In the process, it describes a set of flexible frameworks that might either be adopted by the political branches or imposed by courts. Chapter 6 also explains why these measures would be effective in securing the Fourth Amendment rights of the people while also preserving ample space for government agencies to pursue legitimate law enforcement and national security goals.

Although this book aims to make substantive contributions to academic and legal debates about surveillance law and the Fourth Amendment, its primary audience is "the people," whose interests the Fourth Amendment aims to protect. It therefore makes no assumptions in terms of expertise. You certainly do not need to be a lawyer or a professor to read this book. All you really need is some intellectual curiosity, a reasonable degree of civic engagement, and perhaps a taste for revolution. With that, let us begin.

Notes

1. J.R.R. Tolkien, The Lord of the Rings 616 (Houghton Mifflin 1994) (1954).
2. For an explanation of oppositional logic in authoritarian regimes, see Jaime Malamud-Goti, Game Without End: State Terror and the Politics of Justice, 83–91 (1996).
3. Select Committee to Study Governmental Operations with Respect to Intelligence Activities, Final Report Together With Additional, Supplemental, and Separate Views, Apr. 26, 1976 (hereinafter "Church Committee Report").
4. Church Committee Report, *supra* note 3, at 289.
5. *Id.* at 292.
6. *Id.* at 289.
7. Tech. & Privacy Advisory Comm. (TAPAC), Safeguarding Privacy in the Fight Against Terrorism, 36–37 (Mar. 2004) (hereinafter TAPAC Report).
8. Terry v. Ohio, 392 U.S. 1, 10 (1968).
9. For a revealing history of how the War on Alcohol and then the War on Drugs have led to dramatic expansions in law enforcement institutions and surveillance programs, see Lisa McGirr, The War on Alcohol: Prohibition and the Rise of the American State (2015).
10. 2 Francis Maseres, The Canadian Freeholder: In Three Dialogues Between an Englishman and a Frenchman, Settled in Canada 243–44 (London, B. White 1779) (commenting on Wilkes v. Wood (1763) 98 Eng. Rep. 489 (KB)).
11. Church Committee Report, *supra* note 3, at 289.
12. *Id.* at 4.
13. *Id.*
14. *National Privacy Ranking 2007 – Leading Surveillance Societies Around the World*, Privacy Int'l, http://observatoriodeseguranca.org/files/phrcomp_sort.pdf
15. *See, e.g.*, Julie Cohen, *What Privacy Is For*, 126 Harv. L. Rev. 1904, 1906 (2013).
16. Georgia v. Randolph, 547 U.S. 103 (2006).
17. Cohen, *supra* note 15, at 1911 ("the development of critical subjectivity is a realistic goal only to the extent that privacy comes into play. Subjectivity is a function of the interplay between emergent selfhood and social shaping; privacy, which inheres in the interstices of social shaping, is what permits that interplay to occur. Privacy is not a fixed condition that can be distilled to an essential core, but rather an interest in breathing room to engage in socially situated processes of boundary management. It enables situated subjects to navigate within preexisting cultural and social matrices, creating spaces for the play and the work of self-making.") (internal citation and quotation marks omitted).
18. Barrington Moore, Jr., Privacy, 14 (1984).
19. ABA Standards For Criminal Justice: Law Enforcement Access To Third Party Records 25-4.1(a) commentary (3d ed. 2013).
20. Moore, *supra* note 18, at 10–11.
21. *Id.*
22. Moore, *supra* note 18, at 6.

23. *Id.*
24. *See, generally,* Neil M. Richards, *The Dangers of Surveillance,* 126 Harv. L. Rev. 1934 (2013).
25. Cohen, *supra* note 15, at 1906.
26. *Id.*
27. Jeremy Bentham, *Panopticon; or, the Inspection-House: Containing the Idea of a New Principle of Construction Applicable to Any Sort of Establishment, in Which Persons of Any Description Are to be Kept under Inspection; and in Particular to Penitentiary-Houses, Prisons, Poor-Houses, Lazarettos, Houses of Industry, Manufactories, Hospitals, Work-Houses, Mad-Houses, and Schools: With a Plan of Management Adapted to the Principle, in* The Works of Jeremy Bentham, 37, 39 (John Bowring, ed. 1778, vol. 4). Some readers may be familiar with the Panopticon from Michel Foucault's famous discussion in Discipline and Punish (1977).
28. Bentham, *supra* note 27, at 40–41.
29. *Id.* at 40.
30. *Id.*
31. *Id.*
32. *Id.* at 41.
33. *Id.* at 44.
34. Michel Foucault, Discipline & Punish, 195–228 (1977).
35. Foucault, *supra* note 34.
36. *Id.*
37. John Frederick Coots & Haven Gillespie, Santa Claus is Coming to Town (1934).
38. Jennifer Golbeck, *Thirty Years after 1984, We're All Being Watched, Nearly All Day, in Ways We Could Never Have Imagined,* Psych. Today, Sept. 2, 2014, www.psychologytoday.com/articles/201409/all-eyes-you (quoting Stanford Psychiatrist Elias Aboujaounde as saying that "We cannot afford to just 'get over [a loss of privacy],' for nothing short of our self-custody seems to be at stake," he says. "At its heart, this is about our psychological autonomy and the maintenance of some semblance of control over the various little details that make us us.").
39. Chris Chambers, *NSA and GCHQ: The Flawed Psychology of Government Surveillance,* The Guardian, Aug. 26, 2013 ("Studying [empirical] evidence leads to a clear conclusion and a warning: indiscriminate intelligence-gathering presents a grave risk to our mental health, productivity, social cohesion, and ultimately our future.").
40. *See* M.J. Smith et al., *Employee Stress and Health Complaints in Jobs with and without Electronic Monitoring,* 22 Applied Econ. 17 (1992).
41. Jeffry Stanton & Janet Barnes-Farrell, *Effects of Electronic Performance Monitoring on Personal Control, Task Satisfaction, and Task Performance,* 8 J. Applied Psych. 738 (1996). *See also* Viktor Mayer-Schönberger, Delete: The Virtue of Forgetting in the Digital Age (2011).
42. Chris Chambers, *NSA and GCHQ: The Flawed Psychology of Government Surveillance,* The Guardian, Aug. 26, 2013 ("Psychology forewarns us that a future of universal surveillance will be a world bereft of anything sufficiently interesting to spy on – a beige authoritarian landscape in which we lose the ability to relax, innovate, or take risks. A world in which the definition of 'appropriate'

thought and behaviour becomes so narrow that even the most pedantic norm violations are met with exclusion or punishment.").
43. Alex Marthews & Catherine Tucker, *The Impact of Online Surveillance on Behavior*, in THE CAMBRIDGE HANDBOOK OF SURVEILLANCE LAW (2017); Alex Marthews & Catherine Tucker, *Government Surveillance and Internet Search Behavior*, http://papers.ssrn.com/sol3/papers.cfm?abstract_id=2412564.
44. Human Rights Watch & American Civil Liberties Union, July 2014, *With Liberty to Monitor All: How Large-Scale US Surveillance is Harming Journalism, Law and American Democracy*, www.hrw.org/sites/default/files/reports/usnsa0714_ForUP load_0.pdf; PEN American Center, *Chilling Effects: NSA Surveillance Drives U.S. Writers to Self-Censor*, Nov. 12, 2013, https://pen.org/sites/default/files/Chilling% 20Effects_PEN%20American.pdf.
45. CHURCH COMMITTEE REPORT, *supra* note 3, at 1 ("Unless new and tighter controls are established by legislation, domestic intelligence activities threaten to undermine our democratic society and fundamentally alter its nature.").
46. United States v. Jones, 132 S.Ct. 945, 956 (2012) (Sotomayor, J., concurring). *See also* Cohen, *supra* note 15, at 1905, 1927 ("Privacy therefore is an indispensable structural feature of liberal democratic political systems." "Privacy furthers fundamental public policy goals relating to liberal democratic citizenship, innovation, and human flourishing."); CHURCH COMMITTEE REPORT, *supra* note 3, at 3 ("When a police system passes beyond these limits, it is dangerous to the proper administration of justice and to human liberty, which it should be our first concern to cherish ... There is always a possibility that a secret police may become a menace to free government and free institutions because it carries with it the possibility of abuses of power which are not always quickly apprehended or understood.") (quoting Justice Harlan Fisk Stone).
47. Marie-Helen Maras, *The Social Consequences of a Mass Surveillance Measure: What Happens When We Become the "Others?"* 40 INT'L J. OF L, CRIME & JUSTICE 65 (2012).
48. *See* Emina Subašića et al., *Leadership, Power and the Use of Surveillance: Implications of Shared Social Identity for Leaders' Capacity to Influence*, 22 THE LEADERSHIP Q. 170 (2011).
49. Marcus Jacob & Marcel Tyrell, *The Legacy of Surveillance: An Explanation for Social Capital Erosion and Persistent Economic Disparity between West and East Germany*, Apr. 15, 2010, http://ssrn.com/abstract=1554604.
50. *See* JEFFREY KAHN, MRS. SHIPLEY'S GHOST: THE RIGHT TO TRAVEL AND TERRORIST WATCHLISTS (2013); Jeffrey Kahn, *Terrorist Watchlists*, in THE CAMBRIDGE HANDBOOK OF SURVEILLANCE LAW (2017).
51. P.C. Vey, THE NEW YORKER, Nov. 14, 2014. Another piece of insightful comedy that challenges blasé responses to threats of broad and indiscriminate government surveillance is John Oliver's interview with Edward Snowden, which is available at www.youtube.com/watch?v=XEVlyP4_11M.
52. One recent study, dubbed the Helsinki Privacy Experiment, suggests the answer. In this study, test subjects lived for six months in homes that were innervated with surveillance cameras and microphones. Subjects were also tracked and their internet activities and communications were closely monitored. By design, none of this surveillance was surreptitious. In a set of preliminary findings, researchers report that subjects initially exhibited discomfort with this constant surveillance,

but those effects diminished over time. More interesting, however, was the fact that all the test subjects developed and deployed adaptations and countermeasures in order to avoid surveillance. In some cases, subjects modified their behaviors when in the presence of surveillance. In others, they stopped engaging in certain activities and behaviors altogether. Subjects also routinely sought out areas that were not under surveillance, particularly when engaging in intimate activities or potentially embarrassing activities – but also just to achieve some relief. This constellation of behaviors demonstrated a strong desire among the test subjects for some degree of privacy. *See* Antii Oulavirta et al., *Long-term Effects of Ubiquitous Surveillance in the Home,* PROC. 2012 ASSOC. COMPUTING MACHINERY CONF. ON UBIQUITOUS COMPUTING, 41 (2012), https://people.mpi-inf.mpg.de/~oantti/pubs/ubicomp2012-oulasvirta.pdf.

53. *See, e.g.,* Sara Peters, *Believe It Or Not, Millennials Do Care About Privacy, Security,* Oct. 13, 2015, www.darkreading.com/endpoint/believe-it-or-not-millennials-do-care-about-privacy-security/d/d-id/1322622; *Millennials Protest against Ineffective Security Practices,* www.intercede.com/latest-news-from-intercede/millennials-protest-against-ineffective-security-practices/; Amanda Hess, *Millennials Aren't Oversharing on Social Media (So What Are They Hiding?),* Oct. 18, 2013, www.slate.com/blogs/xx_factor/2013/10/18/millennials_on_social_media_young_people_are_incredibly_savvy_about_internet.html; Daniel Rothberg, *Millennials, Bad at Being Private, Value Privacy,* L.A. TIMES, June 21, 2013, http://articles.latimes.com/2013/jun/21/news/la-ol-millennials-private-value-privacy-20130620; Jay Stanley, *Do Young People Care About Privacy?,* Apr. 29, 2013, www.aclu.org/blog/do-young-people-care-about-privacy; Dan Tynan, *Millennials Do Care About Internet Privacy, They're Just Smarter About It,* Apr. 22, 2013, www.itworld.com/article/2709866/it-management/millennials-do-care-about-internet-privacy--they-re-just-smarter-about-it.html; Chris Jay Hoofnagle et al., *How Different Are Young Adults from Older Adults When It Comes to Information Privacy Attitudes and Policies?* Apr. 14, 2010, http://ssrn.com/abstract=1589864.
54. *See, e.g.,* DANAH BOYD, IT'S COMPLICATED (2014).
55. United States v. Jones, 132 S.Ct. 945 (2012).
56. Jones, 132 S.Ct. at 964 (Alito, J., concurring).
57. *Id.*
58. Jones, 132 S.Ct. at 956 (Sotomayor, J., concurring).
59. Renée McDonald Hutchins, *Tied Up in Knotts? GPS Technology and the Fourth Amendment,* 55 UCLA L. REV. 409, 444 (2007).

1

Our Age of Surveillance

Until quite recently, threats to the Fourth Amendment right of the people to be secure against unreasonable searches and seizures came from physical searches and seizures. These threats persist, but in the twenty-first century, we face a whole new class of threats. Today, law enforcement officers and other government agents have access to a wide variety of new and emerging technologies that allow them to conduct searches and seizures without physically intruding upon our persons, houses, papers, or effects. These technologies mark the advent of our age of surveillance. In this chapter we examine some of these modern means and methods. In the chapters that follow we will ask whether the Fourth Amendment has a role to play in limiting government access to these techniques and technologies.

Tracking Technologies in an Age of Surveillance

Contemporary conversations about government surveillance technologies trace to a Supreme Court case decided in 2012 called *United States v. Jones*,[1] which we discussed briefly in the Introduction. In that case, police officers in the District of Columbia attached small tracking devices to several cars owned and operated by suspects in a major drug conspiracy. These devices pinpointed their locations by using the network of satellites in geosynchronous orbit above the Earth that comprise the Global Positioning System (GPS). The devices transmitted that location information to receiving equipment operated by investigators. That location information was then transferred to a police computer, where it was aggregated and compiled in order to render a complete and detailed record of the suspects' movements over the course of four weeks, including regular visits to locations associated with the conspiracy.

The technology used by officers in *Jones* may be familiar to some readers. Investigators used a similar technology during the second season of David Simon's series *The Wire* to track suspects associated with a drug organization. Based on the tracked suspects' patterns of travel over the course of several weeks, those fictional investigators were able to target locations associated with the conspiracy and to identify new suspects. With the benefit of that information, they eventually seized illegal narcotics and arrested several participants in the conspiracy. All of this was accomplished from the comfort of the officers' base of operations. None of the investigators had to leave the office or spend cold nights in unmarked cars tailing suspects or conducting stakeouts. Their GPS devices and computers did all the hard work.

Law enforcement officers are not the only people to use GPS-enabled trackers. These devices are available to consumers interested in tracking pets, children, spouses, computers, keys, or just about anything else one might want to locate or monitor. GPS technology is embedded in many of the technologies we use on a daily basis. The navigation systems in cars use GPS, which allows these devices to determine our precise locations, chart directions, and even monitor speed. OnStar and similar services use GPS devices in our cars. Smartphones use GPS technology and many cellphone applications access and use this location information – sometimes even if the application itself has nothing to do with location, such as Angry Birds, Brightest Flashlight, Pandora, and even dictionary apps. Many flip phones are also GPS enabled. An increasing range of wearable technologies such as health monitors use GPS to determine how far their wearers walk, run, or bike. GPS is so ubiquitous, in fact, that readers probably have at least one personal GPS tracker on or near them at all times – many readers routinely have several, calculating and logging their precise locations on a constant basis.

Many users of electronic devices do not know, or at least do not think about, how many GPS-enabled tracking devices they live with on a daily basis. They just enter a destination into their navigation systems, open an app on their phones to find the closest coffee shop, or beam with pride when their watch tells them they have walked five miles. Even when users do think about the fact that their cars, computers, and personal devices can pinpoint their locations and track their movements over time, they assume that this information is private or otherwise inaccessible to the government. This assumption is wrong.

We routinely, if unwittingly, share location information gathered by our electronic devices. Some of this sharing is through metadata. Metadata comprises a range of invisible information associated with and embedded in electronic files. The metadata associated with pictures taken using smartphones and cameras often contain location information. Whenever a user shares these pictures, she also shares the metadata, including where the picture was taken and when. Unless users take the time to examine the settings on their devices, metadata associated with tweets, Facebook postings, and text messages will also contain embedded location information. Many devices and applications also share location information automatically. Cellular phones constantly share location information with cellular networks. Applications like Google Maps continuously share location information, which allows them to perform tasks like calculating traffic flow (if Google sees that there are lots of smartphones stopped on a highway, then it concludes that there is a traffic jam). Social networking apps gather and share location information with "friends" and commercial partners, which allows sellers to target offers based on where a user goes or might happen to be at any particular time. As part of the "internet of things,"[2] smart devices also share location information with other smart devices, allowing your refrigerator to send a reminder to buy milk when you are near the grocery store and your thermostat to adjust the temperature in your house when it sees that you are on your way home. Many apps are just leaky, generating large volumes of what former Director of the Central Intelligence Agency (CIA) and head of the National Security Agency (NSA), General Michael Hayden, has described as our "digital exhaust."[3] That location information is free and available to anyone who has the inclination and know-how to collect it.

Many government agencies are so inclined and they know how to gather location information generated by GPS-enabled devices on both a routine and a case-by-case basis. In a moment, we will discuss some of the "Big Data" programs operated by state and federal agencies. Many of these programs can and do gather location information from our devices,[4] allowing government agents to track individuals directly by gathering and interpreting data that is generated, shared, or leaked by our devices.[5] Government agents can also gain access to location data generated by GPS-enabled devices through third parties, including the app makers and service providers with whom we share location information in order to obtain goods and services. Finally, government agents can simply look at our social network sites, which often disclose where we are and store a rich history of where we have been.

This may all seem like paranoid fantasy, but the facts prove otherwise. For example, several programs uncovered among documents leaked by former security contractor Edward Snowden reveal that the NSA is "piggybacking on the tools that enable Internet advertisers to track consumers using 'cookies' and location data to pinpoint targets for government hacking and to bolster surveillance."[6] Another program "aggregates leaked location-based service/location-aware application data to infer IP address geo-locations."[7] The NSA's infamous telephonic metadata program, which we will discuss at length in a moment, also gathers location information that is embedded in or could be inferred from the metadata it receives from telephone companies.[8]

When law enforcement agencies cannot get location and tracking information through these surreptitious means, they can get it from third-party service providers such as Twitter, Google, and Facebook. Service providers and commercial partners track consumers' geolocation to facilitate their provision of goods and services. More and more, those third parties share that information with the government, even if sometimes unwittingly. As a consequence, it is a pretty solid bet that a government agent knows where you are right now, or could find out with minimal effort if she cared to look, because you have a smartphone in your pocket, a tablet in your bag, a GPS-enabled device on your wrist, or you are sitting in your car.

GPS is not the only tracking technology available to law enforcement and other government agencies that are interested in tracking cell phones and their users. Cellular phones function by linking to wireless networks through cellular base transceiver stations. Because service providers often deploy these transceivers on towers or in arrays deployed on tall buildings, people usually refer to them by their more colloquial name: cell towers. Whenever your phone is powered on, it is in communication with local cell towers. Your cellular service provider uses the strength of the signal between your phone and local towers to calculate your location. This cell site location information (CSLI) can be quite precise, particularly in areas that have a high density of cell towers. CSLI is even more precise if a provider uses multiple towers to triangulate the location of a phone, rivaling or surpassing the accuracy of GPS.[9]

Cellular service providers generate CSLI as part of their normal course of business in order to route calls using the strongest available signal, to account for interference, and to avoid signal congestion. Service providers are also required to generate CSLI so that emergency response personnel will know where to go should you use your phone to call 911. In addition to allowing real-time location and tracking, service providers also store CSLI. This historical CSLI shows where your device has been, how it got there, and how long it stayed for periods going back weeks, months, or years. As the United States Supreme Court pointed out recently, CSLI can therefore be used to "reconstruct someone's specific movements down to the minute, not only around town but also within a particular building."[10]

Although government agents do not have direct access to CSLI or historical CSLI, they can get this information from cellular service providers fairly easily. In some cases they just have to ask, but in most cases a subpoena issued by a prosecutor or grand jury is more than enough.[11] As a matter of current Fourth Amendment law, they do not have to get a warrant, which is what would be required to search your home.[12] As a consequence, law enforcement makes liberal use of CSLI, and particularly historical CSLI, in their investigations free from stringent Fourth Amendment constraints.

Another tracking technology that is rapidly expanding governmental surveillance capacities is Radio Frequency Identification (RFID). RFID tags contain unique identity information that can be read by specialized devices. RFID tags come in a variety of shapes and sizes ranging from key fobs to tiny chips to cylinders the size of rice grains. RFID tags have become ubiquitous in recent years. Their most common use is to track goods. For example, a shirt made in Vietnam might have an embedded RFID tag, which would then allow that shirt to be tracked from packaging, shipping, delivery to a retail store, display, and all the way through to sale. RFID tags are also embedded in everything from computers to office supplies to pants as a security measure to protect against workplace theft and shoplifting. Apartment buildings, schools, dorms, and offices control entry using RFID tags embedded in key fobs or access cards. These entry control systems allow facility managers to track who comes, who goes, and when. Drivers use RFID tags to pay tolls or to enter secure parking garages. Mass transit riders use RFID to pay their fares. Increasingly, credit cards and identification cards, including driver's licenses and passports, have embedded RFID tags. Pet owners have RFID tags implanted in their dogs, cats, and horses. People also use RFID – or a similar technology called Near-Field Communication – as a means of payment. The quick pay fobs used by retailers and Apple Pay both use these technologies. People have also started experimenting with implanting RFID devices under their skin, which allows them to unlock doors and pay for dinner with a wave of their hands.

Some readers may be vaguely aware that they are carrying around RFID tracking devices in key fobs and identification cards. They are probably completely unaware, however, that many of their clothes, bags, and other consumer items also have embedded RFID tags. Although these tags may be artifacts of supply-chain monitoring, they remain present and active, offering anyone with the inclination and know-how to "read" not just our identification and credit cards, but our papers and effects.

RFID technologies are inherently leaky. Using relatively inexpensive hardware and information widely available on the Internet almost anyone can read information from the various RFID tags we carry in our pockets and on our persons. In recognition of this fact, there is now a cottage industry in countermeasures, including RFID blocking wallets, purses, computer cases, and passport holders. Few people actually use these security devices, many or most of which may not be very effective in the first place. As a consequence, a lot of your stuff is talking to the world. The question, then, is "Who is listening?"

Because RFID tags are linked to us through what we carry and what we wear, they offer government agencies a unique opportunity to track just about everyone or to monitor who is entering and leaving buildings, transportation hubs, stadiums, or passing by on the sidewalk. For example, immigration agents at border crossings check RFID tags, which have been embedded in US passports since at least 2007. Some government buildings also use RFID to limit access and to track the movements of people inside. In terms of its potential, however, the technology is basically limitless. We all carry these devices and RFID readers are more and more common. To the extent it is not already true, then, we will soon live in a world where the government will be able to track us every time we leave the house by using our wallets, keys, electronic devices, and even our clothes.

In response to all of this developing potential, some readers might ask, "So what?" After all, tracking is hardly new. In fact, stakeouts and tails – both forms of tracking – are long-standing staples in law enforcement practice, but nobody seems to worry too much about these means and methods.[13] Moreover, the information gathered by both traditional and more modern means of tracking is predominately open to public view. Law enforcement officers conducting tracking operations are just gathering the same information we make available to passersby on a routine basis. Although modern means of tracking may be more efficient than traditional methods, which require significant commitments of labor, personnel, and materiel, the information is the same. Why, then, should any of this bother us if the new technology does nothing more than enhance law enforcement efficiency?[14]

The answer is in the technology itself and its ability to effect material changes in our personal lives and democratic culture. Traditional tracking methods are very expensive and labor-intensive. They can easily involve dozens of officers, multiple cars, and even aerial support, not to mention thousands of personnel hours. As a consequence, sustained efforts to track persons using traditional means are quite rare.[15] Law enforcement agencies will commit these kinds of resources only in cases where they already have good reason to target particular persons and only if the crimes involved are sufficiently significant to justify the expenditure.

In contrast to traditional means and methods, modern tracking technologies are highly scalable and grow less and less expensive all the time. They run automatically and autonomously. They gather information constantly, analyze it repeatedly using computer algorithms, and store it forever, all without taxing limited labor resources.[16] As a consequence, law enforcement officers and other government officials no longer need to make hard decisions about who to track, when, or for how long. Modern means and methods give them the capacity to track all of us, all the time, everywhere we go without needing to justify their interest in any one of us in particular. This kind of broad, pervasive, and utterly indiscriminate surveillance is something that simply cannot be achieved using traditional means of tracking. It is also the very definition of a surveillance state.

The difference in terms of surveillance potential between traditional tracking methods and modern tracking technologies is not merely quantitative; it is qualitative in terms of its effects on us, our daily lives, and our society.[17] In a world where law enforcement only has access to traditional tracking methods, the vast majority of us can go about our daily lives completely secure in the fact that we have never been, are not, and never will be subjected to extended governmental surveillance. By contrast, granting government agents unfettered access to modern tracking technologies means that all of us must live with the daily reality that we are or very well might be tracked wherever we go and whatever we do. This kind of panoptic existence effects material changes in our basic assumptions about daily life and has deleterious effects on us as individuals and on the dynamics of our democratic society. Justice Sotomayor emphasized many of these concerns in the *Jones* case, pointing out that

> [a]wareness that the Government may be watching chills associational and expressive freedoms. And the Government's unrestrained power to assemble data that reveal private aspects of identity is susceptible to abuse. The net result is that GPS monitoring – by making available at a relatively low cost such a substantial quantum of intimate information about any person whom the Government, in its unfettered discretion, chooses to track – may "alter the relationship between citizen and government in a way that is inimical to democratic society."[18]

Faced with the possibility of constant tracking, some readers might seek solace in the hope that they are unworthy of this kind of government attention. For example, you might believe that you are not doing anything wrong, so the government will not bother tracking you. This, of course, reflects twentieth-century thinking. The fact that we are not doing anything wrong provides considerable protection against government tracking in a world where limits on resources and capacities require law enforcement and other government agencies to make choices about who to track. That logic no longer holds.

Although we may not be doing anything wrong, law enforcement and other government agents can now track all of us with little effort and at low cost. In fact, it may be harder and more expensive for systems carrying out broad and indiscriminate surveillance to avoid tracking particular persons or groups.[19] That flip, from a world where we can assume that the government only tracks people for good and sufficient reasons to a world where we can assume that the government is tracking all of us all the time for no particular reason, is what marks the qualitative difference between the life we know and life in an age of surveillance. That shift matters quite a bit both for us individually and for our democratic society.

Drones in an Age of Surveillance

There is perhaps no image more evocative of a surveillance state than a remote eye in the sky casting its watchful gaze across the world, capturing everyone and everything in its broad, indiscriminate, and unblinking stare.[20] That image is now a reality with the advent of unmanned aerial vehicles (UAVs), often called drones. UAVs first came to public attention as tools of war.[21] Perhaps the most famous of these warrior UAVs are Predator drones, which have been deployed in Iraq, Afghanistan, Pakistan, and Yemen, among other conflict zones, serving as platforms for both surveillance and offensive action.

The Obama administration was particularly aggressive in its use of military UAVs, conducting hundreds of attacks that killed thousands of terrorist suspects and civilians.[22]

Although drones got their start in war zones, they have become fixtures in domestic airspace as well.[23] The Department of Homeland Security operates Predator drones along the US border with Mexico to assist in immigration control.[24] The Environmental Protection Agency uses drones to monitor the condition of land and water as well as to ensure compliance with administrative regulations. Emergency responders deploy UAVs to assist with firefighting, search and rescue, and disaster response. The private sector uses drones for applications ranging from livestock management to real estate sales.[25] Photojournalists use drones to capture images of public events. Private citizens fly them for fun. Companies like Domino's Pizza and Amazon have even experimented with drones as ways to deliver goods.

Advancements in drone technology have fueled this proliferation, which will accelerate in the coming years.[26] Drones now come cheap. For a few hundred dollars, anyone can buy a drone equipped with high-powered cameras capable of detailed surveillance. Many of these consumer drones can be controlled easily by even the rankest of amateurs with a smartphone or tablet.[27] As a consequence, drones have become an increasingly common feature in public spaces.[28]

Given the relatively low cost and virtually unlimited potential of drones as both a surveillance and weapons platform, it should come as no surprise that domestic law enforcement agencies have invested in drones. Local police forces routinely deploy drones at public events like parades and festivals to monitor potential risks and to record video that can be used for later analysis.[29] They use drones to monitor traffic and to spot speeders and reckless drivers. Police use drones to conduct more targeted, covert surveillance as well.[30] Some drones used for these purposes can be as small as insects, rendering them virtually invisible to innocent citizens and suspects alike.[31] Other drones are capable of fully autonomous flight, allowing for long-term deployment or as a means to conduct continuous surveillance without any need for direct human control.[32] Although many of these more specialized drone technologies can be quite expensive, prices are plummeting. In the relatively near future, drones may be nearly as familiar in public airspace as airplanes, helicopters, or even birds. With the rise of drones, we therefore face a world dominated by thousands of eyes in our skies.

Although it may be reasonable now for most of us most of the time to assume that we are not subject to surveillance by drones, that security is surely short-lived. The reality is that as drones become more sophisticated and less expensive, law enforcement and other government agencies will rely on them more and more often as a means to leverage limited human resources, improve efficiency, and expand their surveillance capacities. In some cases, these drones will be easy to spot. In many cases they will not, either because they are so small or because they operate at high altitudes. As a consequence, even when we cannot see drones, chances are that they will be there, constantly watching, monitoring, and recording. This is the seemingly inevitable reality of our age of surveillance.

The idea that police and other government agents are or very well may be watching us from aerial platforms is unsettling, to say the least. It certainly has the Big Brother aspect that characterizes life in a surveillance state. For that reason, granting law enforcement and other government agencies unlimited licenses to deploy and use UAVs threatens to effect fundamental changes to the basic conditions of individual and collective life.[33] The natural question, then, is whether this kind of constant surveillance is inevitable or whether the Fourth Amendment's guarantee against threats of unreasonable search and seizure might set some reassuring limits.

Cell Site Simulators in an Age of Surveillance

Early generation analogue cellular phones were essentially handheld radios. The only real difference was that by using a telephone company as intermediary cellular phones could communicate over distances far greater than their native carrying capacities would otherwise allow. As a consequence of this basic technical design, early generation cellular phones were highly vulnerable to passive surveillance. With a modified radio scanner, just about anyone could eavesdrop on cellular phone conversations in their immediate areas without leaving any traces of their snooping.[34] Cognizant of this vulnerability, Congress directed the Federal Communications Commission in 1992 to regulate the sale of devices capable of intercepting cellular phone signals.[35] Unfortunately, those regulations did little to stop private snooping and did nothing at all to stop snooping by law enforcement officers or other government agents.

Any need for Congress to regulate further the interception of analogue cellular phone signals was rendered moot by the move to digital technologies in the 1990s. That is both because interpreting digital signals raises more technical hurdles and because service providers started embedding encryption technologies in their network infrastructures. By digitizing and encrypting cellular phone communications, cellular phone companies more or less put casual snoops out of business. For at least two reasons, that technological shift did little or nothing to stop government spying, however. The first is weak encryption. The second is that government agents gained access to more sophisticated spying hardware, including cell site simulators.

As law professor Stephanie Pell and technologist Chris Soghoian report in their seminal article on cell site simulators, some cellular networks do not use any encryption at all.[36] Among those that do, the most commonly used encryption algorithm is known as A5/1. A5/1 is ubiquitous in second-generation or "2G" networks and, at the time, provided fairly good security. Unfortunately, A5/1 was publicly broken by researchers in 1999.[37] In the intervening years, the technology needed to intercept and decrypt A5/1-encrypted cellular phone communications in real time became cheap and widely available. As a consequence, eavesdropping on cellular phone conversations was well within the reach of anyone with the time and inclination. That included law enforcement and other government agencies.

Since 2009, most major cellular phone providers have slowly migrated their network infrastructures away from 2G to third generation (3G) and now fourth generation (4G) technologies. In addition to faster data transmission speeds, that shift allows many of these networks to adopt newer, more robust encryption protocols such as the A5/3 algorithm and, eventually, A5/4.[38] Although government spy agencies like the NSA probably have the capacity to decrypt communications protected using A5/3, it has not been cracked publicly in the same way as A5/1. This means that most users who have a 3G- or 4G-enabled phone and also are connected to a 3G or 4G network can feel fairly secure from threats of passive eavesdropping by casual snoops or local law enforcement. The problem is that users do not always have updated technology or access to updated networks. Moreover, they remain vulnerable to surveillance and even eavesdropping by agents and agencies using more active surveillance devices such as cell site simulators.

Cell site simulators are sometimes referred to as International Mobile Subscriber Identity (IMSI) catchers or by using one of several colorful model names such as "Dirtbox,"[39] "Triggerfish," "Stingray," and "Hailstorm."[40] In essence, cell site simulators behave like the cellular base stations that form the backbone of cellular networks. Usually mounted on towers or the tops of buildings, cellular base stations are the conduits through which users send and receive voice, text, and data communications. Whenever a cellular phone is turned on, it is constantly in contact with service networks through local cellular base stations by sending and receiving information that includes device identification numbers, telephone numbers, and location information. This constant communication allows service providers to coordinate communications, direct cellular signals through the closest, least congested, or most powerful base stations, and therefore to provide users with the most reliable service. As is required under federal law, communication between user devices and local base stations also allows providers to locate users in the event of a 911 call or other emergency.

Because cell site simulators impersonate a user's cellular network, they can gather all the same information that is routinely shared with network base stations. This includes the device identification numbers and phone numbers associated with every device within range, the locations of those devices, and the contents of any communications. This information can be a boon to investigators. It allows them to locate suspects' phones and, therefore, suspects themselves.[41] It also allows them to identify the phones being used by known suspects in order to apply for wiretap orders.[42] This is particularly useful in situations where suspects use disposable "burner" phones. In some cases, it may also allow officers to identify suspects in the first instance by cross-referencing lists of phones in the vicinity of a crime with databases such as criminal history and property records.[43] But this is neither the limit of cell site simulators' capacities nor the limit of their usefulness for government surveillance.

In addition to capturing information about telephones operating in their vicinities, most cell site simulators in use by law enforcement, such as the Harris Corporation's Stingray, have the capacity to eavesdrop on calls, texts, and internet activity. In some cases, these capacities are limited by the fact that the cell site simulators available to many law enforcement agencies operate on 2G technology. 3G- and 4G-enabled phones would therefore preferentially bypass a Stingray in favor of a legitimate service network featuring 3G or 4G capacities. Cell site simulators, such as the Harris Corporation's Hailstorm, have the capacity to act like 3G and 4G base stations. Even here, however, the capacity to intercept content is limited. Most 3G and 4G phones use A5/3 encryption when communicating with 3G and 4G base stations, including any cell site simulators posing as 3G or 4G base stations. As of yet, A5/3 remains sufficiently secure to prevent decryption by imposter devices. That does not mean, however, that 3G and 4G phones are entirely secure.

All cellular phones, even the most modern, are designed to work seamlessly with older networks. This backward compatibility enables them to function in areas where upgrades have not been made to the local network or where more advanced networks are down or overloaded. Most users are familiar with this functionality having seen small icons on their phones indicating whether they are on, say, 4G or the Edge. Cell site simulators in use by domestic government agencies and law enforcement have the capacity to mask or block other cell towers, thereby presenting themselves as the best, or only, available cell tower. As a consequence, all phones in range of these devices are forced to connect to the cell site simulator, which, in turn, presents itself as part of a 2G network. All connected phones respond accordingly, downgrading their encryption protocols to A5/1. These "roll back attacks" render phones captured by a cell site simulator utterly transparent, allowing law enforcement to listen to calls, read texts, and monitor internet usage, all in real time.[44]

It is hard to imagine a surveillance technology more suited to broad and indiscriminate surveillance than cell site simulators. By design, they gather information relating to *all* cellular phones within their geographic areas of operation. In most urban areas, that includes hundreds or thousands of phones belonging to residents and passersby.[45] These devices are also portable. In fact, most are installed in cars or sport-utility vehicles. This mobility allows law enforcement agencies to conduct focused monitoring in a particular area, to scan systematically large areas, to troll at random, or to track suspect phones when they are in motion. That means that, over the course of a relatively short investigation, officers will gather identification information, user data, and location information on tens of thousands of phones and their owners while also potentially having access to the contents of their voice, text, and data communications.

Cell site simulators are not only indiscriminate, but they are also increasingly widespread. Devices like the Stingray were designed for use by intelligence agencies engaged in foreign operations where operatives did not always have access to user information or the contents of cellular phone conversations through lawful means like warrants, subpoenas, and wiretap orders.[46] It did not take long, however, for domestic law enforcement agencies to join the club. According to the Electronic Privacy Information Center, which sued the Federal Bureau of Investigation (FBI) under the Freedom of Information Act seeking information about the domestic use of Stingrays and other cell site simulators, federal agents were deploying and using these devices by at least 1995.[47] As of 2016, at least thirteen separate federal agencies operating on domestic soil had cell site simulators at their disposal, including the FBI, the NSA, most branches of the armed services, the Drug Enforcement Administration, Homeland Security, and the Internal Revenue Service.[48]

State law enforcement agencies were slower to adopt cell site simulators due primarily to prohibitive cost and limited access. As with all technologies, the price has dropped significantly in recent years to the point where most local law enforcement agencies can afford to own cell site simulators. Even those who cannot buy them still have access through partnerships and other agreements with federal agencies like the FBI and Homeland Security. As a result, we know that state or local law enforcement agencies in at least twenty-two states have ready access to cell site simulators.[49] That number is likely quite a bit higher, however.[50] We just cannot know for sure because the deployment and use of cell site simulators is shrouded by strict rules of secrecy enforced by the Department of Justice and Homeland Security.

Under agreements with the Department of Justice and in accordance with rules promulgated by the Federal Communications Commission, the Harris Corporation, which is the primary supplier of cell site simulators in the United States, will only sell or lease their wares to government and law enforcement agencies. Moreover, any state or local law enforcement agency that buys, rents, or otherwise takes possession of a cell site simulator must enter into an agreement with the Department of Justice and Homeland Security. Under the terms of these agreements, those state and local agencies cannot disclose the nature and operation of the devices or expose their use in official court documents.[51] This means that police investigators must hide their use of cell site simulators in court documents and investigatory reports.[52] This may be accomplished by omission or by attributing information gathered by cell site simulators to "confidential sources."[53] In cases where defendants have nevertheless discovered what is afoot, local prosecutors have gone so far as to drop criminal charges in order to avoid exposing the use of cell site simulators to judicial review.[54]

Despite these efforts to preserve secrecy, journalists and activists have documented the fact that cell site simulators are in frequent use. For example, information secured by investigative reporters shows that the Baltimore Police Department used cell site simulators at least 4,300 times between 2007 and 2015 – or more than twice a day over the course of eight years.[55] Although less is known about the frequency of use in other areas of the country due to those nondisclosure agreements enforced by the Department of Justice, reliable reporting suggests that Baltimore is not an outlier.[56]

As a consequence of their indiscriminate nature, widespread deployment, and frequency of use, the chances are that everyone reading this book who has owned or used a cellular phone since 2007 has been surveilled by a cell site simulator at least once. For readers who have visited urban areas or have passed through or by sensitive security areas like airports, government offices, prisons, and military facilities, chances are you have been surveilled multiple times. For those living in urban areas or who regularly pass by or through sensitive security areas, surveillance by cell site simulators is probably a routine fact of daily life. None of us ever knows, of course. That is because these devices act like normal cellular base stations. You have therefore probably never had any reason to suspect that you are being spied upon,[57] save perhaps a time or two when your phone seems inexplicably to have access only to a 2G network.

Cell site simulators became a point of controversy in 2015 as a result of several investigative news reports. In the wake of this media attention, the Department of Justice directed its own agents to refrain from using cell site simulators without first getting a warrant based on probable cause.[58] The Department of Homeland Security subsequently followed suit.[59] That is a completely voluntary policy, however. Some federal statutes, including the Electronic Communications Privacy Act and the Wiretap Act, may regulate the use of cell site simulators to gather contents of communications, but those laws were not written to cover these devices, and therefore fail to provide much guidance or protection.[60] A few states have also passed laws governing the use of cell site simulators by their law enforcement agencies.[61] One state appellate court has also held that police officers in that state must get a warrant before deploying or using cell site simulators.[62] As it stands, however, there are no nationwide laws or federal constitutional rules governing the deployment and use of cell site simulators.

Unlike physical searches of homes or the use of infrared heat detection devices, both of which are governed by the Fourth Amendment, law enforcement's use of Stingray devices is entirely at their discretion or limited only by the fickle leanings of the political branches. Moreover, even where the use of cell site simulators is limited by law or policy, it does not provide very much protection for innocent persons. That is because the devices, by nature and design, gather information about every phone inside their areas of operation, gathering "incidental" information about thousands of perfectly innocent users every time they are deployed and used. It is akin to suspecting that one tenant in an apartment building may have a marijuana plant in his closet and then allowing law enforcement to search every apartment in the building.

In light of the surveillance capacities of cell site simulators, their widespread use, the paucity of statutory regulations, and the utter absence of constitutional limitations, each of us and all of us live under the constant threat that our personal information, our locations, our movements, and even the contents of our cellular communications, whether as voice, text, or data, are subject to government surveillance for good reasons, bad reasons, or for no reasons at all. It is hard to imagine a better example of conditions characteristic of a surveillance state or a means and method of government surveillance more in need of Fourth Amendment regulation.

Big Data in an Age of Surveillance

Big Data is an umbrella term applied to technologies and programs that aggregate, store, and analyze large amounts of information of different kinds from a variety of sources. The scale of Big Data programs can be massive – on the order of not just terabytes (most consumer hard drives hold one or two terabytes) but petabytes (one quadrillion bytes or one thousand terabytes), exabytes (one quintillion bytes or one million terabytes), zettabytes (one sextillion bytes or one billion terabytes), and even yottabytes (one septillion bytes or one trillion terabytes).[63] In order to manage, organize, and analyze this amount of information, Big Data programs utilize computer algorithms, including machine-learning algorithms, which adapt over time based on their iterative experiences with data and human operators.[64] These algorithms sort through large data sets in order to find meaningful needles in the haystack, identify patterns, categorize persons and things, spot potential threats, monitor trends, reconstruct past events, and predict future events.

Big Data is huge and omnipresent. In the commercial sector, companies like Netflix and Amazon use Big Data to recommend movies, books, and products. Google uses Big Data to fill ad space on websites with advertisements uniquely targeted to each user. Retailers use Big Data to identify customers and to develop and refine products. Financial institutions use Big Data to assess the credit worthiness of customers and potential customers. Big Data is particularly useful in these efforts because it often identifies unexpected correlations that serve as strong signals of particular interests, tendencies, tastes, or character traits. For example, Target made the news in 2012 after it used Big Data to determine that female customers who start buying unscented lotion are more likely to be pregnant.[65] Armed with that information, Target sent advertisements and coupons for other pregnancy and baby-related goods to these customers – in at least one case spoiling the surprise! Financial institutions using Big Data have also found that people who buy protective pads to put under the feet of their furniture tend to be very good credit risks.[66]

Big Data is useful for more than just consumer marketing. For example, epidemiologists use Big Data to project disease outbreaks and the progression of infections through populations.[67] Researchers also use Big Data in the form of biostatistics to identify disease risk factors and early intervention strategies by aggregating and analyzing data relating to genetics, medical history, and lifestyle.[68] In order to facilitate these important public health efforts, the Affordable Care Act requires providers and insurers to gather and report anonymized health information, which is aggregated and used for research purposes and for wellness programs.[69] Big Data is also very useful in helping financial institutions and insurers in their efforts to identify and prevent fraud.[70]

Big Data is not an unadulterated good, however. It can also be quite dangerous.[71] Particularly in light of its predictive powers, Big Data can be used not only to serve but also to manipulate and control.[72] For example, Big Data can be used by marketers and search engines to identify personal trigger points and to direct consumer choice, often by exploiting irrational bias.[73] Big Data also yields both false negatives and false positives, resulting in unjust and even dangerous outcomes.[74] For example, it may incorrectly identify a potential homebuyer as a poor credit risk, effectively denying that person the opportunity to purchase a home. It may also falsely identify someone as a security risk, leading to denial of employment opportunities and limitations on the ability to travel.[75] There is also considerable evidence that many Big Data programs tend to disadvantage traditionally marginalized groups, perpetuating cycles of social, political, and economic injustice.[76] In recognition of these dangers, commentators have compared Big Data to the surveillance state described in George Orwell's *1984*, both because of its reach and because of its potential to repress and control.[77]

Given its power and potential, it is no surprise that government agencies at all levels have invested in Big Data in a big way. Big Data efforts at the local level trace back to 1994, when New York City Police Commissioner William Bratton introduced a data-driven policing model called "CompStat." CompStat aggregates a variety of data to identify crime hotspots, predict criminal activity, and strategically deploy police resources.[78] Most major police departments have since adopted some form of data-driven policing. Still, New York continues to lead the way, most recently with a program called the Domain Awareness System (DAS). Developed in collaboration with Microsoft, DAS aggregates and analyzes information from a wide variety of government and private databases, video streams from thousands of security cameras, and images from license-plate readers, toll plazas, and traffic cameras.[79] Given the scope of its surveillance capacities, DAS has been compared to Big Brother from George Orwell's *1984*. Confronted with this comparison, then Mayor Michael Bloomberg bragged that "We're not your mom and pop's police department anymore."[80]

New York is not the only local law enforcement agency to invest big in Big Data. Chicago has a similar system,[81] as does Alabama, which it operates in collaboration with Google.[82] Boston has been developing a system in collaboration with IBM that has real-time facial recognition capabilities.[83] Local law enforcement agencies around the country collaborate with federal authorities in a variety of information sharing environments, or ISEs, which are sometimes called fusion centers.[84] Housed in strategic locations all over the country, fusion centers facilitate the collection, aggregation, and analysis of data from sources including surveillance records, flight manifests, health records, and information relating to online activities.[85] ISEs permit local, state, and federal agencies to access and cross-reference information from these different sources.

There are databases that contain records of real estate transactions. Airlines and train operators have lists of passengers and toll service providers have records of cars that travel through their plazas. There are security cameras in public buildings and on public streets that monitor our comings and goings. Information from these sources was once kept in discrete silos. Moreover, data storage was once very expensive. Now ISEs and similar Big Data programs break down those barriers and the cost of data storage has plummeted. As a result, we now live in a world where Big Data can accomplish what Professor Christopher Slobogin has dubbed "panvasive" searches[86] and technologist Roger Clarke has called "mass dataveillance."[87]

In support of law enforcement, private contractors have joined the Big Data game. Some technology companies like Microsoft and Google collaborate with state and local law enforcement to develop and market Big Data technologies. Other companies have positioned themselves as data brokers that contract with law enforcement and government agencies to conduct Big Data searches.[88] Researcher Chris Hoofnagle has colorfully described these corporate data brokers as "Big Brother's Little Helpers" in recognition of both the scope of their dataveillance capacities and the fact that government agencies and law enforcement are among their most important clients.[89]

Big Data programs have access to an ever-widening variety of information sources. Credit histories, criminal records, property archives, consumer purchases, and internet searches are all gathered, stored, and mined. So, too, is data generated by devices comprising the "Internet of Things."[90] The Internet of Things encompasses items like our smartphones, computers, tablets, and wearable devices like fitness trackers and smart watches, which not only know where we are but also know how fast our hearts are beating. It also includes smart devices like televisions, thermostats, and even refrigerators that use Wi-Fi and Bluetooth to connect to other devices and to the Internet. There are even internet-enabled toys, like Hello Barbie, and home assistants, like Amazon's Alexa, that actively solicit and gather information. All of these devices gather, store, stream, and share a wide range of data, including when we arrive at home, what lights are on in the house, what we are talking about,[91] and whether we are running low on milk. Big Data stands ready to gather and analyze all of this information.

Big Data is not only interested in data from your device; it wants your body. As Professor Margaret Hu has shown, law enforcement and other government agencies have pressed to integrate biometric data as part of their broader efforts to "bureaucratize" surveillance.[92] That data may be in the form of something as familiar as your fingerprints or palm prints, but biometric markers also encompass the unique patterns of blood vessels on our retinas, DNA, facial features, bodily habits like gate and posture, voice prints, and even heartbeats. This is all data that we routinely disclose, and is therefore easy for Big Data programs to access, distribute, store, and analyze. Take fingerprints as an example.

Although law enforcement has been gathering fingerprints, uploading them into national databases, and using them for identification purposes for decades, the most common means of acquiring fingerprints was in the context of postarrest booking procedures. As a consequence, most of us could feel pretty certain that our fingerprints were not on file. That is no longer the case. Now we are required to give fingerprints in contexts ranging from school registration to professional licensing exams to employment background checks. Some of us even use our fingerprints to access our computers, phones, or tablets. As a result, it is a fair bet that one or more Big Data programs have access to your fingerprints.

More common still as a means of identification are our faces. Whether we apply for a driver's license, voter identification card, or a passport, we submit a picture that is digitized, analyzed, and shared across a range of databases. Leveraging that resource, programs like New York's Domain Awareness System now have the ability to identify us as we walk along the street using facial recognition software. Other systems that will be able to identify us by scanning our eyes from a distance of forty feet or more are under development.[93] The dystopian worlds depicted in films like *Minority Report* and *Enemy of the State* are therefore no longer science fiction.

By far the most notorious of the governmental Big Data programs are those revealed in documents leaked by former government contractor Edward Snowden in 2013. Boasting colorful names and acronyms, these programs document a sustained effort by the NSA, the FBI, the CIA, the Department of Homeland Security, the Department of Defense, and other units of the federal government to develop a comprehensive domestic surveillance program.[94] Take, for example, PRISM, under which the federal government compelled major internet service providers and technology companies to provide information relating to internet communications and internet activity.[95] In addition to PRISM, the NSA has also surreptitiously tapped into the physical components of these companies' cloud computing networks, gaining access to user data while it was in transit between secure data centers.[96]

XKEYSCORE, another high-profile program revealed in the Snowden documents, provided government analysts with the capacity to mine content and metadata generated by e-mail, chat, browsing activities, and "leaky" apps through a global network of servers and internet access points operated by private entities.[97] ESCHELON, which was a joint effort with Britain, Canada, Australia, and New Zealand, intercepted and stored the contents of digital communications.[98] STELLARWIND accessed e-mail metadata.[99] EVILOLIVE redirected internet traffic through government-controlled servers and switches in order to gather data and metadata generated by internet activity.[100] UPSTREAM, an umbrella program encompassing efforts like BLARNEY, FAIRVIEW, OAKSTAR, and STORMBREW, "Leverage[d] unique key corporate partnerships to gain access to high-capacity international fiber-optic cables, switches and/or routes throughout the world."[101] Programs like WELLSPRING, TUNDRAFREEZE, and PINWALE gathered and stored images of faces from electronic communications, websites, and social media, which could be cross-referenced with detailed satellite imagery to establish user locations.[102] PICES gathered biometric data at border crossings.[103]

Although these are just a few examples of the surveillance programs revealed in the Snowden leaks, they document a sustained effort by government agencies to aggregate as much data as they can, largely on an indiscriminate basis. These programs gathered the contents of communications, the specifics of internet activities, and the metadata associated with communications and internet activities. These programs also demonstrate a sustained effort to gather information relating to offline activities, such as financial transactions and movement through physical space by exploiting smartphone apps. Although some of these programs appear to have been dismantled, altered, or moved in the face of public criticism, there is no doubt that many of the same capabilities remain, have been reincarnated elsewhere, or easily could be revitalized. In short, it is a fairly safe bet that the government can, is already, or soon will be collecting enough data on a contemporary and perpetual basis to monitor everywhere we go and everything we do, say, or write when using or in the company of technology.[104]

These data-gathering efforts generate massive amounts of information. This data is aggregated into databases like DISHFIRE[105] and TRACFIN,[106] which store intercepted text messages and financial transaction records. These databases are housed in massive data storage facilities.[107] Of course, all of this gathered and stored data is worth very little without some way to mine it and analyze it. Law enforcement and intelligence agencies are therefore in the business of developing efficient and powerful analysis technologies that leverage supercomputers and analytic algorithms. For example, PREFER facilitates the scanning of large text databases.[108] RHINEHART, VoiceRT, Byblos, and SPITFIRE are parts of a continuing effort to decode and scan real-time and historical voice data.[109] BLACKBOOK conducts large-scale semantic data analysis, converting raw information into meaningful outputs.[110] CATALYST and APSTARS compile data profiles of entities and individuals and then document relationships among them. SKYNET and GHOSTFIRE conduct cloud-based analysis of bulk data, including "geospatial, geotemporal, pattern-of-life, and travel analytics."[111]

By far the most famous of the Big Data surveillance technologies revealed in the Snowden documents was the Section 215 telephonic metadata collection program operated by the NSA and the FBI in collaboration with major communications companies like AT&T and Verizon until June 2015, when it was modified by the USA Freedom Act.[112] Telephonic metadata refers to non-content information relating to telephone calls. This usually includes the numbers of the callers, the time and date of the call, the duration of the call, and routing information. For traditional landlines, routing information reveals location. In the case of cellular phones, that routing information provides general geographic location. The metadata associated with cellular phone calls can also include cell site location data discussed earlier.[113] Depending on the devices and the networks involved, telephonic metadata may also include GPS location information.[114]

Starting in October 2001, the NSA, with the cooperation of major telephone service providers, began collecting in bulk telephonic metadata associated with domestic telephone calls. That program was authorized by a presidential order issued by George W. Bush in the immediate aftermath of the terrorist attacks of September 11, 2001. That order also provided authority for the NSA to gather metadata associated with domestic internet communications and the contents of some international communications. That data was then stored and analyzed by the NSA on its own behalf and for other federal agencies, such as the FBI.

Although the October 2001 presidential order was justified by claims of emergency in the aftermath of the terrorist attacks of September 11, 2001, and therefore meant to provide only short-term authority, it was periodically renewed, allowing the NSA to continue gathering bulk telephonic metadata. Concerned with public scrutiny of surveillance programs, prompted by a series of high-profile stories in the *New York Times* in late 2005 and early 2006, the Bush administration and its corporate partners decided to seek judicial authority for the program. On behalf of the NSA, Department of Justice lawyers filed requests with the Foreign Surveillance Intelligence Court (FISC or FISA court)[115] for orders directing major communications companies to provide bulk telephonic metadata on an ongoing basis to the NSA. Those requests cited legislative authority for the program in Section 215 of the USA Patriot Act, as amended in 2006.[116] The bulk telephonic metadata program thus came to be known as the 215 program.

Documents leaked by Edward Snowden show that Verizon was one partner in the bulk metadata collection program. Although the NSA has declined to confirm other corporate partners, investigative reporting by the *New York Times*, the *Guardian*, and the *Washington Post* show that every major domestic telecommunications company provided telephonic metadata to the NSA under this program. The best available evidence therefore suggests that the NSA has gathered metadata associated with a substantial proportion of calls made or received using domestic telecommunications networks since at least 2006.

This effort was indiscriminate. In fact, the telephonic metadata program was indiscriminate by design. As the government explained to the FISA court in 2006, "investigators do not know *exactly* where the terrorists' communications are hiding in the billions of telephone calls flowing through the United States today, [but] we do know that they *are there*, and if we archive the data now, we will be able to use it in a targeted way to find the terrorists tomorrow."[117]

According to reports and documents disclosed by the NSA in the wake of the Snowden revelations, intelligence analysts were not permitted to run searches of the archived telephonic metadata on a purely discretionary basis; neither were they allowed to run algorithmic computer software to analyze all information in the archive, at least within the bounds of that specific program.[118] They were, instead, limited to querying the database using search terms or "seeds," usually in the form of telephone numbers. The process of identifying seed numbers required that a designated supervisory official find reason to suspect a connection between the seed and terrorist activity. Once designated as a seed, analysts could query the database for all calls to or from that number, all calls to or from any number that had communicated with the seed number, all calls to or from any number that had communicated with any number that had communicated with the seed number, and all calls to or from any number that had communicated with any number that had communicated with any number that had communicated with the seed number. In NSA parlance, this meant searching three "hops" from the seed number.

As a result, any query of the database could easily produce tens or hundreds of thousands of hits.

Under the terms of the court orders authorizing the Section 215 program, the NSA agreed to keep data in its archives for no longer than five years. There was an exception for any data that had been retrieved by a query, however. The NSA preserved authority to hold that data indefinitely in a separate database. Not surprisingly, that database was subject to additional analysis with many fewer constraints. For example, there was no process for approving or limiting search terms for queries directed to this database. For a period of three years or so from 2006 until 2009, an unauthorized automated system queried data coming into the system from telecommunications partners, sending calls associated with seeds and numbers three hops from seeds into this targeted database. As a consequence, this database was larger, broader, and less discriminate than officials indicated in their original submissions to the FISA court, allowing the NSA to gather, store indefinitely, and search at their discretion telephonic metadata associated with millions of innocent communications among millions of innocent Americans.

In essence, the Section 215 program allowed the NSA to gather and store all call data associated with every call made every day by every person whose calls were routed through domestic telecommunications infrastructures for well over a decade. It is hard to imagine a better definition of broad and indiscriminate surveillance. To be sure, government agencies have maintained that the program was reasonable because government agents were limited in terms of when and how they could access the raw database. Principally, they point to the fact that the data archive produced by the Section 215 program could only be queried using specific "seeds" and only to three-degrees of separation. That certainly sets some limits, but fewer than one might think.

Imagine, for example, the quite likely event that one or more of the "seed" numbers used to query the database was in contact with a fast-food restaurant, cab company, retail seller, or any number of other innocuous but common contacts we might describe as social hubs. From there, the NSA gathered, stored, and analyzed without constraint all contacts with each of those hubs and all contacts with those who contacted each of those in contact with the hubs. That ends up being a very broad net. Indeed, it is virtually certain that each and all of us have call records stored in the purportedly focused database, where government agents have virtually unfettered discretion to conduct searches and analysis.

Along with other provisions of the USA Patriot Act, Section 215 expired in June 2015. In its place, Congress passed, and President Obama signed, the USA Freedom Act, which purports to set limits on the collection and use of telephonic metadata. Specifically, the USA Freedom Act does not provide authority for further bulk collection of telephonic metadata associated with purely domestic communications by the NSA. The USA Freedom Act did not eliminate bulk storage of telephonic metadata, however. It instead shifted that task from the government to telecommunications companies, relying on them to store telephonic metadata on their own servers.[119] USA Freedom then allows NSA and the FBI to seek orders from the FISA court directing those companies to search their databases using approved search terms – the results of which are then passed to the government. The scope of those searches is now somewhat more limited as well in that they extend to two "hops" rather than three. These are modest reforms to be sure, but they are reforms.[120]

After passage of the USA Freedom Act, the NSA's bulk telephonic metadata program has once again gone dark. We do not know the scope and dimension of its current efforts to gather, store, and analyze telephonic metadata associated with domestic communications. Based on what we know about the Section 215 program, and the light hand in terms of reforms imposed by the USA Freedom Act, we can nevertheless place some safe bets: Telecommunications companies collect and store all telephonic metadata associated with all telephone calls made or received using domestic infrastructures. Those companies preserve that data for at least five years so that it will be available to the NSA, the FBI, and other federal agencies. Through directed searches aimed at these databases, the NSA continues to amass telephonic metadata associated with millions of telephone calls in databases stored on its own servers. That metadata is preserved indefinitely and is available for analysis, limited only by the discretion of NSA authorities and the agencies for whom they provide information and intelligence. In short, we are all probably subject to ongoing surveillance by the NSA through the gathering and storage of telephonic metadata. At the very least, the breadth and scope of the program leaves all of us and each of us insecure against the threat that we very well might be under surveillance.

Like the other technologies discussed in this chapter, granting an unlimited license for law enforcement and other government agencies to deploy and use Big Data puts us on the path to a surveillance state. If we are forced to live in a world where we know that the government is or very well may be gathering bits and bytes of information ranging from very personal health data to our digital pocket lint, then that surely will lead to deleterious effects in our daily lives as individuals and members of a democratic society. As was mentioned in the Introduction, economists Catherine Tucker and Alex Marthews documented what some of these effects might look like in a recent study of online search behavior in the wake of the Snowden revelations.[121] As they show, there was a significant reduction in the use of search terms independently rated as likely to lead to "trouble" with the government in the period after the Snowden leaks, demonstrating the very impact on freedom, expression, exploration, and personal development identified in the Introduction as among the deleterious effects of life in a surveillance state.

Stop and Frisk in an Age of Surveillance

"Stops" and "frisks" are seizures of persons and limited searches of their bodies and possessions. Stops entail the detention of citizens by law enforcement officers. Stops often involve the use of physical force but fall short of full custodial arrests. Stops are justified when officers have reason to suspect that a person has engaged, is engaging in, or is about to engage in a crime. Stops allow officers to detain suspects in order to ask questions or to take other reasonable investigative steps designed to confirm or dispel their suspicions. Frisks allow officers to pat a person's outer clothing and to conduct a cursory inspection of personal property within his reach and control in a search for weapons. Frisks are justified when officers have reason to suspect that a person has a weapon and poses a danger to officers or the public.

Despite their limited nature, there is no contest that stops and frisks constitute significant intrusions upon the security of persons in their persons and effects.[122] Imagine, for a moment, walking along the sidewalk and being approached in an aggressive manner by two armed police officers. Both officers have their hands on their weapons. They are pointing at you and shouting. Confused, you stop. Maybe you look over your shoulder to see who they are talking to. Then it becomes clear. They are talking to you. One officer steps in front of you and puts his hand firmly on your shoulder. The other officer assumes a position several steps behind you, just outside your peripheral vision. Their voices finally come into focus, enough for you to understand what they are saying.

They are yelling now. "Why didn't you stop when we told you to stop?" they want to know. You try to stammer something out, but before you can, they are asking you questions in rapid fire:

> "Where are you coming from?"
> "Where are you going?"
> "What are you doing here?"
> "Why are you so nervous?"
> "What do you have in your pocket?"

With that last question, your hand instinctively goes toward your pocket, which holds your cellular phone. The officer behind you immediately steps forward, seizes your arm, twists it behind you, and presses you roughly, face first, against a nearby brick wall.

You are immobilized and helpless. He is demanding to know what is in your pocket and if it is something that might hurt him. What could he possibly mean? You are trying to think, but it's impossible to gather any thoughts much less muster a response. Your nervous system is flooded with cortisol and norepinephrine, your body with adrenaline. You are in full fight or flight mode. Instinctively you try to pull free. "Don't you fucking move!" the officer screams in your ear as he pushes you into the wall, scraping your cheek and chest against the rough bricks. Then you see the other officer. He has his gun drawn now. What is happening!? The officers are both yelling at you.

> "Stop fighting!"
> "Calm down or we'll have to hurt you!"

But you're not fighting! How could you possibly be calm!? You feel hands running down your sides and legs, up your inseam to your crotch, over your buttocks, along your waistline, up your chest, and down the small of your back. What is going on!? You hear an officer asking whether you can stay calm if he lets go of your arm. You emit something like a hyperventilated sob. He releases your arm, steps back, and orders you to sit down on the sidewalk. After five more minutes of questions you still don't understand, they seem to be satisfied. They order you to move along and then they head off down the sidewalk. Only then do you realize that a small crowd has gathered. Some folks have their phones out, recording and probably livestreaming your helpless degradation for the world to see over the Internet.

This is a stop and frisk.

In addition to constituting intrusions unto themselves, stops and frisks often mark punctuated events in escalating encounters between law enforcement officers and citizens. For example, an officer may observe a person loitering on a street corner. Suspicious, the officer may watch until she sees him engage in "furtive movements." At that point, she might approach him, identify herself as a police officer, and order him to stop, raise his hands, and place them on a nearby wall. The officer might then ask why he is on the corner, what he is doing, where he is going, and why he was engaged in those furtive movements. If, during the course of this interrogation, the officer sees the suspect's eyes darting toward his jacket pocket, she might pat down that pocket along with the rest of the suspect's outer clothing to determine whether he has a weapon. If, in the course of that frisk, she feels something hard in that pocket that plausibly could be a knife or other weapon, then she can retrieve that item from the suspect's pocket. If, upon further inspection, that item turns out to be a pipe along with several vials of crack cocaine, then she can arrest the suspect for unlawful possession of a controlled substance and possession of drug paraphernalia. As we shall see, however, it is quite rare that stops or frisks turn up any evidence of criminality or result in an arrest. The vast majority of stops and frisks target innocents – people just like you and me. The New York City Police Department's (NYPD) stop and frisk program provides a useful example.

According to official statistics released by the NYPD, officers conducted 97,296 stops in 2002, the first year Michael Bloomberg was mayor. That number may seem strikingly high. It is worth remembering, however, that this was just after the terrorist attacks of September 11, 2001, which killed thousands of New Yorkers. In the immediate aftermath of those attacks, the city was in an extended state of emergency. In that environment of heightened vigilance, it is no surprise that officers would have a lower threshold for conducting stops and frisks. What is far more surprising is that 2002 would set the low watermark for stops and frisks for the decade that followed.

The number of stops conducted by NYPD officers rose precipitously in the years after 2002, reaching 500,000 in 2006 and eventually peaking at 685,724 documented stops in 2011. Measured against the population at the time, that means that over 8 percent of New Yorkers were stopped and questioned by law enforcement in 2011. These were not mere conversations on the street. Each of these stops entailed enough use of force to warrant official documentation as a constitutional event. It is therefore certain that there were more, and likely many more, citizen–law enforcement interactions that constituted stops but simply were not documented, either because the officers involved did not bother with the paperwork or because the stops were so routine from the officers' points of view that they did not seem to warrant documentation. The citizens in question probably saw things very differently, of course.

In 2011, of the 685,724 documented stops conducted by the NYPD, 381,704 also included a frisk. That means New Yorkers were subjected to frisks at a rate over 4.5 percent when measured across the population of the city at that time. That might not seem high in the abstract, but consider this: According to NYPD statistics, the total number of crimes categorized as major felonies perpetrated in 2011, including homicide, rape, robbery, felony assault, burglary, and grand larceny, including auto theft, was 106,669. That means New Yorkers were over six times more likely to be stopped and questioned by law enforcement in 2011 than they were to be victims of a major felony. They were almost four times more likely to be frisked by law enforcement than to be the victim of a major felony.

By its sheer breadth, the NYPD's stop and frisk program threatened the security of the people of New York in their persons and effects against searches and seizures. We might nevertheless regard this kind of broad search and seizure program as reasonable if it resulted in high rates of arrest or was successful in seizing large numbers of illegal firearms. Unfortunately, the data shows that the program was not merely overbroad but also so indiscriminate and so lacking in focus that it was unreasonable.[123] For example, the 685,724 stops conducted by the NYPD in 2011 yielded only 40,883 arrests – a success rate of less than 6 percent. Of those arrests, by far the most common were for possession of marijuana, which represented more than 12 percent of arrests. Given this high proportion of marijuana arrests, some critics have suggested that New York's stop and frisk program is more accurately described as a "marijuana arrest program."[124]

This is not to imply that New York's stop and frisk program did not yield some important law enforcement achievements.[125] For example, in 2011 it resulted in thousands of arrests for crimes against persons, including assault (although it is not clear how many of those involved assaults on officers provoked, in part, by a stop or frisk). Officers also seized 780 illegal guns. The problem is that those achievements account for a vast minority of stops and frisks performed under the program. The yield rate of 780 guns for 685,724 stops alone suggests a program that is broad and indiscriminate. That excess is even more apparent, however, when compared to gun recovery numbers from prior years. For example, in 2003 the NYPD recovered 604 guns during 160,851 stops. It is hard to justify as "reasonable" an aggressive stop and frisk program that subjects half a million more citizens to search and seizure in order to find and seize 176 more guns.

New York's stop and frisk program only looks more unreasonable after accounting for race. In 2011, over 86 percent of those stopped and frisked were identified in NYPD data as Black or Latino while only 9 percent were identified as white. High rates of stops by race might be expected in neighborhoods and precincts where Blacks and Latinos comprise a majority of the population. Even in majority white neighborhoods, however, Blacks and Latinos were dramatically overrepresented among those stopped by police in 2011. For example, in the 19th Precinct, which covers the tony Upper East Side, Blacks and Latinos comprise only 9 percent of the overall population. Moreover, the overall rate of stops in the 19th Precinct was relatively low in 2011 as compared to the city as a whole – only 2.5 percent by population. Despite this relatively low rate of stops, and the small proportion of minorities in the population of the 19th Precinct, Blacks and Latinos were dramatically overrepresented as subjects of stops. According to official reports, 71 percent of those stopped by officers in the 19th Precinct in 2011 were Black or Latino. That same pattern was replicated in other predominately white areas of the city, such as the 17th Precinct, which was just shy of 8 percent Black and Latino in 2011, and the 6th Precinct, which was 8 percent Black and Latino. Despite their relatively low representation in the overall population of these districts, Blacks and Latinos were the subjects of over 71 percent of stops in the 17th Precinct and almost 77 percent of stops in the 6th Precinct.

In 2012, New York's stop and frisk policy became an issue of nationwide controversy, leading to a federal lawsuit against the NYPD. William de Blasio made reforming the stop and frisk program a centerpiece of his 2013 campaign for mayor. After assuming office in 2014, Mayor de Blasio initiated a number of reforms, some of which are being supervised by Judge Analisa Torres of the United States District Court for the Southern District of New York. In the interim, the number of reported stops conducted by the NYPD dropped precipitously to 46,235 in 2014. Overall success rates for stops and frisks also improved, if modestly, from 12 percent to 19 percent, but the racial profiles of those who being stopped and frisked remained essentially constant: 53 vs. 55 percent black, 34 vs. 29 percent Hispanic, and 9 vs. 12 percent white in 2011 and 2014, respectively.

Although reductions in the rates of stop and frisk are heartening in a sense, the court-appointed monitor assigned by Judge Torres to oversee the NYPD's stop and frisk program issued a report in July 2015 raising some doubts as to the reliability of these numbers. According to his report, officers now routinely fail to document stops and frisks or mischaracterize them as simple street encounters in order to avoid official reporting requirements and, therefore, administrative scrutiny.[126] Despite this underreporting, there is no doubt that stops and frisks have declined dramatically in New York. Unfortunately, that decline seems to be more a result of thoughtless reaction rather than thoughtful, durable reform. According to the July 2015 report filed with Judge Torres by the court-appointed monitor, many officers now fear legal and supervisory retaliation for conducting stops and frisks.[127] The result is a situation where some officers are over-policing, some are under-policing, and any data beyond anecdote that we might use to assess the overall reasonableness and effectiveness of New York's stop and frisk program is highly suspect, if not wholly unreliable. This situation should make all New Yorkers feel insecure against the threat of unreasonable searches, unreasonable seizures, and preventable crimes.

New Yorkers are also no more secure now from programs of broad and indiscriminate search and seizure than they were in 2011. That is because there are no new or additional legal regulations or protections in place offering security against a renewed policy of widespread stop and frisk. Quite to the contrary, the rapid reduction in stops and frisks appears to be the result of a top-level policy to reduce stops and frisks that is no less thoughtful or rational than the policy decisions that underwrote the rapid rise of stops and frisks during the first decade of the twenty-first century. New York's stop and frisk program therefore offers us an instructive case study that shows how leaving some means and methods of search and seizure to the largely unfettered discretion of law enforcement poses a risk to the security of the people by opening the door to programs of broad and indiscriminate search and seizure.

Although New York provides us with a useful case study of stop and frisk programs, it is far from unique. To the contrary, the NYPD's stop and frisk program offers a snapshot of stop and frisk policies and practices across the country, and particularly in urban areas.[128] In most population centers, police engage in shockingly high numbers of stops and frisks. The vast majority of those stops and frisks produce no arrests or other evidence of criminal activity, and the targets are predominately Blacks and Latinos.

Racial disparities in stop and frisk programs raise a number of concerns. First, there is the obvious potential that overt racism is playing a role. This may account for the practices of some small proportion of officers. For the most part, however, the workings of implicit bias probably explain much of the disparity. The role of implicit bias in social judgments and interactions is well documented.[129] Numerous studies have shown that, no matter one's racial background, we are far more likely to attribute negative character traits and the potential for antisocial behavior to phenotypically Black and Hispanic persons.[130] For most of us, these responses are preconscious and never erupt as racist thoughts or conscious racial bias. Implicit bias nevertheless plays a prominent role in our perceptions of others and our engagements with strangers. In the case of police officers, implicit bias probably accounts for much of the racial disparity in stop and frisk programs. As products of our society, officers just naturally look more closely at Black and Latino citizens and are far more likely to attribute nefarious motives to them and their actions.

It is, of course, no solace at all for members of minority groups to hear that their unequal treatment at the hands of stop and frisk programs is probably attributable to implicit bias rather than outright racism. The incidents are no less demeaning; the systematic discrimination is no less alienating; and their basic senses of security in public places are no less threatened. The result is entirely predictable: tense and sometimes violent interactions between law enforcement agencies and members of minority groups. We have seen the consequences of years and decades weighted by the daily incidents that form broader patterns of discriminatory treatment and label all Blacks as suspects and render all Black bodies constantly vulnerable to seizure and search. Black and Latino citizens and residents simply do not trust law enforcement. When young Black men die at the hands of law enforcement, the incidents become catalysts for collective expressions of outrage and demands for justice, both for the fallen and for a society too long defined by racial injustice.

Although it would be too much to blame the deaths of Michael Brown in Ferguson, Missouri, Eric Garner on Staten Island, New York, and Freddie Gray, Jr., in Baltimore, Maryland, on stop and frisk programs run amok, they no doubt played an important role. After all, these incidents all began as stops and frisks. Stops and frisks, the threat of being stopped and frisked, and awareness of racial targeting in stop and frisk programs, all play a defining part in law enforcement engagements with minority groups, individuals' conceptions of themselves, their constructions of social status, and their views of law enforcement as an institution.[131] More broadly, residents of many neighborhoods designated as "high crime" have been living in an effective state of constant surveillance at least since the advent of data-driven policing and expanded stop and frisk programs. Their views on, and relationships with, the agents of that surveillance are evident in both simmering tensions and moments of eruptive violence. In short, life in a surveillance state is in many ways the norm for many members of minority groups and many residents of targeted neighborhoods, which has begotten a murderous relationship between citizens and law enforcement. Their experiences foretell in an immediate and visceral way the life that lies ahead for all of us in an age of surveillance.

Conclusion

Given the breadth and largely indiscriminate nature of modern-day surveillance programs, and the threats these programs pose to the right of the people to be secure against unreasonable searches and seizures, it is natural to wonder what role the Fourth Amendment might play in effecting stable controls. Unfortunately, as we will see in Chapter 2, current doctrine largely protects modern surveillance technologies and contemporary stop and frisk programs from effective Fourth Amendment review.

Notes

1. 132 S. Ct. 945 (2012).
2. Kevin Ashton, *That – Internet of Things, Thing*, RFID J., June 22, 2009, www.rfidjournal.com/articles/view?4986.
3. Michael Hayden, *American Intelligence in the Age of Terror: A Conversation with Michael V. Hayden*, AM. ENTERPRISE INST., Mar. 25, 2016, www.youtube.com/watch?v=CMUlopfggyg.
4. Ashkan Soltani et al., *NSA Uses Google Cookies to Pinpoint Targets for Hacking*, WASH. POST, Dec. 10, 2013, www.washingtonpost.com/news/the-switch/wp/2013/12/10/nsa-uses-google-cookies-to-pinpoint-targets-for-hacking/; *NSA Signal Surveillance Success Stories*, WASH. POST, Dec. 10, 2013, http://apps.washingtonpost.com/g/page/world/nsa-signal-surveillance-success-stories/647/#document/p3/a135602.
5. Hayden, *supra* note 3.
6. Soltani et al., *supra* note 4.
7. Bruce Schneier, *Everything We Know about How the NSA Tracks People's Physical Location*, THE ATLANTIC, Feb. 11, 2014, www.theatlantic.com/technology/archive/2014/02/everything-we-know-about-how-the-nsa-tracks-peoples-physical-location/283745/.

8. James Risen & Laura Poitras, *N.S.A. Gathers Data on Social Connections of U.S. Citizens*, N.Y. TIMES, Sept. 28, 2013, www.nytimes.com/2013/09/29/us/nsa-examines-social-networks-of-us-citizens.html.
9. *See* Stephanie Pell, *Location Tracking, in* THE CAMBRIDGE HANDBOOK OF SURVEILLANCE LAW (David Gray & Stephen Henderson, eds. 2017).
10. Riley v. California, 134 S.Ct. 2473, 2490 (2014).
11. United States v. Graham, 796 F.3d 332 (4th Cir. 2015), *reh'g en banc granted*, 624 Fed. App'x 75 (Oct. 28, 2015), *argued* Mar. 23, 2016.
12. *See, e.g.*, United States v. Carpenter, __ F.3d __ (6th Cir. 2016; *In re Smartphone Geolocation Data Application*, 977 F.Supp.2d 129, 147 (E.D.N.Y.2013). *But see* United States v. Graham, 796 F.3d 332, 350 (4th Cir.) *reh'g en banc granted*, 624 F. App'x 75 (4th Cir. 2015). Although current Fourth Amendment law does not restrict law enforcement access to CSLI, some state courts have held that a warrant is required under their state constitutions. *See, e.g.*, Commonwealth v. Augustine, 4 N.E.3d 846 (Mass. 2014). Some state legislatures have also passed laws requiring warrants to access CSLI. *See, e.g.*, CalECPA, SB 178 (2016); Md. Crim. Proc. Code § 1-203-1 (2015). The American Civil Liberties Union maintains a map showing state law regulations of CSLI and historical CSLI. *See* www.aclu.org/map/cell-phone-location-tracking-laws-state. None of these state decisions or state statutes governs federal agents or law enforcement authorities in other states. Thus, the state of the law with respect to CSLI is very much in flux. As a consequence, federal law enforcement and many local law enforcement agencies have begun making it a practice to secure a warrant before seeking real-time CSLI and historical CSLI.
13. Relying on robust empirical studies documenting perceived privacy risks, Professor Christopher Slobogin has argued that traditional human surveillance does raise privacy concerns, and therefore should be subject to constitutional regulation. *See, e.g.*, Christopher Slobogin, *Making the Most of United States v. Jones in a Surveillance Society: A Statutory Implementation of Mosaic Theory*, 8 DUKE J. CON. L. & PUB. POLY 1, 27 (2012).
14. *See, e.g.*, United States v. Knotts, 460 U.S. 276, 284 (1983) ("Insofar as respondent's complaint appears to be simply that scientific devices such as the beeper [tracking device] enabled the police to be more effective in detecting crime, it simply has no constitutional foundation. We have never equated police efficiency with unconstitutionality, and we decline to do so now.").
15. United States v. Jones, 132 S.Ct. 945, 963 (2012) (Alito, J., concurring) ("In the pre-computer age, the greatest protections of privacy were neither constitutional nor statutory, but practical. Traditional surveillance for any extended period of time was difficult and costly and therefore rarely undertaken.").
16. United States v. Jones, 132 S.Ct. 945, 955–56 (2012) (Sotomayor, J., concurring) (noting that with modern GPS tracking technologies "The Government can store such records and efficiently mine them for information years into the future").
17. United States v. Knotts, 460 U.S. 276, 283–84 (1983) (indicating that "dragnet-type law enforcement practices" such as "twenty-four hour surveillance of any citizen in this country . . . without judicial knowledge or supervision" "should ever occur," then "different constitutional principles may be applicable").
18. United States v. Jones, 132 S.Ct. 945, 955–56 (2012) (Sotomayor, J., concurring) (internal quotation marks and citation omitted).

19. In a similar vein, one might claim that "Because I'm not doing anything wrong, I don't care who watches me." As we saw in the Introduction, however, that is a view that few people truly hold. It is therefore more rationalization than it is reason. Moreover, the available social science research shows that the kind of constant surveillance enabled by contemporary tracking technologies has very negative psychological and social consequences.
20. J.R.R. TOLKIEN, THE LORD OF THE RINGS 616 (Houghton Mifflin 1994) (1954) ("The Eye: that horrible growing sense of a hostile will that strove with great power to pierce all shadows of cloud, and earth, and flesh, and to see you: to pin you under its deadly gaze, naked, immovable.").
21. Marc Blitz et al., *Regulating Drones under the First and Fourth Amendments*, 57 WM. & MARY L. REV. 49, 53–54 (2015).
22. Charlie Savage & Scott Shane, *U.S. Reveals Death Toll from Airstrikes Outside War Zones*, N.Y. TIMES, July 1, 2016, www.nytimes.com/2016/07/02/world/us-reveals-death-toll-from-airstrikes-outside-of-war-zones.html; Micah Zenko, Opinion, *Obama's Embrace of Drone Strikes Will Be a Lasting Legacy*, N.Y. TIMES, Jan. 12, 2016, www.nytimes.com/roomfordebate/2016/01/12/reflecting-on-obamas-presidency/obamas-embrace-of-drone-strikes-will-be-a-lasting-legacy.
23. *See* Lev Grossman, *Drone Home*, TIME MAG., Feb. 11, 2013, at 28, 31–33; Jennifer Lynch, *Are Drones Watching You?*, ELECTRONIC FRONTIER FOUND., Jan. 10, 2012, www.eff.org/deeplinks/2012/01/drones-are-watching-you. In the United States, "50 companies, universities, and government organizations are developing and producing some 155 unmanned aircraft designs." *Id.* In 2010, expenditures on unmanned aircraft in the United States exceeded 3 billion dollars and are expected to surpass 7 billion dollars over the next ten years. *Id.*
24. Grossman, *supra* note 23, at 31.
25. Blitz et al., *supra* note 21, at 54.
26. *See* ASS'N FOR UNMANNED VEHICLE SYS. INT'L, THE ECONOMIC IMPACT OF UNMANNED AIRCRAFT SYSTEMS INTEGRATION IN THE UNITED STATES 2 (2013) (estimating that the drone industry will be worth over $80 billion by 2025).
27. *See* Jill Scharr, *Indiegogo-Funded Ghost Drone Has Scary-Good Tilt Controls*, TOM'S GUIDE, Jan. 8, 2015, 1:34 AM, www.tomsguide.com/us/ghost-drone-specs-price,news-20240.html; Grossman, *supra* note 23, at 28.
28. *See* Lynch, *supra* note 23 ("[S]ome have forecast that by the year 2018 there will be 'more than 15,000 [unmanned aircraft systems] in service in the U.S., with a total of almost 30,000 deployed worldwide.'").
29. Grossman, *supra* note 23, at 28, 32.
30. Peter Finn, *Domestic Use of Aerial Drones by Law Enforcement Likely to Prompt Privacy Debate*, WASH. POST, Jan. 23, 2011, www.washingtonpost.com/wp-dyn/content/article/2011/01/22/AR2011012204111.html.
31. *See* Adam Piore, *Rise of the Insect Drones*, POPULAR SCI., Jan. 29, 2014, www.popsci.com/article/technology/rise-insect-drones.
32. *The Robot Overhead*, ECONOMIST, Dec. 6, 2014, at 11.
33. *Cf.* INTERNATIONAL HUMAN RIGHTS AND CONFLICT RESOLUTION CLINIC (STANFORD LAW SCHOOL) & GLOBAL JUSTICE CLINIC (NYU SCHOOL OF LAW), LIVING UNDER DRONES: DEATH, INJURY, AND TRAUMA TO CIVILIANS FROM US DRONE PRACTICES IN PAKISTAN

80–103, Sept., 2012, http://chrgj.org/wp-content/uploads/2012/10/Living-Under-Drones.pdf (documenting the severe psychological, social, cultural, and economic effects of constant drone surveillance in Pakistan).
34. *See* H.R. REP. NO. 105-425, at 5 (1998), www.gpo.gov/fdsys/pkg/CRPT-105hrpt425/pdf/CRPT-105hrpt425.pdf ("the Subcommittee on Telecommunications, Trade, and Consumer Protection held a hearing on cellular privacy on February 5, 1997 ... Prior to the witnesses' testimony, a technological demonstration was conducted to highlight the ease with which scanning equipment can be 'readily altered' to intercept cellular communications").
35. *See* Amendment of Parts 2 and 15 to Prohibit Marketing of Radio Scanners Capable of Intercepting Cellular Telephone Conversations, 8 FCC Rcd. 2911 (1993).
36. Stephanie K. Pell & Christopher Soghoian, *Your Secret StingRay's No Secret Anymore: The Vanishing Government Monopoly over Cell Phone Surveillance and Its Impact on National Security and Consumer Privacy*, 28 HARV. J.L. & TECH. 1, 51–53 (2014).
37. *Id.* at 52–53 (citing Alex Biryukov et al., *Real Time Cryptanalysis of A5/1 on a PC*, FAST SOFTWARE ENCRYPTION WORKSHOP (2000), http://cryptome.org/a51-bsw.htm).
38. As of 2016, A5/4 was not yet in wide commercial use.
39. Matt Cagle, *Dirtbox over Disneyland? New Docs Reveal Anaheim's Cellular Surveillance Arsenal*, Jan. 27, 2016, www.aclunc.org/blog/dirtbox-over-disneyland-new-docs-reveal-anaheim-s-cellular-surveillance-arsenal.
40. "Triggerfish," "Stingray," and "Hailstorm" are names of devices manufactured by the Harris Corporation, a major military and law enforcement contractor.
41. *See* Larry Greenmeier, *What Is the Big Secret Surrounding Stingray Surveillance?*, SCI. AM., June 25, 2015, www.scientificamerican.com/article/what-is-the-big-secret-surrounding-stingray-surveillance/ (quoting former federal magistrate judge Brian Owsley).
42. *See id.* (quoting former federal magistrate judge Brian Owsley).
43. *See id.* (quoting former federal magistrate judge Brian Owsley).
44. Pell & Soghoian, *supra* note 36, at 12–13.
45. Investigations of Baltimore City's use of Stingray devices have revealed thousands of instances where officers used the devices but failed to disclose that use to courts, defendants, or even prosecutors. *See* Justin Fenton, *Legal Challenge Alleges Authorities Withheld Police Use of Stingray Surveillance*, BALT. SUN, Sept. 4, 2015, www.baltimoresun.com/news/maryland/baltimore-city/bs-md-ci-stingray-challenge-20150904-story.html.
46. Greenmeier, *supra* note 41.
47. *EPIC v. FBI - Stingray / Cell Site Simulator*, ELEC. PRIVACY INFO. CTR., http://epic.org/foia/fbi/stingray/ (last visited Apr. 5, 2016).
48. Nicky Woolf & William Green, *IRS Possessed Stingray Cellphone Surveillance Gear, Documents Reveal*, THE GUARDIAN, Oct. 26, 2015, www.theguardian.com/world/2015/oct/26/stingray-surveillance-technology-irs-cellphone-tower; *Stingray Tracking Devices: Who's Got Them?*, ACLU, www.aclu.org/map/stingray-tracking-devices-whos-got-them#agencies (last visited Apr. 6, 2016).
49. Woolf & Green, *supra* note 48; Reuters, *US Justice Department Tightens Rules on Cellphone Tracking Devices*, THE GUARDIAN, Sept. 3, 2015, www.theguardian.com/us-news/2015/sep/03/us-justice-department-tightens-rules-cellphone-tracking-devices; *Stingray Tracking Devices*, *supra* note 48.

50. Reuters, *supra* note 49.
51. Timothy Williams, *Covert Electronic Surveillance Prompts Calls for Transparency*, N.Y. TIMES, Sept. 28, 2015, www.nytimes.com/2015/09/29/us/stingray-covert-electronic-surveillance-prompts-calls-for-transparency.html?_r=0; Jessica Glenza & Nicky Woolf, *Stingray Spying: FBI's Secret Deal with Police Hides Phone Dragnet from Courts*, THE GUARDIAN, Apr. 10, 2015, www.theguardian.com/us-news/2015/apr/10/stingray-spying-fbi-phone-dragnet-police.
52. This can be accomplished in number of ways. Sometimes officers use the devices in a purely investigative mode without an intention to use the information they gather in open court. For example, officers might activate the device in the vicinity of a political rally or other public gathering. If they discover any information that is helpful in an investigation, then they may simply credit that information to a "confidential source." In the context of a more focused investigation, officers may also seek a "pen trap" order under the Pen Register Act. These orders, issued by courts on the basis of reasonable suspicion rather than the more demanding probable cause standard governing search warrants and wiretap orders, were designed in an era of landlines where law enforcement would need the cooperation of a telephone company to gather basic user and call information. Most scholars and judges to whom the question has been squarely put agree that laws governing pen registers simply do not reach cell site simulators. *See* State v. Andrews, 227 Md. App. 350 (Md. Ct. Spec. App. 2016) (holding that pen register orders are not sufficient to license the deployment and use of cell cite simulators); Greenmeier, *supra* note 41 (quoting former federal magistrate judge Brian Owsley as arguing that pen register orders are not sufficient to license the deployment and use of cell site simulators). Unfortunately, most judges signing these orders think they are allowing traditional pen trap operations aided by telephone companies, not licensing the use of a cell site simulator because many officers do not disclose the true nature of their activities in their applications.
53. *See* Fenton, *supra* note 45.
54. Williams, *supra* note 51; *See* Fenton, *supra* note 45.
55. Justin Fenton, *Baltimore Police Used Secret Technology to Track Cellphones in Thousands of Cases*, BALT. SUN, Apr. 9, 2015, www.baltimoresun.com/news/maryland/baltimore-city/bs-md-ci-stingray-case-20150408-story.html.
56. *NYPD Has Used Stingrays More than 1,000 Times Since 2008*, NYCLU, Feb. 11, 2016, www.nyclu.org/news/nypd-has-used-stingrays-more-1000-times-2008; Alison Knezevich, *Baltimore Co. Police Used Secretive Phone-Tracking Technology 622 Times*, BALT. SUN, Apr. 9, 2015, www.baltimoresun.com/news/maryland/crime/blog/bs-md-co-county-stingray-20150409-story.html; Nathan Freed Wessler, *ACLU-Obtained Documents Reveal Breadth of Secretive Stingray Use in Florida*, ACLU, Feb. 22, 2015, www.aclu.org/blog/free-future/aclu-obtained-documents-reveal-breadth-secretive-stingray-use-florida (documenting use of cell site simulators in several Florida jurisdictions).
57. *See* Aff. of Supervisory Special Agent Bradley S. Morrison at 1, United States v. Rigmaiden, 844 F. Supp. 2d 982 (D. Ariz. 2012) (No. 08-cr-00814) (noting that cell site simulators gather information "from all wireless devices in the immediate are of the FBI device that subscribe to a particular provider ... including those of innocent, non-target devices.").

58. *See* US Dep't of Justice, Guidance: Use of Cell-Site Simulator Technology, Sept. 3, 2015, www.justice.gov/opa/file/767321/download.
59. *See* US Dep't of Homeland Security, Policy Directive 047-02, Oct. 19, 2015, www.dhs.gov/sites/default/files/publications/Department%20Policy%20Regarding%20the%20Use%20of%20Cell-Site%20Simulator%20Technology.pdf.
60. Glenza & Woolf, *supra* note 51 (quoting former federal judge Brian Owsley).
61. Maryland delegates recently proposed a bill to regulate cell site simulators. H.D. 904, 2016 Leg., 436th Sess. (Md. 2016), http://mgaleg.maryland.gov/2016rs/bills_noln/hb/fhb0904.pdf. Among the other states limiting law enforcement access to cell site simulators are Virginia, Minnesota, Utah, and Washington. Va. Code § 19.2-70.3; Minn. Stat. § 626A.28; Utah Code § 77-23c; Wash. Rev. Code § 9.73.270. On October 29, 2015, Rep. Jason Chaffetz introduced a bill that would criminalize the use of cell site simulators without a warrant based on probable cause. As of May 2016, that bill has not passed into law. H.R. 3871 (114th Cong. 2016), www.gpo.gov/fdsys/pkg/BILLS-114hr3871ih/pdf/BILLS-114hr3871ih.pdf.
62. State v. Andrews, 227 Md. App. 350 (Md. Ct. Spec. App. 2016).
63. James Bamford, *The NSA Is Building the Country's Biggest Spy Center*, Wired Mag., Mar. 15, 2012, www.wired.com/2012/03/ff_nsadatacenter/.
64. Frank Pasquale, The Black Box Society (2015); Joshua A.T. Fairfield & Christoph Engel, *Privacy as a Public Good*, 65 Duke L.J. 385 (2015).
65. *See* Charles Duhigg, *Psst, You in Aisle 5*, N.Y. Times, Feb. 19, 2012, at MM30 (recounting how Target uses publicly available databases and market analytics to identify women who are in the early stages of pregnancy).
66. Steve Henn, *If There's Privacy In the Digital Age, It Has a New Definition*, All Things Considered, NPR Mar. 3, 2014, www.npr.org/sections/alltechconsidered/2014/03/03/285334820/if-theres-privacy-in-the-digital-age-it-has-a-new-definition.
67. Shannon Kempe, *The Big Data Contagion*, Dataversity, June 21, 2012, www.dataversity.net/the-big-data-contagion/.
68. *See* Meredith Barrett et al., *Big Data and Disease Prevention*, 10 Big Data 168 (2013).
69. Patient Protection & Affordable Care Act, Pub. L. No. 111-48, § 4302, 124 Stat. 119, 578 (2010). *See also* David Gray, Danielle Keats Citron, & Liz Clark Rinehart, *Fighting Cybercrime After* United States v. Jones, 103 J. Crim. L. & Criminology 745, 766-67 (2013).
70. *See* Gray, Citron, & Rinehart, *supra* note 69, at 770-82.
71. Pasquale, *supra* note 64, at 119-20; Danielle Keats Citron & Frank Pasquale, *Network Accountability for the Domestic Intelligence Apparatus*, 62 Hastings L.J. 1441, 1443 (2011).
72. United States v. Jones, 132 S. Ct. 945, 954-56 (2012) (Sotomayor, J., concurring) (warning that granting government "unfettered discretion" to gather "comprehensive record[s]" that disclose details of "familial, political, professional, religious, and sexual associations," "chills associational and expressive freedoms" while "alter[ing] the relationship between citizen and government in a way that is inimical to a democratic society"); Jack M. Balkin, *The Constitution in the National Surveillance State*, 93 Minn. L. Rev. 1, 2 (2008) ("Government's most

important technique of control is no longer watching or threatening to watch. It is analyzing and drawing connections between data."); David Gray & Danielle Citron, *The Right to Quantitative Privacy*, 98 MINN. L. REV. 62, 82 (2013).
73. *See* Ryan Calo, *Digital Market Manipulation*, 82 GEO. WASH. L. REV. 995 (2014).
74. Citron & Pasquale, *supra* note 71, at 1443; Danielle Keats Citron, *Technological Due Process*, 85 WASH. U. L. REV. 1249, 1273–77 (2008) (exploring inaccuracies of automated decision-making governmental systems including "No Fly," public benefits, and "dead beat" parent matching systems).
75. Jeffrey Kahn, *Terrorist Watchlists*, in THE CAMBRIDGE HANDBOOK OF SURVEILLANCE LAW (David Gray & Stephen Henderson, eds. 2017); JEFFREY KAHN, MRS. SHIPLEY'S GHOST: THE RIGHT TO TRAVEL AND TERRORIST WATCHLISTS (2013); Citron, *supra* note 74, at 1273–77.
76. PASQUALE, *supra* note 64.
77. Gray & Citron, *supra* note 72, at 76 n.88 (quoting GEORGE ORWELL, NINETEEN EIGHTY-FOUR 4 (1949)); Dan Roberts & Spencer Ackerman, *Anger Swells After NSA Phone Records Court Order Revelations*, THE GUARDIAN, June 6, 2013, www.theguardian.com/world/2013/jun/06/obama-administration-nsa-verizon-records (quoting the ACLU's Jameel Jaffer as characterizing the NSA's telephonic surveillance program as being "beyond Orwellian"); *cf.* Florida v. Riley, 488 US 445, 466 (1989) (Brennan, J., dissenting) ("The Fourth Amendment demands that we temper our efforts to apprehend criminals with a concern for the impact on our fundamental liberties of the methods we use. I hope it will be a matter of concern to my colleagues that the police surveillance methods they would sanction were among those described 40 years ago in George Orwell's dread vision of life in the 1980's."); Bill Keller, Op-Ed., *Living with the Surveillance State*, N.Y. TIMES, June 17, 2013, www.nytimes.com/2013/06/17/opinion/keller-living-with-the-surveillance-state.html?_r=0 (likening the Domain Awareness System, an interconnected system of CCTV cameras and law enforcement databases in Britain, to Orwell's "Big Brother" of *Nineteen Eighty-Four*).
78. For a critique of the preventative policing model that underwrites Compstat and aggressive stop and frisk programs, *see* Jeffrey Fagan, Tom Tyler, & Tracey Meares, *Street Stops and Police Legitimacy in New York*, in COMPARING THE DEMOCRATIC GOVERNANCE OF POLICE INTELLIGENCE: NEW MODELS OF PARTICIPATION AND EXPERTISE IN THE UNITED STATES AND EUROPE 203 (Jacqueline Ross and Thierry Delpeuch, eds. 2016).
79. N.Y.C. POLICE DEPARTMENT, PUBLIC SECURITY PRIVACY GUIDELINES, Apr. 2, 2009, www.nyc.gov/html/nypd/downloads/pdf/crime_prevention/public_security_privacy_guidelines.pdf; Chris Dolmetsch & Henry Goldman, *New York, Microsoft Unveil Joint Crime-Tracking System*, BLOOMBERG NEWS, Aug. 8, 2012, 6:19 PM, www.bloomberg.com/news/articles/2012-08-08/new-york-microsoft-unveil-joint-crime-tracking-system; *see also* Balkin, *supra* note 72, at 2 (reporting on plans to "mount thousands of cameras throughout Lower Manhattan to monitor vehicles and individuals").
80. *NYPD's 'Domain Awareness' Surveillance System, Built by Microsoft, Unveiled by Bloomberg*, HUFFINGTON POST, Aug. 9, 2012, 12:51 PM, www.huffingtonpost.com/2012/08/09/nypd-domain-awareness-surveillance-system-built-microsoft_n_1759976.html?.

81. *"The Array of Things": Chicago Implements City-Wide Big Data Project*, Dataconomy, June 24, 2014, http://dataconomy.com/the-array-of-things-chicago-implements-city-wide-big-data-project/.
82. Lee Peck, *Mobile Police Intelligence Growing Through "Project Shield,"* Fox10tv, Dec. 15, 2015, www.fox10tv.com/story/30761700/mobile-police-intelligence-growing-through-project-shield.
83. Nestor Ramos, *City Used High-Tech Tracking Software at '13 Boston Calling*, Bos. Globe, Sept. 8, 2014, www.bostonglobe.com/metro/2014/09/07/boston-watching-city-acknowledges-surveillance-tests-during-festivals/Sz9QVurQ5VnA4a6Btds8xH/story.html.
84. Report of the Technology and Privacy Advisory Committee, Safeguarding Privacy in the Fight Against Terrorism 37–39 (2004), www.fredhcate.com/Publications/TAPAC_Report%20Final.pdf [hereinafter TAPAC Report].
85. Citron & Pasquale, *supra* note 71, at 1443; US Dep't of Justice, Health Security: Public Health and Medical Integration for Fusion Centers 8 (2011), www.it.ojp.gov/GIST/159/File/health%20security%20appendix.pdf.
86. Christopher Slobogin, *Panvasive Surveillance, Political Process Theory and the Nondelegation Doctrine*, 102 Geo. L.J. 1721 (2014).
87. Roger A. Clarke, *Information Technology and Dataveillance*, 31 Comm. ACM 498, 502–04 (1988).
88. *See* Danielle Citron, *Big Data Brokers as Fiduciaries*, Concurring Opinions, June 19, 2012, 5:08 PM, www.concurringopinions.com/archives/2012/06/big-data-brokers-as-fiduciaries.html.
89. Chris Jay Hoofnagle, *Big Brother's Little Helpers: How ChoicePoint and Other Commercial Data Brokers Collect and Package Your Data for Law Enforcement*, 29 N.C. J. Int'l L. & Com. Reg. 595 (2004).
90. *See* Andrew Ferguson, *The Internet of Things and the Fourth Amendment of Effects*, 104 Cal. L. Rev. 805 (2016).
91. Dominic Crossley, *Samsung's Listening TV is Proof that Tech Has Outpaced Our Rights*, The Guardian, Feb. 13, 2015, www.theguardian.com/media-network/2015/feb/13/samsungs-listening-tv-tech-rights.
92. Margaret Hu, *Biometric Surveillance and Big Data Governance*, in The Cambridge Handbook of Surveillance Law (David Gray & Stephen Henderson, eds. 2017). Margaret Hu, *Biometric Cybersurveillance*, 88 Ind. L. J. 1475 (2013).
93. Robinson Meyer, *Long-Range Iris Scanning is Here*, Atlantic, May 13, 2015, www.theatlantic.com/technology/archive/2015/05/long-range-iris-scanning-is-here/393065/.
94. *See* James Bamford, The Shadow Factory: The NSA from 9/11 to the Eavesdropping on America 177–96 (2009); James Bamford, *The Black Box: Inside America's Massive New Surveillance Centre*, Wired UK, Mar. 30, 2012, www.wired.co.uk/magazine/archive/2012/05/features/the-black-box; James Risen & Eric Lichtblau, *Bush Lets US Spy on Callers Without Courts*, N.Y. Times, Dec. 16, 2005, www.nytimes.com/2005/12/16/politics/bush-lets-us-spy-on-callers-without-courts.html; Michael Isikoff, *The Fed Who Blew the Whistle*, Newsweek Dec. 12, 2008, www.thedailybeast.com/newsweek/2008/12/ 12/the-fed-who-blew-the-whistle.html.

95. Privacy & Civil Liberties Oversight Bd., Report on the Surveillance Program Operated Pursuant to Section 702 of the Foreign Intelligence Surveillance Act 33–34 [hereinafter PCLOB Report on 702] (2014), www.pclob.gov/library/702-Report.pdf. According to noted security expert Professor Laura Donohue, "PRISM draws [data] from Microsoft, Google, Yahoo!, Facebook, PalTalk, YouTube, Skype, AOL, and Apple – some of the largest e-mail, social network, and communications providers – making the type of information that could be obtained substantial: e-mail, video and voice chat, videos, photos, stored data, VoIP, file transfers, video conferencing, notifications of target activity (for example, logins), social networking details, and special requests." Laura Donohue, *Section 702 and the Collection of International Telephone and Internet Content*, 38 Harv. J. Law & Pub. Pol'y 117, 120–21 (2015). *See also NSA Files*, The Guardian, www.theguardian.com/world/interactive/2013/nov/01/snowden-nsa-files-surveillance-revelations-decoded#section/3 (last visited Apr. 7, 2016).

96. Bamford, *supra* note 94, at 212–33; Barton Gellman & Ashkan Soltani, *NSA Infiltrates Links to Yahoo, Google Data Centers Worldwide, Snowden Documents Says*, Wash. Post, Oct. 30, 2013, www.washingtonpost.com/world/national-security/nsa-infiltrates-links-to-yahoo-google-data-centers-worldwide-snowden-documents-say/2013/10/30/e51d661e-4166-11e3-8b74-d89d714ca4dd_story.html.

97. Glenn Greenwald, *XKeyscore: NSA Tool Collects "Nearly Everything a User Does on the Internet,"* The Guardian, July 31, 2013, www.theguardian.com/world/2013/jul/31/nsa-top-secret-program-online-data; James Ball, *Angry Bird and Leaky Phone Apps Targeted by NSA and GCHQ for User Data*, The Guardian, Jan. 28, 2014, https://theintercept.com/2015/05/21/nsa-five-eyes-google-samsung-app-stores-spyware/.

98. Jane Perrone, *The Echelon Spy Network*, The Guardian, May 29, 2001, www.theguardian.com/world/2001/may/29/qanda.janeperrone.

99. Glenn Greenwald & Spencer Ackerman, *NSA Collected US Email Records in Bulk for More than Two Years Under Obama*, The Guardian, June 27, 2013, www.theguardian.com/world/2013/jun/27/nsa-data-mining-authorised-obama. Although some early reports suggested that the NSA was gathering and storing every communication passing through internet choke points, more recent reporting suggests that companies were performing searches based on NSA selectors and sending e-mails produced by those searches to the NSA. *See* Charlie Savage, *N.S.A. Gets Less Web Data Than Believed, Report Suggests*, N.Y. Times, Feb. 17, 2016, at A16, www.nytimes.com/2016/02/17/us/report-says-networks-give-nsa-less-data-than-long-suspected.html; Office of the Inspector General of the Nat'l. Sec. Agency, Final Report of the Audit on the FISA Amendments Act §702 Detasking Requirements 92, Nov. 24, 2010, www.documentcloud.org/documents/2712306-Savage-NYT-FOIA-IG-Reports-702-2.html. *But see* Siobhan Gorman & Jennifer Valentino-DeVries, *New Details Show Broader NSA Surveillance Reach*, Wall St. J., Aug. 20, 2013, www.wsj.com/articles/SB10001424127887324108204579022874091732470?mg=id-wsj (reporting that the NSA instead requests blocks of traffic based on certain geographic indicators, and then copies the traffic and keeps communications based on "strong selectors," which could include an e-mail address or a "large block of computer

addresses that correspond to an organization it is interested in. In making these decisions, the NSA can look at content of communications as well as information about who is sending the data.").

100. Glenn Greenwald & Spencer Ackerman, *How the NSA is Still Harvesting Your Online Data*, THE GUARDIAN, June 27, 2013, www.theguardian.com/world/2013/jun/27/nsa-online-metadata-collection; Pierluigi Paganini, *Stellar Wind, Prism, EvilOlive, ShellTrumpet, US Massive Surveillance*, SECURITY AFF., June 29, 2013, http://securityaffairs.co/wordpress/15689/intelligence/stellar-wind-prism-evilolive-shelltrumpet-surveillance.html.
101. *See* NSA Files, *supra* note 95.
102. James Risen & Laura Poitras, *N.S.A. Collecting Millions of Faces from Web Images*, N.Y. TIMES, May 31, 2014, www.nytimes.com/2014/06/01/us/nsa-collecting-millions-of-faces-from-web-images.html?_r=0; Scott Shane, *No Morsel Too Minuscule for All-Consuming NSA*, N.Y. TIMES, Nov. 2, 2013, www.nytimes.com/2013/11/03/world/no-morsel-too-minuscule-for-all-consuming-nsa.html?pagewanted=2&_r=2&ref=international-home.
103. Risen & Poitras, *supra* note 102.
104. *See id.*; Isikoff, *supra* note 94; Risen & Lichtblau, *supra* note 94.
105. Shane, *supra* note 102.
106. *Id.*
107. *See* Bamford, *supra* note 94, at 80, 82–83.
108. *NSA Dishfire Presentation on Text Message Collection – Key Extracts*, THE GUARDIAN, Jan. 16, 2014, www.theguardian.com/world/interactive/2014/jan/16/nsa-dishfire-text-messages-documents.
109. Dan Froomkin, *The Computers Are Listening*, THE INTERCEPT, May 5, 2015, https://theintercept.com/2015/05/05/nsa-speech-recognition-snowden-searchable-text/.
110. *Director of National Intelligence Blackbook Semantic Data Management Presentations*, PUBLIC INTELLIGENCE, Mar. 29, 2012, https://publicintelligence.net/director-of-national-intelligence-blackbook-semantic-data-management-presentations/.
111. *Skynet: Applying Advanced Cloud-Based Behavior Analytics*, THE INTERCEPT, May 8, 2015, https://firstlook.org/theintercept/document/2015/05/08/skynet-applying-advanced-cloud-based-behavior-analytics/.
112. Although the program had been in operation in some form since 2001, it came to pubic notoriety as the centerpiece of the Snowden controversy. The program has since been the subject of considerable debate and litigation. Much of that attention has abated since the passage of the USA Freedom Act in June 2015, which appears to have altered the structure of the program while preserving its breadth and sweep. We will discuss the merits of these reforms in Chapter 6.
113. *How the NSA is Tracking People Right Now*, WASH. POST, www.washingtonpost.com/apps/g/page/world/how-the-nsa-is-tracking-people-right-now/634/ (last visited Apr. 7, 2016).
114. Despite its availability, the NSA denies gathering location information as part of the 215 program.
115. The FISA court was established as part of the Foreign Intelligence Surveillance Act of 1978. That law was passed in the wake of an investigation conducted by the

Church Committee, a Senate Select Committee chaired by Senator Frank Church to investigate foreign and domestic intelligence programs conducted by the Nixon administration. Among the programs uncovered by the Church Committee were efforts to surveil United States citizens on domestic soil in violation of the Constitution and federal law. As part of a bundle of reforms in the wake of the Church Committee's investigations, Congress established the Foreign Intelligence Surveillance Court, which was charged with reviewing and approving warrant applications for covert surveillance. FISA court proceedings are ex parte, which means that it only hears from government lawyers when considering applications, and top secret, which means that few, if any, surveillance efforts approved by the court are ever subject to scrutiny. On at least one occasion, former NSA Director General Michael Hayden has indicated that he would be comfortable with a more adversarial process when the FISA Court is considering surveillance programs as opposed to individual warrants. See Michael Hayden, Cybersurveillance in the Post-Snowden Age, presented at Wash. & Lee School of Law, Jan. 23, 2015, www.youtube.com/watch?v=VUEuWiXMkBA&list= UUZbc1ac1UNZJzmk_nTb1RhA.
116. That section of the law provides for gathering "..." as part of "... investigations." In addition to its scope and nature, critics of the Section 215 program contend that the statute in no way provides for ongoing bulk collection of telephonic metadata.
117. PRIVACY & CIVIL LIBERTIES OVERSIGHT BOARD, REPORT ON THE TELEPHONE RECORDS PROGRAM CONDUCTED UNDER SECTION 215 OF THE USA PATRIOT ACT AND ON THE OPERATIONS OF THE FOREIGN INTELLIGENCE SURVEILLANCE COURT 43 (2014), www.pclob.gov/library/215-Report_on_the_Telephone_Records_Program.pdf (citing 2006 Memo at 8).
118. Contrast this program with others, such as BLACKBOOK, SKYNET, and GHOSTFIRE, *supra* notes 110–11, which entail not just data storage but sophisticated analysis.
119. The USA Freedom Act does not require telephone companies to store metadata. Under rules promulgated by the Federal Communications Commission, telephone companies must store all metadata associated with billing for eighteen months, *see* 47 C.F.R. § 42.6; but the current telephonic metadata program otherwise relies on the good graces of telephone companies.
120. Far more exciting from a civil liberties and Fourth Amendment point of view is a provision for the appointment of a "special advocate" assigned to bring some degree of adversarial process to the Foreign Intelligence Surveillance Court. USA FREEDOM Act of 2015, Pub. L. No. 114-23 § 401(i)(2)(A), 129 Stat. 268, 279 (2015).
121. Alex Marthews & Catherine Tucker, *Government Surveillance and Internet Search Behavior*, in THE CAMBRIDGE HANDBOOK OF SURVEILLANCE LAW (David Gray & Stephen Henderson, eds. 2017), http://ssrn.com/abstract=2412564.
122. Terry v. Ohio, 392 U.S. 1, 16–17 (1968).
123. *See* Fagan et al., *supra* note 78.

124. NEW YORK CIVIL LIBERTIES UNION, 2012 STOP AND FRISK REPORT 18 (2012), www.nyclu.org/files/releases/2012_Report_NYCLU.pdf.
125. Some supporters of aggressive stop and frisk policies argue that they are successful in reducing overall crime rates because they deter potential offenders. We will discuss these arguments in Chapter 6. For now, it is enough to note that there is no reliable and convincing evidence bearing this argument out. See, e.g., David Greenberg, *Studying New York City's Crime Decline: Methodological Issues*, 31 JUSTICE QUARTERLY 54 (2014).
126. PETER L. ZIMROTH, FIRST REPORT OF THE INDEPENDENT MONITOR 7–8, July 9, 2015, https://ccrjustice.org/sites/default/files/attach/2015/07/Floyd%20Monitors%20Report%207%209%202015.pdf.
127. *Id.* at 8–9.
128. See, e.g., United States Department of Justice, Civil Rights Division, *Investigation of the Baltimore City Police Department*, Aug. 10, 2016, www.justice.gov/opa/file/883366/download; Chicago Police Accountability Task Force, Recommendations for Reform: Restoring Trust between the Chicago Police and the Communities They Serve, April 2016, https://chicagopatf.org/wp-content/uploads/2016/04/PATF_Final_Report_4_13_16-1.pdf; American Civil Liberties Union of Illinois, Stop and Frisk in Chicago, March 2015, www.aclu-il.org/wp-content/uploads/2015/03/ACLU_StopandFrisk_6.pdf; United States Department of Justice, Civil Rights Division, *Investigation of the Newark Police Department*, July 22, 2014, www.justice.gov/sites/default/files/crt/legacy/2014/07/22/newark_findings_7-22-14.pdf; American Civil Liberties Union of Massachusetts, *Black, Brown and Targeted*, Oct. 2014, https://aclum.org/app/uploads/2015/06/reports-black-brown-and-targeted.pdf; Plaintiffs' Fifth Report to Court and Monitor on Stop and Frisk Practices, Bailey v. City of Philadelphia (2013) (C.A. No. 10-5952), www.aclupa.org/download_file/view_inline/2230/198; United States Department of Justice, Civil Rights Division, *Investigation of the Seattle Police Department*, Dec. 16, 2011, www.justice.gov/sites/default/files/crt/legacy/2011/12/16/spd_findletter_12-16-11.pdf.
129. MAHZARIN R. BANAJI, BLINDSPOT: HIDDEN BIASES OF GOOD PEOPLE (2013); Andrew Scott Baron & Mahzarin R. Banaji, *The Development of Implicit Attitudes: Evidence of Race Evaluations from Ages 6 and 10 and Adulthood*, 17 PSYCHOL. SCI. 53 (2006); Marianne Bertrand & Sendhil Mullainathan, *Are Emily and Greg More Employable than Lakisha and Jamal? A Field Experiment on Labor Market Discrimination*, 94 AM. ECON. REV. 991 (2004); Irene V. Blair et al., *Assessment of Biases Against Latinos and African Americans Among Primary Care Providers and Community Members*, 103 AM J. PUB. HEALTH 92 (2013); Jennifer L. Eberhardt et al., *Seeing Black: Race, Crime, and Visual Processing*, 87 J. PERSONALITY & SOC. PSYCHOL. 876 (2004).
130. BANAJI, *supra* note 129; Baron & Banaji, *supra* note 129; Bertrand & Mullainathan, *supra* note 129; Blair et al., *supra* note 129; Eberhardt et al., *supra* note 129.
131. *See* Fagan et al., *supra* note 78; Chicago Police Accountability Task Force, *Recommendations for Reform: Restoring Trust between the Chicago Police and the Communities They Serve*, April 2016, at 6, https://chicagopatf.org/wp-content/uploads/2016/04/PATF_Final_Report_4_13_16-1.pdf. For some deeply affecting first-person accounts of the effects of contemporary stop and frisk programs on

individuals, *see Stop and Frisk – Ivan's Story*, www.youtube.com/watch?v=j6TqBpRux0g, *Stop and Frisk: The High School Senior*, www.youtube.com/watch?v=01rsXYIXOrU, *Stop and Frisk: The Police Officer*, www.youtube.com/watch?v=tt4O62_VXs4; *Stop and Frisk: The Pastor*, www.youtube.com/watch?v=XfcHk53Puxg.

2

The Fourth Amendment in the Twentieth Century

To the extent that some or all of the surveillance technologies and programs described in Chapter 1 seem like they are overreaching, unjustified, unreasonable, or even illegal, the next natural question is where we might look for some source of restraint. One obvious possibility would be the Fourth Amendment's protections against "unreasonable searches and seizures." Unfortunately, as this chapter explains, all of these technologies and programs are exempt from effective Fourth Amendment regulation under existing doctrine. To make a place for the Fourth Amendment in our age of surveillance will therefore require a revolution in Fourth Amendment law.

When I teach the Fourth Amendment, students are gobsmacked to find out how limited is the scope of its protection. Like most relatively well-informed citizens who have the good fortune of living in middle- and upper-middle-class American society, they carry with them a sense that the Constitution provides protections that line up roughly with their instincts about things like liberty and justice, privacy and security. They are shocked to find out that Fourth Amendment doctrine runs quite contrary to many of their common intuitions. In a passage famous among professors who teach criminal procedure, Scott Sunby describes the basic state of affairs:

> To maintain privacy, one must not write any checks nor make any phone calls. It would be unwise to engage in conversation with any other person, or to walk, even on private property, outside one's house. If one is to barbecue or read in the backyard, do so only if surrounded by a fence higher than a double-decker bus and while sitting beneath an opaque awning. The wise individual might also consider purchasing anti-aerial spying devices if available (be sure to check the latest Sharper Image catalogue). Upon retiring inside, be sure to pull the shades together tightly so that no crack exists and to converse only in quiet tones. When discarding letters or other delicate materials, do so only after a thorough shredding of the documents (again see your Sharper Image catalogue);

ideally, one would take the trash personally to the disposal site and bury it deep within. Finally, when buying items, carefully inspect them for any electronic tracking devices that may be attached.[1]

In this chapter we will trace the various lines of Supreme Court decisions that are responsible for this upside-down state of affairs. As we do, it will be tempting to become cynical about both the police and the Fourth Amendment. You should fight that sense of despair. There is cause for disappointment in the current state of Fourth Amendment law. But it would be wrong to give up hope on the Fourth Amendment itself. Like the Constitution as a whole, the Fourth Amendment is our ancestral birthright. It constrains the natural tendencies of governments, including law enforcement, to expand their reach and control. The Constitution and the Fourth Amendment therefore stand as critical bulwarks against the tyranny and despotism that drove our forebears to break from their colonial masters and to establish a new nation committed to core principles of self-government and limited state power.

We live in a time where we have drifted away from this vision. To make the Fourth Amendment relevant in our age of expanding surveillance will therefore require a bit of a revolution in Fourth Amendment law. Before entering upon that battle, however, it is important to first understand where we are and how we got here. Only with that historical perspective can we chart a course forward. The goal of this chapter is to provide that perspective.

The Origins of the Fourth Amendment: A Very Brief History

We will have occasion later on to revisit in some detail the historical context in which the Fourth Amendment was drafted and adopted. For now, it is enough to remember that the Fourth Amendment was not part of the original Constitution. Like the rest of the Bill of Rights, the Fourth Amendment is the product of the First Congress, where it was drafted and adopted as part of a grand bargain among Federalists, who by and large stood in favor of establishing a strong central government, and Anti-Federalists, who remained much more skeptical. Each of the first ten amendments responds in one way or another to objections raised by Anti-Federalists during the process of drafting and ratifying the Constitution.

The Fourth Amendment traces to experiences in England and the colonies with general warrants and writs of assistance. General warrants and writs of assistance provided executive agents with what amounted to unlimited licenses to conduct searches and seizures without fear of being held accountable for their conduct. General warrants became infamous in a series of cases decided in the early 1760s. One of these, *Entick v. Carrington*,[2] has been "described as a monument in English freedom undoubtedly familiar to every American statesman at the time the Constitution was adopted, and considered to be the true and ultimate expression of constitutional law with regard to search and seizure."[3]

At about the same time general warrants were under scrutiny in England, citizens of the colonies were complaining about writs of assistance, which were a special form of general warrant. Although writs of assistance would have been illegal under English common law, colonial authorities claimed that the Townshend Acts of 1767 denied those common-law protections to the colonists. In a series of lawsuits that included Paxton's Case and the Malcolm Affair, a group of colonists led by former Advocate General of the Admiralty James Otis challenged the legality of writs of assistance. In the course of this litigation, Otis delivered an hours-long oration condemning writs of assistance before an audience of future revolutionary luminaries, including John Adams. Adams would later remark that this speech marked "the first scene of the first act of opposition to the arbitrary claims of Great Britain." "Then and there," Adams recalled, "the child of Independence was born."[4]

In response to controversies over general warrants and writs of assistance, the several colonies adopted provisions in their various constitutions banning general warrants and writs of assistance. During the ratification debates, many prominent commentators expressed concerns that the newly created federal government might override or simply ignore these state-level constitutional rights. In order to quiet these concerns, proponents of the Constitution agreed that the First Congress would draft and pass an amendment setting limits on the authority of federal agents to conduct searches and seizures. To reinforce that agreement, many of the first states to ratify the Constitution submitted signing statements, describing their visions of the constitutional constraints that should be imposed on searches and seizures.

This is how the Fourth Amendment came to be. It was drafted and adopted in response to concerns about the authority of government agents to conduct the kinds of broad and indiscriminate searches without fear of accountability that were licensed by general warrants and writs of assistance. But, as we shall see, the Fourth Amendment does more than simply ban general warrants and writs of assistance. It guarantees a more general "right of the people to be secure in their persons, houses, papers, and effects against unreasonable searches and seizures" and commands that this right "shall not be violated."

The Fourth Amendment in the Twentieth Century

For the better part of a century after it was ratified, the Fourth Amendment mostly lay fallow. There were very few cases brought before the Supreme Court involving Fourth Amendment issues. That is due largely to three factors. First, the Fourth Amendment did not purport to establish anything particularly new or radical in the way of rights. In fact, its basic protections were found in long-established English common law, which banned general warrants and allowed citizens to sue government agents if they trespassed upon private property without sufficient cause or reasonable justification. At the direction of the crown, the colonial government had abrogated some of these common-law rights by statute, denying American colonists protections of home and hearth guaranteed to their brethren on the Isles. Among other offenses, denial of these rights was cited as grounds and motivation for the American Revolution. The Fourth Amendment played an important role in guaranteeing those rights for citizens of the newly formed United States of America, but it did not break any new ground. It simply enshrined a set of well-understood common-law protections.

The second reason there were so few Fourth Amendment cases until the late eighteenth century is that there were very few agents whose activities required review and regulation. There were no established, organized, professional police agencies in the late eighteenth century, either in Britain or in the Americas. Progenitors of the modern police force had appeared elsewhere in Europe, but the idea of uniformed police officers patrolling public streets sparked outrage in England, which had long preferred a much looser system of civilian watches, constables, and solitary sheriffs. Our forebears inherited that skepticism. As a consequence, organized police forces did not begin to appear in the United States until the middle part of the nineteenth century, and then only in a few major cities like New York, Boston, and Philadelphia. It was not until the early twentieth century that police departments, uniformed police officers on patrol, and professional police detectives became commonplace features of American life. As we shall see, their arrival led to more, and more frequent, engagements between citizens and law enforcement, which, in turn, led to more constitutional litigation relating to searches and seizures.

The third reason we do not see many Fourth Amendment cases in the Supreme Court until the late nineteenth century and early twentieth century is that the Fourth Amendment did not apply to the states or any officers of state governments until the early twentieth century. During the first hundred years of our history, there were a handful of federal agents engaged in efforts to combat customs evasion, but the massive federal security and law enforcement apparatus we have today simply did not exist. The vast majority of the law enforcement officers who came on the scene starting in the late nineteenth century worked for localities and states. As written and ratified, the Fourth Amendment applied only to the federal government and did not purport to bind local and state officials. That did not change until 1949, when, in a case called *Wolf v. Colorado*,[5] the Supreme Court held that the Fourth Amendment is "incorporated" to the states through the Fourteenth Amendment, which prohibits the states from depriving "any person of life, liberty, or property, without due process of law."[6]

The Early Twentieth Century: A Physical Approach to Search and Seizure

Despite the fact that it was not incorporated to the states until the middle part of the twentieth century, Fourth Amendment issues began making a more regular appearance on the Supreme Court's docket around the turn of the twentieth century in response to the emergence and expansion of law enforcement agencies at both the federal and the state levels.[7] In these early cases, the Court took a very conservative view of the Fourth Amendment's reach and scope, defining "search" and "seizure" in physical terms that mirrored the common law of trespass. As a consequence, Fourth Amendment rights in these early years were linked to property rights and founding era concerns about government interference with "persons, houses, papers, and effects."[8]

Boyd v. United States, which was decided in 1886, provides a useful example.[9] The *Boyd* case marks familiar territory for search and seizure law: import taxes.[10] Boyd was charged by the federal government with failing to pay customs taxes on twenty-nine cases of plate glass imported from England. As part of its investigation, the government applied for a court order compelling Boyd to hand over bills of lading, invoices, and other documents establishing the purchase price and value of that glass. In its application, the government cited a federal statute authorizing courts to issue such orders. Mr. Boyd complied under protest, allowing him to challenge the constitutionality of the statute and its application in his case. That challenge eventually made its way to the Supreme Court.

Writing for the Supreme Court in *Boyd*, Justice Joseph Bradley had no difficulty finding that compelling Boyd to produce his papers to government officers was a "search" and "seizure" for Fourth Amendment purposes. Justice Bradley further deemed the search and seizure unreasonable. Recalling pre-Revolutionary experiences with writs of assistance and English experiences with general warrants, Justice Bradley saw the physical taking and examination of a person's personal or business papers as directly akin to searches for political pamphlets in the general warrants cases and searches for imported goods in the writs of assistance cases. Concerned with the broad authority granted to law enforcement, Justice Bradley held that the statute violated Boyd's Fourth Amendment rights. Although the Court would later change its views on the constitutional status of orders compelling the production of documents, the key point is that, almost a century after the Fourth Amendment was ratified, the Court focused on physical invasions and physical seizures.

Through the early part of the twentieth century, the Supreme Court continued to maintain this traditional understanding of searches and seizures. *Olmstead v. United States*,[11] decided in 1928, provides a vivid and notorious example. The advent of national prohibition in 1920 promoted rapid growth in two now-familiar American institutions: organized crime and federal law enforcement, including the Bureau of Investigation (FBI). The FBI came under the direction of John Edgar Hoover in 1924.[12] Among the many revolutions Hoover promoted was the use of wiretapping to monitor and gather evidence against criminal organizations.

In *Olmstead*, FBI agents targeted a large-scale bootlegging operation engaged in the importation and distribution of Canadian liquor. The principal in that operation was Roy Olmstead, a former star on the Seattle police force (crime apparently paid better!). To gather evidence against Olmstead, including dates and times of liquor deliveries, federal agents installed a recording device on the telephone lines that serviced Olmstead's house. Evidence from that wiretap was used both to intercept illegal shipments and to convict Olmstead and his associates for multiple violations of federal laws. Olmstead argued that installing and using a wiretapping device constituted a "search" under the Fourth Amendment, and therefore required a warrant. Because the investigators did not have a warrant, or any other form of judicial permission, Olmstead sought to suppress these recordings at trial.

Writing for a five-justice majority, Chief Justice William Howard Taft held that intercepting Olmstead's telephone conversations was not a "search" under the Fourth Amendment because the wiretapping technology did not physically intrude into Olmstead's home. Instead, the device had been installed on transmission lines owned and operated by the telephone company and located in public space. Absent some kind of physical intrusion into Olmstead's property, Chief Justice Taft held that the Fourth Amendment provided no protection. This despite the fact that the wiretap allowed agents to listen to conversations that Olmstead and his associates believed were private. No matter how intrusive, unexpected, or offensive this kind of government spying might be, the *Olmstead* Court held that it simply did not raise any Fourth Amendment issues absent a physical intrusion upon a protected "person, house, paper, or effect."

Justice Louis Brandeis wrote a spirited dissent in *Olmstead* that would eventually provide a blueprint for contemporary Fourth Amendment law.[13] Before joining the Court, Brandeis coauthored an influential article in the *Harvard Law Review* decrying the declining state of privacy in American society.[14] Brandeis's concern in that article was with the salacious turn taken by many tabloids, which were obsessed then, as they are now, with documenting and reporting on the foibles, follies, and daily lives of socialites in major cities like Boston and New York. Brandeis and his law partner, Samuel Warren, argued that these kinds of invasions of personal privacy should be restrained. For similar reasons, Justice Brandeis argued that federal agents' eavesdropping using wiretaps should be subject to Fourth Amendment restraints.

As Brandeis pointed out in his article, and in his dissenting opinion in *Olmstead*, the advent of technologies such as photography, telephones, and recording devices carried with them both promise and the potential for abuse. Given the new forms of privacy invasions made possible by these technologies, Justice Brandeis argued that it would be anachronistic to require physical invasion as a predicate for either private tort actions or constitutional challenges to government surveillance. Although taking and publishing revealing photographs, eavesdropping, and recording conversations did not require the "force and violence" necessary to invade property, Justice Brandeis believed that they nevertheless compromised the sanctity of citizens' thoughts, beliefs, and emotions as well as the "individual security" they invested in their private activities, including talking on the telephone.[15] Lest the Fourth Amendment become little more than a dead letter, Justice Brandeis argued that Fourth Amendment law must keep pace with changing times by protecting citizens' privacy from government intrusions, whether by physical invasions or more modern means.

In the years after *Olmstead*, the Court remained committed to the view that the Fourth Amendment governed only physical intrusions. *Goldman v. United States*,[16] decided in 1942, provides a ready example. In that case, federal law enforcement officers broke into the offices of an attorney suspected of fraud. Officers installed a remote listening device, attached by wires through a wall to an adjoining office where the officers set up a listening post. That device did not work. Agents therefore relied on a "detectaphone" – a highly sensitive microphone that was attached to the exterior of an adjoining wall. With that device, officers overheard meetings between Goldman and his coconspirators. Thanks to this evidence, the government was able to secure convictions against Goldman and his associates.

On appeal, the defendants argued that their Fourth Amendment rights were violated by the unlawful entry into the office and by the use of the detectaphone. The Court agreed with them as to the first point, but found that the illegal entry had failed to produce any evidence – the device did not work, after all. The Court therefore found that it was a violation that did not affect in any material way either the investigation or the trial. As to the detectaphone, the Court followed its reasoning in *Olmstead*. Because using the detectaphone did not require a physical intrusion into the private office, the Court held that its use was neither a search nor a seizure for purposes of the Fourth Amendment.

Justice Francis Murphy wrote a probing dissent in the *Goldman* case. Justice Murphy, who is perhaps best known for his condemnation of the government's internment of Japanese-Americans during World War II,[17] argued in *Goldman* that the Fourth Amendment provides protections against more than just physical invasions of private spaces that our founders experienced or could have imagined.[18] Although the detectaphone did not require a physical trespass, Justice Murphy pointed out that "the search of one's home or office no longer requires physical entry, for science has brought forth far more effective devices for the invasion of a person's privacy than the direct and obvious methods of oppression which were detested by our forebears and which inspired the Fourth Amendment."[19] "Surely the spirit motivating the framers," he continued, "would abhor these new devices no less."[20]

Although Justice Murphy was not able to persuade a majority of his brethren in *Goldman*, his concerns about the encroachment upon privacy enabled by surveillance technologies were prescient. As Justice Potter Stewart reported for the Court in *Silverman v. United States*, eavesdropping technology had advanced to the point in 1961 that parabolic microphones allowed officers to eavesdrop at a long distance and technology then close on the horizon would allow them to listen to conversations in closed rooms and through open windows from across busy city streets.[21] Despite the immediate threats to privacy posed by these technologies, the Court in *Silverman* still saw no need to abandon its strictly physical view of Fourth Amendment searches and seizures. It was therefore willing to hold that the use of a "spike microphone" inserted into the party wall of a townhouse until it made contact with a heating duct implicated the Fourth Amendment because the device physically penetrated into the defendant's home. The Court nevertheless seemed comfortable with eavesdropping technology that simply gathered faint and inaudible sound waves from a lawful vantage point because these devices were nothing more than a more advanced version of the detectaphone used in the *Goldman* case.

The Mid-Twentieth Century: The Katz Revolution

Six years after the *Silverman* case, Justice Stewart and the Court changed direction in the landmark case *Katz v. United States*.[22] Charles Katz was a bookie who used a public pay phone to make and receive illegal bets. This particular phone was housed in an enclosed glass booth with a door, which Katz would shut while conducting his business. Wise to his misdeeds, federal agents surreptitiously attached an "electronic ear" to the outside of the booth, enabling them to record Katz's incriminating conversations. The booth did not belong to Katz. Although he appears to have monopolized it much of the time, it was public. Katz therefore could not claim that his property rights were violated or that he suffered a physical trespass when the agents attached their device to the booth. Moreover, the listening device did not penetrate into the phone booth, much like the detectaphone used in *Goldman*. Given these facts, the officers surveilling Katz likely thought they had avoided any entanglement with the Fourth Amendment. After all, there was no physical intrusion into the phone booth, and, even if there had been, Katz did not have a property interest in the booth that would allow him to claim it as his "house" or "effect." They turned out to be quite wrong.

Writing for the Court in *Katz*, Justice Stewart rejected the narrow view of search that had prevailed since *Olmstead*, holding that the Fourth Amendment "protects people, not places." Although the officers had not engaged in any physical violation of Katz's person, home, or possessions, Justice Stewart found that they had violated Katz's reasonable expectations of privacy in his telephone conversations. Referring to prevailing social norms relating to public telephone booths, Justice Stewart reasoned that any person who enters a phone booth, "shuts the door behind him, and pays the toll that permits him to place a call is surely entitled to assume that the words he utters into the mouthpiece will not be broadcast to the world."[23] "To read the Constitution more narrowly," Justice Stewart continued, would "ignore the vital role that the public telephone has come to play in private communication."[24] The fact that there had been no invasion of Katz's property was irrelevant, according to Justice Stewart. So long as Katz's reasonable expectations of privacy had been violated, there was a search. Thus, the Court in *Katz* departed from the long line of cases, including *Olmstead* and *Goldman*, where it had defined searches and seizures as requiring some form of physical intrusion.

Although Justice Stewart wrote the majority opinion in *Katz*, it was a concurring opinion by Justice John Marshall Harlan II that would have the broadest impact. There, Justice Harlan described a two-pronged test for determining whether government action constitutes a "search" for purposes of the Fourth Amendment: First, the activity must violate a subjectively manifested expectation of privacy. Second, that expectation must be "one that society is prepared to recognize as reasonable." In Mr. Katz's case, he had subjectively manifested an expectation of privacy in his telephone conversations by entering an enclosed booth and shutting the door. Furthermore, his expectations were perfectly reasonable in light of the physical structure of the booth and broader social norms and practices regarding the use of telephones in telephone booths. In subsequent cases, the Supreme Court adopted Justice Harlan's two-pronged test when determining whether government actions constitute a "search" under the Fourth Amendment.

The *Katz* doctrine marks an important adaptation of constitutional doctrine to changes in law enforcement practices. Absent *Katz*, the concept of Fourth Amendment search likely would have remained limited by the law of trespass. As a consequence, the deployment and use of wiretaps and similar electronic spying technologies might have remained within the unfettered discretion of law enforcement. As it stands, *Katz* and another 1967 case called *Berger v. New York*[25] impelled adoption of the Wiretap Act.[26] Passed in 1968, the Wiretap Act requires that law enforcement officers secure a warrant before installing a wiretap. The Wiretap Act is now part of a broader piece of legislation called the Electronic Communications Privacy Act,[27] which provides additional protections against the use of electronic devices to intercept data or to access stored data. It is therefore safe to say that, absent *Katz* and *Berger*, we would live in a very different world where police officers could routinely listen to our telephone conversations and monitor the contents of our e-mails, texts, and other electronic communications whenever it suited their fancies.

The Late Twentieth Century, Part I: The Consequences of Katz

Katz marked a watershed moment in Fourth Amendment law, providing important protections against some twentieth-century surveillance techniques and technologies. Unfortunately, the *Katz* test has proven inadequate to the task of regulating the means, methods, and technologies that have come to define our contemporary age of surveillance. This is due largely to three doctrines that emerged in the years after *Katz*: the public observation doctrine, the third-party doctrine, and doctrine of Fourth Amendment standing. Together, these doctrines seem to leave most of the tracking, surveillance, and data aggregation technologies discussed in Chapter 1 beyond the scope of effective Fourth Amendment review.

The Public Observation Doctrine

Elaborating the role of reasonable expectations of privacy when assessing Fourth Amendment interests, the *Katz* Court opined that "What a person knowingly exposes to the public, even in his own home or office, is not a subject of Fourth Amendment protection."[28] In the context of that case, this meant that Mr. Katz did not have any reason to expect that his presence or movements in the phone booth would remain private. That is because the booth was in a public place and the door and sides were composed partially of glass, which provided any passerby an opportunity to observe Katz and his conduct inside the booth. Justice Stewart therefore concluded that "What [Katz] sought to exclude when he entered the booth was not the intruding eye, but the uninvited ear."[29] On that basis, officers could watch him without running afoul of the Fourth Amendment, but needed to secure a warrant before employing a surreptitious listening device to eavesdrop on his conversations.

As the Court's analysis in *Katz* suggests, there may sometimes be gaps between subjective expectations of privacy and reasonable expectations of privacy. Consider an all-too common contemporary circumstance. We have all had the experience of sitting next to someone talking on a cellular phone in an airport, restaurant, or park. The topics of these conversations are sometimes quite personal, involving the details of a loved one's health crisis or the crumbling of a relationship. Caught up in a moment of solipsistic immersion, they may believe that they are having a private conversation when, in fact, they are sharing the intimate details of their lives with everyone around them. If the topic of the conversation was not the details of a recent romantic dalliance but, instead, a planned drug deal, and a police officer happened to overhear, then any claims of subjective expectations of privacy would be in vain because it is objectively unreasonable to expect that telephone conversations conducted in full hearing of anyone who happens to walk by are private. Thus, to render expectations of privacy in telephone conversations objectively reasonable, we must withdraw from public hearing by entering a home, an office, or a phone booth.

This gap between subjective expectations of privacy and objectively reasonable expectations of privacy is central to the public observation doctrine. In straightforward terms, the public observation doctrine holds that law enforcement officers may make visual, aural, or olfactory observations from any lawful vantage point without implicating the Fourth Amendment. These efforts are neither searches nor seizures by Fourth Amendment standards because they do not violate objectively reasonable expectations of privacy. Officers making these observations are simply watching, listening to, or smelling what citizens have exposed to the public, and therefore cannot hope to maintain as private.

To understand the scope of the public observation doctrine and the law enforcement practices it licenses, let us consider a few examples.

1. A police officer standing on a public sidewalk looks through the window of a private home and sees a marijuana plant growing in the window. Is this a search? Under the public observation doctrine, it is not. The horticulturalist in question has exposed the plant to public view, and therefore has no reasonable expectation of privacy as against officers' making observations that could be made by any member of the public who might also be standing on that sidewalk.[30]
2. A police officer parks a "cherry picker" truck like those used by tree trimmers and power companies on a public street, climbs into the basket, and raises himself twenty feet into the air to look through the window of a third-floor apartment. From that vantage point, the officer sees a marijuana plant growing inside. Is this a search? Under the public observation doctrine, it is not. Although our pot grower might not expect to have anyone looking through his third-floor window, and few members of the public could or would be able to look through his window, the fact is that there are tree trimmers, power-line maintenance workers, painters, road crews, photographers, and any number of people who might park a cherry picker across the street and, in the course of their activities, glance through the window and see that merry pot plant. It would therefore be objectively unreasonable for anyone in that apartment to expect privacy unless they draw the shades.[31]
3. Suspicious that people are using the stalls in public bathrooms to consume drugs, officers make a habit of ambling through and even loitering about so they can look inside the stalls through the slight gaps between the doors and walls. They sometimes even lean down to look through the gaps between the doors and the floor. Is this a search? According to the public observation doctrine, it is not. That is because any member of the public can make the same observations from the same vantage points. In fact, people often do, if only to see whether the stall is empty. It is therefore unreasonable from a Fourth Amendment point of view to deny government agents the opportunity to look as well.[32]
4. Law enforcement officers come along the street on garbage day and rummage through cans set out on the curb to be picked-up. During the course of their dumpster diving, they find all manner of revealing matter, including love notes, seminude photos of residents, and the remnants of a marijuana plant. Is this activity a search? Under the public observation doctrine, it is not. Although

we might hope that our garbage will go straight to the landfill or incinerator without anyone looking through it, the fact is that any member of the public or, for that matter, any interested bear or raccoon has access to our garbage cans.[33] So long as officers do not invade private property to access a garbage can, they can look through the contents without fear of committing a Fourth Amendment search.

5. Police officers suspect that, behind a fence, in the backyard of a home, there is a marijuana plant growing. To get a better look, they fly over in a helicopter and hover for several minutes at low altitude. Is this a search? Under the public observation doctrine, it is not. Although few helicopters make low-flying passes over our backyards, as long as the officers operate in navigable airspace, they are in a place where any member of the helicopter flying public might also pass. It is therefore unreasonable for anyone to expect that they will not be observed in their backyards from helicopters, airplanes, or even satellites.[34] The Court has also held that it would make no difference were officers to use high-powered binoculars or a telescope to make their observations from a higher altitude.[35]

6. Drug enforcement agents suspect that a methamphetamine manufacturer is acquiring chemicals from a local supply warehouse. With the cooperation of the warehouse operators, officers install a radio beeper tracking device in a container of chemicals, which is then sold to the suspect during his next visit. With the assistance of that beeper, the agents track the suspect for the better part of an afternoon until he finally stops at a remote cabin. Is this a search? By now it should come as no surprise that it is not. As the Court concluded in *United States v. Knotts*, "A person traveling in an automobile on public thoroughfares has no reasonable expectation of privacy in his movements from one place to another" because, by definition, he has exposed those movements to public view.[36]

The hypotheticals and actual cases documenting the scope of the public observation doctrine are virtually endless, but these few examples provide a vivid picture of its scope. For many people, the picture is unsettling. Most go about their daily lives with a sense of anonymity or obtuse oblivion when they are in public spaces. This affords an expectation that we are not being watched or tracked – at least not for extended periods of time across different spaces and contexts.[37]

We might expect that the Fourth Amendment would reflect those instincts and expectations. As these examples show, however, it does not – at least under current doctrine.

Many of the techniques, programs, and technologies discussed in Chapter 1 fall outside Fourth Amendment review and regulation as a consequence of the public observation doctrine. Consider GPS tracking. If the government installed a GPS-enabled tracking device on every car, cellular phone, portable computer, tablet, and MP3 player sold in the United States at the time of manufacture, then it seems that there would be no Fourth Amendment bar on tracking those devices as they move through public spaces.[38] That is because these efforts would not reveal any information that was not knowingly exposed to others. We might hope and expect that we are not being tracked through our devices, but that expectation appears to be unreasonable, at least insofar as the tracking is limited to following our public movements. By the same rationale, public tracking with RFID tags would not raise any Fourth Amendment concerns. GPS devices and RFID tags may be more effective and efficient than the radio beeper device used in the *Knotts* case – particularly when linked to computer systems capable of storing the massive amounts of data that would be produced – but their deployment and use would be no less constitutional, thanks to the public observation doctrine.

The result is the same for visual surveillance technologies. Suppose that police install a network of closed-circuit television cameras in and around a park where, rumor has it, illegal drugs are bought and sold. Most of the cameras are mounted to trees and light poles, but some are carried by small drones, which patrol the airspace over the park. Images recorded by these cameras feed into a server, allowing officers to monitor events in real time. All of this seems to be perfectly constitutional because none of this conduct constitutes a "search" under the public observation doctrine. Citizens may come to the park to read, picnic, or to enjoy an intimate moment expecting that they will have some level of privacy. But under current Fourth Amendment doctrine, their expectations are entirely unreasonable. That is because the park is a public place, visible at any time by passersby. So long as the cameras only capture what a member of the public might observe from any of these vantage points, nothing the officers see can constitute a Fourth Amendment search. Nothing changes if officers store all of the images recorded by their cameras for later scrutiny or analysis.

Now imagine that police expand the program by installing a network of surveillance cameras all over town. Mounted on permanent structures, police cars, and drones, these cameras cover every inch of public space, providing complete and constant visual surveillance of all spaces and activities that are exposed to public view. The images from all these cameras are then fed into a central facility and stored on networked servers. As a consequence, the police have a complete visual record of everything that happens in spaces exposed to public view going back to the system's start. This visual record allows officers to track the historical movements of anyone and everyone who either moves through public spaces or leaves their blinds open. Does this system offend the Fourth Amendment?

Under the public observation doctrine, even this kind of broad, indiscriminate, and pervasive surveillance does not raise any Fourth Amendment concerns. One might worry about the dramatic gains in efficiency provided by a system like this, but the Supreme Court has been quite clear that technological efficiency alone does not change the Fourth Amendment calculus. For example, in the *Knotts* case mentioned earlier, Justice White wrote for the Court that "we have never equated police efficiency with unconstitutionality, and we decline to do so now" where "scientific devices such as the beeper enabled the police to be more effective in detecting crime."[39] One might also worry that the degree of efficiency between radio trackers and broad surveillance systems is different, such that the sheer amount of information gathered would trigger Fourth Amendment regulation.[40] Unfortunately, the public observation doctrine seems to make it impossible to draw such a distinction.[41] After all, as one prominent commentator has pointed out, it is impossible to add zero to zero and get anything other than zero.[42] Thus, no matter how much information police may gather using visual surveillance technologies, they cannot violate reasonable expectations of privacy so long as every frame and image falls within the bounds of the public observation doctrine.

Based on this analysis, it seems that surveillance systems, no matter how sophisticated and pervasive, escape Fourth Amendment scrutiny as long as the information they gather falls within the broad compass of the public observation doctrine. This includes programs, like New York's Domain Awareness System, that aggregate information from public and private surveillance cameras and license-plate readers. It includes technologies like cell site location, RFID readers, and GPS-enabled tracking, all of which fall outside the scope of

Fourth Amendment scrutiny insofar as they are used to gather information that is exposed to the public.

For most people, this result is troubling. To its credit, the Supreme Court seems to share that feeling. In the *Knotts* case, the Court made a note of the possibility that "dragnet-type law enforcement practices" such as "twenty-four hour surveillance of any citizen ... without judicial knowledge or supervision" might be subject to "different constitutional principles."[43] More recently, in the *Jones* case, five sitting justices signaled their own concerns about extended surveillance using contemporary technologies like GPS-enabled tracking devices.[44] The Court itself has yet to translate these concerns into law, however.

The Third-Party Doctrine

The second line of cases arising from *Katz* that plays a prominent role in debates about contemporary surveillance technologies is the third-party doctrine. The third-party doctrine holds that if we share information with a third party, and the government gains access to that information through the third party, then the Fourth Amendment is not implicated. To see the third-party doctrine in action, imagine that Bart is planning a bank robbery. Bart needs someone to drive the getaway car, so he enlists Steve "Wheelman" Smith, widely recognized as the best driver in the business. Steve agrees to participate. A day before the caper, Steve is arrested for a minor drug offense. In exchange for leniency on his drug charge, he tells officers all about Bart's planned bank robbery. Acting on instructions from the police, Steve arrives the next day at the appointed rendezvous to pick Bart up and then drives to the bank. Unknown to Bart, Steve is wearing a small microphone, which allows police officers in a nearby van to eavesdrop on everything said in the car. During their drive, Bart rehearses his plan in detail. Police officers listen to and record every word. Bart is then arrested and charged with attempted bank robbery.

Have the police violated Bart's reasonable expectations of privacy? He certainly did not want anyone to know about his plans, least of all the police. He also expected Steve to keep his secret. Perhaps he even swore Steve to secrecy. Given these circumstances, it seems perfectly reasonable for Bart to expect that Steve would keep his mouth shut. If that is right, then the police officers' offer of an incentive to Steve, and Steve's subsequent violation of Bart's trust, looks like a violation of Bart's reasonable expectations of privacy. It would seem to follow that Bart's Fourth Amendment rights have been violated.

The eavesdropping device only seems to make matters worse for the police. In many ways, the microphone used in our hypothetical looks like the electronic ear used on the telephone booth in *Katz*. After all, Bart entered the car and closed the door with the purpose of excluding the "uninvited ear." He therefore expected that everything he said in the car would be private. The last thing on his mind was the possibility that the police were listening to every word he said. It therefore seems that the officers conducted a "search" when they eavesdropped on Bart's conversation with Steve.

Given the close parallels between our hypothetical and *Katz*, one can be forgiven for thinking that using a confidential informant to report on private conversations and asking that informant to wear a "wire" so officers can listen to and record those conversations violates the Fourth Amendment. According to the third-party doctrine, however, none of this is even a "search." To see why, let us consider *United States v. Hoffa*.[45]

In *Hoffa*, famed union leader and organized crime figure James Hoffa was convicted of jury tampering for bribing jurors during a criminal trial. The critical evidence used to convict Hoffa of jury tampering came from Edward Partin, a local union official who testified that Hoffa discussed bribing jurors in his presence. Unbeknownst to Hoffa, Partin was working as a government informer. In that role, Partin made frequent reports about these conversations to federal agents and eventually testified about them at Hoffa's trial. On appeal to the Supreme Court, Hoffa argued that Partin was acting as a government agent and that his failure to disclose that fact violated Hoffa's reasonable expectations of privacy in conversations with Partin and in conversations that took place in Partin's presence. The Court rejected that argument, noting that Hoffa's expectations relied "upon his misplaced confidence that Partin would not reveal his wrongdoing" and concluding that the Fourth Amendment does not protect a "wrongdoer's misplaced belief that a person to whom he voluntarily confides his wrongdoing will not reveal it."[46]

Based on *Hoffa*, it seems clear that Bart has no grounds to argue that his Fourth Amendment rights were violated. Bart trusted Steve. Based on that trust, he voluntarily disclosed information to Steve. Steve later was revealed to be a turncoat, but that just means that Bart's trust was misplaced. In other words, his subjective expectations of privacy were violated. His trust in Steve does not translate into reasonable expectations of privacy, however. Thus, Bart may have a bone to pick with Steve, but he cannot claim that his reasonable expectations of privacy were violated when Steve snitched to the police.

The reasoning in the *Hoffa* case has been extended to cover circumstances where codefendants, government informers, and undercover police officers testify about what they have seen or heard.[47] It has also been applied to allow the use of body-wires and surreptitious recording devices during police investigations.[48] As long as at least one party to the conversation knows that police are listening-in or recording what is said, the Court has had no difficulties in holding that the Fourth Amendment rights of the other parties are neither implicated nor violated. As in *Hoffa*, their misplaced trust defeats any claim of reasonable expectations of privacy.

Most people are not too bothered by cases like *Hoffa*. That is in part because the basic concept has some intuitive appeal. We may be disappointed when a friend divulges our secrets, but we hold that friend responsible. We usually do not blame or seek to punish the audience for this kind of gossip. That same instinct underlies *Hoffa* and its progeny. The facts in these cases also seem pretty foreign or remote. Most of us do not engage in criminal conspiracies. We therefore figure that the government is not interested in "flipping" our friends, sending undercover officers to befriend us, or paying acquaintances to inform on us. Finally, most of us are pretty careful about whom we trust, and with what information. Together, these factors mean that most of us, most of the time, need not worry that the government is getting information about us through third parties. We trust friends and colleagues. Even if that trust is misplaced, the government is probably not interested in us anyway.

Although few people would object to the third-party doctrine if it only applied in cases like *Hoffa*, another line of cases are more likely to raise concerns. Those involve institutions like banks, credit card companies, and telephone service providers. In these cases, there is no misplaced trust. They represent themselves as trustworthy institutions with whom we can share sensitive and personal information. One might assume that it is reasonable to expect that personal information shared with these third parties is protected by the Fourth Amendment. This is not so.

Consider, as examples, *California Bankers Association v. Schulz*,[49] which was decided in 1974, and *United States v. Miller*,[50] decided in

1976. In both of these cases, government investigators subpoenaed banks seeking customers' sensitive financial, account, and transaction information. Those customers surely shared that information with their banks with the subjective expectation that it would be kept private. Given the nature of banks and their roles in society, we might also conclude that these customers' subjective expectations of privacy were perfectly reasonable. The Supreme Court did not see it that way, however.

In both *California Bankers Association* and *Miller*, the Supreme Court held that government agents can subpoena transaction records from banks without violating customers' reasonable expectations of privacy. In the Court's view, customers voluntarily share information with their banks. Customers also know that transaction information is shared with counterparties who receive checks or are paid by credit card. Customers might hope and assume that their banks will not reveal the details of their financial transactions to the government, but, according to the Court, every customer "takes the risk, in revealing his affairs to another, that the information will be conveyed by that person to the government."[51] That risk is assumed, the Court continued, "even if the information is revealed on the assumption that it will be used only for a limited purpose and the confidence placed in the third party will not be betrayed."[52] Applying the logic from these two cases, the Court later held that individuals have no reasonable expectations of privacy in the records associated with telephone calls. Any "person who uses the phone," the Court opined in *Smith v. Maryland*, decided in 1979, "assume[s] the risk that the [telephone] company would reveal to the police the numbers he dialed."[53]

Together, these cases provide the foundation for the third-party doctrine. The third-party doctrine is sometimes summarized by the proposition that we lose all reasonable expectations of privacy in information we share with third parties.[54] This goes a bit too far. Were this the case, then *Katz* itself was wrongly decided. After all, Katz shared everything he said with those whom he called from that pay phone. If, by sharing that information, he lost all reasonable expectations of privacy in his conversations, then law enforcement's use of an electronic ear to eavesdrop on him could not be a Fourth Amendment search. It therefore cannot be the case that we lose all expectations of privacy in information we share with third parties. The third-party doctrine is therefore better understood as holding that, if you share information with a third party, then you have no Fourth Amendment complaint if the government gains access to that information by lawful means. Sometimes the third party will simply volunteer the information. Sometimes the government will ask for it. Other times, the government will compel disclosure through a subpoena or perhaps by calling the third party to testify in a grand jury or in open court. In all these circumstances, the Fourth Amendment does not limit government access.

In combination with the public observation doctrine, the third-party doctrine plays a critical role in protecting many contemporary surveillance programs from Fourth Amendment scrutiny. For example, courts have cited it as grounds for allowing government access to cell site location data[55] and historical cell site location data without a warrant.[56] Courts have cited the third-party doctrine when granting law enforcement access to location information held by social media services. For example, during a series of protests in New York held in 2011 under the slogan "Occupy Wall Street," several people were investigated for inciting others to violate the law by blocking traffic, parading without permits, and, in some cases, engaging in violence. Among those under investigation was a man named Malcolm Harris, who was arrested on charges of disorderly conduct while marching on the Brooklyn Bridge. As part of its investigation, the Manhattan District Attorney's Office subpoenaed the social networking site Twitter for information relating to Mr. Harris's tweets over a three-month period, including his subscriber information and the times, dates, and locations of his tweets. Both Twitter and Mr. Harris resisted that subpoena, arguing that Mr. Harris shared this information with Twitter solely in order to use Twitter's services and on the understanding that Twitter would keep the information confidential. Applying the third-party doctrine, a New York Court found that Harris had no Fourth Amendment grounds for objecting to the subpoena.[57]

Mr. Harris's case is by no means exceptional. Internet Service Providers routinely receive requests from government agents for information about their customers' internet activities. These requests do not constitute searches under the third-party doctrine. So, too, requests from law enforcement for user information from search engines and other internet companies. In fact, these requests have become a common routine for law enforcement agencies in recent years. For example, Google and Yahoo report receiving tens of thousands of requests for user information from federal, state, and local law enforcement every year.[58] No matter the promises these companies might have made to their customers, the third-party doctrine means that those who use these services have no reasonable expectations of privacy in the web searches they conduct or the pages they visit and read.

The third-party doctrine is also the primary constitutional justification for the National Security Agency's (NSA) telephony metadata program, which we discussed in Chapter 1. Under this program, the NSA and the Federal Bureau of Investigation gathered call records associated with domestic telephone calls. Under the third-party doctrine, this effort appears to fall outside the scope of Fourth Amendment review or regulation.[59] That is because we have no reasonable expectations of privacy in those call records by virtue of the third-party doctrine.

The third-party doctrine has also been cited in support of other government information-gathering programs. For example, government agencies routinely gather and store information about air travel, amassing records documenting who flies, where, and how often. Law enforcement agencies have access to information gathered by EZ Pass and other companies through which customers pay tolls on public roadways. Under the auspices of the Affordable Care Act, the Department of Health and Human Services gathers patient, disease, and treatment information. In addition to discrete information-gathering programs, government agencies also make use of Big Data technologies, which aggregate or cross-reference otherwise discrete silos of data and then apply analytic tools for a wide range of purposes, including crime detection, emergency preparedness, and to promote efficient delivery of services. By definition, these programs are completely indiscriminate in their collection, aggregation, and analysis of information, sweeping the innocent in with the guilty. They are also perfectly constitutional, at least under current doctrine, because all the information gathered, stored, and analyzed was at one point gathered from a third party with whom the information was shared voluntarily. Gathering, aggregating, and storing that information is therefore not regarded as a "search" under current Fourth Amendment doctrine.

Fourth Amendment Standing

To bring a lawsuit in federal court, a plaintiff must show that he has an interest at stake. This "standing" requirement derives from Article III of the Constitution, which governs the judiciary. A plaintiff has standing if he has suffered, or is at impending risk of suffering, a specific injury; this injury or risk of injury is the result of an action by the defendant; and that the court can provide some form of remedy for that injury. In the context of cases alleging harms arising from violations of Fourth Amendment rights, the Supreme Court also requires that a plaintiff show that he has Fourth Amendment standing. After *Katz*, the Court has interpreted Fourth Amendment standing as a requirement that plaintiffs show that they have suffered a personal violation of their subjectively manifested and reasonable expectations of privacy.[60]

Rules governing Fourth Amendment standing have been applied most often in cases where officers search homes, cars, or effects that normally enjoy Fourth Amendment protections. For example, in *Rawlings v. Kentucky*,[61] the defendant tried to exclude from evidence at trial drugs discovered during an unlawful search of his girlfriend's purse. The Supreme Court held that he did not have standing to challenge that search or to request relief because he did not have a reasonable expectation of privacy in the purse. His girlfriend did, but he did not. Because the illegal search did not violate *his* reasonable expectations of privacy, the Court held that *he* did not have standing to challenge the government's actions. Similarly, the Court held in *Minnesota v. Carter*[62] that two out-of-town visitors who visited an apartment to package drugs did not have standing to challenge a search of that apartment because they did not have reasonable expectations of privacy in the premises.

Although the Fourth Amendment standing requirement may seem perfectly *reasonable* at first blush, it has led to some results that can only be described as *unreasonable*. *United States v. Payner*[63] is among the most egregious. In that case, federal agents suspected that Payner was using the services of a Bahamian bank to hide income and avoid paying taxes. The agents could not gather enough evidence to prove their suspicions in court, so they hit upon a plan to steal banking records that might help their case. When one of the bank's vice presidents came to Miami on business, they arranged for him to go on a date with a woman recruited by the agents. While the vice president was away from his hotel room, a private investigator working with the government broke in, stole the banker's briefcase, and took it to a locksmith, who then opened the lock. The private investigator then took the briefcase and its contents to an Internal Revenue Service agent, who made photocopies of all the documents. At trial, Payner objected to the introduction of these stolen documents as evidence against him because they were the fruits of an illegal search. Although the Supreme Court agreed that the agents' conduct was illegal and unconstitutional, it nevertheless held that Payner did not have standing to complain. It was not his hotel room or his briefcase that were invaded, after all. The government was allowed to profit from their illegal search because Payner's personal reasonable expectations of privacy were not violated.

The rules governing Fourth Amendment standing have prevented citizens from challenging contemporary surveillance programs. The most notorious case on point is *Clapper v. Amnesty International*.[64] The plaintiffs in *Clapper* were attorneys and human rights activists who regularly represented or otherwise worked with international clients and partners. They brought suit to challenge a 2008 amendment to Section 702 of the Foreign Intelligence Surveillance Act.[65] That amendment granted broader authority for national security agencies to intercept electronic communications when at least one of the parties was a noncitizen located abroad. The plaintiffs in *Clapper* alleged that, due to the nature of their international work, they were subject to surveillance under Section 702. They therefore challenged the constitutionality of Section 702 and any surveillance programs operating under its authority.

The Supreme Court held that the plaintiffs in *Clapper* lacked standing to challenge Section 702. The problem was that the plaintiffs could not prove that they had actually been subject to surveillance under the secret program. They strongly suspected that they were, but their claim was based on speculation rather than hard facts. In normal circumstances, the plaintiffs could have remedied this situation through the discovery process that is part of all civil lawsuits. In this case, however, the government maintained that any surveillance programs that might exist under the authority of 702 would be top secret, and therefore immune from discovery. The Supreme Court agreed. Despite the obvious Catch-22, the Court held that the plaintiffs in *Clapper* had not demonstrated standing to challenge Section 702 and could not reasonably hope to access the evidence necessary to prove that they had standing.[66]

Although the Supreme Court's analysis in *Clapper* focused on Article III standing, Fourth Amendment standing loomed in the background. Because the plaintiffs could not prove that they had actually been surveilled, they also could not prove any violations of their personal expectations of privacy.

The Fourth Amendment standing doctrine makes it quite difficult to challenge contemporary surveillance programs, even if they are broad, indiscriminate, and lead to unreasonable results. That is because current doctrine takes a very personal view of Fourth Amendment rights that focuses on individual persons rather than "the people" as a whole. As a result, there is no way for "the people," or an individual acting on behalf of the people, to challenge government surveillance programs absent a showing of personal violation of personal rights. Current rules governing Fourth Amendment standing also limit the scope of relevant evidence in cases where plaintiffs allege that their rights have been violated. Because the rules governing standing require courts to assess searches and seizures on a case-by-case basis, courts must focus exclusively on the facts particular to each specific case. Evidence tending to show that an overall program is unreasonable in that it yields lots of false positives or exhibits patterns of discriminate impact is therefore irrelevant from a Fourth Amendment point of view because it does not illuminate whether a specific stop, say, was supported by reasonable suspicion. Even terribly broken systems sometimes get it right. Third, current rules governing Fourth Amendment standing make it nearly impossible to sue for reforms on a programmatic level. Under current doctrine, individual plaintiffs may only seek relief for themselves in order to vindicate their personal Fourth Amendment rights. A plaintiff therefore can seek a court order barring government agents from surveilling him, but cannot demand broader reforms that might achieve greater security for the people as a whole.[67]

The Late Twentieth Century, Part II: Terry v. Ohio

The *Katz* case marked a revolution in Fourth Amendment law. Many Fourth Amendment progressives welcomed that revolution because *Katz* seemed to provide significantly broader protections for citizens. After all, by expanding the definition of "search" to include not just physical intrusions but also invasions of reasonable expectations of privacy, *Katz* widened the scope of law enforcement activities subject to Fourth Amendment regulation. As we have seen, that revolution has faltered. The public observation doctrine and the third-party doctrine mark two of the most important stumbles. The consequences are now evident. Despite the apparent promise of *Katz*, the people have been left vulnerable to many of the means, methods, and technologies that define our twenty-first-century age of surveillance. *Katz* is not solely responsible for this state of affairs, however.

One year after *Katz* was decided, the Supreme Court initiated a second revolution in Fourth Amendment law with a case called *Terry v. Ohio*.[68] In *Terry*, the Court faced a simple question: May police officers stop, question, and frisk citizens on the street without a warrant, without probable cause, and, perhaps, without even needing to justify themselves on Fourth Amendment grounds at all? To understand the importance of this question, it is necessary to take a broader perspective on daily engagements between police officers and citizens.

Police officers have a wide variety of engagements with citizens on the street every day. Many of these encounters are friendly and banal. An officer assisting pedestrians at a crosswalk during the morning rush hour may wish passersby a good day. An officer might stop to assist a mother folding her stroller before getting on the municipal bus. He may buy a cup of coffee from the local shop and engage staff and fellow customers in small talk. None of these encounters constitute searches or seizures. There are no physical intrusions, no efforts to gather information for law enforcement purposes, and no invasions of subjectively manifested and reasonable expectations of privacy. They therefore do not raise any Fourth Amendment questions and likewise do not require any particular justification.

On the other end of the spectrum, there are engagements between law enforcement officers and citizens that clearly constitute searches and seizures. For example, if an officer enters a home to look for stolen stereo equipment, rummages through a briefcase to look for cocaine, or removes the contents of a citizen's pockets in hopes of finding a marijuana cigarette, then there is no doubt that the officer has conducted a search. In each of these cases, the officer has physically intruded into a constitutionally protected area (a "person, house, paper, or effect") for the purpose of finding evidence of a crime. In so doing, the officer has also violated subjectively manifested, and perfectly reasonable, expectations of privacy. Likewise, if a police officer commands a citizen to stop, places her in handcuffs, informs her that she is under arrest, and then transports her to the police station to be held pending arraignment, then there is no doubt that the citizen has been seized for purposes of the Fourth Amendment. In this case, the officer has materially interfered with liberty and freedom of movement under color of law.

Between a friendly hello, which lies on one end of the Fourth Amendment spectrum, and a full custodial arrest and physical search, which lies on the other, there are a wide variety of engagements between citizens and law enforcement that involve some invasions of privacy or some level of explicit or implied coercion yet fall short of the levels of intrusion entailed by custodial arrests and physical searches. Stops and frisks lie somewhere in this middle ground. Stops occur when a police officer invokes her authority to command someone to stop. Police officers usually conduct stops where they suspect that something suspicious or criminal may be afoot. They will then ask questions or take other investigative steps to confirm or dispel their suspicions. Sometimes during the course of a stop, a police officer may be concerned that the person with whom she is engaged is armed and potentially dangerous. In these circumstances, she might like to determine whether her suspicions are well founded by conducting a frisk. Frisks involve an officer's patting down the outside of a suspects clothing or personal items to determine by touch whether a weapon is present.

The first question for the Supreme Court in *Terry* was whether stops and frisks are searches and seizures for Fourth Amendment purposes. That question was particularly important given the rules and limitations governing searches and seizures at that time. By the time *Terry* was decided, the Supreme Court had established three important rules governing searches and seizures. First, searches and seizures required probable cause. For searches, this meant that officers needed probable cause to believe that evidence of a crime would be found in the place to be searched at the time of the search. For arrests, this meant that officers needed probable cause to believe that the person arrested was committing or had committed a crime. Second, the Court had expressed a strong preference for warrants. For searches, that preference was quite strong, particularly with respect to searches of highly protected areas like homes. For arrests, the preference was less strong because the circumstances of many arrests make getting a warrant difficult or impossible. The third, which is commonly referred to as the "exclusionary rule," dealt with failures by police officers to obey the first two rules. If officers did not have probable cause to conduct search or to effect an arrest, or if they failed to get a warrant when one was required, then any evidence discovered as a result would be excluded from the prosecution's case at trial no matter how reliable and material that evidence might be.

One might wonder where these requirements come from. We will explore this question at greater depth in Chapter 5. For now, it is enough to note that the probable cause requirement, the warrant requirement, and the exclusionary rule were all well established when *Terry* was decided in 1968. This meant that there was a considerable amount at stake in the question of whether stops and frisks constituted seizures and searches under the Fourth Amendment. If stopping a citizen to inquire into his business was treated as a "seizure," asking him questions constituted a "search," and conducting a brief pat down to find weapons was also a "search," then it seemed that law enforcement officers would be required to show probable cause before conducting a stop or frisk. They might even need to get a warrant. If they did not have probable cause, or failed to get warrant, then they would face the prospect of losing any evidence they might discover pursuant to the exclusionary rule.

Although this result might have been wonderful with respect to the security of the people against government searches, it would have been a disaster for the people's interests in effective law enforcement. By definition, stops and frisks are investigative tools. They are designed to determine whether there is criminal activity afoot at a point in time when there is not enough evidence to show probable cause. If officers were required to show probable cause before conducting stops and frisks, then they would be considerably more limited in their ability to detect and perhaps prevent crime. Subjecting stops and frisks to the probable cause and warrant requirements would also entail a high degree of judicial micromanagement, effectively barring or limiting the use of stops and frisks as a tool for detecting and preventing crime.

Alternatively, if the *Terry* Court decided that only full custodial arrests and physically intrusive searches for evidence constituted "seizures" and "searches" for purposes of the Fourth Amendment, then that would have had the effect of leaving a wide range of interactions between police and citizens, including stops and frisks, beyond the reach of any Fourth Amendment restraints at all. Although that result would be a boon for law enforcement, it would have posed a significant threat to the security of the people in their persons, houses, papers, and effects against unreasonable searches and seizures. That is because it would have granted an unlimited license for officers to stop and frisk anyone they pleased for bad reasons, for insufficient reasons, or for no reasons at all without serious concerns that they would be held accountable by courts.

The Supreme Court in *Terry* sought a middle course between these extremes by reimagining the Fourth Amendment landscape. Prior to *Terry*, courts had a fairly narrow view of the Fourth Amendment and its regulatory potential. Searches and seizures were understood in reference to physically invasive searches and custodial arrests. All searches and seizures required probable cause, and courts preferred that officers secure warrants before conducting most searches. In *Terry*, the Court painted a much more complicated picture, engaging a broader range of police activities, but also providing for less stringent controls and regulations along that spectrum. More specifically, the Court held that stops and frisks are seizures and searches, and therefore fall within the ambit of Fourth Amendment regulations. At the same time, however, the Court held that stops and frisks do not require probable cause and are not subject to the warrant requirement. For stops and frisks, the Court instead held that reasonable suspicion will do. The Court reached this result on the basis of its assessment of what is reasonable in the context of evolving encounters between police officers and citizens.

As it is described by the Court in *Terry*, the principal goal of the Fourth Amendment is to ensure that searches and seizures are reasonable. Reasonableness, according to the Court, entails a fact-intensive, case-by-case assessment of (1) the privacy interests of a citizen implicated by police conduct; (2) law enforcement interests in their own safety and in detecting, preventing, and prosecuting crime; and (3) whether law enforcement conduct in a particular circumstance strikes a reasonable balance between those sometimes competing interests. An arrest constitutes the most severe form of intrusion on the privacy interests of a citizen. To justify an arrest as reasonable, officers must therefore demonstrate that there are compelling law enforcement interests at stake by pointing to specific facts and evidence sufficient to show probable cause to believe that the arrestee has committed a crime. Police officers must also run the gauntlet of judicial review when conducting arrests, either by securing a warrant before the arrest or by participating in a postarrest hearing where a neutral magistrate will make an independent assessment as to whether there was probable cause to make an arrest.

By comparison, stops are much less intrusive, and therefore require only reasonable suspicion. They also do not require warrants or any other form of prior judicial review. Similarly, searches that involve physical intrusions into constitutionally protected areas raise serious privacy concerns, and therefore require probable cause to believe that evidence will be found in the place to be searched at the time of the search. Many such searches are also subject to the warrant preference, which requires officers to test their claims of probable cause before a neutral magistrate before conducting their search. By comparison, frisks are much less intrusive, and therefore require only reasonable suspicion that the suspect is armed and potentially dangerous. As with stops, frisks are not subject to the warrant preference, and therefore do not require prior judicial review.

The *Terry* decision concretized a number of important principles of Fourth Amendment law that have had lasting effects on the security of the people from unreasonable searches and seizures. First and foremost, it established reasonableness as the principal metric for evaluating the constitutionality of searches and seizures. The probable cause requirement, the warrant preference, and the exclusionary rule suggest a degree of rule-based formalism. The *Terry* Court turned away from this technical, rule-bound approach, choosing instead a more fluid and open framework for evaluating Fourth Amendment questions based on reasonableness.

Second, the Court defined reasonableness in reference to the competing interests of citizens and law enforcement at stake in searches and seizures. By definition, all searches and seizures threaten the privacy interests of the citizen whose person, house, paper, or effect is searched or seized. At the same time, searches and seizures are critical tools in the context of ongoing efforts by law enforcement to detect, prevent, and prosecute crime. After *Terry*, courts have assessed the reasonableness of searches and seizures by weighing these competing interests to determine whether an appropriate balance has been struck in each particular case.

Third, courts after *Terry* have assessed reasonableness on a case-by-case basis, focusing on the particular facts and circumstances surrounding an individual search or seizure. This approach is reinforced by the rules governing Fourth Amendment standing we discussed earlier.

Finally, the *Terry* Court required that courts assess the reasonableness of searches and seizures from an objective point of view. This means that the subjective intentions or beliefs of officers conducting searches and seizures do not matter. What matters is whether, based on the facts and circumstances presented to them, they acted reasonably.

Together, these changes in Fourth Amendment law have licensed a range of intrusive practices and policies while also limiting the capacities of courts to impose Fourth Amendment constraints on means, methods, practices, and policies of search and seizure. Contemporary stop and frisk programs provide the most notorious examples.

The rules announced in *Terry* work to preserve the largely unfettered discretion of police officers to conduct stops and frisks without regular or effective judicial review. Foremost among these is the focus after *Terry* on assessing reasonableness on a case-by-case basis. This means that statistics documenting the overall failure rates of stop and frisk programs, their geographic focuses, and racial biases are not relevant when a suspect challenges her own stop and frisk. It may be comically obvious that a stop and frisk program under which 90 percent of subjects are perfectly innocent of any wrongdoing is not serving law enforcement interests in detecting, preventing, and prosecuting crime. So too, it is painfully obvious that such programs fail to strike a reasonable balance between the interests of the people in privacy and physical security and the interests of law enforcement in crime detection. After *Terry*, however, these are answers to the wrong questions. The only question relevant to the Fourth Amendment under *Terry* is whether, in each individual case, officers can point to some objective facts or observations that are sufficient to show reasonable suspicion in the circumstance. The broader context is simply not relevant.

These consequences of *Terry* for Fourth Amendment doctrine reach far outside the stop and frisk context. Take, for example, *Whren v. United States*.[69] In that case, two plainclothes police officers observed a truck occupied by two young black men transiting a "high crime area" in Washington, D.C. The officers observed the truck stop for too long at an intersection, then turn abruptly before accelerating at what officers described as an "unreasonable speed." Based on these observations, the officers stopped the truck citing probable cause to believe that the driver had violated local traffic ordinances. When they approached the passenger compartment of the truck, the officers observed plastic bags of what proved to be crack cocaine inside. At trial, and again on appeal, Whren and his codefendant argued that the officers' true motivations for stopping their truck was suspicion based on racial profiling and that the alleged minor traffic violations served as a mere pretext for a stop based on race. Writing for the Court in *Whren*, Justice Antonin Scalia held that the officers' true motives were irrelevant from a Fourth Amendment point of view. All that mattered was that, based on the immediate facts presented to the officers, they had reasonable grounds to effect a stop.

In subsequent years, the Court has expanded on *Whren*. For example, in *Devenpeck v. Alford*,[70] the Court confronted a case where a suspect recorded his conversation with a police officer. The officer took offense and arrested him for recording their conversation despite the fact that the suspect produced proof in the form of court opinions showing that he was perfectly within his rights to make that recording. As it turned out, the suspect was right. The officer had arrested him for something that was not illegal. Despite that mistake, the Court held that the arrest was perfectly reasonable under the Fourth Amendment because there was sufficient evidence at the scene to prove that the suspect had committed another crime. Here again, the true motives of the officer did not matter.

Virginia v. Moore[71] offers yet another example of how the basic framework of Fourth Amendment analysis prescribed by *Terry* has affected the scope of Fourth Amendment review. In that case, David Lee Moore was stopped by police officers on suspicion of driving with a suspended license. It turned out that he was, in fact, driving with a suspended license, which was punishable by a fine and jail time. The officers then arrested Moore and searched him incident to that arrest, whereupon they discovered that he was carrying sixteen grams of crack cocaine. All of this would have been perfectly lawful save for one fact: Virginia law explicitly prohibited the officers from arresting Moore for driving on a suspended license. They were instead obliged to issue a summons. They could only arrest Moore if he refused to discontinue the violation or the officers otherwise had good grounds to believe that he would not appear on the summons. Prosecutors in the case never seriously contended that any of these conditions were met. In other words, they conceded that the arrest was illegal under Virginia law. Nevertheless, Justice Scalia, writing for the Court, held that there was no Fourth Amendment violation. That is because, on the facts before them, the officers had probable cause to believe that Moore had committed a crime. No matter their motivations, violations of state law, or the likelihood that the officers had followed a policy and practice of using minor traffic violations as pretexts for escalating their encounters with citizens suspected of drug crimes, all that mattered to the Court were the objective facts of the particular case. The Court simply was not interested in taking a broader view.

Conclusion

We live in an age of surveillance. Government agents and their private sector collaborators have new and unprecedented technological capacity to monitor and track all of us and each of us everywhere we go and in everything we do. For most of us, the threats of broad and indiscriminate surveillance posed by these technologies may seem abstract – more fiction than science. As we saw in Chapter 1, however, that is naïve.

All of us have been and are subject to government surveillance. Moreover, many of us routinely are subject to surveillance that is more visceral and immediate in the form of stops and frisks, which are a routine feature of daily life for far too many innocent and law-abiding citizens. Faced with these present and looming threats to security in our bodies, homes, property, and information, it is tempting to turn to the Fourth Amendment for some succor. As we have seen in this chapter, however, that path holds little promise.

Many of the means, methods, and practices that form the core of our emerging surveillance state exploit gaps in contemporary Fourth Amendment doctrine. Primary among these are the public observation doctrine, the third-party doctrine, rules governing Fourth Amendment standing, and the stop and frisk doctrine. Individually and in concert, these jurisprudential products of the twentieth century threaten to make the Fourth Amendment a dead letter in the twenty-first century. This apparent crisis in Fourth Amendment law has not gone unnoticed.

The Supreme Court appears to appreciate both the challenges to and the critical role of the Fourth Amendment in our age of surveillance. This was evident in *United States v. Jones*, the GPS tracking case decided in 2012.[72] In that case, Justices Ginsburg, Breyer, Alito, Sotomayor, and Kagan expressed deep concerns about the impact of contemporary surveillance technologies on Fourth Amendment rights. They nevertheless failed to identify what changes they would make to Fourth Amendment doctrine or how those changes might be justified or applied. In this sense, *Jones* issued an invitation for policymakers, judges, activists, and scholars to come forward with proposals. The next chapter reviews some of the most influential responses to this invitation.

Notes

1. Scott Sunby, *Everyman's Fourth Amendment: Privacy or Mutual Trust between Government and Citizen?*, 94 COLUM. L. REV. 1751, 1789–90 (1994).
2. (1765) 95 Eng. Rep. 807 (KB).
3. United States v. Jones, 132 S. Ct. 945, 949 (2012) (citations and internal quotation marks omitted).
4. Riley v. California, 134 S.Ct. 2473, 2494 (2014) (quoting 10 WORKS OF JOHN ADAMS 247–48 (C. Adams ed. 1856)).
5. Wolf v. Colorado, 338 U.S. 25 (1949). There is a case to be made that *Wolf* also assumes rather than holding that the Fourth Amendment applies to the states. If that

view is correct, then the Fourth Amendment was not incorporated until 1961, when the Court decided *Mapp v. Ohio*, 367 U.S. 643 (1961). For present purposes, nothing turns on which of these two dates marks the official incorporation of the Fourth Amendment to the states.
6. The basic framework for this process of incorporation is laid out in Chicago, Burlington & Quincy R.R. Co. v. City of Chicago, 166 U.S. 226 (1897).
7. *See* Chapter 4.
8. *Jones*, 132 S. Ct. at 949–50.
9. 116 U.S. 616 (1886).
10. It was in service of customs collections that colonial magistrates issued the writs of assistance that so angered our founders and led to the inclusion of the Fourth Amendment among the Bill of Rights. A century after the founding, those concerns appear to have remained very much alive.
11. 277 U.S. 438 (1928).
12. For a fascinating account of the role that prohibition had in fueling the rise of American law enforcement institutions, see LISA MCGIRR, THE WAR ON ALCOHOL: PROHIBITION AND THE RISE OF THE AMERICAN STATE (2015).
13. Olmstead v. United States, 277 U.S. 438, 471 (1928) (Brandeis, J., dissenting).
14. Samuel Warren & Louis Brandeis, *The Right to Privacy*, 4 HARV. L. REV. 193 (1890).
15. *Olmstead*, 477 U.S. at 473–74 (Brandeis, J., dissenting).
16. 316 U.S. 129 (1942).
17. *See* Korematsu v. United States, 323 U.S. 214, 233 (1944) (Murphy, J., dissenting).
18. *Goldman*, 316 U.S. at 139 (Murphy, J., dissenting).
19. *Id.*
20. *Id.*
21. 365 U.S. 505, 508–09 (1961).
22. 389 U.S. 347 (1967).
23. *Katz*, 389 U.S. at 352.
24. *Id.*
25. 388 U.S. 41 (1967).
26. 18 U.S.C. § 2510 *et seq.* (2012).
27. Pub. L. No. 99–508 (1986).
28. 389 U.S. at 351.
29. 389 U.S. at 352.
30. *See* California v. Ciraolo, 476 U.S. 207 (1986); United States v. Bellina, 665 F.2d 1335 (4th Cir. 1981).
31. *See id.*
32. *See* United States v. Delaney, 52 F.3d 182 (8th Cir. 1995).
33. *See* California v. Greenwood, 486 U.S. 35 (1988).
34. Florida v. Riley, 488 U.S. 445 (1989).
35. Dow Chemicals Co. v. United States, 476 U.S. 227 (1986).
36. United States v. Knotts, 460 U.S. 276 (1983).
37. *See* United States v. Maynard, 615 F.3d 544, 563 (D.C. Cir. 2010).
38. *See* United States v. Jones, 132 S. Ct. 945, 954 (2012) (Sotomayor, J., concurring).
39. 460 U.S. at 284.
40. *See* United States v. Jones, 132 S. Ct. 945, 964 (2012) (Alito, J., concurring).

41. *See id.* (leaving these questions for another day).
42. Orin S. Kerr, *The Mosaic Theory of the Fourth Amendment*, 111 MICH. L. REV. 311 (2012).
43. 460 U.S. at 283-84.
44. United States v. Jones, 132 S. Ct. 945, 954 (2012) (Sotomayor, J., concurring); United States v. Jones, 132 S. Ct. 945, 962-64 (2012) (Alito, J., concurring).
45. 385 U.S. 293 (1966).
46. 385 U.S. at 302.
47. Lewis v. United States, 385 U.S. 206 (1966) (undercover officers); Lopez v. United States, 373 U.S. 427 (1963).
48. United States v. White, 401 U.S. 745 (1971).
49. 416 U.S. 21 (1974).
50. 425 U.S. 435 (1976).
51. *Id.* at 443.
52. *Id.*
53. 442 U.S. 735, 744 (1979).
54. *See, e.g.,* United States v. Jones, 132 S. Ct. 945, 957 (2012) (Sotomayor, J., concurring) (opining that "it may be necessary to reconsider the premise that an individual has no reasonable expectation of privacy in information voluntarily disclosed to third parties").
55. *See, e.g.,* United States v. Skinner, 690 F.3d 772 (6th Cir. 2012), cert. denied, 133 S. Ct. 2851 (2013); In re Application of the United States for an Order for Authorization to Obtain Location Data Concerning an AT & T Cellular Telephone, 2015 WL 1842761 (N.D. Miss. Mar. 30, 2015); In re Smartphone Geolocation Data Application, 977 F.Supp.2d 129 (E.D.N.Y.2013); Devega v. State, 286 Ga. 448 (2010).
56. *See, e.g.,* United States v. Davis, __ F. 3d. __ (11th Cir. 2016); United States v. Chavez, 2016 WL 740246 (D. Conn. Feb. 24, 2016).
57. People v. Harris, 945 N.Y.S.2d 505 (N.Y. Crim. Ct. 2012).
58. *See* Google Transparency Report, www.google.com/transparencyreport/userdatarequests/legalprocess/.
59. *See* ACLU v. Clapper, 959 F. Supp. 2d 724 (S.D.N.Y. 2013), *aff'd in part, remanded in part, and vacated,* 785 F.3d 787 (2d Cir. 2015). *But see* Klayman v. Obama, 957 F. Supp. 2d 1 (D.D.C. 2013), vacated and remanded 800 F.3d 559 (D.C. Cir. 2015).
60. Rakas v. Illinois, 439 U.S. 128 (1978).
61. Rawlings v. Kentucky, 448 U.S. 98 (1980).
62. Minnesota v. Carter, 525 U.S. 83 (1998).
63. 447 U.S. 727 (1980).
64. Clapper v. Amnesty International, 133 S.Ct. 1138 (2013).
65. The amendment is lodged at 50 U.S.C. § 1881a. For a careful and complete critical history of Section 702 and the surveillance programs it has spawned, *see* Laura Donohue, *Section 702 and the Collection of International Telephone and Internet Content,* 38 Harv. J. L. & Pub. Pol. 117 (2014).
66. Plaintiffs seeking to challenge government surveillance programs continue to run into the wall erected by *Clapper. See, e.g.,* Jewel v. National Security Agency, No. C 08-04373, (Feb. 10, 2015) (applying rules governing standing and the "state secrets" doctrine to dismiss challenges to NSA surveillance programs).

67. The limits imposed by Fourth Amendment standing doctrine were born out in *Floyd v. City of New York*, 959 F.Supp. 2d 540 (S.D.N.Y. 2013). In that case, individual plaintiffs sought to challenge the constitutionality of the NYPD's stop and frisk program. Although Judge Sheindlin was sympathetic, she struggled to find a way to make compelling evidence of programmatic unreasonableness relevant when Fourth Amendment law required that she analyze each incident of stop and frisk individually.
68. 392 U.S. 1 (1968).
69. 517 U.S. 806 (1996).
70. 543 U.S. 146 (2004).
71. 553 U.S. 164 (2008).
72. 132 S. Ct. 945 (2012).

3

Some Competing Proposals

The Court had the chance to chart a course for the Fourth Amendment in our twenty-first-century age of surveillance in *United States v. Jones*.[1] In that case, law enforcement officers attached a GPS-enabled tracking device to Jones's car in an effort to connect him to a drug conspiracy. The officers then tracked his movements over the course of four weeks. They collected thousands of pages of data documenting everywhere Jones had gone during those four weeks, including regular visits to locations associated with the drug conspiracy. Based in part on this evidence, Jones was convicted at trial. He filed an appeal, which ultimately ended up in the Supreme Court.

Jones presented the perfect opportunity for the Court to decide whether the Fourth Amendment might impose some restraints on the government's use of modern surveillance technologies. The Court demurred, however, and instead resolved the case on much narrower grounds. Specifically, the Court focused on the fact that law enforcement officers touched Jones's car in order to install their tracking device. Writing for the majority, Justice Antonin Scalia held that this physical intrusion constituted a search for purposes of the Fourth Amendment. Because the officers did not have a valid warrant giving them authority to effect such an intrusion, the Court held that they had violated Jones's Fourth Amendment rights. Given that this holding resolved the controversy, the Court saw no reason to reach the additional question whether officers' use of the device to track Jones constituted a Fourth Amendment search.

The majority opinion in *Jones* was important for a number of reasons, not least because it clarified the place of *Katz v. United States* in Fourth Amendment law.[2] The real action in the case, however, was in the concurring opinions written by Justice Sonia Sotomayor and Justice Samuel Alito. Justice Sotomayor joined the majority opinion written by Justice Scalia, but wrote separately to express her concerns about granting law enforcement unfettered discretion to use advanced surveillance technologies that do not require a physical intrusion, such as tracking technologies that exploit the GPS chips native to our electronic devices and data aggregation technologies that gather information previously shared with third parties.[3] In her concurrence, Justice Sotomayor suggested that meeting these challenges would require the Court to fundamentally rethink its commitments to doctrines discussed in Chapter 2, including the third-party doctrine.[4]

Although Justice Sotomayor joined the majority opinion in *Jones*, Justice Alito did not. He wrote a separate concurring opinion, which Justices Ruth Bader Ginsburg, Stephen Breyer, and Elena Kagan joined.[5] In that opinion, Justice Alito focused on the duration of the surveillance to which Jones was subjected and the volume of information gathered over that time. In Justice Alito's view, we simply do not expect that anyone, much less the government, is engaging in long-term surveillance of *us*. On that basis, Justice Alito concluded that Jones had a reasonable expectation of privacy that was violated when officers tracked him for four weeks and gathered thousands of pages of data documenting his movements in precise detail.[6]

Although five justices supported the general proposition that the Fourth Amendment should have something to say about twenty-first-century surveillance technologies in *Jones*, there was no consensus regarding how to go forward. Many commentators therefore read *Jones* as a warning shot of sorts, putting legislatures and law enforcement on notice that a revolution is coming.[7] *Jones* was also an invitation, affording an opportunity for legislatures and civil society to offer proposals.[8] A number of scholars and commentators have answered that invitation. This chapter will explore some of the most promising of these.

Although there is considerable variation among them, post-*Jones* proposals for rethinking the Fourth Amendment generally fall into one of five basic categories: market-based approaches that favor self-help; proposals that focus on how much information is gathered; proposals that focus on how long surveillance is conducted; proposals that focus on the nature or content of information that is gathered; and proposals that focus on the means and methods, including advanced technologies, that are used to conduct surveillance. Although all of these proposals have strengths and weaknesses, the most promising path forward is to focus on means and methods of surveillance with the goal of regulating the government's use of technologies capable of facilitating programs of broad and indiscriminate surveillance, thereby preserving the right of the people to be secure against threats of unreasonable search.

The People vs. the Government: The Market-Based Approach

Despite the Fourth Amendment's noble place in the history of our republic, there is a significant contingent of privacy advocates who do not think it can provide much protection in our age of surveillance. In their view, the Fourth Amendment – or, at any rate, Fourth Amendment doctrine – simply is not up to the task of addressing modern privacy challenges.[9] Some of these critics are equally skeptical of the political branches, which have proven to be incapable of reining in law enforcement and security agencies as they pursue ever-more expansive and invasive surveillance programs.[10] The technologies and programs discussed in Chapter 1 provide credible evidence that this skepticism is well placed. So far, at least, many of these programs have flourished free of any real constitutional or legislative restraints.

In the absence of real constitutional, legislative, or executive solutions, the best hope for protecting privacy in the modern era may rest with the people themselves. Most of the twenty-first-century challenges discussed in Chapter 1 trace to technological innovations that facilitate programs of broad and indiscriminate surveillance. If technology is the problem, then it might make sense to seek technological solutions. If consumers demand privacy protections, then technology companies, device manufacturers, and service providers will rise to meet that demand, both by incorporating privacy protections into their products and by producing new countermeasures.

In support of a market-based approach, advocates can cite some hopeful examples. Foremost among these are advances in encryption technology. Apple and Google were much in the news in 2016 because they met consumer demands for privacy protections by incorporating sophisticated encryption into their devices with the goal of rendering them immune both to government intrusions and to malicious hackers. Encryption is also playing a more prominent role in protecting the privacy of data transmission. Service providers like Apple and Silent Circle offer secure end-to-end encryption for texts and voice mail. For a while, at least, Silent Circle and a company called Lavabit provided encrypted e-mail services. Tor provides a means to prevent tracking and to preserve anonymity while using the Internet. All of these products and services exist to meet consumer demands for privacy and security against both government and private snooping.

Although these products and services show the ability of the market to address consumer demands for privacy protections in the digital age, they are not sufficient to guard against the kinds of methods and programs, described in Chapter 1, absent the support of robust constitutional protections. A pure market-based approach pits consumers against government snoopers, resulting in an arms race between surveillance technologies and countersurveillance technologies. In the words of former NSA and CIA Director General Michael Hayden, it's "game on."[11] Consumers gain access to encryption, and then government agencies endeavor to break that encryption.[12] As consumers migrate to products that allow for anonymous or secure internet browsing, the government develops technologies designed to pierce that anonymity.[13] Absent some way to restrain the government's efforts to develop and deploy new and more sophisticated surveillance technologies, consumers can never be sure who is winning this race. Because we can never know whether the technologies we deploy to protect ourselves against government intrusions are providing any real protection, it is just impossible for them to afford any sense of security against threats of unreasonable searches and seizures.

Adding to these concerns is the fact that government and law enforcement agencies routinely target technology companies precisely because they try to meet market demands for privacy protections. For example, the Federal Bureau of Investigation (FBI) secured a court order against Apple in 2016 demanding that the company write software that would enable the government to circumnavigate security and encryption software on a user's iPhone. Apple contested that order with the assistance of dozens of supporters from business, civil liberties groups, and the professoriate. The FBI eventually dropped its suit after they found a contractor who could break into the target phone, but the question is sure to arise again with another phone running another operating system with different security protocols and different encryption software.

The Apple encryption controversy of 2016 is not an isolated case. Google, Yahoo, and other major search engines receive thousands of demands each year for user information, including web pages visited and the search terms used. Telephone service providers respond to thousands of demands each year from law enforcement agencies for information about users' calls. These requests are so routine that all the major telephone service providers have dedicated portals that allow law enforcement to request and obtain this information online.

One might ask whether these examples show a market failure or a market opportunity for new services and providers. Unfortunately, companies that have sought to exploit this opportunity have not fared well. Take, as an example, the e-mail service provider Lavabit. Lavabit prided itself on protecting the privacy of its customers and providing secure communications. After being peppered with requests and then court orders demanding user information, Lavabit shuttered its doors in 2013 rather than compromise its business model. Seeing the "writing on the wall," e-mail service provider Silent Circle followed suit, shutting down its secure e-mail service in order to avoid having to disclose user information.[14] Despite the demand for privacy services, it therefore looks like incessant government intrusion makes any business model built on meeting these demands short-lived. At any rate, reliance on the market does not seem to be enough to guarantee the security of the people against threats of government intrusion. We also need some way to restrain the government.

Another market-based solution to the challenges posed by contemporary surveillance means, methods, and programs might be to opt out entirely. Prosecutors took this position before the Maryland Court of Special Appeals in a 2016 case called *State v. Andrews*, which tested the legality of cell site simulators.[15] In its brief to the court, the Maryland Attorney General promoted self-help. If you do not want law enforcement officers to track you by tracking your cellular phone, the Attorney General argued, then you should just turn your phone off and take out the battery. For several reasons, this approach should be rejected. We live in a digital age where it is impossible to both participate in society and to avoid leaving a data trail. As journalist Julia Angwin has shown, it takes hundreds of hours to limit our data profiles, and, even then, the results are imperfect.[16] More importantly, however, it exacts unacceptable costs to our liberty interests. We should not have to withdraw from society and the wonders of the digital age in order to secure basic rights guaranteed to us by the Fourth Amendment.[17] This would mean letting technology rob us of our birthright.

In *Kyllo v. United States*, which addressed the constitutionality of using heat detection devices to monitor the interior of homes, Justice Scalia argued that "the power of technology to shrink the realm of guaranteed privacy" must be limited lest we "permit police technology to erode the privacy guaranteed by the Fourth Amendment."[18] The alternative proposed by the government in the *Andrews* case would have citizens "retir[e] to the cellar, cloak[] all the windows with thick caulking, turn[] off the lights and remain[] absolutely quiet."[19] If this is where the market approach leads us, then "we must ask what we will have saved if we cede significant ground to a bunker mode of existence, retaining only that sliver of privacy that we cannot envision a madman exploiting."[20] Fortunately, as Professor Tony Amsterdam has pointed out, "This much withdrawal is not required in order to claim the benefit of the [Fourth] amendment because, if it were, the amendment's benefit would be too stingy to preserve the kind of open society to which we are committed and in which the amendment is supposed to function."[21] Forced withdrawal from the world to maintain privacy would mean sacrificing the public sphere and civil society as cornerstones of a functioning democracy.[22]

What this discussion shows is that technology and other market responses alone are not sufficient to protect the people against threats of unreasonable search and seizure absent some sort of legal protections for privacy-enhancing technology and privacy-preserving products. If the government is free to develop surveillance technologies with the goal of penetrating encryption or other privacy-enhancing technologies, and law enforcement has a broad license to deploy and use this technology in secret and without meaningful legislative or judicial restraints, then technology cannot provide any meaningful or lasting protections. If the government is free to compel service providers to disclose user information or to penetrate their own encryption, then consumers simply cannot rely on companies' promises to maintain customer privacy. This is not to suggest that technology and other market innovations are not part of the solution. Rather, the point is that the only way the market can provide real and reliable solutions to challenges posed by contemporary surveillance technologies is if there are also some complementary constitutional or legislative restraints on government surveillance. Free enterprise alone is just not sufficient to combat the threats posed by contemporary surveillance technologies. We need free enterprise backed by rights. In this circumstance, the most promising source for those rights is the Fourth Amendment.

How Much Is Too Much? The Mosaic Theory

A majority of justices in *Jones* expressed sympathy for what has come to be known as the "mosaic theory." The fundamental insight behind the mosaic theory is that we can maintain reasonable expectations of Fourth Amendment privacy in certain quantities of information and data even if we lack reasonable expectations of privacy in the constituent parts of that whole.[23]

The mosaic theory traces to a decision written by Judge Douglas Ginsburg of the United States Court of Appeals for the District of Columbia Circuit in the *Jones* case before it went to the Supreme Court.[24] At the Court of Appeals, the government relied on the public observation doctrine to defend their long-term use of a GPS tracking device to monitor Jones's movements. In advancing their position, prosecutors relied heavily on the Supreme Court's decision in *United States v. Knotts*.[25] *Knotts* held that the use of a radio beeper tracking device to monitor the movements of a suspect over public streets is not a search because we have no reasonable expectations of privacy in our movements over public streets. Although the prosecutors in the *Jones* case acknowledged that GPS devices are much more effective and efficient than the radio tracking device at issue in *Knotts*, they maintained that the public observation doctrine applied because the information gathered by GPS trackers and radio trackers is fundamentally the same: movements of a suspect over public streets.

Writing for a unanimous panel, Judge Ginsburg rejected the analogy between the radio tracking device used in *Knotts* and the GPS device used in *Jones*. Although both devices monitored movements through public space, Judge Ginsburg expressed deep concerns regarding how long officers used the GPS device, the fact that the device enabled constant surveillance, and the overall quantity of information officers gathered using their GPS device. According to Judge Ginsburg, *Knotts* "held only that '[a] person traveling in an automobile on public thoroughfares has no reasonable expectation of privacy in his movements from one place to another,' not that such a person has no reasonable expectation of privacy in his movements whatsoever, world without end."[26] In order to clarify the distinction, Judge Ginsburg advanced an approach to assessing reasonable expectations of privacy under the Fourth Amendment that has come to be called the mosaic theory.

The insight underlying the mosaic theory is straightforward. Although we might understand in the abstract that a member of the public, and therefore law enforcement, could observe our public movements at any point in time, "A reasonable person does not expect anyone to monitor and retain a record of every time he drives his car, including his origin, route, destination, and each place he stops and how long he stays there; rather, he expects each of those movements to remain 'disconnected and anonymous.'"[27] The kind of long-term, constant tracking conducted by the officers in *Jones* violated this reasonable expectation. On that basis, Judge Ginsburg and his panel concluded that the use of a GPS device to track Jones for four weeks constituted a search under the Fourth Amendment because it went well past the kinds of relatively short-term and largely incidental monitoring we might expect of law enforcement or any member of the public.

The phrase "mosaic theory" comes from national security debates. In defending the need to maintain secrecy with respect to means, methods, and sources of intelligence gathering, the government has argued that revealing even seemingly small or trivial pieces of information relating to intelligence practices presents real dangers to national security because those pieces can be aggregated by foreign governments and enemies into a more revealing whole.[28] So too, Judge Ginsburg argued, the bits and pieces of information gathered by contemporary surveillance technologies like GPS-enabled tracking devices allow the government to assemble revealing images of us and our lives. As he points out:

> Prolonged surveillance reveals types of information not revealed by short-term surveillance, such as what a person does repeatedly, what he does not do, and what he does ensemble. These types of information can each reveal more about a person than does any individual trip viewed in isolation. Repeated visits to a church, a gym, a bar, or a bookie tell a story not told by any single visit, as does one's not visiting any of these places over the course of a month. The sequence of a person's movements can reveal still more; a single trip to a gynecologist's office tells little about a woman, but that trip followed a few weeks later by a visit to a baby supply store tells a different story. A person who knows all of another's travels can deduce whether he is a weekly church goer, a heavy drinker, a regular at the gym, an unfaithful husband, an outpatient receiving medical treatment, an associate of particular individuals or political groups – and not just one such fact about a person, but all such facts.[29]

Although the Supreme Court declined to endorse the mosaic theory in *Jones*, five justices indicated strong sympathies for Judge Ginsburg's views. For example, Justice Sotomayor wondered "whether people reasonably expect that their movements will be recorded and aggregated in a manner that enables the Government to ascertain, more or less at will, their political and religious beliefs, sexual habits, and so on."[30] She also expressed concerns about "entrusting to the Executive, in the absence of any oversight from a coordinate branch, a tool so amenable to misuse, especially in light of the Fourth Amendment's goal to curb arbitrary exercises of police power to and prevent a too permeating police surveillance."[31] In a similar vein, Justice Alito, writing for himself and

Justices Ginsburg, Breyer, and Kagan, pointed out that citizens do not now expect "constant monitoring of the location of a vehicle for four weeks."

The mosaic theory has been the target of trenchant criticism on conceptual, doctrinal, and practical grounds. One of the most forceful of these objections came from Judge Sentelle, who is Judge Ginsburg's colleague on the District of Columbia Circuit Court of Appeals. In the normal course of events, circuit courts of appeals judges hear cases in panels of three. When particularly controversial or difficult cases come before these courts, they may also elect to sit *en banc*, which means that the case will be heard, or reheard, by all the active judges of the court. After Judge Ginsburg's panel ruled against the government, prosecutors filed a motion requesting that the District of Columbia Circuit Court of Appeals hear the Jones case *en banc*. That motion ultimately was denied, but Judge Sentelle wrote an opinion dissenting from that decision of the court.[32] In his opinion, Judge Sentelle took aim at the mosaic theory on conceptual grounds, arguing that it was incoherent.

The mosaic theory claims that, in some cases, certain aggregations of information may implicate reasonable expectations of privacy even though the constituent parts do not.[33] In Judge Sentelle's view, that basic premise is nonsense. After all, "The sum of an infinite number of zero-value parts is also zero."[34] Defenders of the mosaic theory might argue that this criticism misses the point. After all, the image of the mosaic does not advocate simple addition. Rather, it suggests that certain aggregations of data are more revealing than the sum of their parts just as a mosaic is more than just an aggregation of broken bits of ceramic and glass. It is therefore not, strictly speaking, the quantity of data that is important under the mosaic theory but the potential revelations that might result as a consequence of aggregating data. To revisit one of Judge Ginsburg's examples, "a single trip to a gynecologist's office tells little about a woman, but that trip followed a few weeks later by a visit to a baby supply store tells a different story."[35]

Even if the mosaic theory can avoid this basic conceptual problem, it still faces serious doctrinal challenges under current Fourth Amendment law. To start, the Supreme Court has never suggested that we might have reasonable expectations of privacy in aggregations of information despite not having reasonable expectations of privacy in the constituent parts. That does not doom the project, of course. Prior to *Katz v. United States*, there was very little suggestion in the Court's precedents that it might treat as searches or seizures conduct that did not entail any kind of physical intrusion into a constitutionally protected area, but that did not stop the *Katz* Court from initiating a revolution in Fourth Amendment law. There is no immediate reason to take the mosaic theory off the table just because it would entail another revolution in Fourth Amendment law – particularly if that revolution is due.

Even assuming that the moment is ripe for a revolution in Fourth Amendment law, it is not immediately clear that the mosaic theory is the best way forward. That is evident when we consider some of the potential doctrinal and practical consequences of the mosaic theory. For example, adopting a mosaic theory would require modifying or discarding both the third-party doctrine and the public observation doctrine. That might not be such a bad thing in light of the roles played by these doctrines in ushering in our present age of surveillance, but it is important to think through the potential consequences this might have for traditional law enforcement techniques such as human surveillance, witness interviews, and the analysis of physical evidence.

The Supreme Court has never held that officers are engaging in searches or seizures for Fourth Amendment purposes when they conduct stakeouts, tail suspects, interview witnesses, or analyze lawfully seized physical evidence. That is because these activities entail neither physical intrusions nor encroachments upon reasonable expectations of privacy. All that might change under the mosaic theory, however. Under a mosaic regime, officers who use traditional investigative means and methods would need to be just as worried about stumbling onto the wrong side of a Fourth Amendment line as would officers using more contemporary means. The mosaic theory therefore appears to risk being overprotective in that it might encroach too much on perfectly legitimate – or, at least, long-standing – law enforcement activities, including not only human surveillance, witness interviews, and the analysis of physical evidence but also public records searches, the use of confidential informants, and undercover operations. After all, just about any investigative means has the potential to gather "too much" information, by itself or in combination with other means, which might implicate mosaic concerns.[36]

The mosaic theory also threatens to punish law enforcement officers and agencies for being good at their jobs. In many ways, good police work is about gathering as much reliable information as is possible. That is how threats are identified and harm is prevented. That is how guilty people are arrested, prosecuted, and punished. Just as importantly, good information helps make sure that innocent people are not wrongly arrested, prosecuted, or punished. In light of this, the mosaic theory creates perverse incentives for law enforcement officers not to investigate too much or to gather too many facts lest they find themselves on the wrong side of a Fourth Amendment line. Advocates can surely respond that the mosaic theory does not set limits on investigations but only defines how far they can go before officers have to get a warrant, but the tension and backward incentives remain. Just as importantly, it highlights just how dramatic is the shift in Fourth Amendment law proposed by the mosaic theory and how momentous the effects would be on established, long-standing, law enforcement practice.

Another problem with the mosaic theory is that, ironically, it may not be sufficiently protective. That is evident in Justice Alito's proposed holding in *Jones*. According to Justice Alito, the problem in *Jones* was not with the methods used by law enforcement officers to track Jones and his coconspirators. The problem was, instead, with how long they used the GPS device and how much information they gathered in the process. Justice Alito would have been perfectly comfortable with "relatively short-term monitoring." What troubled him was "longer term GPS monitoring."[37] The problem with this approach is that it would effectively grant law enforcement officers unfettered license to track anyone they pleased using a GPS device or any other means so long as they did not do so for too long and did not gather too much information. That would leave each of us and all of us to wonder whether we are being monitored or tracked by government agents at any given moment. This hardly seems consistent with the Fourth Amendment's guarantee of security for the people against unreasonable searches and seizures.

On this point, at least, Chief Justice John Roberts seems to agree. During oral argument in *United States v. Jones*, the Solicitor General relied on the public observation doctrine to defend the officers' use of GPS tracking devices. In response, Chief Justice Roberts asked whether:

> You think there would also not be a search if you put a GPS device on all of our cars, monitored our movements for a month? You think you're entitled to do that under your theory? ... you could tomorrow decide [to] put a GPS device on every one of our cars, follow us for a month; no problem under the Constitution?[38]

His point, of course, was that granting law enforcement officers and agencies unfettered access to these kinds of surveillance technologies would effectively license broad and indiscriminate surveillance, allowing the government to monitor anyone, anywhere, at any time, for good reasons, for bad reasons, or for no reasons at all. It is hard to imagine a more direct threat to the Fourth Amendment right of the people to be secure against unreasonable searches. In the face of these threats, the mosaic theory can guarantee only that government agents are not gathering too much information about us. That is cold comfort indeed if it remains the case that the government may well be watching, tracking, and surveilling any of us or all of us at any particular moment.

Another critique of the mosaic theory focuses on its lack of guidance for law enforcement. Professor Orin Kerr has pressed this point quite persuasively.[39] Under current doctrine, police officers know that entering a home constitutes a search, but that looking through an open window from a lawful vantage point does not. They know that tapping a phone is a search, but that asking a telephone company for the metadata associated with a suspect's telephone calls is not. Furthermore, they know what they must do to render a search legal, whether that is getting a warrant, a judicial order, or preparing themselves to justify their conduct in a later court proceeding. The mosaic theory muddies the water considerably by putting officers at constant risk of stumbling across a Fourth Amendment line simply because they are too successful in using a means that is not otherwise subject to Fourth Amendment regulation. As Professor Kerr has pointed out, that danger is amplified if an officer utilizes multiple investigative means such as human surveillance, public records searches, and witness interviews because it would be hard in the midst of an active investigation for officers to assess whether they have discovered too much information.[40] By contrast, officers can easily keep track of what to do before deploying particular means of information gathering. For example, they know that they generally need to get a warrant before conducting a physical search of a home.

Most of the practical and doctrinal challenges to the mosaic theory trace back in one way or another to a basic line-drawing problem. If mosaic theorists want to stake a claim that gathering too much information triggers Fourth Amendment protections, then they must come forward with a clear, coherent, workable, and doctrinally responsible test for determining how much is too much.[41] Assuming that mosaic advocates can meet this demand, questions would still remain regarding how we might act to vindicate mosaic interests. For example, would officers need a warrant before conducting a search that crosses the mosaic boundary, or would it be sufficient to justify their conduct after the fact? If officers violated a mosaic right, then would the fruits of their investigation be subject to exclusion at trial? If so, then how much information would be excluded? Would we need to exclude all evidence produced by an investigation that violated mosaic rights, or would it be sufficient to exclude just enough evidence to get the overall investigation back below the mosaic threshold? If this sort of a limited exclusionary rule would suffice, then how would we decide what to trim? The difficulty of these questions should give us pause before adopting the mosaic theory as our new Fourth Amendment standard.[42]

How Long Is Too Long? The Durational Approach

In *Jones*, Justice Alito advocates for a durational approach to determining whether the deployment and use of surveillance technologies are subject to Fourth Amendment review. "Under this approach," he writes, "relatively short-term monitoring of a person's movements on public streets accords with expectations of privacy that our society has recognized as reasonable. But the use of longer term GPS monitoring in investigations of most offenses impinges on expectations of privacy."[43]

Justice Alito's durational approach is particularly important to consider because it appears to have garnered the support of a majority of sitting justices on the Supreme Court. Justices Ginsburg, Breyer, and Kagan, all signed Justice Alito's concurring opinion. Although Justice Sotomayor did not join Justice Alito's concurring opinion, she endorsed his durational test in her concurring opinion, writing that "I agree with Justice Alito that, at the very least, 'longer term GPS monitoring in investigations of most offenses impinges on expectations of privacy.'"[44] Thus, there appear to be at least five justices ready to endorse duration of surveillance as a means for vindicating their shared concerns about the impact of contemporary surveillance technologies on Fourth Amendment interests.

Although Justice Alito's durational approach appears to have majority support in the Supreme Court, it does not have the force of law because it was not the majority opinion of the Court. That may be for good reason. Justice Alito's durational test faces many of the same conceptual, doctrinal, and practical challenges faced by the mosaic approach.[45]

For example, as Justice Scalia pointed out in his majority opinion for the Court in *Jones*, the Supreme Court has long held that "mere visual observation [from a lawful vantage point] does not constitute a search."[46] When officers on the beat conduct stakeouts or tail suspects, they are doing no more than any member of the public can do. Would conducting lawful human surveillance of this sort become unlawful merely because it went on for an extended period of time? Strangely, Justice Alito does not seem to think it would. He notes that extended human surveillance is expensive in terms of resources, and therefore quite rare, but does not appear to suggest that long-term human surveillance violates reasonable expectations of privacy.[47] He nevertheless maintains that conducting that same surveillance using advanced tracking technologies such as GPS does violate reasonable expectations of privacy. If, however, it is the duration of surveillance that is concerning, then it is hard to see how the means would matter.

The durational approach also seems to suffer from some version of the mathematical impossibility highlighted by Judge Sentelle in his critique of the mosaic approach. That is particularly evident in Justice Alito's conclusion that "relatively short-term monitoring of a person's movements on public streets accords with expectations of privacy that our society has recognized as reasonable."[48] If the value in terms of privacy expectations assigned to short-term tracking is zero, and the value associated with long-term tracking is something greater than zero, then the durational approach appears to be adding zeros to get something greater than zero. Thus, Judge Sentelle's point – that the "sum of an infinite number of zero-value parts is also zero"[49] – goes just as much against the durational approach as it does the mosaic theory.

Justice Alito and other advocates of the durational approach might respond to these conceptual objections by relying on the same insights that underlie the mosaic theory. In fact, the best way to think of the durational approach may be as a means to operationalize the mosaic theory rather than as a distinct proposal unto itself. Even if this is right, however, the durational approach must still face serious doctrinal concerns. Foremost among these is the potential violence that a durational constraint on investigations might do to a whole range of investigative practices that are well established under Supreme Court law. Human surveillance is certainly one of these, but we can also add witness interviews, gathering physical evidence, analyzing physical evidence, and records searches – in fact, just about any investigative practice or combination of practices might well trigger Fourth Amendment consequences under a durational approach if they go on for "too long."

Proponents might respond by arguing that this dramatic reconfiguration of Fourth Amendment doctrine and law enforcement practice is necessary and appropriate given the rise of technologically enhanced surveillance means and methods. If the concern is with modern surveillance technologies, however, then the durational approach is far too blunt an instrument. The better course would seem to be to focus on these new threats rather than upending more than a century of established law and police practice. Put differently, it may well be true that you need to break a few eggs to make an omelet, but the durational approach seems to call for throwing the whole carton against the wall.

Beyond these conceptual and doctrinal concerns, the durational approach also faces serious practical challenges. As Justice Scalia argued in *Jones*, line-drawing problems are foremost among them. For example, Justice Alito does not explain "why a 4-week investigation is 'surely' too long."[50] We are therefore left to wonder whether monitoring for two hours, two days, or two weeks might be acceptable. To his credit, Justice Alito recognizes that these line-drawing problems exist, and therefore advises officers to get a warrant if ever they are uncertain.[51] But that just begs the question as to where the point of uncertainty lies. It therefore forces officers to operate in a constant zone of uncertainty, which risks mistakes. For some officers in some cases these mistakes will come at the cost of Fourth Amendment interests because they will wait too long to get a warrant. In other cases the mistakes will come at the cost of legitimate law enforcement goals as officers refrain from pursuing their investigations for fear of accidentally tripping over a Fourth Amendment line. Whichever way you look at it, greater clarity is the answer to practical line-drawing problems, but clarity is what is missing from the durational approach.

Professor Christopher Slobogin has come forward with a proposal that would resolve many of these practical difficulties.[52] He presents his proposal in the form of a model statute governing surveillance. In keeping with the natural consequences of mosaic theory, his proposed statute does not distinguish between methods of surveillance. Thus, human surveillance, whether as a stakeout or a traditional tailing operation, has just as much potential to be a Fourth Amendment "search" as GPS tracking.[53] What matters instead is how long officers conduct their surveillance. In embracing this agnosticism as to means and methods, Professor Slobogin accepts the fact that the durational approach would have broad doctrinal and practical consequences for traditional law enforcement practices. In his view, however, this is a good thing. By Professor Slobogin's lights, it just does not make sense to draw distinctions between human surveillance and electronic surveillance. Both constitute "searches" by any reasonable definition, and both have the potential to threaten reasonable expectations of privacy. He would therefore put them on equal footing from a Fourth Amendment point of view.[54]

To solve practical problems posed by the durational approach, Professor Slobogin recommends that we draw clear, bright lines. His proposal preserves the warrant requirement for all searches already subject to Fourth Amendment regulation, such as home searches and wiretaps. He goes further, however, subjecting surveillance that is not traditionally covered by the Fourth Amendment, such as tailing suspects or tracking public movements, to constitutional review based on the duration of the search. Under his proposal, all targeted surveillance that lasts longer than forty-eight hours in the aggregate would require a warrant issued by a detached and neutral magistrate and backed by probable cause.[55] Surveillance that lasts between twenty minutes and forty-eight hours in the aggregate would require a court order based on a standard of reasonable suspicion.[56] Surveillance that lasts less than twenty minutes in the aggregate would only require some good faith basis.[57] Targeted data surveillance, whether conducted directly or through third parties, would be subject to similar time constraints, with forty-eight hours again marking the trigger point for the warrant requirement.[58]

The great virtue of Professor Slobogin's proposal is its clarity and ease of application. That clarity comes with costs, of course, along some of the conceptual and doctrinal dimensions discussed above. For example, Professor Slobogin's proposal would require dramatic modifications to the third-party doctrine and the public observation doctrine. In Professor Slobogin's view, this is all to the good, but, when weighing the options, these are certainly costs to consider. Another potential difficulty with Professor Slobogin's proposal, as with any bright line approach to implementing the mosaic theory, is that it ignores the actual mosaics of information aggregated during any particular investigation. Thus, it may well turn out in practice that surveillance for a few minutes in one case produces a very revealing mosaic while surveillance for a week in another turns up next to nothing. The durational approach therefore runs the risk of imposing undue limits on law enforcement while failing to provide any real protections for the fundamental citizen interests at stake.

None of this is meant to condemn Professor Slobogin's proposal or any other attempt to implement the durational approach. The point, instead, is that any such effort will entail compromises and that these compromises inevitably will have consequences for Fourth Amendment doctrine, law enforcement practice and, ultimately, the security of the people against unreasonable searches and seizures. Given the nature and scope of the conceptual, doctrinal, and practical challenges raised by the durational approach, there is good reason to at least exercise caution, and perhaps to look for alternatives.

Protecting the Right Information: The Content-Based Approach

Another group of proposals offered in the wake of the Supreme Court's invitation in *United States v. Jones* focus not on the quantities of information gathered by government surveillance or the duration of government surveillance but on the nature of the information that is gathered. Three such proposals deserve special attention. The first has been advanced by prominent First Amendment scholar Neil Richards.[59] In Richards's view, the real interests at stake in law enforcement's use of contemporary surveillance technologies are not Fourth Amendment reasonable expectations of privacy but First Amendment interests in freedom of thought and expression. He has therefore argued that we should regulate government surveillance activities according to the nature of information that will be gathered and the degree to which government access to that information will compromise intellectual freedom. Under this approach, surveillance that seeks or would reveal information directly related to intellectual or expressive pursuits would be tightly constrained, perhaps by requiring a warrant issued by a detached and neutral magistrate based on probable cause. By contrast, this approach would allow for looser controls if surveillance seeks or would reveal information that is less closely related to, or even completely detached from, the intellectual and expressive pursuits protected most fiercely by the First Amendment.

The second content-based approach to regulating government surveillance that warrants close attention is the product of a special task force of the American Bar Association (ABA).[60] The ABA has a long history of convening committees and task forces to examine existing and emerging legal challenges with the goal of proposing rules and standards designed to meet those challenges. One of these ABA task forces convened in 2006 to tackle the problem of law enforcement access to third-party records. The effort could not have been more prescient. Over the course of seven years, the task force, composed of judges, prosecutors, defense attorneys, and academics, gathered input from a wide range of interested parties. Their efforts culminated in a set of model standards published in 2013. Those standards propose a graduated scheme of judicial and administrative controls on law enforcement access to records held by third parties based on how "private" is the information in those records. Thus, access to records deemed to contain "highly" private information would require a warrant backed by probable cause; access to records that contain "moderately" private information would require a court order based on reasonable suspicion; records that contain "minimally" private information could only be accessed using a subpoena issued by a prosecutorial agency after it determines that the records are relevant to ongoing investigation; and, finally, records that contain information not deemed private would be freely accessible to law enforcement so long as investigators could justify the need to view those records for some legitimate purpose.

A third content-based approach that warrants some attention has been advanced by Professor Jack Balkin and several of his colleagues at Yale's Information Society Project, including Kiel Brennan-Marquez.[61] Rather than focus directly on the content of information at risk, these scholars take a collateral course targeting the sources of that information. More specifically, they identify a class of parties and entities they describe as "information fiduciaries." Information fiduciaries are those entrusted with personal, intimate, or private information on the understanding that they will keep that information private. Depending upon the nature of the relationship implicated, the level of trust involved, and the degree of privacy at stake, this approach would limit the ability of law enforcement agents to gather material through information fiduciaries, whether a bank, a social media service, or an e-commerce company like Amazon.

Content-based approaches to identifying and vindicating concerns raised by contemporary surveillance technologies boast an intuitive appeal. For starters, they do not indulge in strained analogies or obscure imagery. They instead focus directly on the interests at stake. Moreover, these interests are easy to understand. Few would dispute that we have weighty interests in lists of books we read, details about the political group meetings we attend, the contents of our diaries, and secrets we share with trusted parties because this is all information closely linked to our personal projects of ethical self-development and our political projects as citizens. Finally, the basic regulatory frameworks suggested by content-based approaches feature an appealing symmetry. It makes sense to provide the most stringent protections when our intellectual, expressive, and most significant privacy interests are most at stake while allowing for looser controls when those interests are less threatened. Despite these advantages, however, there are very good reasons to worry that these content-based approaches will create more problems than they solve.

Taking a content-based approach to regulating contemporary surveillance technologies would cut against a very important thread of Fourth Amendment doctrine. For the most part, the Fourth Amendment has always been concerned with *how* law enforcement officers gather information. By contrast, it has been largely unconcerned with *what kinds* of information are gathered.[62] For example, in *Kyllo v. United States*,[63] the Supreme Court was asked whether using a heat detection device to monitor hot spots in a home – which might be indicative of a marijuana growing operation – constituted a "search" for purposes of the Fourth Amendment. The government argued that it was not a search because the device itself was not sophisticated enough to show any "private activities" or "intimate details" of the home.[64] Writing for the majority, Justice Scalia roundly rejected the invitation to parse Fourth Amendment interests based on what might be revealed by a particular investigative means or method. In the Court's view, the home enjoys the highest levels of constitutional protections regardless of what we may be doing at any particular moment, be it washing the dishes or having sex.[65] Whether utterly banal or intensely personal, the Court maintained that we have a reasonable expectation of privacy in everything we do outside of public view in our homes. The Court reaffirmed that content neutrality in a 2014 case called *Riley v. California*.[66] There, the Court held that police officers must secure a warrant before accessing the contents of cellular phones. In so holding, the Court declined to distinguish between smartphones and "flip" phones despite the fact that smartphones contain more, and more intimate, information than flip phones.[67] Were it to adopt a content-based approach to assessing and protecting Fourth Amendment interests at stake in our age of surveillance, the Court would have to abandon this established history of remaining neutral with respect to degrees of privacy involved in our various legal activities. That would mean not only overturning a long line of doctrine; it would also be unwise.

There are good reasons the Court has declined to engage in assessing or weighing degrees of privacy interests in its Fourth Amendment jurisprudence. We live in a diverse society where people are free to define for themselves what constitutes value and to pursue their own conceptions of the good life. As a consequence of this diversity, different people have different views on what sorts of information must be protected as private and what constitutes valuable expression. This diversity is not happenstance. It is a consequence of constitutional design.

One of the principal concerns of Anti-Federalists during the ratification debates in 1787 was that handing governing authority over to a democratic process would allow a majority to exercise tyrannical control over minorities.[68] The Constitution and the Bill of Rights, including the First and Fourth Amendments, guard against this possibility by enforcing government neutrality with respect to differences among citizens' various conceptions of value and the good life, thereby securing space for minorities to survive and flourish.[69] The Court's commitment to value neutrality in its Fourth Amendment jurisprudence is an extension of this basic constitutional commitment. If the Court were to abandon that neutrality and start assessing, weighing, and valuing the privacy interests at stake in information and activities, then it would inevitably have to pick winners and losers by privileging some views on privacy and expressive value over others. That is not only anti-constitutional, but it is also antidemocratic.

That the content-based approach would license courts to challenge basic constitutional commitments to value neutrality should give us pause. First, it raises serious practical concerns.[70] Do contributions to a private chat room dedicated to feline fur styling implicate intellectual freedom? Are these postings highly private, moderately private, or not private at all? If participants in the chat room agree to maintain the privacy and confidentiality of the chat room, does that make them information fiduciaries? The example might seem silly, but it is hard to see, from a practical point of view, how we would answer these questions. More concerning, however, is the fact that the project entailed in answering these questions is inherently oppressive in that it would require choosing among competing conceptions of the good life.[71] It would therefore require the Court to value some groups over others.

Particularly in the current environment, where the Court is deeply politicized, there is no way to insulate this process of picking winners and losers from politics. Those dangers are amplified by the fact that much of our contemporary political discussion is dictated by the demands of a perpetual War on Terror, which seems to require greater and greater sacrifices of liberty, purportedly in the name of security.[72] The very real risk entailed in the content-based approach is therefore that the Fourth Amendment will become a tool of oppression rather than a steadfast defender of freedom. Surely, that is not the role we want the Fourth Amendment to play in our age of surveillance.

How is the Information Gathered? A Technology-Centered Approach

The mosaic theory, the durational approach, and the content-based approach all share a common feature: their focus on what information is gathered. In one way or another, all of these approaches seek to assign some value to this information, even if tangentially in the case of the durational approach, which really just seeks to operationalize the mosaic approach. That shared focus is a source of shared dangers. It creates conceptual problems for all three approaches. It puts all three approaches on the wrong side of long-standing Fourth Amendment doctrine. It raises serious practical concerns relating to line drawing or assigning value. It also exposes the potential that each of these approaches might end up harming the very rights and interests that seem to be most threatened in our age of surveillance.

In light of these difficulties and dangers, Professor Danielle Citron and I have argued that, rather than focusing on *what* information is gathered, we should focus instead on *how* information is gathered.[73] In our view, what is troubling about life in our age of surveillance is the prospect of living in a world where each of us and all of us are subject to the constant and real threat of broad and indiscriminate surveillance.[74] After all, it is hard to imagine a situation more contrary to the Fourth Amendment right of the people to be secure against unreasonable searches and seizures than life in a surveillance state. The principal sources of these threats lie in the prospect of granting law enforcement and other government agents an unlimited license to deploy and use modern surveillance technologies. If this is the source of the threat, then it makes good sense to address the threat directly by limiting law enforcement's access to these technologies.

A technology-centered approach has many advantages. As compared to proposals that focus on what information is gathered, a technology-centered approach does not pose any particular conceptual challenges. It does not require adding "zero-value parts" to achieve a value greater than zero. Neither does it rely on strained metaphors to explain the dangers or threats to privacy and Fourth Amendment interests. A technology-centered approach also does not face the same sorts of doctrinal objections that plague the other proposals discussed in this chapter. Quite to the contrary, it is completely consistent with the long line of Supreme Court cases, including *Kyllo v. United States*, in which the Court has focused on means and methods when applying the Fourth Amendment.

Recall that, in *Kyllo*, the government argued that its heat detection device could not reveal any "intimate" activities, and that using it therefore did not constitute a "search" for purposes of the Fourth Amendment. Writing for the Court in *Kyllo*, Justice Scalia declined the invitation to adopt this content-based approach to assessing Fourth Amendment interests and rights. He chose instead to focus on the technology itself. "The question," according to the Court, was "what limits there are upon this power of technology to shrink the realm of guaranteed privacy."[75] The answer, according to the Court, is that "obtaining by sense-enhancing technology any information regarding the interior of the home that could not otherwise have been obtained without a physical intrusion into a constitutionally protected area constitutes a search."[76] In order to secure the right of the people to be secure against the threat of unreasonable searches posed by these technologies, the *Kyllo* Court limited law enforcement's ability to deploy and use heat detection devices by requiring officers to secure a warrant.

A technology-centered approach would follow the tack taken by the Court in *Kyllo*. In doing so, it would remain consistent with the general approach taken by the Court when applying the Fourth Amendment more or less since its adoption. As we saw in Chapter 2, the primary targets for the Fourth Amendment in 1791 were physical searches of "persons, homes, papers, and effects." Although primitive in technological terms, experiences with general warrants and writs of assistance taught our founders that granting to government agents unfettered discretion to conduct physical searches and seizures threatened the security and liberty of everyone. In response, the Fourth Amendment bars general warrants, sets limits on specific warrants, and guarantees a more general right of the people to be secure against unreasonable searches and seizures.

The Supreme Court maintained this founding-era focus on means and methods of government intrusion through the nineteenth century and into the early part of the twentieth century. This was the era when the Court defined "search" and "seizure" in terms of physical intrusion. Throughout this era, the Court continued to focus on how information was gathered rather than what information was gathered.

As we saw in Chapter 2, *Katz v. United States* initiated a revolution in Fourth Amendment law. Despite that revolution, the Court maintained its focus on the means and methods of government surveillance. Recall that in *Katz* officers used an electronic ear to eavesdrop on conversations in a public telephone booth.[77] Despite the fact that the conversations involved dealt with illegal activities rather than intimate or intellectual pursuits, the Court maintained its focus on the means and method of government intrusion, holding that *use of the device* violated Katz's reasonable expectations of privacy. The Court's post-*Katz* cases have stayed the course. As examples, in *United States v. Knotts*[78] and *United States v. Karo*[79] the focus was on radio beepers used as tracking devices. In *Smith v. Maryland* the question was whether using a pen register to gather telephone metadata constituted a search.[80] The list goes on.

Despite the many shifts and changes in the Court's Fourth Amendment jurisprudence over the last 225 years, it has always asked whether using a means or method of government surveillance in particular circumstances constitutes a search or seizure. By contrast, it has never focused on the content of what was discovered to determine whether a search occurred.[81] Although novel, a technology-centered approach fits within this basic framework. As a consequence, it faces many fewer potential doctrinal and practical problems as compared to the mosaic theory, the durational approach, or content-based approaches.

Because it conforms in a general way to the Supreme Court's established focus on means and methods, the technology-centered approach is much less likely to require dramatic alterations to existing law enforcement practices like human surveillance. Under current doctrine, tailing a suspect and staking out his home and place of business do not constitute searches so long as officers conduct their surveillance from lawful vantage points. If the Court adopts some version of the mosaic theory, the durational approach, or the content-based approach, then human surveillance would come under Fourth Amendment scrutiny in ways that run contrary to existing doctrine and practice. By contrast, a technology-centered approach would not require expanding the scope of the Fourth Amendment to encompass human surveillance. That is because, as Justice Alito pointed out in *United States v. Jones*, human surveillance is "costly" and "rarely undertaken" because it "require[s] a large team of agents, multiple vehicles, and perhaps aerial assistance."[82] Precisely because human surveillance as a means and method is so limited in terms of its scalability, it cannot facilitate broad and indiscriminate surveillance as a practical matter. Preserving law enforcement's unfettered access to human surveillance would therefore not run afoul of the Fourth Amendment under a technology-centered approach. By contrast, GPS tracking and similar means and methods would trigger Fourth Amendment concerns precisely because they are highly scalable, removing practical constraints on the ability to conduct broad and indiscriminate surveillance.

Perhaps in recognition of its conceptual, doctrinal, and practical advantages, the Supreme Court appeared to endorse a technology-centered approach in *Riley v. California*, decided in 2014.[83] Recall that the question in *Riley* was not whether law enforcement should be able to deploy and use contemporary surveillance technologies but, rather, whether law enforcement should be able to search the contents of cellular phones without a warrant. In order to search a person, his personal effects, or his home for evidence, police officers usually must obtain a warrant from a detached and neutral magistrate based on probable cause. In *Riley*, the government argued that it should be able to search cellular phones seized from arrestees without a warrant pursuant to the search incident to arrest rule. The search incident to arrest rule provides that officers may, secondary to a lawful arrest, search an arrestee and any items or areas within his immediate reach and control at the time of the arrest without first securing a warrant. The question for the Court in *Riley* was whether that exception, which has been applied to things like wallets, bags, and desk draws, extends to cellular phones. Applying a technology-centered approach, the Court held that it does not.

The focus of the Court's analysis in *Riley* was on the features of cellular phones that distinguish them as a technology from items and areas usually covered by the search incident to arrest rule. Although wallets, bags, and desks are all "effects" or part of "houses," subject to

Fourth Amendment protections, they are limited in terms of the kinds and amounts of information they can and do contain. Writing for the Court in *Riley*, Chief Justice John Roberts pointed out that cellular phones are very different. Unlike low-tech vessels like wallets, cellular phones can hold a vast amount of information in many different forms. This is particularly true of "smartphones," which contain not only detailed records of calls made and received but the contents of text and e-mail communications, histories of internet activity, historical location information, photographs, videos, books, and documents. These phones also serve as portals to additional troves of information kept in third-party servers, which are sometimes referred to as the "cloud." Based on these distinguishing features of cellular phones as a technology, the Court held that they deserve a higher degree of Fourth Amendment protection than wallets, bags, and desk drawers. As a result, the Court held that cellular phones cannot be searched incident to a lawful arrest. As is noted above, however, the Court refused to assign different values to the kinds or amount of information different phones or kinds of phones might hold. It therefore recognized an important distinction between taking a technology-centered approach and a content-based approach, favoring a focus on technologies.

Conclusion

None of this is meant to suggest that a technology-centered approach does not face problems of its own. It surely does. There are real questions about its constitutional pedigree. Whether applying a traditional physical intrusion test or the reasonable expectations of privacy standard, most Fourth Amendment cases focus on the facts of a particular case and whether the citizen at bar can claim a violation of her rights. There are as of yet no "different constitutional principles" that would allow threats of broad and indiscriminate surveillance posed by "dragnet type law enforcement practices"[84] to trigger Fourth Amendment concerns much less underwrite rules that would limit access to these kinds of means and methods. Chapters 4 and 5 will address these challenges by advancing a theory of the Fourth Amendment that focuses on the fundamentally collective nature of Fourth Amendment rights and the imperative command that the "right of the people to be secure ... against unreasonable searches and seizures *shall not* be violated."

In addition to fundamental theoretical difficulties, a technology-centered approach also faces its own practical challenges. Among these are (1) identifying the technologies that threaten the collective right of the people to be secure against unreasonable searches, and (2) finding effective means for preserving that right of the people while also accommodating legitimate law enforcement needs. Chapters 4 and 5 will address these problems by proposing a clear test that can be applied to determine whether a particular search technology triggers Fourth Amendment regulation. Chapter 6 will apply this test to the means, methods, and technologies discussed in Chapter 1.

Notes

1. 132. S. Ct. 945 (2012).
2. As is evidenced by Justice Alito's concurrence in *Jones*, many judges and scholars assumed that *Katz* displaced the physical interpretation of the Fourth Amendment that prevailed into the middle part of the twentieth century. See *Jones*, 132 S. Ct. at 959 (Alito, J., concurring) ("*Katz v. United States* ... finally did away with the old approach, holding that a trespass was not required for a Fourth Amendment violation."). The majority opinion in *Jones* made clear that, rather than replacing it, *Katz* erected an edifice on top of the traditional physical approach providing additional protections for citizens. 132 S. Ct. at 950–51.
3. 132 S. Ct. at 956–57 (Sotomayor, J., concurring).
4. *Id.* at 957.
5. 132 S. Ct. at 957 (Alito, J., concurring).
6. *Id.* at 965.
7. *Id.* at 963–64 (expressing a preference for legislative action to regulate law enforcement's use of contemporary surveillance technologies in the mode of the Wiretap Act, which passed in 1968, the year after *Katz*).
8. *Id.* at 962–63.
9. *See, e.g.*, Orin S. Kerr, *The Mosaic Theory of the Fourth Amendment*, 111 MICH. L. REV. 311 (2012).
10. 132 S. Ct. at 957 (Alito, J., concurring).
11. Michael V. Hayden, *American Intelligence in the Age of Terror: A Conversation with Retired General Michael V. Hayden*, Mar. 25, 2016, www.aei.org/wp-content/uploads/2016/03/160325-AEI-Gen-Hayden-on-American-Intelligence.pdf.
12. *Secret Documents Reveal N.S.A. Campaign Against Encryption*, N.Y. Times, Sept. 5, 2013, www.nytimes.com/interactive/2013/09/05/us/documents-reveal-nsa-campaign-against-encryption.html?_r=1&; Nicole Perlroth, Jeff Larson, & Scott Shane, *N.S. A. Able to Foil Basic Safeguards of Privacy on Web*, Sept. 5, 2013, www.nytimes.com/2013/09/06/us/nsa-foils-much-internet-encryption.html.
13. Documents released as part of the Snowden disclosures report programs like Turbulence, Turmoil, Tumult, and TorStinks, all of which target technologies

designed to preserve the anonymity of internet users. *See* www.theguardian.com/world/2013/oct/04/tor-attacks-nsa-users-online-anonymity; https://edwardsnowden.com/wp-content/uploads/2013/10/tor-stinks-presentation.pdf – actual document

14. Somini Sengupta, *2 E-Mail Services Shut Down to Protect Customer Data*, N.Y. TIMES BITS BLOG, Aug. 8, 2013, 11:15 PM, http://bits.blogs.nytimes.com/2013/08/08/two-providers-of-encrypted-e-mail-shut-down/?_r=0.
15. Reply Brief of Appellant at *3, State v. Andrews, 227 Md. App. 350, 2016 WL 1254567 (Md. Ct. Spec. App. 2016), *brief available at* 2016 WL 910249.
16. *See* JULIA ANGWIN, DRAGNET NATION: A QUEST FOR PRIVACY, SECURITY, AND FREEDOM IN A WORLD OF RELENTLESS SURVEILLANCE (2014).
17. DANIELLE KEATS CITRON, HATE CRIMES IN CYBERSPACE 224 (2014); Danielle Keats Citron, *Cyber Civil Rights*, 89 B.U. L. REV. 61, 105 (2009); *cf.* Palmieri v. Lynch, 392 F.3d 73, 96–97 (2d Cir. 2005) (Straub, J., dissenting) ("[F]orcing homeowners to shutter windows and completely enclose yards or else diminish the privacy they enjoy in their homes and curtilage. I simply cannot imagine that the drafters of the Fourth Amendment dictated such dark and cloistered lives for citizens.").
18. 533 U.S. 27, 34 (2001); *see also* Anthony G. Amsterdam, *Perspectives on the Fourth Amendment*, 58 MINN. L. REV. 349, 384 (1974) ("Fortunately, neither *Katz* nor the fourth amendment asks what we expect of government. They tell us what we should demand of government.").
19. Amsterdam, *supra* note 18, at 402.
20. Renée McDonald Hutchins, *Tied Up in Knotts? GPS Technology and the Fourth Amendment*, 55 UCLA L. REV. 409, 464 (2007).
21. Amsterdam, *supra* note 18, at 402.
22. *See Jones*, 132 S. Ct. at 956 (Sotomayor, J., concurring) (arguing that granting law enforcement "unfettered discretion" to use tracking technologies "may 'alter the relationship between citizen and government in a way that is inimical to democratic society") (internal quotation marks omitted); Thomas M. Crocker, *The Political Fourth Amendment*, 88 WASH. U. L. REV. 303, 369 (2010) ("[P]lacing pressure on persons to return to their individual 'private' worlds to seek refuge from government searches and surveillance diminishes the public sphere's security.").
23. David Gray & Danielle Citron, *The Right to Quantitative Privacy*, 98 MINN. L. REV. 62 (2013).
24. United States v. Maynard, 615 F.3d 544 (D.C. Cir. 2010), *aff'd sub nom.* United States v. Jones, 132 S. Ct. 945 (2012). The case changed names because Mr. Maynard elected not to join in Jones's petition of certiorari to the Supreme Court.
25. 460 U.S. 276 (1983).
26. *Maynard*, 615 F.3d at 557.
27. *Id.* at 563.
28. CIA v. Sims, 471 U.S. 159, 178 (1985).
29. *Maynard*, 615 F.3d at 562 (footnote omitted).
30. *Jones*, 132 S. Ct. at 956 (Sotomayor, J., concurring).
31. *Id.* (internal citation and quotation marks omitted).
32. 625 F.3d 766 (2010) (Sentelle, C.J., dissenting).

33. *Jones*, 132 S. Ct. at 964 (Alito, J., concurring); *Maynard*, 615 F.3d at 558.
34. *Jones*, 625 F.3d at 769 (Sentelle, C.J., dissenting).
35. *Maynard*, 615 F.3d at 562.
36. Kerr, *supra* note 9, at 311.
37. *Jones*, 134 S. Ct. at 964 (Alito, J., concurring).
38. Transcript of Oral Argument at 9-10, United States v. Jones, 132 S. Ct. 945 (2012) (No. 10-1259).
39. Kerr, *supra* note 9, at 331-32.
40. *Id.* at 334-35.
41. David Gray & Danielle Citron, *A Shattered Looking Glass: The Pitfalls and Potential of the Mosaic Theory of Fourth Amendment Privacy*, 14 N.C. J.L. & TECH. 381, 408 (2013).
42. Kerr, *supra* note 9, at 340-43.
43. 132 S. Ct. at 964 (Alito, J., concurring).
44. 132 S. Ct. at 955 (Sotomayor, J., concurring). One might wonder why, if she agreed with him, Justice Sotomayor did not just sign Justice Alito's opinion. We may never know, but the most likely explanation is that she did not want to risk confusion about the controlling law coming out of *Jones*. With one clear majority opinion that garnered five votes, it is clear that Justice Scalia's opinion is the one and only controlling opinion. Two opinions that each garnered five votes would have made things much less clear. There is also the very real possibility that Justice Sotomayor preferred not to jump too soon into the complex questions raised by Justice Alito's durational test. By taking the narrower path charted by the majority opinion, but at the same time penning a probing concurrence that explores the challenges posed by contemporary surveillance technologies to Fourth Amendment law, Justice Sotomayor opened the floor for the legislative branch, the executive branch, and civil society to weigh in before the Supreme Court takes action.
45. 132 S. Ct. at 953-54 (majority opinion).
46. 132 S. Ct. at 953.
47. 132 S. Ct. at 963 (Alito, J., concurring).
48. *Id.* at 964.
49. *Jones*, 625 F.3d at 769 (Sentelle, J., dissenting).
50. 132 S. Ct. at 954 (majority opinion).
51. 132 S. Ct. at 964 (Alito, J., concurring).
52. Christopher Slobogin, *Making the Most of United States v. Jones in a Surveillance Society: A Statutory Implementation of Mosaic Theory*, 8 DUKE J. CONST. L. & PUB. POL'Y 1, 24-25, special issue (2012).
53. To his great credit, Professor Slobogin was not fresh to the table in taking this view. Quite to the contrary, he has been warning readers about the dangers of government surveillance for years and has always included among his targets human surveillance. *See* CHRISTOPHER SLOBOGIN, PRIVACY AT RISK 119-36 (2007).
54. Slobogin, *supra* note 52, at 13.
55. *Id.* at 25.
56. *Id.*
57. *Id.*
58. *Id.* at 28.

59. *See, e.g.*, Neil M. Richards, *The Dangers of Surveillance*, 126 HARV. L. REV. 1934, 1935 (2013). For an extended critique of Professor Richards's views, see Danielle Citron & David Gray, *Addressing the Harm of Total Surveillance: A Reply to Professor Neil Richards*, 126 HARV. L. REV. F. 262 (2013).
60. ABA STANDARDS FOR CRIMINAL JUSTICE: LAW ENFORCEMENT ACCESS TO THIRD PARTY RECORDS 6 (3d ed. 2013). For an extended critique of these standards, see David Gray, *The ABA Standards for Criminal Justice: Law Enforcement Access to Third Party Records: Critical Perspectives from a Technology-Centered Approach to Quantitative Privacy*, 66 OKLA. L. REV. 919 (2014).
61. *See, e.g.*, Jack Balkin, *Information Fiduciaries and the First Amendment*, 49 U.C. DAVIS L. REV. (forthcoming 2016); Kiel Brennan-Marquez, *Fourth Amendment Fiduciaries*, 84 FORDHAM L. REV. 611 (2015).
62. The notable exception is found in a line of cases dealing with drug-sniffing dogs. In these cases, the Court has held that targets have no reasonable expectations of privacy in criminal activities. *See, e.g.*, Illinois v. Caballes, 533 U.S. 405; United States v. Place, 462 U.S. 696 (1983). Even in these cases, however, the Court ends up focusing on the means of conducting searches. In particular, it holds that the use of a well-trained and reliable drug-sniffing dog is not a "search" for purposes of the Fourth Amendment because that dog can detect only evidence of criminal conduct and reveals nothing about lawful activities.
63. 533 U.S. 27 (2001).
64. 533 U.S. at 37.
65. There is one notable exception to this rule. The Supreme Court has held that we have no reasonable expectations of privacy in illegal activities. *See* United States v. Place, 462 U.S. 696 (1983). Although the Court has only applied this rule in cases involving drug-sniffing dogs, which the Court has characterized as *sui generis, see* Illinois v. Caballes, 543 U.S. 405, 409 (2005), the rule itself appears to allow law enforcement officers to deploy and use any device that is only capable of detecting criminal activities without running afoul of the Fourth Amendment. *See* Richard Myers, *Detector Dogs and Probable Cause*, 14 GEO. MASON L. REV. 1 (2006). *See also* Hope Walker Hall, Comment, *Sniffing Out the Fourth Amendment: United States v. Place – Dog Sniffs – Ten Years Later*, 46 ME. L. REV. 151 (1994). None of the technologies discussed in this book fall within the protections of this doctrine because they are capable of detecting both legal and illegal activities.
66. Riley v. California, 134 S. Ct. 2473 (2014).
67. *Id.* at 2492–93.
68. *See* THE FEDERALIST NOS. 10, 51.
69. *See, e.g.*, THE DECLARATION OF INDEPENDENCE para. 2 (U.S. 1776) ("We hold these truths to be self-evident, that all men are created equal, that they are endowed by their Creator with certain unalienable Rights, that among these are Life, Liberty and the pursuit of Happiness.").
70. Citron & Gray, *supra* note 59, at 267.
71. *Id.* at 267–68.
72. Danielle Keats Citron & Frank Pasquale, *Network Accountability for the Domestic Intelligence Apparatus*, 62 HASTINGS L.J. 1441, 1479–80 (2011); Daniel J. Solove, *Data Mining and the Security-Liberty Debate*, 75 U. CHI. L. REV. 343, 350 (2008).

73. *See, e.g.,* Gray & Citron, *supra* note 23; Gray, *supra* note 60; Citron & Gray, *supra* note 59, at 268; David Gray, Danielle Citron, & Liz Clark Rinehart, *Fighting Cybercrime After* United States v. Jones, 102 J. CRIM. L. & CRIMINOLOGY 745 (2013); Gray & Citron, *supra* note 41.
74. Susan Freiwald was the first to propose breadth and indiscriminateness as standards for evaluating the Fourth Amendment interests at stake in contemporary surveillance technologies during her award-winning talk at the 2012 Privacy Law Scholars Conference. *See* Susan Freiwald, The Four Factor Test (Jan. 2013) (unpublished manuscript), http://works.bepress.com/cgi/viewcontent.cgi?article=1012&context=susan_freiwald.
75. Kyllo v. United States, 533 U.S. 27, 34 (2001).
76. *Id.* at 34 (internal quotation marks omitted).
77. 389 U.S. 347 (1967).
78. 460 U.S. 276 (1983).
79. 468 U.S. 705 (1984).
80. 442 U.S. 735 (1979).
81. The so-called "mere evidence" rule is not to the contrary. There is no doubt that seizing "mere evidence" constitutes a search. That, in fact, is the core of the rule itself as it was announced in Boyd v. United States, 116 U.S. 616 (1886), and Gouled v. United States, 255 U.S. 298 (1921), where the Court held that statutes and warrants allowing for the search and seizure of personal documents are constitutionally infirm.
82. 132 S. Ct. at 945, 963 (2012) (Alito, J., concurring).
83. 134 S. Ct. 2473 (2014).
84. United States v. Knotts, 460 U.S. 276, 284 (1983).

4

Fourth Amendment Remedies as Rights

We live in an age of surveillance where law enforcement and other government agents increasingly rely on means and methods that facilitate programs of broad and indiscriminate search or seizure. Some of these means and methods are in the form of new and emerging technologies like GPS tracking, drones, networked surveillance cameras, and large-scale data aggregation and analysis. Some, such as stop and frisk, are established parts of the law enforcement toolbox, but have expanded on a programmatic level beyond the reach of effective constitutional control. As a consequence, we, the people, now live with the reality of constant and pervasive surveillance that leaves us insecure in our persons, houses, papers, and effects against threats of unreasonable search and seizure.

These challenges present us with two options. First, we might accept the fact that these technologies and programs are beyond the scope of effective Fourth Amendment regulation. As Justice Oliver Wendell Holmes wrote in a related context, this would "reduce the Fourth Amendment to a form of words."[1] It would also mean accepting life in a surveillance state. That would be anathema to core principles that define America as a political society and Americans as a people. The other option is to reconsider the direction taken by Fourth Amendment doctrine in the twentieth century. This is the path we will take in this chapter.

Paradoxically, the path forward leads us first to the past in an effort to determine how the Fourth Amendment would have been understood at the founding. By conducting a close reading of the Fourth Amendment and interpreting its language in the light of historical context, this chapter argues that the Fourth Amendment guarantees a collective right to prospective remedies that are sufficient to preserve the security of the people against threats of unreasonable search and seizure.

A Note on Method

When applying constitutional provisions to contemporary questions, judges, elected officials, and scholars generally employ some form of either "living constitutionalism" or originalism. Living constitutionalists argue that the Constitution is not necessarily found in the surface text. It lives instead in principles underlying the text. By focusing on these principles, living constitutionalists show how the meaning of the Constitution can change over time to meet new challenges, to accommodate "evolving standards of decency,"[2] to preserve basic democratic norms,[3] and to promote the constitutional aspiration to achieve a "more perfect union."[4] For example, segregation laws once were regarded as constitutional by the Supreme Court.[5] Our views on race, justice, and equality evolved over time until we recognized that these practices violated core constitutional principles of justice and equality. In recognition of that shift, courts now treat segregation laws as unconstitutional violations of due process and equal protection under the Fifth and Fourteenth Amendments.[6] To cite another example, it was once perfectly constitutional to inflict the death penalty on perpetrators who committed their crimes as juveniles.[7] Our views on culpability and punishment changed over time, however, revealing the cruelty inherent in this practice. As a result, the Supreme Court now holds that the death penalty is cruel and unusual in violation of the Eighth Amendment when applied to juvenile offenders.[8]

Living constitutionalism has obvious attractions as we face contemporary surveillance practices. It allows us to look past the constraining text and identify basic principles, such as a right to privacy, that are capacious enough to address new programs and technologies. In the Fourth Amendment context, it marries nicely with the general framework of reasonable expectations of privacy, promising the development of "different constitutional principles" sufficient to deal with "dragnet-type law enforcement practices."[9] Adopting living constitutionalism might also allow the meaning of the Fourth Amendment to change and grow in order to accommodate new discoveries from fields such as neuroscience and psychology, which continue to teach us about ourselves, our needs, and the conditions necessary for human flourishing.

Despite the intuitive appeal of living constitutionalism, there are good reasons to be wary of relying on this interpretive method. Social practices and community standards change and evolve over time. This means that constitutional principles or constitutional protections built on these shifting foundations are equally temporary. Moreover, changes in community standards are not always felicitous. They sometimes work to the disadvantage of the people, which would have the effect of contracting the scope of Fourth Amendment protections.[10] Justice Antonin Scalia was famously skeptical of living constitutionalism on these grounds, arguing that "A society that adopts a bill of rights is skeptical that 'evolving standards of decency' always 'mark progress,' and that societies always 'mature,' as opposed to rot."[11] His concerns are particularly salient in the present context. As new surveillance technologies emerge and expand, they can lead to reductions in our common expectations of privacy.[12] Privacy scholars refer to this phenomenon as "technological determinism." In *Kyllo v. United States*, Justice Scalia warned that the Court should guard against technological determinism by refusing to "permit police technology to erode the privacy guaranteed by the Fourth Amendment."[13]

Living constitutionalism also raises serious philosophical and political concerns. Constitutions are, by nature, counter-majoritarian documents. Their entire purpose is to restrain the political branches. The role of the judiciary in our system of checks and balances is to enforce these constitutional boundaries, no matter how unpopular. This is, in part, why federal judges enjoy life tenure. Liberated from the vagaries of the political process, federal judges can make the hard decisions, denying the electorate its policy preferences if those preferences run afoul of the Constitution without needing to worry about losing their jobs in the process. That is all well and good. It is quite another matter, however, for the judiciary to act as an unelected legislature, imposing its own policy preferences under the guise of ever-changing "reasonable expectations of privacy." That would not only be counter-majoritarian, but it would also be antidemocratic, converting our constitutional democracy into an oligarchy.

In light of these and other concerns with living constitutionalism, many judges and scholars favor originalism. Originalists are primarily interested in the text of the Constitution and what it meant when it was adopted. Originalism should not be confused with intentionalism, which attempts to divine the intentions of those who wrote the Constitution. Originalists are concerned instead with the common public meaning of the Constitution – how it would have been read and understood by the average reader at the time. For example, an originalist would be most interested in understanding how the text of the Fourth Amendment would have been understood in 1791, when it was ratified.

Originalists acknowledge that their method limits the Supreme Court's ability to constitutionalize some important, positive shifts in our prevailing views on social justice. Originalists maintain, however, that it is better to have a stable, reliable set of constitutional norms that provide a set of stable, reliable protections for citizens, and stable, reliable limitations on the political branches.[14] From this perspective, originalists are much like Odysseus,[15] who tied himself to the mast of his ship so he would not be tempted by the sirens' calls to approach the Sirenum scopuli.[16] So too, originalists seek to bind us to something stable and unchanging so we can resist the temptations of the moment, which often drive us to abandon principle in favor of expediency or to serve momentary political demands at the expense of fundamental rights.[17]

As a method, originalism starts with giving words their most straightforward, non-technical meanings. This usually entails consulting historical dictionaries to determine what words would have meant to readers at the time. Originalists also apply rules called canons of interpretation, such as *noscitur a sociis* (which translates, roughly, as "it is known by its associates") and *ejusdem generis* (again, roughly, "of the same kind"). These canons remind us to read words in the context of the sentences and paragraphs where they appear. Other canons advise reading words and sentences in their broader context, favoring interpretations that preserve consistency and coherency across a document. There are also canons that provide for consulting exogenous sources, such as prior drafts, related laws, or historical evidence of the problems and challenges constitutional provisions were designed to address. Originalists do not consult these sources to determine what those who wrote a law or a constitution meant to achieve, however. That would be to revert to intentionalism. They instead use these sources to better understand what the text would have meant to those who read it at the time on the assumption they would have understood it in the broader context of contemporary challenges and controversies.

To be sure, originalism has its critics. Some argue that it reduces us to rule by the "dead hand" of our founders, who lived in very different times. Others contend that originalism renders the Constitution inflexible and incapable of dealing with contemporary challenges and circumstances. Critics also point out that many of our founders had abhorrent views on critical questions of social justice, including slavery, racism, and gender equality that should bind us in our contemporary pursuits of justice. Others point out that it is not obvious that questions of original public meaning have determinate answers, which leaves room for judges to substitute their own policy preferences for those of the majority under the guise and cover of historical interpretation. Despite these concerns, this chapter will adopt public meaning originalism as its method for two reasons.

First, despite its potential problems, originalism at least holds out the possibility of binding judges, and therefore the political branches, to a set of stable, objective constraints. To the extent the Constitution and the Bill of Rights are meant to serve as a set of precommitments, protecting us against the temptations of the moment, originalism at least tries to tether itself to something stable.[18] By contrast, theories embracing living constitutionalism leave all three branches of government vulnerable to the sirens' songs of political expediency. As our founders well understood, these melodies are particularly tempting in times of emergency, when urgency may make it easy to justify compromising core rights and values.[19]

Second, public meaning originalism is extremely influential.[20] Even after the death of Justice Scalia, a majority of the sitting justices on the United States Supreme Court have explicitly endorsed public meaning originalism, have expressed sympathy with the basic approach, or have shown deep skepticism with unbounded living constitutionalism. According to one recent poll, most ordinary citizens also favor originalist approaches to constitutional interpretation.[21] Purely as a practical matter, it is therefore essential to take originalism seriously. This does not mean that other approaches are without influence. But the fact of the matter is that most living constitutionalists are already convinced that Fourth Amendment doctrine needs to be modified to address contemporary surveillance technologies. The skeptics tend to be originalists; so it is worth seeing whether that skepticism is well grounded.[22]

Out of concern for both principle and practicality, this chapter will employ the tools of public meaning originalism to determine the meaning of the Fourth Amendment. The results are illuminating. As we will discover, the Fourth Amendment establishes a collective right to prospective remedies. The primary goal of these remedies is to limit the discretion of government agents to deploy and use means and methods of search and seizure capable of facilitating programs of broad and indiscriminate search and seizure because these programs leave the people vulnerable to threats of unreasonable search and seizure. By limiting that discretion, the Fourth Amendment is able to guarantee that most people, most of the time, are secure against threats of unreasonable search and seizure. In the chapters that follow, we shall explore how this reading can help chart a course for the Fourth Amendment in an age of surveillance.

The Two Clauses of the Fourth Amendment

The Fourth Amendment features two distinct clauses. The first, often referred to as the reasonableness clause, provides that

> [t]he right of the people to be secure in their persons, houses, papers, and effects, against unreasonable searches and seizures, shall not be violated

The second, known as the warrant clause, provides that

> and no Warrants shall issue, but upon probable cause, supported by Oath or affirmation, and particularly describing the place to be searched, and the persons or things to be seized.

This division is no accident. Consider the original draft of the Fourth Amendment, submitted to the First Congress by a committee chaired by James Madison. It provided that

> [t]he rights of the people to be secured in their persons, their houses, their papers, and their other property from all unreasonable searches and seizures, shall not be violated by warrants issued without probable cause, supported by oath or affirmation, or not particularly describing the places to be searched, or the persons or things to be seized.[23]

Madison's draft would only have protected the right of the people to be secure from searches and seizures conducted pursuant to warrants that failed to satisfy the requirements of probable cause, oath and affirmation, and particularity. It would not have regulated unreasonable searches and seizures conducted in the absence of a warrant or unreasonable searches and seizures conducted under the authority of proper warrants. Speaking on the floor of the First Congress, Representative Egbert Benson from New York[24] protested that, in light of these deficits, the Madison draft did not provide sufficient protections. To remedy the situation, Benson proposed dividing the text into two clauses using the now-familiar language "and no warrants shall issue."[25] The First Congress ultimately adopted his proposal, resulting in the Fourth Amendment we have today.

What is the relationship between the two clauses? The modern Supreme Court regards reasonableness as the "touchstone" of the Fourth Amendment. It views the warrant clause as subordinate, regulating only searches conducted pursuant to warrants. This reading certainly makes sense given the text. The reasonableness clause comes first. It also imposes a broad prohibition on threats to the people's right to security against unreasonable searches and seizures. The warrant clause comes second. It is narrower in scope, regulating only in those circumstances where officers pursue warrants as licenses to search or seize. The Court's reading of the reasonableness clause as predominate also gives due weight to the Fourth Amendment's drafting history. The canon of interpretation *expressio unius est exclusio alterius* advises that the expression of one thing implies the exclusion of the alternative. As the editors of the leading treatise on statutory interpretation have put the point, "when people say one thing, they do not mean something else."[26] Given Congressman Benson's efforts to separate the two clauses, the two drafts must have had different meanings for eighteenth-century readers such that the language that was ratified had the effect of excluding that which it replaced. Otherwise, why would he have bothered? In this case, the final text effected a general prohibition against threats to the people's security from unreasonable searches and seizures. That is in contrast with the original draft, which was much narrower.[27] Based on both grammar and history, then, we should read the Fourth Amendment as guaranteeing to the people an overarching right to be secure from unreasonable searches and seizures and imposing a subordinate prohibition on warrants issued on less than probable cause, in the absence of oath or affirmation, and without sufficient particularity.

But if the reasonableness clause provides such broad protections, then why not stop there? Why bother with the second clause? The answer is found in the context of then contemporary events. The Fourth Amendment was adopted against the backdrop of controversies surrounding the use of general warrants in England and writs of assistance in the colonies.[28] Eighteenth-century common law allowed magistrates to issue warrants based on sworn oath or affirmation demonstrating good and sufficient reasons justifying a search for specific things in a particular place.[29] The primary advantage of common-law warrants was that they provided immunity from trespass suits.[30] As a consequence, eighteenth-century common law expressed a preference of sorts for warranted searches.[31] In exchange for submitting to an application process that included scrutiny by a judicial officer, describing the reasons for search under oath, and accepting limitations on the scope of their discretion, government officials conducting searches could avoid the risk of civil liability. Those same incentives also provided valuable protection for the people against threats of unreasonable search and seizure by discouraging searches conducted without prior judicial approval, overbroad searches, and searches conducted on the whim of a particular official. Government agents either got warrants or they exposed themselves to potential civil liability. Either way, the interests of the people were protected.

General warrants and writs of assistance provided government agents with the same immunity from civil action afforded by common-law warrants but imposed none of the procedural safeguards. In contrast to common-law warrants, which specified where searches would be conducted and for what, general warrants and writs of assistance granted government agents broad and unlimited discretion to search whenever and wherever they liked. Common-law warrants required that searches should be justified by good and sufficient reasons, established by sworn oath or affirmation, but general warrants and writs of assistance granted government agents authority to conduct searches on a whim, out of malice, or as part of efforts to suppress political or religious freedoms. While common-law warrants were issued by magistrates or justices of the peace, executive officials, such as secretaries of state, had the authority to issue general warrants. Writs of assistance gave their bearers additional authority to command the assistance of others to participate in a search, including civilians and household servants. General warrants and writs of assistance therefore stole from the people both the right to sue and protections afforded by common-law warrants, exposing them to threats of unreasonable searches and seizures while also denying them any form of redress.

General warrants trace their origins to the fourteenth century. These early iterations allowed innkeepers to search guests for counterfeit money and untaxed goods. In the fifteenth century, Parliament granted broad authority to members of the trades to seize and destroy defective or substandard goods. Drawing on this precedent, the infamous Star Chamber authorized the stationers and printers' guild, chartered in 1557 as The Worshipful Company of Stationers and Newspaper Makers, to search, seize, and arrest those who used the printed word to engage in sedition. During the reigns of Elizabeth I, James I, and Charles I, the Star Chamber became more and more aggressive in its attempts to silence critics of the crown, including pamphleteers. General warrants played an important role in these efforts.

Although the Star Chamber was abolished by the Habeas Corpus Act in 1640, the threat of general warrants quickly resurfaced. The Licensing Press Act of 1662 authorized secretaries of state to issue general warrants in an effort to identify and punish publishers and pamphleteers who criticized the Crown. The Licensing Press Act expired in 1695, but the practice of executives issuing general warrants in sedition cases continued.[32]

Controversies surrounding general warrants in Britain came to a head in a series of mid-eighteenth-century cases involving efforts by agents of King George III to silence some of his most vocal critics, including John Wilkes and John Entick. Wilkes and Entick published newsletters and bills criticizing the King and his policies. Their criticism focused on several controversial taxes, including an excise on hard cider. In an effort to silence them, George Montagu-Dunk, the Second Earl of Halifax, issued general warrants authorizing his agents and messengers to search for evidence relating to the publication of the offending pamphlets and to arrest those responsible on charges of seditious libel. Under authority of these warrants, Halifax's minions searched the homes and offices of Wilkes, Entick, and others suspected of publishing materials critical of the crown.

In a series of cases now referred to as the general warrants cases, the printers, Wilkes, and Entick sued the agents who searched their homes and seized their property under authority of warrants issued by the Earl of Halifax. Several of these cases were heard by Charles Pratt, Lord Chief Justice of the Court of Common Pleas. Chief Justice Pratt is sometimes referred to as "Lord Camden" in light of his ascendency to the House of Lords as Earl of Camden in 1765. Justice Pratt used the occasion to condemn general warrants. He was particularly concerned with the broad grants of "discretionary power" provided by general warrants for "messengers to search wherever their suspicions may chance to fall," which he saw as a threat to "the person and property of every man in this kingdom," and "totally subversive of the liberty of the subject."[33] He refused to grant the defendants any form of immunity from suit and allowed substantial jury verdicts to stand.

The general warrants cases established the illegality of general warrants under the common law. This common-law rule was subject to abrogation by statute, however. The Licensing Press Act, which would have granted Lord Halifax authority to issue general warrants, had lapsed by 1762, but

Justice Pratt acknowledged that it could be renewed.[34] It never was. Unfortunately for the American colonists, the Licensing Press Act was not the only law purporting to authorize general warrants. In 1696, Parliament granted broad authority for the King's agents in the colonies to seek writs of assistance authorizing customs officials to search for and seize contraband goods. Writs of assistance became a rather notorious tool in the New England colonies, and particularly Massachusetts, where officials overseeing the port of Boston used them to clamp down on efforts to circumvent revenue laws.

Writs of assistance authorizing searches for contraband goods in Massachusetts came up for renewal in 1761. Then Advocate Attorney General of the Admiralty Court James Otis was charged to defend them, but resigned his commission, choosing instead to represent a group of merchants contesting the legality of writs of assistance in the colonies. The most famous of Otis's cases is known as Paxton's Case. In the course of these representations, Otis made an impassioned speech of over four hours during which he decried general warrants as "the worst instrument of arbitrary power, the most destructive of English liberty and the fundamental principles of law, that ever was found in an English lawbook." Otis lost the case, and new writs issued, but his efforts were not wasted. According to John Adams, who was in the audience that day, Otis's oration marked "the first scene of the first act of opposition to the arbitrary claims of Great Britain."[35] "Then and there," Adams continued, "the child Independence was born."[36]

The founding generation was quite keen to prohibit general warrants and writs of assistance. As a consequence, eight of the original colonies barred general warrants and writs of assistance in their founding constitutions.[37] In light of this history, and the plain meaning of the text, the best way to read the warrant clause is as a ban on general warrants and writs of assistance. It would be a mistake, however, to read the warrant clause as limiting the scope of the reasonableness clause. General warrants certainly threaten the security of the people against unreasonable searches and seizures, and therefore run afoul of the reasonableness clause. The reasonableness clause is much broader, however, providing more general protections for the people against policies and practices that threaten the right of the people to be secure against unreasonable searches and seizures.

Given the predominate role of the reasonableness clause in the Fourth Amendment, it is critical to understand the nature and the scope of its protections. In keeping with our commitment to apply the methods of public meaning originalism, we must therefore try to understand how the reasonableness clause would have been understood by readers in 1791. In the sections that follow, we will do precisely that, beginning with the first two words.

"The right..."

The Fourth Amendment starts with the two-word phrase "The right." According to Samuel Johnson's *Dictionary of the English Language*,[38] often cited as an authoritative source for the meaning of English words during the founding era,[39] "right," when used as a noun, referred to a "just claim," "that which justly belongs to one," a "property" or "interest," a "power" or "prerogative," or an "immunity" or "privilege." By these definitions, "The right" as it is used in the Fourth Amendment probably meant to readers in 1791 something quite close to what it means to readers today.

This does not quite exhaust our inquiry. Words live in the world. They therefore carry connotations from their uses in common parlance, in specialized fields of study, and in connection with significant events, all of which contribute to public meaning. To understand the meaning of "The right" in the Fourth Amendment, it is therefore important to go beyond dictionary definitions to consider then contemporary sources and events that would have informed readers' understanding of the text. Specifically, we would be well served to understand how Renaissance and late eighteenth-century political theorists understood and applied the concept of rights to the extent that these authors and their work influenced prevailing views on fundamental questions of social and political justice in the founding era. We should also try to understand the role that rights and rights claims played in the revolutionary movement, which also would have informed eighteenth-century readers' understanding of the text.

In terms of political philosophers, there is perhaps no one who had more influence on our eighteenth-century forebears than John Locke.[40] The centerpiece of Locke's political philosophy is the idea of a social contract between government and the governed, who together, as a people, comprise a "Body Politick."[41] To explain the role of a social contract in political society, Locke posited the existence of a state of nature where there was no society, no state, and no government. In this state of nature, each person was absolutely free, subject only to the demands of her own reason. These demands were few but universal, describing a set of mutual restraints in the form of basic rights, including the right to life, the right to liberty, and the right to property. Together, these rights and restraints comprise the natural law. In order to ensure our enjoyment of basic rights and to guarantee respect for the natural law, Locke argued that we exit the state of nature and enter into political society by way of a social contract.[42] In their turn, political societies then enter into contracts establishing governments and submitting themselves to governmental authority.[43]

Contracts are premised on the free consent of parties.[44] In keeping with the idea of a social contract, Locke was therefore concerned with consent as the foundation of political legitimacy. In his view, consent served at least two important purposes. First, it described a rule of politics. To achieve and preserve legitimacy, Locke argued that governments must secure the consent of the governed. He therefore favored democracy as a model of political rule. Consent also serves as a regulatory ideal by which we can measure societies and governments. For example, no rational being would agree to a social contract that unnecessarily impinged upon natural rights. Autocratic or repressive regimes that fail to respect and protect natural rights therefore cannot claim legitimacy because they cannot claim to have the rational consent of the governed.[45] Where the lived realities of life in a state fail to conform to the basic demands of a rational social contract, Locke maintained that the people have an absolute right to alter or overthrow their government by political means or, if necessary, revolution.

The influence of Locke's political philosophy on the founding generation is evident in the opening lines of the Declaration of Independence, which asserts the "self-evident" truth that "all men are created equal" and endowed with "certain inalienable Rights," including "Life, Liberty, and the Pursuit of Happiness." The Declaration of Independence goes on to maintain that the just powers of government derive from "the consent of the governed," and asserts the "Right of the People" to dissolve any government that fails to secure these rights. A more concise summary of Locke's political philosophy would be hard to find.

Locke's influence carried through to the Constitution. For example, the Constitution makes clear that it is a contract from its opening line. "We the People of the United States," reads the Preamble, "in Order to form a more perfect Union, establish Justice, insure domestic Tranquility, provide for the common defence, promote the general Welfare, and secure the Blessings of Liberty to ourselves and our Posterity, do ordain and establish this Constitution for the United

States of America."[46] From these opening phrases, the Constitution goes on to describe the basic terms of this contract, including the establishment of democratic processes by which the consent of the governed can be secured and the division of powers between an executive and a legislature, all of which Locke promotes in his *Second Treatise of Government*.[47]

Although the main text of the Constitution reads like a realization of Locke's ideal of a social contract, it is notably silent on issues of basic rights. By contrast, most of the state constitutions that predated the Constitutional Convention of 1787 contained lengthy declarations of rights. This omission caused considerable controversy during the ratification process. Critics of the strong central government proposed by the Constitution worried that their natural rights, and those rights secured to them as citizens of their respective states, might be threatened or overridden by the federal government. In order to quell those concerns, the First Congress committed to amending the Constitution to include a bill of rights. Without that promise, it is virtually certain that the Constitution would not have been ratified in many state conventions.

Absent some clear evidence to the contrary, this history suggests that the best reading of "The right" in the Fourth Amendment is as a reference to and enshrinement of fundamental natural or political rights in the Lockean tradition. When late eighteenth-century Americans read the phrase "The right" in the Fourth Amendment, they therefore knew that it referred to a fundamental "interest," "prerogative," or "power" linked to natural rights, collective projects of self-governance, or both. As such, we may expect that the rights protected in the Bill of Rights generally, and the Fourth Amendment specifically, will have close ties to basic rights in physical security, liberty, the peaceful possession and enjoyment of property,[48] or the conditions necessary to meaningful participation in public politics.[49] By contrast, it would be quite surprising to find that the rights secured by the Fourth Amendment are frivolous or mere contingencies of the times, akin to rights created by present-day entitlement programs.

"The right of the people..."

One of the principal tenets of textual interpretation, and therefore public meaning originalism, holds that the meaning of words is determined by their context in phrases, sentences, paragraphs, and texts. Although a peek at the dictionary and a basic understanding of the framers' conceptual world may set us on the track to understanding a particular word or phrase, we must read those words in broader context within the text. This is certainly true of the phrase "The right" in the Fourth Amendment, which appears as part of the more revealing phrase "The right of the people." As we shall see in this section, "the people" appears several times in the original Constitution and the Bill of Rights, each time referring to the nation or society as a whole. It plays that same role in the Fourth Amendment, making clear that the right to be secure against unreasonable searches and seizures is a collective right of the people rather than a right of individual persons.

In keeping with the methods of public meaning originalism, we start with plain meaning. According to Samuel Johnson's *Dictionary of the English Language*, "people" would have been understood in 1791 as referring to "a nation" or "those who compose a community." In this regard, "people" can be understood in contrast to "person," which eighteenth-century readers would have understood to mean an "Individual or particular man or woman."[50] This does not quite settle the matter, however. There is, after all, some ambiguity even in the dictionary meaning of "people." Read as "a nation," "people" might refer to a group collectively, such as in the sentence "Cambodia is home to the Khmer people." By contrast, "those who compose a community" might be read as referring to people generically, as in the sentence "When it rains, people tend to stay inside." Fortunately, the text of the Fourth Amendment resolves this potential ambiguity.

The Fourth Amendment does not read "The right of *people* to be secure..." It instead reads "The right of *the people* to be secure." One very important canon of interpretation originalists cite often is *noscitur a sociis*, or "a word is known by the company it keeps."[51] This canon reflects the basic rule of most semantic systems that the meaning of a word is determined in part by syntax. Abiding basic rules of English grammar, and the canon *noscitur a sociis*, we therefore cannot ignore the presence of that definite article in the Fourth Amendment or the modifying force it has on the meaning of "people."

"The" meant in 1792 what it means now. It is "The article noting a particular thing."[52] Modified by "the," we may therefore assume that readers in 1791 would have understood "the people" in the Fourth Amendment as a reference to the nation or community as a whole, as in the phrase "We the people of the United States..."[53] As a matter of plain meaning, we therefore have good reason to believe that those who read the Fourth Amendment in 1791 would have understood from its opening phrase that it recognizes a collective "claim," "property," "interest," "power," "prerogative," or "immunity" held by the people of the United States as whole. This has important implications. For example, to claim Fourth Amendment protections a person must be a member of "the people" in good standing.[54] Moreover, individuals can only exercise Fourth Amendment rights through and by virtue of that membership.[55] Most importantly, however, this reading of the Fourth Amendment corrects a common misconception about the nature of Fourth Amendment rights.

There is a common myth holding that the Fourth Amendment recognizes only individual rights of persons rather than a collective right of the people as a whole.[56] This misconception not only runs contrary to the plain text of the Fourth Amendment it also ignores both the Fourth Amendment's place in the Constitution and the historical context in which it was drafted and adopted.[57]

The Constitution, inclusive of the Bill of Rights, describes an undeniably collective enterprise.[58] That is evident from the first phrases of the Preamble,[59] which read:

> We the People of the United States, in Order to form a more perfect Union, establish Justice, insure domestic Tranquility, provide for the common defence, promote the general Welfare, and secure the Blessings of Liberty to ourselves and our Posterity, do ordain and establish this Constitution for the United States of America.

Those who read this language at our founding would have understood these as the opening phrases of a social contract in the Lockean tradition between a people and its government. By its terms, that contract is by and for the nation as a whole, now and into perpetuity. Moreover, this collective view makes perfect sense in light of the times. After all, we had just won a revolution by which, in the language of the Declaration of Independence, "one people ... dissolve[d] the political bands which ha[d] connected them with another [people]."[60]

The collective enterprise described in the Preamble is in marked contrast to its immediate predecessor: the 1781 Articles of Confederation. As compared to the Constitution, the Articles of Confederation rejected the proposition that there was a "People of the United States," favoring instead a contract of "mutual friendship and intercourse among the people of the different States."[61] The government formed by the Articles of Confederation ultimately failed, leading to the Philadelphia

Convention of 1787 and the Constitution we have today. The decision by the founding generation to turn away from the Articles of Confederation would have informed eighteenth-century readers' understanding of the Constitution. They simply could not have missed the significance of an opening paragraph explicitly introducing a collective contract by and among the people of the nation as a whole.

The Preamble's focus on "the people" carries through to Article I and portions of the Bill of Rights. Article I, Section 2 provides that "The House of Representatives shall be composed of Members chosen every second Year by the People of the several States,"[62] which specifically contemplates "the people acting collectively" to approve their representatives.[63] More important from a textualist point of view is the fact that "the people" in Article I is modified by the phrase "of the several States." That same modification appears in Amendment XVII, which provides that senators shall be "elected by the people [from each state]." These modifications suggest the need to clarify for readers the fact that "the people" referred to in Article I and Amendment XVII is not the same as "the people" referred to in the Preamble. To reinforce the point, Amendment X provides that "The powers not delegated to the United States by the Constitution, nor prohibited by it to the States, are reserved to the States respectively, or to the people," drawing a sharp line for readers between "the people" of the United States as a whole, and "the people" of the individual states.[64]

The drafting history of the Fourth Amendment provides further evidence that the "right of the people" would have been understood as referring to a collective rather than purely individual right. The plain language of the Fourth Amendment describes a "right of the people"[65] not a "right of each person" or "every subject." That is not happenstance. Those who drafted the Fourth Amendment in 1791 had two models to choose from.[66] The first was offered by Article Ten of the 1776 Pennsylvania Declaration of Rights, which provided that "the people have a right to hold themselves, their houses, papers, and possessions free from search and seizure."[67] The second came from the Massachusetts and New Hampshire Bills of Rights, each of which provided that "[e]very subject has a right to be secure from all unreasonable searches and seizures."[68] The First Congress ultimately chose an approach modeled after the Pennsylvania Declaration of Rights. That choice would have been particularly significant for those who read the Fourth Amendment in 1791 given the parentage of the Massachusetts Bill of Rights.

John Adams is widely hailed as the intellectual father of the Fourth Amendment.[69] His work on search and seizure for the Massachusetts constitution was groundbreaking and later served as a blueprint for the Fourth Amendment.[70] Despite Adams's influence on the overall structure and content of the Fourth Amendment, the First Congress ultimately chose Pennsylvania's "the people" rather than Adams's "every subject."[71] This choice would have stood out to then contemporary readers, adding yet more weight to the claim that the Fourth Amendment would have been understood in 1791 as describing a collective right of "the people" rather than an individual right of each "person" or each "subject."[72]

The decision to follow the Pennsylvania model is even more significant in terms of original public meaning if we take a closer look at the Pennsylvania Declaration of Rights. Very much in the Lockean tradition, the preamble of the Pennsylvania Declaration makes clear its aim of protecting collective rights as well as individual rights. "[A]ll government," it reads, "ought to be instituted and supported for the security and protection of the community as such, and to enable the individuals who compose it, to enjoy their natural rights."[73] In keeping with that goal, the Pennsylvania Declaration sometimes uses "the people" or "the community" and sometimes uses "all men" or "every member" in order to draw distinctions between rights that rest primarily with the "community as such" and those that lie with "the individuals who compose it."[74] Table 4.1 shows this arrangement.

Table 4.1 shows a clear pattern in the allocation of rights within the Pennsylvania Declaration.[75] Rights assigned to individuals – such as the right to freedom of worship, the right to own property, and the right to fair criminal process – link directly to the natural rights of persons in the state of nature, personal projects of ethical self-development, or individual engagements with state power. They guarantee liberty of thought and belief, rights in property, and basic rights of bodily security. In keeping with the Lockean tradition, a just state must respect and preserve these basic individual rights as a condition of legitimacy.[76] No rational person would consent to being governed by a state that sought to control her beliefs, steal her property, or abuse her body. It is therefore no surprise that Pennsylvanians established these limits on the powers of their newly formed government, binding it according to the basic demands of natural law.

Table 4.1 *Pennsylvania Bill of Rights*

Collective Rights	Individual Rights
Art. III "[T]he people of this state have the sole, exclusive and inherent right of governing and regulating the internal police of the same."	Art. "[A]ll men are born equally free and independent . . ."
Art. V "[T]he community hath an indubitable, unalienable and indefeasible right to reform, alter or abolish government, in such manner as shall be by that community judged most conducive to the public weal."	Art. II "[A]ll men have a natural and unalienable right to worship Almighty [God], according to the dictates of their own consciences and understanding . . ."
Art. VI "[T]he people have a right, at such periods as they may think proper, to reduce their public officers to a private station, and supply the vacancies by certain and regular elections."	Art. VIII "[E]very member of society hath a right to be protected in the enjoyment of life, liberty and property . . . no part of a man's property can be justly taken from him or applied to public uses, without his own consent or that of his legal representatives . . ."
Art. XIII " . . . the people have a right to freedom of speech, and of writing and publishing their sentiments: therefore the freedom of the press ought not to be restrained."	Art. IX "[I]n all prosecutions for criminal offences, a man hath a right to be heard by himself and his council . . ."
Art. XVI "[T]he people have a right to assemble together to consult for their common good, to instruct their representatives, and to apply to the legislature for redress of grievances by address, petition or remonstrance."	Art. XI ("[I]n controversies respecting property, and in suites between man and man, the parties have a right to trial by jury . . ."
Art. X. "That the people have a right to hold themselves, their houses, papers, and possessions free from search and seizure, and therefore warrants without oaths or affirmations first made, affording a sufficient foundation for them, and whereby any officer or messenger may be commanded or required to search suspected places, or to seize any person or persons, his or their property, not particularly described, are contrary to that right, and ought not to be granted."	Art. XV ("[A]ll men have a natural inherent right to emigrate from one state to another that will receive them . . ."

Rights secured for the people by the Pennsylvania Declaration – such as the right to hold elections, the right to free speech, and the right to assemble – represent basic political rights essential to collective projects of self-governance where the primary goal is to secure the free consent of the governed. This makes good sense. After all, the political contracts that form governments in the Lockean tradition are not among individuals but rather are entered into by the people as a whole in the form of a Body Politick.[77] It therefore makes sense that rights regulating the relationship between society and government would lie first with the people as a whole rather than individual persons because it is the people as a whole who is the primary party in interest.[78]

This does not mean that collective rights guaranteed to the people as a whole do not provide important protections for individuals as well. They surely do. But these individual guarantees are derivative of the collective right rather than freestanding individual rights. Consider the right of the people to elect their representatives guaranteed in Article I of the Constitution. This collective right necessarily secures to individuals the right to contribute meaningfully to the process of selecting representatives, usually by voting. The obverse is not true, however. The right to vote does not mean one has the right to elect one's own representatives. I cannot complain that my right to participate in electoral politics has been violated simply because my candidate lost. So long as the electoral process is fair and yields a winner, the collective right to elect representatives is vindicated, even for the losers.

Like the Pennsylvania Declaration of Rights, the US Constitution and the Bill of Rights allocate some rights to "the people" and others to individuals. Consider Table 4.2:

As did the Pennsylvania Declaration of Rights before it, the US Constitution tends to rest political rights, such as the right to elect representatives and the right to assemble and petition the government, with "the people." By contrast, it reserves to individual "persons" more personal protections, such as the right to a jury trial and rights in property. Tellingly, the Fourth Amendment right to security against unreasonable search and seizure is guaranteed to "the people." This choice bespeaks a founding-era understanding that security from unreasonable search and seizure is linked to collective projects of self-governance.[80] This may seem strange to the modern mind, but it accurately reflects then contemporary perceptions of the threats addressed by the Fourth Amendment.

Table 4.2 *United States Constitution*

Collective Rights	Individual Rights
Art. I, Sec. 2 "The House of Representatives shall be composed of members chosen every second year by the people of the several states …"	Amend. III "No Soldier shall, in time of peace be quartered in any house, without the consent of the Owner, nor in time of war, but in a manner to be prescribed by law."
Amend. I "Congress shall make no law … abridging … the right of the people peaceably to assemble, and to petition the Government for a redress of grievances.	Amend. V: "No person shall be held to answer for a capital, or otherwise infamous crime, unless on a presentment or indictment of a Grand Jury, except in cases arising in the land or naval forces, or in the Militia, when in actual service in time of War or public danger; nor shall any person be subject for the same offence to be twice put in jeopardy of life or limb; nor shall be compelled in any criminal case to be a witness against himself, nor be deprived of life, liberty, or property, without due process of law; nor shall private property be taken for public use, without just compensation."
Amend. II " … the right of the people to keep and bear Arms, shall not be infringed."[79]	
Amend IV: "The right of the people to be secure in their persons, houses, papers, and effects, against unreasonable searches and seizures, shall not be violated … ".	Amend VI: "In all criminal prosecutions, the accused shall enjoy the right to a speedy and public trial, by an impartial jury of the State and district wherein the crime shall have been committed, which district shall have been previously ascertained by law, and to be informed of the nature and cause of the accusation; to be confronted with the witnesses against him; to have compulsory process for obtaining witnesses in his favor, and to have the Assistance of Counsel for his defence."
Amend. IX: "The enumeration in the Constitution, of certain rights, shall not be construed to deny or disparage others retained by the people."	
Amend X: "The powers not delegated to the United States by the Constitution, nor prohibited by it to the States, are reserved to the States respectively, or to the people."	

The Fourth Amendment's role in protecting the political rights of the people is evident in the history of events that gave rise to its inclusion in the Bill of Rights.[81] Like many provisions of the Bill of Rights, the Fourth Amendment was motivated by founding-era struggles with abuses of power.[82] As we saw earlier in this chapter, the Fourth Amendment's principal bêtes noires were general warrants and writs of assistance.[83] British courts famously rejected general warrants in the general warrants cases.[84] Those cases, which would have been widely known in late eighteenth-century America,[85] demonstrated the corrosive impact of broad search and seizure powers on political freedoms. There, agents of the Crown used general warrants to target and silence prominent pamphleteers who criticized the King and his policies.[86] In striking down those warrants, Chief Justice Pratt noted the general threats to liberty of conscience and thought posed by general warrants.[87] He then reasoned that nobody, whether innocent or guilty,[88] could feel secure if forced to live under a regime where executive agents had the authority to engage in programs of broad and indiscriminate search.[89] As he pointed out, if a government can grant "discretionary power ... to messengers to search wherever their suspicions may chance to fall ... it certainly may affect the person and property of every man in this kingdom."[90] In a similar vein, James Otis attacked general warrants in his famous 1761 speech as "destructive of English liberty" because they grant "a power that places the liberty of every man in the hands of every petty officer."[91]

Given this context, it is fitting that the Fourth Amendment secures a "right of the people" rather than a right of each person or every subject. The historical goal, after all, was to provide for the general security of the nation and society as a whole against threats posed by the existence of general warrants and writs of assistance.[92] Reflecting on this history, Professor Tony Amsterdam has written that the "evil" targeted by the Fourth Amendment "was general: it was the creation of an administration of public justice that authorized and supported indiscriminate searching and seizing."[93] That reading certainly fits the text and its times.

Founding-era concerns with the general impact of search and seizure practices have carried over to the modern era.[94] In 1948, Justice Jackson advised that "The right of officers to thrust themselves into a home is also a grave concern, not only to the individual but to a society which chooses to dwell in reasonable security and freedom from surveillance."[95] The role of collective interests is particularly evident in the Court's modern exclusionary rule jurisprudence,[96] which focuses on securing the general right of the people by deterring law enforcement officers from engaging in unreasonable searches and seizures.[97]

When our forebears read "the people" in the Constitution and the Bill of Rights they understood it as referring to the American people as a political unit. "We the people" established the United States of America as a political entity headed by a central government. At the same time, "We the people" worried about the possibility that the federal government might grow too powerful and autocratic. "We the people" therefore set limits on federal powers by guaranteeing some rights to the people, securing other rights to individuals, and reserving to the people authority not specifically granted to the federal government. Among these limits, the Fourth Amendment is best understood as guaranteeing a collective right – of a piece with the right to representative government, the right to assemble, the preservation of unenumerated rights, and the reservation of powers not delegated to the federal government.[98]

As a matter of fortuity, an originalist reading of the Fourth Amendment accords nicely the views of some contemporary living constitutionalists. For example, Justice Stephen Breyer has written extensively about his approach to constitutional interpretation, which seeks to maximize what he describes as "active liberty."[99] In contrast to liberty as simple freedom from unwarranted governmental coercion, active liberty emphasizes the democratic necessity of citizens' " 'active and constant participation in collective power.' "[100] In Breyer's view, the Constitution embodies a commitment to certain "ancient and unchanging ideals"[101] essential to preserving and expanding active liberty while protecting against the tyranny of the majority. Faith to these ideals, he argues, is essential to the proper functioning of our participatory democracy.[102] When interpreting the Constitution, Justice Breyer believes that judges should focus on the consequences for active liberty[103] with an eye on the overall goal of preserving conditions amenable to democratic participation. At least in the case of the Fourth Amendment, taking the text and history seriously yields a reading wholly amenable to Justice Breyer's version of living constitutionalism because it links rights against unreasonable search and seizure with other political rights.

Although the Fourth Amendment protects a collective right of the people rather than individual rights of each person, it provides important protections for individuals as well. As with the right of the people to elect their representatives, which entails a right of individuals to vote or otherwise contribute to the process of selection, rights reserved to "the people" provide protections for individuals as well.[104] All of us and each of us therefore have a right to be free from unreasonable search and seizure.[105] Individuals certainly have the right to challenge instances of government action and policies of search and seizure. But when a member of "the people" challenges a governmental search or seizure, she does not stand for herself alone. By invoking the protection of our collective right she also stands for "the people" as a whole.[106]

By way of summary, this section has shown that the Constitution wrestles with fundamental and timeless political challenges relating to the powers of government, limits on those powers, and the relationships between citizens, each other, and the state. In the process, it recognizes a people who claim some rights for themselves as "one Body Politick." The Constitution also reserves rights for individual members of that whole. As a matter of original public meaning, those choices were made clear to then contemporary readers by the plain language of the text. The Fourth Amendment right to be secure against unreasonable searches and seizures is one of the rights reserved to the people as a whole.[107] That is evidenced both by the plain language of the Fourth Amendment and the historical context in which it was drafted, adopted, and ratified. As that historical moment shows, then contemporary readers would have understood the Fourth Amendment as protecting rights held by "the people" as a whole against the government.[108]

This has important implications for the doctrine of Fourth Amendment standing. The Supreme Court has held that only individuals who suffer violations of their personal expectations of privacy may challenge a search or seizure. Furthermore, the Court limits the scope of these challenges to the facts of a particular search or seizure. As a result, individual litigants have a hard time challenging programs and policies. Taking seriously the text and history of the Fourth Amendment reveals that this is upside down. The Fourth Amendment is concerned primarily with policies and practices, such as general warrants and writs of assistance. Individual cases may provide examples of these kinds of policies and practices in action, as did the search of John Entick's home in the general warrants cases, but the primary concern is the threat against the right of the people these instances represent.

"The right of the people to be secure in their persons, houses, papers, and effects..."

If the Fourth Amendment aims to secure a collective right protecting the interests of the people in collective projects of self-governance, then the natural question is "What is that right?" Here again, the answer lies in the text. The right guaranteed to the people by the Fourth Amendment is the right "to be secure in their persons, houses, papers, and effects." In late eighteenth-century America, "to be" meant what it means now, "To have some certain state, condition, [or] quality." "Secure" too had a familiar meaning: "Free from fear [or] danger." The first definition of "person" in Samuel Johnson's 1768 *Dictionary of the English Language* is an "Individual or particular man or woman," but, given the collective dimension of the Fourth Amendment right, and the fact that the text reads "persons" rather than "person," most contemporary readers would have moved to Johnson's next entry, defining "person" as a "Man or woman considered as opposed to things." As a textual matter, and applying the canon of *noscitur a sociis*, that makes good sense given that "persons" is the first in a list otherwise comprised of things, including "houses" ("A place wherein a man lives; a place of human abode"), "papers" ("Substance on which men write and print"), and "effects" ("Goods; moveables").

By its plain language, the Fourth Amendment guarantees a collective right of the people to live in a state or condition characterized by freedom from fear or danger against some manner of threat to themselves, their living spaces, their written and printed materials, and their personal property.[109] Our forebears' interest in preserving this state of security and tranquility reflects their preoccupation with the threat to collective security posed by general warrants and writs of assistance.[110] Critics in the Americas and England knew that the kinds of broad, indiscriminate, and purely discretionary searches licensed by general warrants and writs of assistance threatened "the person and property of every man in this kingdom,"[111] and their "right[s] of personal security, personal liberty and private property."[112] Reflecting on that history a century after the founding, Justice Joseph Bradley noted that

> [t]he principles laid down in [the general warrants cases] affect the very essence of constitutional liberty and security. They reach farther than the concrete form of the case then before the court, with its adventitious circumstances; they apply to all invasions on the part of the government and its employees of the sanctity of a man's home and

the privacies of life. It is not the breaking of his doors, and the rummaging of his drawers, that constitutes the essence of the offence; but it is the invasion of his indefeasible right of personal security, personal liberty, and private property, where that right has never been forfeited by his conviction of some public offence, – it is the invasion of this sacred right which underlies and constitutes the essence of Lord Camden's judgment.[113]

Americans who read the Fourth Amendment in 1791 would have understood that it sought to secure a basic set of protections against threats to them, their homes, their writings, and their property that would leave them as "well-guarded as a prince in [their] castle[s]."[114] The next question is, then, what sort of threats against the security of the people did the Fourth Amendment target? The answer to this question lies in the phrase "searches and seizures."

"The right of the people to be secure in their persons, houses, papers, and effects against ... searches and seizures..."

The right of the people to be secure in their persons, houses, papers, and effects guaranteed by the Fourth Amendment is not absolute. The Fourth Amendment guarantees freedom from fear against "searches and seizures." It does not provide security against conduct that cannot fairly be described as a search or a seizure. But what constitutes a "search" or a "seizure" for purposes of the Fourth Amendment?

Samuel Johnson's 1792 *Dictionary of the English Language* defines "search" as "To examine; to try; to explore; to look through" and, citing John Locke, no less, "To make inquiry" or "To seek; to try to find." It further defines "seizure" as "The act of "tak[ing] possession of," "The act of taking forcible possession of," "grasp[ing], or "lay[ing] hold on." Thus, as a matter of plain meaning, "search" in the Fourth Amendment would have been understood by most founding-era readers in fairly colloquial terms as examining, seeking, or trying to find a person, exploring a house, looking through papers, or examining personal property. Similarly, "seizure" would have been understood in 1791 as taking forcible possession of a person, house, paper, or item of personal property.

These definitions of search and seizure reflect the historical context in which the Fourth Amendment was drafted and adopted. As we have seen, the general warrants cases in England and the writs of assistance cases in the colonies informed eighteenth-century readers' understanding of the Fourth Amendment. In these cases, government agents entered, explored, and looked through homes and businesses in search of seditious literature or contraband goods. In the course of those searches, they took possession by force of papers, personal property, and persons. Given the historically important roles played by these cases, this is probably the kind of conduct that would have come to mind when then contemporary readers came across the phrase "searches and seizures" in the Fourth Amendment.

Original public understandings of "search" and "seizure" stand in stark contrast to the technical definitions of "search" and "seizure" that define modern Fourth Amendment jurisprudence. As we saw in Chapter 2, the Supreme Court in *Katz v. United States* abandoned colloquial definitions of "search" and "seizure" for an inquiry focused on whether a government agent violates a subjectively manifested expectation of privacy that society recognizes as reasonable. This shift may have been rights-protective on the facts of that case. Unfortunately, the *Katz* test has spawned a series of doctrines that have left the people vulnerable to an expanding range of increasingly panvasive search techniques and technologies. The solution lies in taking seriously the original public meaning of "search" and "seizure."

As compared to the *Katz* test, a plain text reading of "search and seizure" hews much more closely to common sense. We have a pretty clear sense of what it means to search or seize, which accords with both dictionary meanings and common parlance. By contrast, the *Katz* definition of "search and seizure" is completely foreign to native speakers today and 1791. Take, for example, the third-party doctrine. The Court has held that when government agents seek, look for, examine, look through, or explore bank records or telephone call logs then this is not a "search" because it does not invade reasonable expectations of privacy. If we take the text of the Fourth Amendment seriously, then that result seems silly because it is silly. Likewise the public observation doctrine, which holds that looking through a garbage can, trespassing on "open fields" to seek evidence, hovering in a low-flying helicopter to examine a backyard, and seeking or trying to find someone as he drives along public streets is not a "search." For anyone whose mind is not poisoned by studying Fourth Amendment law, these are all textbook examples of what it means to search.

The *Katz* test also exhibits a deep confusion about the relationship between "unreasonable" and "search and seizure" in the text of the Fourth Amendment. *Katz* defines search and seizure in terms of reasonableness. It posits that "searches" are, by definition, "unreasonable" because they violate reasonable expectations of privacy. *Katz* therefore implies that there is no such thing as a "reasonable" search for purposes of the Fourth Amendment. If the conduct is "reasonable," then, according to *Katz*, it is not a "search." That is not only silly, but it also makes a mess of the phrase "unreasonable searches and seizures." After all, why include the adjective "unreasonable" if all searches and seizures are by definition unreasonable?

Taking the text seriously cleans up this mess quite nicely. As written, the Fourth Amendment guarantees security against unreasonable searches and seizures. It is therefore at the point of assessing whether a search is or may be "unreasonable" that courts should be concerned with reasonableness, not, as the *Katz* Court has had it, at the point of determining the meaning and scope of "search" and "seizure." If we take the text seriously, then, we should first determine whether government action constitutes examining, exploring, looking through, making inquiry, seeking, trying to find, taking possession of, grasping, or laying hold on. If it does, then we can move on to ask whether that act of searching or seizing threatens the right of the people to be secure against unreasonable searches and seizures. Jumping straight to assessments of reasonableness when defining search and seizure not only puts the cart before the horse, but it also forgets the horse entirely. Staying true to the text therefore requires abandoning both the third-party doctrine and the public observation doctrine.

"The right of the people to be secure in their persons, houses, papers, and effects against unreasonable searches and seizures . . ."

Although "search" and "seizure" would not have carried the weight of any technical meaning for most eighteenth-century American readers, "unreasonable" may well have had a more specialized meaning based on the use of "reasonable" in eighteenth-century common law,[115] and particularly in cases involving searches or seizures. As a methodological matter, we should nevertheless begin with the plain meaning of the words.

Samuel Johnson's 1792 *Dictionary of the English Language* defined "unreasonable" as "Not agreeable to reason," "Exorbitant; claiming or insisting on more than is fit," or "Greater than is fit; immoderate."

To answer the question begged by the first definition, Johnson's dictionary defined "reason" as "The power by which man deduces one proposition from another, or proceeds from premises to consequences," "Right; justice," or "Moderation." Thus, our forebears would have read "unreasonable" in the Fourth Amendment as describing a failure to conform to the demands of rational analysis or action ill-fitted to the circumstances. Unreasonable searches and seizures would, then, have been understood as searches and seizures conducted in the absence of good and sufficient reasons. The text itself only takes us this far. It is silent as to what kinds of reasons might count as good reasons and what sorts of reasons might be sufficient to justify searches or seizures. For eighteenth-century readers, that gap would have been filled by their formative experiences with general warrants and writs of assistance.

By 1791, common-law courts in England had roundly rejected general warrants as "unreasonable."[116] On this side of the Atlantic, James Otis famously railed against writs of assistance, marking "the first scene of the first act of opposition to the arbitrary claims of Great Britain."[117] In keeping with this history, the first draft of the Fourth Amendment submitted to the First Congress defined the right of security against unreasonable searches as a right to be free from the fear of searches conducted pursuant to general warrants.[118] That approach reflected language in several states' ratification statements[119] and parallel provisions in many state constitutions.[120] Although the final draft of the Fourth Amendment took a broader view of "unreasonable searches and seizures," the warrant clause remained, establishing a specific prohibition on general warrants.[121] In the context of investigating the original public meaning of "unreasonable searches and seizures," it is therefore important to understand why common-law courts and revolutionary-era critics thought ill of general warrants and writs of assistance because their *reasoning* would have informed then contemporary readers' understandings of what constituted an unreasonable search and seizure for purposes of the Fourth Amendment.

By definition, general warrants and writs of assistance were not specific as to the places to be searched or the goods, papers, and persons to be seized,[122] authorizing searches "without naming any person whatsoever in the warrant."[123] This raised serious concerns for eighteenth-century jurists. Relying on authorities like Sir Matthew Hale, common-law courts held that "such an uncertain warrant [is] void; and there is no case or book to the contrary."[124] Courts in post-Revolutionary America continued to identify lack of specificity as a hallmark of unreasonableness, striking down warrants that purported to allow searches of "all suspected places, stores, shops and barns"[125] rather than "limit[ing] the search to such particular place or places, as [the magistrate], from the circumstances, shall judge there is reason to suspect [that contraband will be found]."[126]

What was it about the generality of general warrants that provoked such strong reactions? It was the fact that they gave executive agents unfettered license to search wherever they pleased, for illegitimate reasons, for insufficient reasons, or no reason at all.[127] For example, the Court in *Money v. Leach*, one of the general warrants cases, held that "It is not fit, that the receiving or judging of the information should be left to the discretion of the officer."[128] In *Wilkes v. Wood*, another of the general warrants cases, Chief Justice Pratt condemned the prospect of "a discretionary power given to messengers to search wherever their suspicions may chance to fall."[129] Echoing these concerns in his speech against writs of assistance in Paxton's Case, James Otis worried that general warrants licensed executive agents to "imprison, or murder any one within the realm."[130] Based on this evidence, eighteenth-century readers would have regarded grants of broad and unfettered discretion as hallmarks of unreasonable searches and seizures.[131]

Because general warrants granted such broad discretion to conduct searches and seizures, those warrants effectively forgave any requirement that government agents provide good and sufficient reasons to justify searches and seizures before the fact. As the famous eighteenth-century legal historian William Blackstone noted in his *Commentaries on the Common Law*, "a justice of the peace cannot issue a warrant to apprehend a felon upon bare suspicion," but must instead "examine upon oath the party requiring the warrant."[132] By contrast, as the court in *Huckle v. Money*, another of the general warrants cases, pointed out, general warrants are unreasonable because they are issued "without any information or charge" establishing good and sufficient reasons to conduct a search or seizure.[133] Fifteen years after the Fourth Amendment was ratified, the United States Supreme Court reaffirmed the fact that baseless warrants were unreasonable, holding that a warrant issued for "want of stating some good cause certain, supported by oath" is unconstitutional.[134] Thus, searches conducted pursuant to general warrants were regarded as unreasonable in the late eighteenth century at least in part because they forgave any obligation to justify a search or seizure before the fact through a process of reason-giving before a neutral arbiter, such as a magistrate.

Another feature of general warrants and writs of assistance that made them unreasonable in the eyes of eighteenth-century courts and commentators was the fact that they excused agents who conducted searches or seizures from justifying their conduct to an independent reviewer after the fact. Under eighteenth-century common law, anyone conducting a search or seizure could be haled into court by the target of that search or seizure and compelled to justify himself by providing good and sufficient reasons for his actions in pain of potential civil liability.[135] General warrants and writs of assistance excused government agents from this common-law requirement by providing them with immunity against lawsuits. General warrants and writs of assistance also forgave any requirement to keep an inventory of the papers or property seized.[136] Finally, agents acting under the authority of general warrants or writs of assistance did not have to appear before a magistrate after conducting a search to explain their actions. This absence of accountability led James Otis to conclude that general warrants amounted to a license for executive agents to "reign secure in [their] petty tyranny, and spread terror and desolation around [them], until the trump of the Archangel shall excite different emotions in [their] soul[s] . . . and whether they break through malice or revenge, no man, no court can inquire."[137]

Eighteenth-century courts and critics also worried that general warrants and writs of assistance would allow government agents to conduct searches and seizures for illegitimate reasons. James Otis warned that "Every one with this writ may be a tyrant," conducting searches and seizures at his whim.[138] In support of his concerns, Otis cited a case where the holder of a writ of assistance – a man named Ware – was convicted of engaging in profanity on the Sabbath. Ware retaliated by searching the homes of the constable who charged him and the justice of the peace who convicted him "from the garret to the cellar" to show them "a little of my power."[139] Courts continued to worry about the possibility of searches conducted for illegitimate reasons in the early years after the Fourth Amendment was ratified and adopted. For example, in 1814 Chief Judge Tapping Reeve of the Connecticut Court of Errors struck down "a warrant to search all suspected places, stores, shops and barns in [town]" because the discretion granted the officers "would open a door for the gratification of the most malignant passions."[140]

To sum up a bit, general warrants and writs of assistance granted unfettered discretion to government agents, allowing them to search wherever and whomever they pleased. General warrants and writs of assistance did not require government agents to explain themselves or their reasons for conducting a particular search or seizure before the fact. They also provided immunity from civil actions and did not otherwise require any sort of procedural review after the fact. These features were what made searches and seizures conducted under the authority of general warrants unreasonable. We should therefore expect that eighteenth-century readers would have had these same considerations in mind when they read the Fourth Amendment.

This understanding of unreasonableness provides additional support for the proposition that the Fourth Amendment should be read as guaranteeing a collective right of the people rather than individual rights of each person. Few colonists were actually the victims of searches under the authority of writs of assistance. Very few had personal experience with the outrage and insecurity that comes from having one's door broken down and drawers rummaged through. What they did know, however, was that the very existence of general warrants and writs of assistance made them ever vulnerable to baseless or even malicious searches or seizures.[141] That general threat was certainly a concern in the general warrants cases, where courts pointed out that the broad powers granted by general warrants "may affect the person and property of every man in this kingdom"[142] and would "destroy all the comforts of society."[143] Those courts further criticized agents of the crown for "exercising arbitrary power, violating Magna Charta, and attempting to destroy the liberty of the kingdom, by insisting upon the legality of the general warrant."[144] Expanding on these concerns, James Otis worried about the rise of a surveillance state licensed by general warrants and a subsequent breakdown in social order where "one arbitrary exertion will provoke another, until society be involved in tumult and in blood."[145] Courts continued to cite the collective concerns raised by general warrants in the early years after ratification.[146] For example, Chief Judge Reeve of the Connecticut Court of Errors opined in 1814 that allowing a general warrant to stand would leave "every citizen of the United States within the jurisdiction ... liable to be arrested and carried before the justice for trial."[147]

As this history shows, the Fourth Amendment was not concerned with individual searches and seizures in isolation. The Fourth Amendment was, instead, concerned with laws and policies that left the people insecure against threats of unreasonable search and seizure by granting broad, unfettered discretion for government agents to search wherever they pleased and to seize whatever they liked without needing to justify their actions in a court of law.[148] This makes good sense. After all, individual searches and seizures, whether unreasonable or not, do not really pose a general threat to the people. Threats to the security of the people arise instead from the possibility that anyone could be subjected to an unreasonable search or seizure at any time. Eighteenth-century jurists and commentators criticized general warrants and writs of assistance because their very existence threatened the "person and property of every man,"[149] the "liberty of every man,"[150] and the security of "society"[151] as a whole.

This is not to suggest that the Fourth Amendment is completely uninterested in particular searches and seizures. Rather, the Fourth Amendment focuses on the features of particular searches and seizures that cast a broader or more general threat. It is particularly interested in the policy or practice that grants license to a particular search or seizure. If such a policy or practice (1) grants too much discretion to government agents; (2) insulates government agents from effective judicial restraint and accountability; or (3) otherwise threatens the right of the people to be secure in their persons, houses, papers, and effects against searches conducted for no reason, for insufficient reasons, or for illegitimate reasons, then that policy or practice violates the Fourth Amendment. Any search conducted pursuant to such a policy also violates the Fourth Amendment because it leaves the people as a whole insecure against threats of unreasonable searches and seizures.

This may seem a bit abstract. The best way to make it more concrete is to consider what it would mean in application. We will spend Chapters 5 and 6 doing just that, but we can get started here by asking what the Fourth Amendment itself did about threats of unreasonable searches and seizures. The answer is found in the last phrase of the reasonableness clause, which provides that the right of the people to be secure against unreasonable searches and seizures "shall not be violated," and the warrant clause, which offers an example of how that imperative can be vindicated by enforcing prospective remedies designed to limit discretion, enforce some form of accountability, and otherwise provide a sense of security for the people against threats of unreasonable search and seizure.

> "The right of the people to be secure in their persons, houses, papers, and effects against unreasonable searches and seizures shall not be violated . . ."

The reasonableness clause ends with a declaration that the collective right of the people to live in a state or condition characterized by freedom from fear or danger that their living spaces will be explored, their written and printed materials looked through or taken, their personal property examined or taken, and their persons sought, examined, or restrained for no reason, insufficient reasons, illegitimate reasons, or based solely on the unfettered discretion of executive agents acting beyond the reach of effective judicial constraint or review "shall not be violated." "Violate" meant to 1791 readers what it means to us today: "to injure; to hurt" or "to infringe." "Shall," by contrast, requires a bit more interpretive care.

Largely absent from twenty-first-century common parlance, the meaning of "shall" may be somewhat mysterious to modern readers. In early English "shall" was an independent verb.[152] It was later relegated to the category of modal auxiliaries, whose exclusive service is to modify the meanings of other verbs.[153] To understand the modal meaning of "shall" it is helpful to consider it in contrast with "will." As compared to "will," "shall" suggests external compulsion as in the commandment "Thou shalt not kill." On the other hand, "will" connotes an internal motive linked to the subject's own motives as in "I will do my best." In terms of their modal usage, these basic meanings of "shall" and "will" appear to have remained fairly stable well into the modern era.[154] That began to change, however, as both "shall" and "will" emerged in constructions designed to communicate what grammarian Cornelius Beach Bradley has described as the "colorless future."[155]

According to Bradley, early English did not have the resources necessary to describe the future in purely neutral terms without implying either command or actions of will.[156] Speakers therefore experimented with various ways to express the idea of colorless futurity, sometimes by using "shall" and "will." As a result, the meanings of "shall" and "will" became somewhat confused over time. "Shall" sometimes was used to communicate compulsion and other times to predict what was to come. Likewise, speakers sometimes used "will" to report internal states of inclination or desire, but other times as a way to predict what was going to happen.

Over time, the overlapping usage of "shall" and "will" that resulted from efforts to construct a colorless future tense broke down the borders between their original modal meanings. As a consequence, native speakers started using "shall" to report not only commands, but also personal plans born of their own wills, as in Douglass MacArthur's famous March 21, 1942, promise "I shall return." Likewise, speakers began to use "will" not only to describe situations where someone acted on her own volition but also in circumstances where action was dictated externally, such as when a parent punishes her child by commanding "You will not go out on Saturday night." By the late twentieth century, common usage had rendered "shall" and "will" so unreliably equivocal in terms of their modal meanings that the federal government's Plain Language Action and Information Network advised those drafting formal documents to abandon "shall" altogether in favor of "must" when they meant to suggest obligation,[157] leaving pure futurity solely to the domain of "will."

One might object that some of these examples simply reflect bad grammar. Like all linguistic conventions, however, grammar evolves over time, accommodating the inevitable evolutions of natural language through usage.[158] This division between formal rules and common usage complicates our quest to understand the meaning of "shall" in the Fourth Amendment. As linguist Charles Fries has noted, eighteenth-century guides to English grammar and usage were more proscriptive than descriptive, which makes them singularly unhelpful if the goal is to determine original public meaning. Moreover, the most authoritative of these guides are far from illuminating. For example, Samuel Johnson defines "shall" as the future tense of "should," which certainly suggests a degree of externally generated obligation rather than mere futurity. Unfortunately, in his essay on usage, prepended to his *Dictionary of the English Language*, he suggests that "shall" may be used in a purely predictive fashion, just like "will,"[159] and Johnson routinely uses "shall" to suggest mere futurity in his own prose.[160] Noah Webster attempted to be more helpful, suggesting in his 1793 *Grammatical Institute of the English Language* that, when used in the future tense, "shall" in the first person merely foretells, while "shall" in the second or the third person commands or promises.[161] Unfortunately, his own usage does not always conform to this rule, as when he writes that he "shall always feel indebted to the man who shall suggest any improvements" and "Here, therefore, shall be added some further examples."[162]

Given all of this confusion, it is no surprise that there is a considerable academic literature on the uses of "shall" and "will," some of which is addressed specifically to the use of "shall" in the US Constitution.[163] We are fortunate, however, in that the meaning and mode of "shall" in legal contexts appear to have been fairly stable through at least the late eighteenth century, where it always communicated the "superior authority in commands and laws" when used in "legislative forms"[164] as in the phrase "thou shalt not kill."

Attributing this modal meaning to "shall" in the Fourth Amendment certainly makes sense in context. The Fourth Amendment is prescriptive rather than predictive. It would therefore be very odd to read the phrases "shall not be violated" and "shall not issue" in the Fourth Amendment as mere predictions of what was not to come rather than commands relying on legal authority. All the more so given that there were instances of unreasonable searches and seizures in the years immediately after the Fourth Amendment was ratified.[165] Each of these failures would prove the Fourth Amendment wrong if it was merely predicting. Given the context and available evidence, we can therefore be fairly safe in assuming that most readers in 1791 would have read the Fourth Amendment as prescribing and commanding rather than projecting and predicting.

With the benefit of this final interpretive insight, we now have before us a pretty clear idea of the original public meaning of the reasonableness clause. Most founding-era readers would have read the reasonableness clause as commanding future governments not to injure or infringe upon the collective right of the people to live free from fear that their living spaces would be explored, their written and printed materials looked through or taken, their personal property examined or taken, and their persons sought, examined, or restrained for no reason, for insufficient reasons, for illegitimate reasons, or based solely on the unfettered discretion of executive agents acting beyond the reach of effective judicial constraint or review. Given the prominent historical place of general warrants and writs of assistance, then contemporary readers would have read the Fourth Amendment as being particularly concerned with laws and policies that licensed programs of broad and indiscriminate search and seizure, granted unfettered discretion to executive agents, allowed for searches in the absence of sufficient cause, or failed to provide some form of accountability. These, after all, were precisely the concerns raised by courts and critics with respect to general warrants and writs of assistance and therefore would have informed eighteenth-century readers' understanding of the Fourth Amendment.

> "The right of the people to be secure in their persons, houses, papers, and effects against unreasonable searches and seizures shall not be violated, and no warrants shall issue, but upon probable cause, supported by oath or affirmation, and particularly describing the place to be searched, and the persons or things to be seized"

If the reasonableness clause issues an imperative command that forbids conduct, policies, and practices that threatened the right of the people to be secure against unreasonable searches and seizures, then the next natural questions run to who has the power to enforce that command and how. The answer is found in the warrant clause.

Our eighteenth-century forebears understood that the road to tyranny often is paved by the best of intentions. As the Maryland Farmer, a prominent founding-era pamphleteer, pointed out in one of his Anti-Federalist broadsides, general warrants are particularly tempting "in those cases which may strongly interest the passions of government."[166] Half a generation before him, the Canadian Freeholder offered similar observations in his commentaries on the general warrants cases, noting that appointed members of the executive are "fond of doctrines of reason of state, and state necessity, and the impossibility of providing for great emergencies and extraordinary cases, without a discretionary power in the crown to proceed sometimes by uncommon methods not agreeable to the known forms of law."[167] Because they understood these quite natural institutional motives common to all executives, our founders sought to guarantee a general right of security from unreasonable searches and seizures through the enforcement of policies and procedures capable of constraining government agents and limiting the discretionary authority of those wielding the truncheon of state power.[168] Eighteenth-century common law and the warrant clause together offer a blueprint for what they had in mind.

Before issuing specific warrants, common-law courts in the eighteenth century usually required that applicants appear before a judicial officer and offer evidence under oath sufficient to provide "strong reason to believe" that contraband would be found in the place to be searched.[169] Questions of "reason and convenience" were not to be "left to the discretion of the officer," but resided instead with a magistrate, who had authority to give "certain directions to the officer."[170] By the late eighteenth century, prospective constraints on searches and seizures imposed by the process of seeking and receiving specific warrants had become so entrenched in the common law that most commentators considered them to be part of the English constitution.[171] Parliament declined to extend those protections to the colonists, however, effectively abrogating rights guaranteed to other British subjects by granting customs agents in the colonies access to writs of assistance. One of the principal concerns confronting those who met in Philadelphia during the hot summer of 1787 was that the proposed federal government might take similar steps, abrogating by federal statute rights guaranteed under the common law and by state constitutions.[172] Those worries carried over to the ratification debates[173] where Anti-Federalists and other constitutional critics worried about granting too much authority to the federal government.[174]

Faced with threats of general warrants, too easy access to more specific warrants, and similar laws and policies allowing searches and seizures licensed "by uncommon methods not agreeable to the known forms of law," the First Congress decided that the only way to guarantee the security of the people was to impose prospective constraints on warranted searches that would be sufficient to guarantee a collective sense of security against "general exploratory searches ... based only on the eagerness of officers to get hold of whatever evidence they may be able to bring to light."[175] This is precisely what the warrant clause does. By banning general warrants and limiting access to specific warrants, the warrant clause promises security for the people against threats of unreasonable searches or seizures conducted under the authority of warrants, thereby allowing all of us and each of us to feel secure in ways that we otherwise could not and would not if government agents had access to general warrants and writs of assistance.[176]

The warrant clause does more than constitutionalize common-law warrant procedures. It also serves as a model for how the imperative command issued by the reasonableness clause can be fulfilled. The reasonableness clause commands that the right of the people to be secure from unreasonable searches and seizures "shall not be violated." Those who read the Fourth Amendment in 1791 understood well that abstract commands are not enough to constrain governments against the temptations of power, privilege, and emergency. They knew that the only way to guarantee the right of the people against threats of legislative encroachment or executive overreach was to establish a constitutional requirement for concrete constraints[177] that would prevent unreasonable searches in the first place.[178] This is precisely what the reasonableness clause does. It guarantees the collective right of the people to prospective constraints on the government and its agents that are sufficient to guarantee that the people can live free from fear of being subjected to unreasonable searches and seizures. Thus, the Fourth Amendment is not merely an instantiation of rights; it is a call to action. It demands that the political branches commit to policies of restraint. Where they fail to do so, the Fourth Amendment requires that courts, acting as constitutional guardians, impose prospective remedial measures sufficient to effectively guarantee the security of the people against threats of unreasonable searches and seizures.[179] In short, the Fourth Amendment guarantees a collective right to prospective remedies.

The warrant clause provides a valuable model of the kinds of prospective remedies that might be sufficient to fulfill the imperative command issued by the reasonableness clause. It sets limits on the discretionary authority of executive agents to conduct searches and seizures. It requires that government agents have good and sufficient reasons for conducting searches and seizures. It lodges authority to judge the merits and sufficiency of these reasons with a neutral party. Finally, it sets limits on the scope of searches and seizures. These features of the warrant clause allow all of us and each of us to live relatively free from fear that government agents will be able to secure authority to engage in programs of broad and indiscriminate search or seizure.

To be sure, those who read and wrote the Fourth Amendment in 1791 understood that protections afforded by the Fourth Amendment come with a cost.[180] As the Pennsylvania Supreme Court reported in 1810:

> It is true, that by insisting on an oath, felons may sometimes escape. This must have been very well known to the framers of our constitution; but they thought it better that the guilty should sometimes escape, than that every individual should be subject to vexation and oppression.[181]

Despite the costs, the founding generation regarded as sacred their basic security against threats that government agents might at any moment search or seize their persons, houses, papers, or effects without sufficient good reasons and free from any form of legal accountability. They therefore adopted and ratified the Fourth Amendment "to prevent the government from functioning as in a police state."[182]

Importantly, the warrant clause does not exhaust the universe of remedial measures licensed by the Fourth Amendment. General warrants and writs of assistance posed the primary threats against the security of the people against unreasonable searches and seizures in the late eighteenth century. The warrant clause addressed general warrants and writs of assistance directly. As we have seen in this chapter, however, the reasonableness clause does more than just ban general warrants. It addresses all threats to the right of the people to be secure against unreasonable searches and seizures – even those unknown in 1791. In this regard, our originalist reading of the Fourth Amendment seems to converge with more activist interpretations that might be advanced by living constitutionalists because it recognizes that fulfilling the imperative command that the right of the people "shall not be violated" requires addressing new and emerging threats of unreasonable search and seizure and enforcing new prospective remedies.

Conclusion

As we will see in the next chapter, the Supreme Court seized upon its Fourth Amendment authority to propound new constitutional remedies several times during the course of the twentieth century. In each of these instances, the Court created prospective remedies designed to deal with new and emerging threats to the Fourth Amendment rights of the people. These experiences have much to teach us about how the courts might respond to some of the threats posed by the means and methods discussed in Chapter 1. In Chapter 6, we shall apply those lessons.

Notes

1. Silverthorne v. United States, 251 U.S. 385, 392 (1920).
2. Trop v. Dulles, 356 U.S. 86, 101 (1958).
3. STEPHEN BREYER, ACTIVE LIBERTY: INTERPRETING OUR DEMOCRATIC CONSTITUTION (2008).
4. U.S. CONST. pmbl.
5. Plessy v. Ferguson, 163 U.S. 537 (1896).
6. Brown v. Bd. of Educ., 347 U.S. 483 (1954).
7. Stanford v. Kentucky, 492 U.S. 361 (1989).
8. Roper v. Simmons, 543 U.S. 551 (2005).
9. United States v. Knotts, 460 U.S. 276, 284 (1983).
10. *See Jones*, 132 S. Ct. at 953.
11. ANTONIN SCALIA, A MATTER OF INTERPRETATION 40–41 (1997).
12. *See Jones*, 132 S. Ct. at 962 (Alito, J., concurring) ("[T]he *Katz* test rests on the assumption that this hypothetical reasonable person has a well-developed and stable set of privacy expectations. But technology can change those expectations.

Dramatic technological change may lead to periods in which popular expectations are in flux and may ultimately produce significant changes in popular attitudes. New technology may provide increased convenience or security at the expense of privacy, and many people may find the tradeoff worthwhile. And even if the public does not welcome the diminution of privacy that new technology entails, they may eventually reconcile themselves to this development as inevitable.").

13. Kyllo v. United States, 533 U.S. 27, 34 (2001).
14. *See* JED RUBENFELD, FREEDOM AND TIME (2001)
15. JON ELSTER, ULYSSES AND THE SIRENS: STUDIES IN RATIONALITY AND IRRATIONALITY 36–47 (1979).
16. HOMER, ODYSSEY XII, 39.
17. David Gray, *Why Justice Scalia Should Be a Constitutional Comparativist ... Sometimes*, 59 STAN. L. REV. 1249, 1266 (2007).
18. *See* RUBENFELD, *supra* note 14.
19. *See infra* at notes 166–10 and accompanying text.
20. *See, e.g.*, William Baude, *Is Originalism Our Law?*, 115 COLUM. L. REV. 2349 (2015).
21. Courtney Such, *Poll: Public Displeased with Supreme Court*, Real Clear Politics, May 20, 2014, www.realclearpolitics.com/articles/2014/05/20/poll_public_displea sed_with_supreme_court_122690.html. The poll, which was conducted by the Mellman Group, http://big.assets.huffingtonpost.com/SupremeCourtPoll2014.pdf.
22. *See, e.g., Jones*, 953–54.
23. James Madison, Speech to the House of Representatives, June 8, 1789, *in* 12 THE PAPERS OF JAMES MADISON 201 (Robert A. Rutland et al., eds. 1979).
24. Thomas Davies has argued that it was Elbridge Gerry of Massachusetts, not Egbert Benson, who lodged this objection and moved to divide the two clauses of the Fourth Amendment. Thomas Y. Davies, *Recovering the Original Fourth Amendment*, 98 MICH. L. REV. 547, 717–18 (1999). As Professor Davies admits, however, there is insufficient conclusive evidence as to whether it was Benson or Gerry. *Id.* Moreover, it does not matter who made the motion. For present purposes, what really matters is that it was made and passed.
25. NELSON B. LASSON, THE HISTORY AND DEVELOPMENT OF THE FOURTH AMENDMENT TO THE UNITED STATES CONSTITUTION 101 (1970).
26. *See* 2A NORMAN J. SINGER & J.D. SHAMBIE SINGER, SUTHERLAND STATUTES AND STATUTORY CONSTRUCTION § 47:24 (7th ed., rev. vol. 2013) (pointing out that drafters of legislation are presumed to know the relevant existing law).
27. *See* Anthony G. Amsterdam, *Perspectives on the Fourth Amendment*, 58 MINN. L. REV. 349, 399 (1974) ("What we do know, because the language of the fourth amendment says so, is that the framers were disposed to generalize to some extent beyond the evils of the immediate past.").
28. Boyd v. United States, 116 U.S. 616, 626–27 (1886) ("Lord Camden pronounced the judgment of the court in Michaelmas Term, 1765, and the law as expounded by him has been regarded as settled from that time to this, and his great judgment on that occasion is considered as one of the landmarks of English liberty. It was welcomed and applauded by the lovers of liberty in the colonies, as well as in the mother country. It is regarded as one of the permanent monuments of the British Constitution, and is quoted as such by the English authorities on that subject

down to the present time. As every American statesman, during our revolutionary and formative period as a nation, was undoubtedly familiar with this monument of English freedom, and considered it as the true and ultimate expression of constitutional law, it may be confidently asserted that its propositions were in the minds of those who framed the Fourth Amendment to the Constitution, and were considered as sufficiently explanatory of what was meant by unreasonable searches and seizures.").

29. Akhil Reed Amar, *Fourth Amendment First Principles*, 107 HARV. L. REV. 757, 778 (1994).
30. *Id.* at 778; 4 WILLIAM BLACKSTONE, COMMENTARIES *288 ("[A] lawful warrant will at all events indemnify the officer, who executes the same ministerially.").
31. Davies, *supra* note 24, at 585-90.
32. *Cf. id.* at 629 (citing Entick v. Carrington (1765), 95 Eng. Rep. 807 (KB), 19 Howell's St. Tr. 1029 (1765)).
33. Wilkes v. Wood (1763) 98 Eng. Rep. 489 (KB). *See also Entick*, 95 Eng. Rep. at 817 ("[W]e can safely say there is no law in this country to justify the defendants in what they have done; if there was, it would destroy all the comforts of society ..."); TELFORD TAYLOR, TWO STUDIES IN CONSTITUTIONAL INTERPRETATION 33, 35 (1969) (recounting how members of Parliament and other elites felt threatened by the use of general warrants in the Wilkes case); Donald L. Doernberg, *"We the People": John Locke, Collective Constitutional Rights, and Standing to Challenge Government Action*, 73 CALIF. L. REV. 52, 57-58 (1985) (noting that "most eighteenth-century liberal doctrines can be traced to Locke and his concept that community power resides in the majority").
34. *Entick; Wilkes*; LASSON, *supra* note 25, at 37.
35. 10 THE WORKS OF JOHN ADAMS, SECOND PRESIDENT OF THE UNITED STATES: WITH THE LIFE OF THE AUTHOR, NOTES AND ILLUSTRATIONS, BY HIS GRANDSON CHARLES FRANCIS ADAMS 248 (C. Adams ed., 1856).
36. Riley v. California, 134 S. Ct. 2473, 2494 (2014).
37. These states were Delaware, Maryland, Massachusetts, New Hampshire, North Carolina, Pennsylvania, Virginia, and Vermont. Connecticut and Rhode Island did not have constitutions in 1789. Connecticut adopted its first constitution in 1818. Rhode Island did not adopt a constitution until 1842. New York, New Jersey, South Carolina, and Georgia all had constitutions, but none addresses searches and seizures. *See* WILLIAM CUDDIHY, THE FOURTH AMENDMENT: ORIGINS AND ORIGINAL MEANING 602-1791, at 852 (2009).
38. SAMUEL JOHNSON, A DICTIONARY OF THE ENGLISH LANGUAGE (10th ed. 1792).
39. District of Columbia v. Heller, 554 U.S. 570, 581 (2008); ANTONIN SCALIA & BRYAN A. GARNER, READING LAW: THE INTERPRETATION OF LEGAL TEXTS 419 (2012) (citing JOHNSON, *supra* note 38, as among "the most useful and authoritative ['contemporaneous-usage dictionaries'] for the English language generally and for the law").
40. Doernberg, *supra* note 33, at 59-66. *See, e.g.*, The Proceedings Relative to Calling the Convention of 1776 and 1790: The Minutes of the Convention that Formed the Present Constitution of Pennsylvania 55 (1776) [hereinafter Pennsylvania

Proceedings] (asserting that legitimate governmental authority is "derived from, and founded on the authority of the people only"); A [MARYLAND] FARMER, NO. 1 (1788) (objecting to the federal constitution on the grounds that it contained no bill of rights, thereby denying citizens the ability to "plead ... and produce Locke, Sydney, or Montesquieu as authority" in defense of "natural right"). DAVID W. MINAR, IDEAS AND POLITICS: THE AMERICAN EXPERIENCE 47 (1964) ("Locke can be regarded as the advance ideologist of the American Revolution. He developed a set of political ideas which has very largely served as the basis for American political values and for the institutional structure which American and British government has since assumed. His importance for American political thought can hardly be overestimated; indeed, there is probably no better short summary of the ideas of Locke than the American Declaration of Independence.").

41. JOHN LOCKE, *Second Treatise, in* TWO TREATISES OF GOVERNMENT AND A LETTER CONCERNING TOLERATION 141–42 (Ian Shapiro, ed. 2003).
42. *Id. Cf.* Entick v. Carrington, 19 Howell's St. Tr. 1029, 1066 (1765) (KB) ("The great end, for which men entered into society, was to secure their property.").
43. Doernberg, *supra* note 33, at 61–62.
44. LOCKE, *supra* note 41, at 141–42.
45. *Id.* at 188–93.
46. At least one prominent originalist has endorsed the idea that Preambles play an important role in interpreting texts.

    See SCALIA & GARNER, *supra* note 39, at 218 ("[T]he preamble of a statute is a key to open the mind of the makers, as to the mischiefs, which are to be remedied, and the objects, which are to be accomplished by the provisions of the statute." (quoting 1 JOSEPH STORY, COMMENTARIES ON THE CONSTITUTION OF THE UNITED STATES § 459, at 326 (2d ed. 1858))).
47. LOCKE, *supra* note 41, at 164, 166, 171–72.
48. William Tudor, *James Otis's Speech on the Writs of Assistance 1761, in* AMERICAN HISTORY LEAFLETS: COLONIAL AND CONSTITUTIONAL NO. 33, at 18, 19 (Albert Bushness Hart & Edward Channing, eds. 1906) ("He asserted that [property] rights were inherent and inalienable. That they never could be surrendered or alienated but by idiots or madmen, and all the acts of idiots and lunatics were void, and not obligatory, by all the laws of God and man." "In short, he asserted [property] rights to be derived only from nature, and the author of nature; that they were inherent, inalienable, and indefeasible by any laws, pacts, contracts, covenants, or stipulations, which man could devise. These principles and these rights were wrought into the English constitution, as fundamental laws.").
49. BREYER, *supra* note 3.
50. JOHNSON, *supra* note 38.
51. SINGER & SINGER, *supra* note 26, at 195; SCALIA, *supra* note 11, at 26.
52. JOHNSON, *supra* note 38.
53. U.S. CONST. pmbl. ("We the People of the United States, in order to form a more perfect union ..."). As a point of comparison, Article I, section 2 refers to "the People of the several States," who have the right to choose their representatives in the House. U.S. CONST. art. I, § 2.

54. *See* Samson v. California, 547 U.S. 843 (2006) (allowing suspicionless searches of parolees); Hudson v. Palmer, 468 U.S. 517 (1984) (allowing routine searches of prisoners' cells).
55. *See* United States v. Verdugo-Urquidez, 494 U.S. 259, 265 (1990) (" '[T]he people' protected by the Fourth Amendment, and by the First and Second Amendments, and to whom rights and powers are reserved in the Ninth and Tenth Amendments, refers to a class of persons who are part of a national community or who have otherwise developed sufficient connection with this country to be considered part of that community."). On this point, the *Heller* Court seems inclined to agree. *See* District of Columbia v. Heller, 554 U.S. 570, 579–81 (2008).
56. *See, e.g., Heller*, 554 U.S. at 579 (asserting that "the right of the people" protected by the Fourth Amendment "unambiguously refer[s] to individual rights, not 'collective' rights, or rights that may be exercised only through participation in some corporate body"); Donald L. Doernberg, *"The Right of the People": Reconciling Collective and Individual Interests Under the Fourth Amendment*, 58 N.Y.U. L. REV. 259, 260 (1983). *But see Heller*, 554 U.S. at 580 (concluding that "the people" as used in the Fourth Amendment "refers to all members of the political community, not an unspecified subset").
57. *See generally* David Gray, *Dangerous Dicta*, 72 WASH. & LEE L. REV. 1181 (2015).
58. Donald Doernberg traces this collective dimension of the Constitution to John Locke and his influence on our Revolutionary forebears and the framing generation. Doernberg, *supra* note 33, at 57–58.
59. As Justice Scalia has noted, preambles are relevant sources for determining textual meaning. SCALIA & GARNER, *supra* note 39, at 217–20.
60. *See, e.g.*, THE DECLARATION OF INDEPENDENCE (U.S. 1776). *See also* Pennsylvania Proceedings, *supra* note 40, pmbl. ("We, the representatives of the freemen of Pennsylvania, in general convention met, for the express purpose of framing such a government, confessing the goodness of the great governor of the universe (who alone knows to what degree of earthly happiness mankind may attain by perfecting the arts of government) in permitting the people of this state, by common consent and without violence, deliberately to form for themselves, such just rules as they shall think best for governing their future society; and being fully convinced, that it is our indispensable duty, to establish such original principles of government, as will best promote the general happiness of the people of this state and their posterity, and provide for future improvements ... do, by virtue of the authority vested in us by our constituents ordain declare and establish the following declaration of rights, and frame of government, to be the constitution of this commonwealth ...").
61. *See* ARTICLES OF CONFEDERATION OF 1781, art. IV.
62. U.S. CONST. art. I, § 2.
63. *See* District of Columbia v. Heller, 554 U.S. 570, 579–80 (2008) (conceding that "the people" as used in Article I "arguably refer[s] to 'the people' acting collectively").
64. U.S. CONST. amend. X. *See also Heller*, 554 U.S. at 579–80 (conceding that "the people" as used in the Tenth Amendment "arguably refer[s] to 'the people' acting collectively").
65. U.S. CONST. amend. IV. In *Heller*, the Court asserts that the Fourth Amendment "unambiguously refer[s] to individual rights, not 'collective' rights, or rights that may be exercised only through participation in some corporate body." 554 U.S. at 579. This, of course, is dicta – and dangerous dicta at that

insofar as the Court's pronouncement was made without the benefit of any record regarding the text and history of the Fourth Amendment. See Gray, *supra* note 57. On a fuller record, the Court would have been hard-pressed to avoid the conclusion that the Fourth Amendment unambiguously refers to collective rights. For example, the dicta in *Heller* violates the first canon of textual interpretation: that words should be given their ordinary meaning. See *Heller*, 554 U.S. at 576-77; SCALIA & GARNER, *supra* note 39, at 69-77. Furthermore, both the historical record and the Court's own jurisprudence suggest that the Fourth Amendment unambiguously refers to individual rights that can only be exercised through membership in a group: "the people." See United States v. Verdugo-Urquidez, 494 U.S. 259, 265-75 (1990). Moreover, as the Court pointed out in *Verdugo-Urquidez*, the framer's use of "the people" in the First, Second, Fourth, Ninth, and Tenth Amendments strikes an important contrast between their use of "person" and "accused" in the Fifth and Sixth Amendments, further suggesting that the Fourth Amendment has critical collective dimensions. 494 U.S. at 265-66. This choice lines up with similar choices made in then-contemporary state constitutions, and particularly the Pennsylvania Declaration of Rights. See *infra* notes 67-68 and accompanying text. The Court's contemporary exclusionary rule cases also focus on the collective dimensions of Fourth Amendment rights, maintaining that exclusion is justified only insofar as it can promote the general security of the people in their persons, houses, papers, and effects. See infra Chapter 5. Ultimately, of course, it is not at all clear that the *Heller* Court would disagree. Just a few sentences after issuing its dangerous dicta, it adopts the more defensible view that "the people" "unambiguously refers to all members of the political community, not an unspecified subset." 554 U.S. at 580.
66. 2A SINGER & SINGER, *supra* note 26, § 47:24 (pointing out that drafters are presumed to know the relevant existing law).
67. PA. CONST., Declaration of Rights, art. X (1776).
68. MA. CONST., Declaration of Rights, art. XIV (1780). The New Hampshire Constitution uses "hath" rather than "has," but is in all other respects identical. See N.H. CONST., art. XIX (1784). See also Ratification Statement from New York (1788) (recommending that the Constitution protect, inter alia, the right of "every freeman ... to be secure from all unreasonable searches and seizures ..."); Ratification Statement from Virginia (1788) (same); Ratification Statement from North Carolina (1788) (same).
69. Thomas K. Clancy, *The Framers' Intent: John Adams, His Era, and the Fourth Amendment*, 86 IND. L.J. 979, 979-80 (2011).
70. Boyd v. United States, 116 U.S. 616, 625 (1886); TAYLOR, *supra* note 33, at 43.
71. See CUDDIHY, *supra* note 37, at 602-791, 729.
72. See SINGER & SINGER, *supra* note 26, at 425-26, 429, 446; YULE KIM, CONG. RESEARCH SERV., NO. 97-589, STATUTORY INTERPRETATION: GENERAL PRINCIPLES AND RECENT TRENDS 42 (2008); R.E.H., Annotation, *Resort to Constitutional or Legislative Debates, Committee Reports, Journals, etc., as Aid in Construction of Statute*, 70 A.L.R. 5 (1931); Richard H. Fallon, Jr., *A Constructivist Coherence Theory of Constitutional Interpretation*, 100 HARV. L. REV. 1189, 1194-209, 1237-45 (1987). *Cf.* United States v. Verdugo-Urquidez, 494 U.S. 259, 265-66 (1990) (assigning significance to choices made by the drafters to use "the

people," "person," and "accused"); SCALIA & GARNER, *supra* note 39, at 256 (acknowledging the canon of interpretation under which "If the legislature amends or reenacts a provision ... a significant change in language is presumed to entail a change in meaning."). The negative implication canon, *expressio unius est exclusio alterius*, holds that a statement's meaning may derive not only from what is said, but also what is not said. SCALIA & GARNER, *supra* note 39, at 107.
73. *See* PA. CONST., pmbl. ("[A]ll government ought to be instituted and supported for the security and protection of the community as such, and to enable the individuals who compose it, to enjoy their natural rights ..."). Differences in phrasing among these different provisions show differences in meaning.
74. KIM, *supra* note 72, at 14–15.
75. That this choice should be afforded significance when interpreting the text is a matter of *in pari materia*. *See* SCALIA & GARNER, *supra* note 39, at 252–55; KIM, *supra* note 72, at 14, 15, 42.
76. *See* Tudor, *supra* note 48, at 18 ("He asserted that [property] rights were inherent and inalienable. That they never could be surrendered or alienated, but by idiots or madmen, and all the acts of idiots and lunatics were void, and not obligatory, by all the laws of God and man.").
77. Doernberg, *supra* note 33, at 60–61.
78. All of this comes into clearer focus if we consider the definitions of basic terms used in Pennsylvania's founding documents. Again relying on Samuel Johnson's *Dictionary of the English Language*, those who read the Pennsylvania Declaration in 1776 would have understood "commonwealth" as "the general body of the people," a collective entity. They, in turn, would have regarded the "nation" in reference to "the people in general." The fact that "the people," "the commonwealth," and "the nation" precede the government, and therefore set the conditions of any contract creating government authority is evident in then-contemporary definitions of key political terms. For example, they regarded "democracy" as "a form of government ... in which the sovereign power is lodged with the people" "republican" as "Placing the government in the people." Conceptually and semantically, it therefore makes sense to think of political rights, which regulate the government, as rights held first by "the people." JOHNSON, *supra* note 38.
79. In District of Columbia v. Heller, 554 U.S. 570 (2008), the United States Supreme Court rejected a plain-text reading of the Second Amendment. Although it is beyond the scope of this book, the Court's reasoning in that case is deeply flawed. Based on the text of the Second Amendment and the historical context in which it was adopted, it is quite clear that eighteenth century readers would have understood the right to bear arms as a political right that was secured to the people as a check on overreaching government power. Those concerns were particularly salient during the ratification debates, where the primary concern was that the newly instituted federal government would overpower state governments, treading on both the sovereignty of states and the rights guaranteed to citizens of those states by their state constitutions. Particularly in light of the important roles played by state and local militias during the Revolution, it therefore comes as no surprise that our founders would have wanted to preserve state and local militias as checks on the federal government. For similar reasons, they were very skeptical of the idea

that the federal government would or could maintain a standing army. This is not to suggest that the Second Amendment does not also protect the rights of individuals to keep and bear arms. It surely does. The point, instead, is that this individual right derives from a collective right to keep and bear arms just as the right to vote derives from the collective right of the people to choose their government. Neither does the plain text of the Second Amendment suggest that an individual must be a member of a militia in order to keep or bear arms. The prefatory clause of the Second Amendment provides important context to be sure, but, as a grammatical matter, it does not limit the extension of "the people" in the second clause. Moreover, it was standard practice in late eighteenth-century America for citizens, whether members of militia or not, to keep firearms in their homes. In short, the *Heller* Court reached the right holding but for the wrong reasons. Justice Scalia, who wrote the majority opinion in *Heller*, could have remained faithful to the original public meaning of the text while also upholding an individual right of members of "the people" to keep and bear arms. As it stands, however, *Heller* reads as an instance of method bowing to results – a sad legacy indeed for the leading originalist of his generation.

80. Goldman v. United States, 316 U.S. 129, 142 (1942) (Murphy, J., dissenting) ("The benefits that accrue from this and other articles of the Bill of Rights are characteristic of democratic rule. They are among the amenities that distinguish a free society from one in which the rights and comforts of the individual are wholly subordinated to the interests of the state. We cherish and uphold them as necessary and salutary checks on the authority of government. They provide a standard of official conduct which the courts must enforce. At a time when the nation is called upon to give freely of life and treasure to defend and preserve the institutions of democracy and freedom, we should not permit any of the essentials of freedom to lose vitality through legal interpretations that are restrictive and inadequate for the period in which we live."); Alexander A. Reinert, *Public Interest(s) and Fourth Amendment Enforcement*, 2010 U. ILL. L. REV. 1461, 1486 (2010).

81. *Boyd*, 116 U.S. 616, 624–25 (1886) ("In order to ascertain the nature of the proceedings intended by the Fourth Amendment to the Constitution under the terms 'unreasonable searches and seizures,' it is only necessary to recall the contemporary or then recent history of the controversies on the subject, both in this country and in England.").

82. TAYLOR, *supra* note 33, at 19.

83. Riley v. California, 134 S. Ct. 2473, 2494 (2014); United States v. Jones, 132 S. Ct. 945, 949 (2012); Berger v. New York, 388 U.S. 41, 49 (1967); *Boyd*, 116 U.S. at 624, 626–27; Davies, *supra* note 24, at 601; TAYLOR, *supra* note 33, at 19, 26, 38; Silas J. Wasserstrom, *The Fourth Amendment's Two Clauses*, 26 AM. CRIM. L. REV. 1389, 1392–93 (1989); Amar, *supra* note 29, at 772.

84. Wilkes v. Wood (1763) 98 Eng. Rep. 489 (KB). Go-Bart Importing Co. v. United States, 282 U.S. 344, 357 (1931); CUDDIHY, *supra* note 37, at 439–40, 446–52; 4 WILLIAM BLACKSTONE, COMMENTARIES *342; Davies, *supra* note 24, at 655.

85. *Boyd*, 116 U.S. at 630 ("Can we doubt that, when the Fourth and Fifth Amendments to the Constitution of the United States were penned and adopted, the language of Lord Camden was relied on as expressing the true doctrine on the subject of

searches and seizures, and as furnishing the true criteria of the reasonable and 'unreasonable' character of such seizures?").
86. TAYLOR, *supra* note 33, at 29–30.
87. *Boyd*, 116 U.S. at 630 ("The principles laid down in this opinion affect the very essence of constitutional liberty and security. They reach farther than the concrete form of the case then before the court, with its adventitious circumstances; they apply to all invasions on the part of the government and its employees of the sanctity of a man's home and the privacies of life."); Amsterdam, *supra* note 27, at 366 ("[T]he specific incidents of Anglo-American history that immediately preceded the adoption of the [Fourth] amendment we shall find that the primary abuse thought to characterize the general warrants and the writs of assistance was their indiscriminate quality, the license that they gave to search Everyman without particularized cause" which threatened "the whole English nation.").
88. *Boyd*, 116 U.S. at 629 ("Whether this proceedeth from the gentleness of the law towards criminals, or from a consideration that such a power would be more pernicious to the innocent than useful to the public, I will not say. It is very certain that the law obligeth no man to accuse himself; because the necessary means of compelling self-accusation, falling upon the innocent as well as the guilty, would be both cruel and unjust; and it would seem that search for evidence is disallowed upon the same principle. Then too, the innocent would be confounded with the guilty.") (quoting Entick v. Carrington, 19 Howell's St. Tr. 1029, 1074 (1765)).
89. *See* JOSIAH QUINCY, JR., REPORTS OF CASES ARGUED AND ADJUDGED IN THE SUPERIOR COURT OF THE PROVINCE OF MASSACHUSETTS BAY BETWEEN 1761 AND 1772, at 489 (1865) (quoting *Boston Gazette*, Jan. 4, 1762, report on *Paxton's Case*) ("[E]very housholder in this province, will necessarily become *less secure* than he was before this writ had any existence among us; for by it, a custom house officer or any other person has a power given him, with the assistance of a peace officer, to enter forcibly into a dwelling house, and rifle any part of it where he shall please to suspect uncustomed goods are lodgd! – Will any man put so great a value on his freehold, after such a power commences as he did before? . . . Will any one then under such circumstances, ever again boast of british honor or british privilege?"). *See also* Osborn v. United States, 385 U.S. 323, 329 n.7 (1966) (The "indiscriminate use of such devices in law enforcement raises grave constitutional questions under the Fourth and Fifth Amendments, and . . . impose[s] a heavier responsibility on this Court in its supervision of the fairness of procedures . . ."); Johnson v. United States, 333 U.S. 10, 17 (1948) ("An officer gaining access to private living quarters under color of his office and of the law which he personifies must then have some valid basis in law for the intrusion. Any other rule would undermine 'the right of the people to be secure in their persons, houses, papers and effects,' and would obliterate one of the most fundamental distinctions between our form of government, where officers are under the law, and the police state where they are the law." (footnote omitted)); David Gray & Danielle Keats Citron, *The Right to Quantitative Privacy*, 98 MINN. L. REV. 62, 73–83 (2013).
90. Wilkes v. Wood (1763) 98 Eng. Rep. 489, 489 (KB). *See also* Entick v. Carrington (1765) 95 Eng. Rep. 807, 817 (KB), 19 Howell's St. Tr. 1029 ("[W]e can safely say

there is no law in this country to justify the defendants in what they have done; if there was, it would destroy all the comforts of society ..."); TAYLOR, *supra* note 33, at 33–35 (recounting how members of Parliament and other elites felt threatened by the use of general warrants in the Wilkes case); Luke M. Milligan, *The Forgotten Right to Be Secure*, 65 HASTINGS L.J. 713, 749–50 (2014) ("Individual decisions to speak or exercise religious rights are based on some assessment of the expected costs and benefits of such actions. Here is the critical point: it is the *potential* for an unreasonable search or seizure – not simply its actuality – that impacts deliberations regarding the exercise of speech or religious rights."); Doernberg, *supra* note 33, at 57–58 (noting that "most eighteenth-century liberal doctrines can be traced to Locke and his concept that community power resides in the majority.").

91. Tudor, *supra* note 48, at 15. In his notes on Otis's speech, John Adams notes that Otis analyzed the Acts of Trade at issue in the Writs of Assistance Case, and "one by one ... demonstrated, that if they were considered as revenue laws, they destroyed all our security of property, liberty, and life, every right of nature, and the English constitution, and the charter of the province." *Id.* at 20.

92. Go-Bart Importing Co. v. United States, 282 U.S. 344, 357 (1931) ("[General searches] are denounced in the constitutions or statutes of every State in the Union."). Marron v. United States, 275 U.S. 192, 195 (1927) ("General searches have long been deemed to violate fundamental rights. It is plain that the amendment forbids them."); *Boyd*, 116 U.S. at 630 ("The principles laid down in this opinion affect the very essence of constitutional liberty and security. They reach farther than the concrete form of the case ...; they apply to all invasions on the part of the government and its employees of the sanctity of a man's home and the privacies of life."); Wasserstrom, *supra* note 83, at 1393 (The founders "sought to prohibit the newly formed government from using general warrants, a device they believed jeopardized the liberty of every citizen."). In his famous argument in the writs of assistance cases, James Otis identified general warrants as "the worst instrument of arbitrary power, the most destructive of English liberty and the fundamental principles of law, that ever was found in an English law book." Tudor, *supra* note 48, at 15. As Donald Doernberg points out, James Otis was among the many founding-era intellectuals who were deeply influenced by John Locke and his collectivist theories of government and political legitimacy. *See* Doernberg, *supra* note 33, at 66 n.86. Among the people in the audience during Otis's speech was John Adams, who would later identify Otis's speech as " 'the first scene of the first act of opposition to the arbitrary claims of Great Britain.' " Riley v. California, 134 S. Ct. 2473, 2494 (2014).

93. Amsterdam, *supra* note 27, at 432–33.

94. Berger v. New York, 388 U.S. 41, 53 (1967) ("The security of one's privacy against arbitrary intrusion by the police – which is at the core of the Fourth Amendment – is basic to a free society.") (quotations and citations omitted).

95. Johnson v. United States, 333 U.S. 10, 14 (1948). *See also* Brinegar v. United States, 338 U.S. 160, 181 (1949) (Jackson, J., dissenting) ("Courts can protect the innocent against such invasions only indirectly and through the medium of excluding evidence obtained against those who frequently are guilty ... So a search against Brinegar's car must be regarded as a search of the car of Everyman."); Camara v. Mun. Ct., 387 U.S. 523, 528 (1967) ("The basic purpose

of [the Fourth] Amendment, as recognized in countless decisions of this Court, is to safeguard the privacy and security of individuals against arbitrary invasions by governmental officials.").
96. Doernberg, *supra* note 56, at 273, 278–80.
97. *See* David Gray, Meagan Cooper & David McAloon, *The Supreme Court's Contemporary Silver Platter Doctrine*, 91 TEX. L. REV. 7 (2012); Doernberg, *supra* note 33, at 105.
98. United States v. U.S. Dist. Court, 407 U.S. 297, 313–14 (1972) ("Historically the struggle for freedom of speech and press in England was bound up with the issue of the scope of the search and seizure power. History abundantly documents the tendency of Government – however benevolent and benign its motives – to view with suspicion those who most fervently dispute its policies."); Amsterdam, *supra* note 27, at 433 ("[T]he phraseology of the [Fourth] amendment, akin to that of the first and second amendments and the ninth, [was not] accidental."); William J. Stuntz, *Warrants and Fourth Amendment Remedies*, 77 VA. L. REV. 881, 902 (1991) ("Indeed, the real harm [illegal] searches cause, the harm that matters most to society as a whole, is the diminished sense of security that neighbors and friends may feel when they learn of the police misconduct. Totalitarian governments do not cow their citizens by regularly ransacking all their homes; the threat is usually enough. At their worst, illegal searches can represent such threats, sending a signal to the community that people who displease the authorities, whether or not they commit crimes, can expect unpleasant treatment."); United States v. Jones, 132 S. Ct. 945, 956 (2012) (Sotomayor, J., concurring) (noting that law enforcement's unfettered access to contemporary surveillance technologies threatens to "alter the relationship between citizen and government in a way that is inimical to democratic society.").
99. BREYER, *supra* note 3.
100. *Id.* at 4–5 (quoting Benjamin Constant, *The Liberty of the Ancients Compared with That of the Moderns*, *in* BENJAMIN CONSTANT, POLITICAL WRITINGS 309, 309–28 (Biancamaria Fontana trans. & ed. 1988)).
101. BREYER, *supra* note 3, at 132.
102. *Id.* at 5–6, 17–34.
103. *Id.* at 17–20.
104. SCALIA & GARNER, *supra* note 39, at 129–31 (citing the canon of interpretation that the plural includes the singular). Pennsylvania Proceedings, *supra* note 40, at 54 ("all government ought to be instituted and supported for the security and protection 'of the community as such, and to enable the individuals who compose it . . .'"). *Cf.* District of Columbia v. Heller, 554 U.S. 570, 580–81 (2008) (concluding that "the people" as used in the Second Amendment describes rights "exercised individually and belong[ing] to all Americans."); *id.* at 636 (Stevens, J., dissenting) (arguing that "the people" in the Second Amendment describes a collective right, but "Surely it protects a right that can be enforced by individuals.").
105. Doernberg, *supra* note 56, at 260. *See also* Camara v. Mun. Ct., 387 U.S. 523, 527 (1967) ("The basic purpose of this Amendment, as recognized in countless decisions of this Court, is to safeguard the privacy and security of individuals against arbitrary invasions by governmental officials. The Fourth Amendment thus gives concrete expression to a right of the people which is 'basic to a free

society.' "); Johnson v. United States, 333 U.S. 10, 14 (1948) ("The right of officers to thrust themselves into a home is also a grave concern, not only to the individual, but to a society which chooses to dwell in reasonable security and freedom from surveillance."); Weeks v. United States, 232 U.S. 383, 392 (1914) (The Fourth Amendment's protection "reaches all alike, whether accused of crime or not, and the duty of giving it force and effect is obligatory upon all entrusted under our Federal system with the enforcement of the laws."). *But see* Minnesota v. Carter, 525 U.S. 83, 88 (1998) ("The [Fourth] Amendment protects persons against unreasonable searches of 'their persons [and] houses' and thus indicates that the Fourth Amendment is a personal right that must be invoked by an individual.").

106. PETER D.G. THOMAS, JOHN WILKES: A FRIEND TO LIBERTY 32 (1996) (quoting Wilkes as claiming that his suit in the famous General Warrants Cases was brought "for the sake of every one of my English fellow subjects."); Reinert, *supra* note 80, at 1487-91; Arnold H. Loewy, *The Fourth Amendment as a Device for Protecting the Innocent*, 81 MICH. L. REV. 1229, 1263-72 (1983). *See also* United States v. White, 401 U.S. 745, 790 (1971) (Harlan, J., dissenting) ("Interposition of a warrant requirement is designed not to shield 'wrongdoers,' but to secure a measure of privacy and a sense of personal security throughout our society."); Brinegar v. United States, 338 U.S. 160, 181 (1949) (Jackson, J., dissenting) ("There may be, and I am convinced that there are, many unlawful searches of homes and automobiles of innocent people which turn up nothing incriminating, in which no arrest is made, about which courts do nothing, and about which we never hear. Courts can protect the innocent against such invasions only indirectly and through the medium of excluding evidence obtained against those who frequently are guilty ... So a search against [the defendant's] car must be regarded as a search of the car of Everyman."); People v. Cahan, 282 P.2d 905, 907 (Cal. 1955) ("Thus, when consideration is directed to the question of the admissibility of evidence obtained in violation of the constitutional provisions, it bears emphasis that the court is not concerned solely with the rights of the defendant before it, however guilty he may appear, but with the constitutional right of all the people to be secure in their homes, persons and effects.").

107. *Heller*, 554 U.S. at 579-81; United States v. Verdugo-Urquidez, 494 U.S. 259, 265 (1990) (" '[T]he people' protected by the Fourth Amendment, and by the First and Second Amendments, and to whom rights and powers are reserved in the Ninth and Tenth Amendments, refers to a class of persons who are part of a national community or who have otherwise developed sufficient connection with this country to be considered part of that community.").

108. Doernberg, *supra* note 56, at 260. *See also Brinegar*, 338 U.S. at 181 (Jackson, J., dissenting) ("[T]he Amendment was directed only against the new and centralized government, and any really dangerous threat to the general liberties of the people can come only from this source. We must therefore look upon the exclusion of evidence in federal prosecutions, if obtained in violation of the Amendment, as a means of extending protection against the central government's agencies.").

109. Richard H. McAdams, Note, *Tying Privacy in Knotts: Beeper Monitoring and Collective Fourth Amendment Rights*, 71 VA. L. REV. 297, 318 (1985) ("A close

reading of the fourth amendment supports the notion that people *as a group* have a right to be confident that the government will not make unreasonable intrusions into their 'persons, houses, papers and effects.'"). *See also* Luke M. Milligan, *The Right "to Be Secure"*: Los Angeles v. Patel, 2015 CATO SUP. CT. REV. 251; Milligan, *supra* note 90, at 738–50.

110. CUDDIHY, *supra* note 37, at 122 ("After the 1640s, moreover, general searches and warrants began to attract criticism simply because the furnished an infinite power of surveillance to searchers that exposed every Englishman's dwelling to perpetual, capricious intrusion.").

111. *Wilkes*, 98 Eng. Rep. at 489. *See also* Entick v. Carrington (1765) 95 Eng. Rep. 807, 817 (KB), 19 Howell's State Trials 1029 ("[W]e can safely say there is no law in this country to justify the defendants in what they have done; if there was, it would destroy all the comforts of society"); TAYLOR, *supra* note 33, at 33–35 (recounting how members of Parliament and other elites felt threatened by the use of general warrants in the Wilkes case); Doernberg, *supra* note 33, at 57–58 (noting that "most eighteenth-century liberal doctrines can be traced to Locke and his concept that community power resides in the majority.").

112. *Boyd*, 116 U.S. at 630. *See also* Milligan, *supra* note 90, at 740 (quoting anonymous commentary on *Paxton's Case*, likely written by James Otis) ("[E]very housholder in this province, will necessarily become less *secure* than he was before this writ had any existence among us; for by it, a custom house officer or any other person has a power given him, with the assistance of a peace officer, to enter forcibly into a dwelling house, and rifle any part of it where he shall please to suspect uncustomed goods are lodgd! – Will any man put so great a value on his freehold, after such a power commences as he did before? ... Will any one then under such circumstances, ever again boast of british honor or british privilege?").

113. *Boyd*, 116 U.S. at 630.

114. Milligan, *supra* note 90, at 741 (quoting John Adams, Appendix A, *in* 2 THE WORKS OF JOHN ADAMS, *supra* note 35, at 3, 14).

115. Davies, *supra* note 24, at 686–93 (arguing that that "unreasonable" in the search and seizure context just meant against the English constitution, or blackletter common law during the founding era).

116. 4 WILLIAM BLACKSTONE, COMMENTARIES *1291 ("A general warrant to apprehend all persons suspected, without naming or particularly describing any person in special, is illegal and void for its uncertainty; for it is the duty of the magistrate, and ought not to be left to the officer, to judge of the ground of suspicion.").

117. ADAMS, *supra* note 35, at 248.

118. *See* Madison, *supra* note 23 ("The rights of the people to be secured in their persons, their houses, their papers, and their other property, from all unreasonable searches and seizures, shall not be violated by warrants issued without probable cause, supported by oath or affirmation, or not particularly describing the places to be searched, or the persons or things to be seized.").

119. *See, e.g.*, Ratification Statement from New York Delegation (1788) ("That every freeman has a right to be secure from all unreasonable searches and seizures of his person, his papers, or his property; and therefore, that all warrants to search suspected places, or seize any freeman, his papers, or property, without information, upon oath or affirmation, of sufficient cause, are grievous and

oppressive; and that all general warrants (or such in which the place or person suspected are not particularly designated) are dangerous, and ought not to be granted."); Ratification Statement from Virginia Delegation (1788) ("That every freeman has a right to be secure from all unreasonable searches and seizures of his person, his papers, and property; all warrants, therefore, to search suspected places, or seize any freeman, his papers, or property, without information on oath (or affirmation of a person religiously scrupulous of taking an oath) of legal and sufficient cause, are grievous and oppressive; and all general warrants to search suspected places, or to apprehend any suspected person, without specially naming or describing the place or person, are dangerous, and ought not to be granted."); Ratification Statement from North Carolina Delegation (1788) ("That every freeman has a right to be secure from all unreasonable searches and seizures of his person, his papers and property; all warrants, therefore, to search suspected places, or to apprehend any suspected person, without specially naming or describing the place or person, are dangerous, and ought not to be granted.").

120. *See, e.g.*, Article XII, Vermont Bill of Rights (1786) ("That the people have a right to hold themselves, their houses, papers and possessions, free from search or seizure: and therefore warrants, without oaths or affirmations first made, affording sufficient foundation for them, and whereby any officer or messenger may be commanded or required to search suspected places, or to seize any person or persons, his, her or their property not particularly described, are contrary to that right, and ought not to be granted."); Article XIX, New Hampshire Bill of Rights (1784) ("Every subject hath a right to be secure from all unreasonable searches and seizures of his person, his houses, his papers, and all his possessions. All warrants, therefore, are contrary to this right, if the cause or foundation of them be not previously supported by oath, or affirmation; and if the order in the warrant to a civil officer, to make search in suspected places, or to arrest one or more suspected persons, or to seize their property, be not accompanied with a special designation of the persons or objects of search, arrest, or seizure; and no warrant ought to be issued but in cases, and with the formalities prescribed by the laws."); Article XIV, Massachusetts Bill of Rights (1780) ("Every subject has a right to be secure from all unreasonable searches, and seizures of his person, his houses, his papers, and all his possessions. All warrants, therefore, are contrary to this right, if the cause or foundation of them be not previously supported by oath or affirmation; and if the order in the warrant to a civil officer, to make search in suspected places, or to arrest one or more suspected persons, or to seize their property, be not accompanied with a special designation of the persons or objects of search, arrest, or seizure: and no warrant ought to be issued but in cases, and with the formalities, prescribed by the laws."); Article XI, North Carolina Declaration of Rights (1776) ("That general warrants – whereby an officer or messenger may he commanded to search suspected places, without evidence of the fact committed, or to seize any person or persons, not named, whose offences are not particularly described, and supported by evidence – are dangerous to liberty, and ought not to be granted."); Article XXIII, Maryland Declaration of Rights (1776) ("That all warrants, without oath or affirmation, to search suspected places, or to seize any person or property, are grievous and oppressive; and all general warrants-to search suspected places, or to apprehend suspected persons, without naming or

describing the place, or the person in special-are illegal, and ought not to be granted."); Article X, Pennsylvania Declaration of Rights (1776) ("That the people have a right to hold themselves, their houses, papers, and possessions free from search and seizure, and therefore warrants without oaths or affirmations first made, affording a sufficient foundation for them, and whereby any officer or messenger may be commanded or required to search suspected places, or to seize any person or persons, his or their property, not particularly described, are contrary to that right, and ought not to be granted."); Article XVII, Delaware Declaration of Rights (1776) ("That all warrants without oath to search suspected places, or to seize any person or his property, are grievous and oppressive; and all general warrants to search suspected places, or to apprehend all persons suspected, without naming or describing the place or any person in special, are illegal and ought not to be granted."); Article X, Virginia Declaration of Rights (1776) ("That general warrants, whereby any officer or messenger may be commanded to search suspected places without evidence of a fact committed, or to seize any person or persons not named, or whose offence is not particularly described and supported by evidence, are grievous and oppressive, and ought not to be granted.").

121. Thomas Davies and Laura Donohue argue that this is all they meant. *See* Davies, *supra* note 24, at 686–93; Laura K. Donohue, *The Original Fourth Amendment*, U. CHI. L. REV. (forthcoming 2016). We can remain agnostic as to whether his history is right or wrong insofar as what the framers intended is largely irrelevant to the project of uncovering original public meaning except insofar as those intentions may have informed readers' understanding of the text. By this test, Davies's intentionalist account is a step too far in that it renders superfluous the first clause of the Fourth Amendment.

122. 4 WILLIAM BLACKSTONE, COMMENTARIES *1291 ("A general warrant to apprehend all persons suspected, without naming or particularly describing any person in special, is illegal and void for its uncertainty.").

123. Huckle v. Money (1763) 95 Eng. Rep. 768 (KB); Wilkes v. Wood (1763) 98 Eng. Rep. 489, 498–99 (KB) ("no offenders' names are specified in the warrant . . .").

124. Money v. Leach (1765) 97 Eng. Rep. 1075, 1088 (KB).

125. Grumon v. Raymond, 1 Conn. 40 (1814).

126. Frisbie v. Butler, 1 Kirby 213 (Conn. 1787).

127. Rice v. Ames, 180 U.S. 371, 374–75 (1901), JOSEPH CHITTY, A PRACTICAL TREATISE ON THE CRIMINAL LAW: COMPRISING THE PRACTICE PLEADINGS, AND EVIDENCE, WHICH OCCUR IN THE COURSE OF CRIMINAL PROSECUTIONS VOL. I, 66 (1836) ("But though there are precedents of general warrants to search all suspected places for stolen goods, these are not at common law legal, because it would be extremely dangerous to leave it to the discretion of a common officer to arrest what persons(r), or search what houses he things fit(s).")

128. Money v. Leach (1765) 97 Eng. Rep. 1075, 1088 (KB). *See also* General D Grey, 7th Geo. 3d, Ch. 46 ("it will be unconstitutional to lodge such a Writ in the Hands of the Officer, as it will give him a discretionary Power to act under it in such Manner as he shall think necessary.").

129. Wilkes v. Wood (1763) 98 Eng. Rep. 489, 498–99 (KB). *See also* Entick v. Carrington (1765) 95 Eng. Rep. 807 (KB) (decision to search and seize was "left to the discretion of these defendants . . .").

CONCLUSION

130. James Otis, Feb. 24, 1767.
131. *See* Delaware v. Prouse 440 U.S. 648, 653–54 (1979) ("The essential purpose of the proscriptions in the Fourth Amendment is to impose a standard of 'reasonableness' upon the exercise of discretion by government officials, including law enforcement agents . . .")
132. 4 WILLIAM BLACKSTONE, COMMENTARIES.
133. Huckle v. Money (1763) 95 Eng. Rep. 768 (KB). *See also* James Otis (noting that general warrants justify searches and seizures on nothing more than "Bare suspicion without oath.").
134. *Ex parte* Burford, 7 U.S. (3 Cranch) 448 (1806).
135. Entick v. Carrington (1765) 95 Eng. Rep. 807, 817 (KB) ("if he will tread upon his neighbor's ground, he must justify it by law").
136. Wilkes v. Wood (1763) 98 Eng. Rep. 489, 498–99 (KB) (striking down general warrant in part because ". . . no inventory is made of the things thus taken away . . .").
137. James Otis, Feb. 24, 1767.
138. *Id.*
139. *Id.*
140. Concerns about the general threats posed by general warrants carried over to the post-founding era. *See, e.g.*, Raymond v. Grummon, 1 Conn. 40 (1814).
141. Frisbie v. Butler, 1 Kirby 213 (Conn. 1787).
142. Wilkes v. Wood (1763) 98 Eng. Rep. 489, 498–99 (KB).
143. Entick v. Carrington (1765) 95 Eng. Rep. 807 (KB).
144. Huckle v. Money (1763) 95 Eng. Rep. 768 (KB).
145. James Otis, Feb. 24, 1767 ("if it should be established, I insist upon it every person, by the 14th Charles Second, has this power as well as the custom-house officers. The words are: 'It shall be lawful for any person or persons authorized,' etc. What a scene does this open! Every man prompted by revenge, ill-humor, or wantonness to inspect the inside of his neighbor's house, may get a Writ of Assistance. Others will ask it from self-defence; one arbitrary exertion will provoke another, until society be involved in tumult and in blood.").
146. *Boyd*, 116 U.S. 616, 630 (1886) (striking down a broad grant of search powers by Congress and noting that "The struggles against arbitrary power in which they had been engaged for more than twenty years, would have been too deeply engraved in their memories to have allowed them to approve of such insidious disguises of the old grievance which they had so deeply abhorred").
147. Concerns about the general threats posed by general warrants carried over to the post-founding era. *See, e.g.*, Raymond v. Grummon, 1 Conn. 40 (1814).
148. Milligan, *supra* note 90, at 738–50; Davies, *supra* note 24, at 552.
149. Wilkes v. Wood (1763) 98 Eng. Rep. 489 (KB).
150. James Otis, Feb. 24, 1767.
151. Entick v. Carrington (1765) 95 Eng. Rep. 807, 817 (KB).
152. Cornelius Beach Bradley, *Shall and Will – An Historical Study*, 42 TRANS. & PROC. AM. PHILOLOGICAL ASS'N 5, 5 (1911).
153. *Id.*
154. Charles C. Fries, *The Periphrastic Future with Shall and Will in Modern English*, 40 PROC. MOD. LANGUAGE ASS'N 963, 978 (1925).
155. Bradley, *supra* note 152, at 11.

156. *Id.* at 9.
157. *Shall and Must*, PLAINLANGUAGE.GOV, www.plainlanguage.gov/howto/word suggestions/shallmust.cfm (last visited Apr. 25, 2016).
158. Bradley, *supra* note 152, at 21.
159. SAMUEL JOHNSON, A GRAMMAR OF THE ENGLISH TONGUE (1812) (suggesting that "I shall [be walking]" is equivalent in meaning with "[I] will be walking.").
160. *See, e.g.*, Johnson ("In this work, when it shall be found that much is omitted, let it not be forgotten that much likewise is performed . . .").
161. NOAH WEBSTER, GRAMMATICAL INSTITUTE OF THE ENGLISH LANGUAGE (1793).
162. *Id.*
163. *See, e.g.*, Nora Rotter Tillman & Seth Barrett Tillman, *A Fragment on Shall and May*, 50 AM. J. LEGAL HIST. 543 (2008–2010).
164. Bradley, *supra* note 152, at 15–16.
165. *See, e.g., Ex parte* Burford, 7 U.S. (3 Cranch) 448 (1806); Frisbie v. Butler, 1 Korby 213 (Conn. 1787).
166. A Maryland Farmer, No. 1 (1788), *reprinted in* 1 THE FOUNDERS' CONSTITUTION 462, 464 (Philip B. Kurland & Ralph Lerner, eds. 1987).
167. 2 FRANCIS MASERES, THE CANADIAN FREEHOLDER: IN THREE DIALOGUES BETWEEN AN ENGLISHMAN AND A FRENCHMAN, SETTLED IN CANADA 243–44 (London, B. White 1779) (commenting on Wilkes v. Wood (1763) 98 Eng. Rep. 489 (KB)). *See also Boyd*, 116 U.S. at 635 (1886) ("Though the proceeding in question is divested of many of the aggravating incidents of actual search and seizure, yet, as before said, it contains their substance and essence, and effects their substantial purpose. It may be that it is the obnoxious thing in its mildest and least repulsive form; but illegitimate and unconstitutional practices get their first footing in that way, namely, by silent approaches and slight deviations from legal modes of procedure.").
168. Florida v. Royer, 460 U.S. 491, 513 (1983) (Powell, J., concurring) ("We must not allow our zeal for effective law enforcement to blind us to the peril to our free society that lies in this Court's disregard of the protections afforded by the Fourth Amendment.") (quoting and citing Coolidge v. New Hampshire, 403 U.S. 443, 455 (1971) (Brennan, J., concurring) ("In times of unrest, whether caused by crime or racial conflict or fear of internal subversion, this basic law and the values that it represents may appear unrealistic or 'extravagant' to some. But the values were those of the authors of our fundamental constitutional concepts.")); Davies, *supra* note 24, at 578–83 (documenting the Founders' concerns with executive discretion).
169. Entick v. Carrington (1765) 95 Eng. Rep. 807 (KB).
170. Money v. Leach (1765) 97 Eng. Rep. 1075, 1088 (KB).
171. Davies, *supra* note 24, at 687.
172. *Id.* at 658.
173. CUDDIHY, *supra* note 37, at 671–91; Davies, *supra* note 24, at 658.
174. *See, e.g.*, A Maryland Farmer, *supra* note 166, at 464 ("[S]uppose for instance, that an officer of the United States should force the house, the asylum of a citizen, by virtue of a general warrant, I would ask, are general warrants illegal by the constitution of the United States? Would a court, or even a jury, but juries are no longer to exist, punish a man who acted by express authority, upon the bare

recollection of what once was law and right? I fear not, especially in those cases which may strongly interest the passions of government, and in such only have general warrants been used."). Go-Bart Importing Co. v. United States, 282 U.S. 344, 357 (1931) ("[General searches] are denounced in the constitutions or statutes of every State in the Union.").
175. United States v. Lefkowitz, 285 U.S. 452, 462 (1932).
176. Davies, *supra* note 24, at 576-77.
177. Camara v. Mun. Ct., 387 U.S. 523, 528 (1967) ("The Fourth Amendment thus gives concrete expression to a right of the people which is basic to a free society.").
178. Davies, *supra* note 24, at 576 ("The Framers sought to *prevent* unjustified searches and arrests from occurring, not merely to provide after-the-fact remedy for unjustified intrusions.")
179. Berger v. New York, 388 U.S. 41, 50-51 (1967); Weeks v. United States, 232 U.S. 383, 391-92 (1914); Boyd v. United States, 116 U.S. 616, 630 (1886).
180. United States v. Di Re, 332 U.S. 581, 595 (1948) ("[T]he forefathers, after consulting the lessons of history, designed our Constitution to place obstacles in the way of a too permeating police surveillance, which they seemed to think was a greater danger to a free people than the escape of criminals from punishment.").
181. This involved a trade-off: Conner v. Commonwealth, 3 Binn. 38, 43-44 (Pa. 1810).
182. Doernberg, *supra* note 56, at 260.

5

Constitutional Remedies

The Fourth Amendment asserts a broad "right of the people to be secure ... against unreasonable searches and seizures" and issues an imperative command that this security "shall not be violated."[1] In Chapter 4, we learned that this sense of collective security can only be guaranteed by instituting and enforcing prospective remedies that eliminate, restrain, or regulate methods, practices, and policies that pose a general threat to the security of the people.[2]

The warrant clause provides an illuminating example of the kinds of threats that raise Fourth Amendment concerns and the sorts of remedial structures that can satisfy the imperative command contained in the reasonableness clause.[3] The warrant clause targets general warrants and writs of assistance, which threatened the right of the people to be secure against unreasonable searches by allowing government agents to search anywhere they please, for good reasons, for illegitimate reasons, or for no reasons at all without providing for any form of legal accountability.[4] The warrant clause met this threat by banning general warrants. It also institutes important limits on warranted searches. By requiring a showing of probable cause, the warrant clause limits access to warrants. By requiring that warrants be issued only from detached and neutral magistrates, the warrant clause constrains executive authority and provides a means of legal accountability.[5] By requiring specificity as to the places to be searched and the property to be seized, the warrant clause limits the discretion of agents acting under the authority of warrants. Together, these remedial measures effectively guaranteed the security of the people from threats of unreasonable search and seizure posed by general warrants and writs of assistance.

Based on their experiences with legislation overriding common-law prohibitions on general warrants, our colonial forebears expected that threats to their security against unreasonable searches and seizures would emerge from time to time as a result of predictable overreaching by the political branches.[6] They were particularly concerned about the tendency of executive agents to justify programs of broad and indiscriminate search and seizure by relying on claims of emergency or executive necessity.[7] They also worried about the willingness of legislatures to ratify executive demands for expansive search powers by passing statutes overriding common-law protections.[8] In the reasonableness clause, the founders therefore provided the courts with a flexible constitutional resource, empowering them to meet emerging challenges by enforcing constitutional restraints on the political branches that are effective in guaranteeing the security of the people, enforceable by courts and government agencies, and parsimonious with respect to their impact on legitimate government interests.[9]

During most of the nineteenth century, the courts had little reason or opportunity to act on their Fourth Amendment authority to guarantee the security of the people against unreasonable searches and seizures by enforcing constitutional remedies. That is because there were no significant new threats to the security of the people against unreasonable searches and seizures. That all began to change in the late nineteenth and early twentieth centuries with the advent of professionalized paramilitary police forces. The courts responded by elaborating and enforcing several important remedial measures such as the *Miranda* prophylaxis, the warrant requirement, and the exclusionary rule. In this chapter, we will examine these examples in order to gain a firmer grasp on the idea of constitutional remedies.

Professional Police Forces: A Twentieth-Century Challenge to the Security of the People

Broad threats to the security of the people against unreasonable searches and seizures posed by cell site simulators, bulk data collection, and contemporary stop and frisk programs may seem novel, but they are not. We have faced similar challenges in the past. The first came in the late eighteenth century when the security of the people was threatened by general warrants and writs of assistance.[10] The Fourth Amendment itself responded to those threats by guaranteeing the people's security against unreasonable searches and specifying a set of constitutional remedies tailored to meet then contemporary challenges. A century later, the right of the people to be secure against unreasonable searches and seizures was threatened by a novel surveillance technology: professionalized, paramilitary law enforcement organizations. The Court's responses to this new threat are instructive as we consider the role of the Fourth Amendment in our twenty-first century age of surveillance.

Most of the law enforcement institutions that define our experiences with state power simply did not exist in late eighteenth-century America.[11] There was no Federal Bureau of Investigation or anything remotely its equivalent.[12] There were no professional police forces or officers charged with detecting, investigating, and prosecuting crime.[13] Some municipalities had constables and night watchmen, but they were mostly a feckless bunch, criticized for sloth and ineptitude rather than overzealous use of power.[14] In fact, the detection, investigation, and prosecution of crimes in eighteenth-century America were mostly private matters mediated by magistrates and grand juries.[15] A citizen might swear out a warrant,[16] which a magistrate would direct a sheriff to enforce,[17] but arrests and prosecutions were seldom, if ever, motivated, organized, or directed by government officials.[18] Most investigations were conducted by private citizens or their hired agents, not police detectives. Interrogations were conducted by grand juries or magistrates in open court, not by professional police investigators behind the closed doors of interview rooms.[19]

In this bygone era, the basic protections afforded by private tort actions and the warrant clause were sufficient to guarantee the security of the people against unreasonable searches and seizures.[20] Private persons and government officials were both subject to lawsuits for trespass.[21] Because these suits left defendants personally liable, they posed a significant deterrent against cavalier, unfounded, and indiscriminate searches. The general warrants cases discussed in Chapter 4 provide a good example. The agents who searched John Wilkes's home were found liable by a jury for the princely sum of £1,000[22] – over £177,000 today.[23] Wilkes also collected £4000 from Lord Halifax, in whose name the general warrant had been issued.[24]

These threats of substantial liability encouraged due care. It also created strong incentives to get warrants. One of the principal advantages of lawful warrants to search or seize under the common law was that they provided immunity from lawsuits. The warrant clause's demanding limitations provided an important complement to the threat of private tort actions, effectively pushing search and seizure proceedings to the courts, where citizens could be sure of the rigorous protections afforded by proceedings conducted in-line with the warrant clause. Then, the world changed.[25] Principal among these changes was the emergence of professional, paramilitary police forces.

Unlike their continental peers, Englishmen in the eighteenth and early nineteenth centuries had deep reservations about the prospect of professional police forces.[26] It is easy to understand why. After all, police forces are, in essence, standing armies that occupy civilian territories on a perpetual basis. As a consequence, England did not begin to charter professional police departments until well into the nineteenth century.[27] Americans were similarly reserved.[28] During the early days of the nineteenth century, law enforcement in the United States remained a largely private affair.[29] That changed in the middle part of the nineteenth century when reformers began agitating for solutions to the increasingly acute problem of urban crime.[30] They had in mind a model of preventative policing pioneered by British Home Secretary, and later Prime Minister, Sir Robert Peel.[31]

In 1829, Peel pressed for the creation of a police department in Greater London.[32] The result was the Metropolitan Police Service, which was housed in a building abutting a street called Great Scotland Yard – thus its famous moniker.[33] As originally conceived, the Metropolitan Police Service was somewhat limited in its authority. In particular, "bobbies" – so named in honor of Peel – were not permitted to conduct investigations for fear that they might abuse that power to pry into the private lives of Londoners, and particularly nobles.[34] Officers instead relied on their visible presence to suppress crime.[35] They wore uniforms bearing permanent emblems and marks of hierarchical rank reminiscent of the military.[36] They patrolled the streets on foot and on horses. All of this was in stark contrast with the essentially private constables and night watchmen previously charged with keeping the peace in London.

Peel's model of a centralized, bureaucratized, ever-present police force slowly took hold in mid-nineteenth-century America.[37] Led by New York, most of America's largest cities had permanent uniformed police forces by 1870.[38] By the early twentieth century, the model of a professional, paramilitary police force had spread to almost every municipality in the country.[39]

The advent of these professional police forces resulted in the creation of new disciplinary regimes[40] and dramatic changes in citizens' daily engagements with state power.[41] Prior to the creation of professional police forces, the state and its capacity to use force were largely an abstraction for most citizens.[42] With uniformed officers on the street, and cadres of professional investigators engaged in identifying and apprehending offenders, state power became a visible, visceral part of the daily tableaus of American life, particularly in cities.[43] Uniformed police officers populating the public sphere also provided the state with a new, far-reaching surveillance apparatus. State power was not merely present, but it was also watching.[44] Finally, officers and investigators asserted a broad license to use force.[45] Police claimed a right to command, to employ violence, to effect forcible seizures of persons, and to enter and search property.[46] More and more, citizens lived with very real threats to security in their persons, houses, papers, and effects that simply had not existed before the emergence of professional police forces.

These new police departments developed their own training models, internal standards, and cultural norms.[47] Chief among these measures was the detection of crime and the apprehension of suspects. Officers were judged by these standards and norms for purposes of pay and promotion, which created incentives to be aggressive and shaped officers' professional personalities.[48] Institutional standards and norms also produced a degree of cultural separation between law enforcement and their communities. Officers assumed a proprietary position as guardians of the peace, setting them apart from and above the citizenry.[49]

The daily realities of law enforcement reinforced that separation. Unlike civilians, the everyday experiences of police officers were defined by the potential for violence.[50] Success and survival were tied to officers' abilities to conform psychologically and socially to law enforcement culture. To join the police department was to join a brotherhood, which entailed duties of faith and fealty.[51] It also provided access to power and status, which, eventually, bred a sense of practiced entitlement,[52] and sometimes even led to corruption and abuse.[53] Police officers and their departments adopted an almost warlike posture.[54] Police departments became "forces."[55] Workdays became "tours of duty."[56] The open display of firearms became a key feature of law enforcement identity as well, even as it became less and less common for citizens to carry guns.

The rise of professional police forces in the United States occasioned more expansive uses of police powers, including search and seizure.[57] Some of these developments were literally pedestrian, such as the advent of the beat cop;[58] but some cast a darker shadow, such as undercover investigations, eavesdropping,[59] investigative detention,[60] custodial interrogation,[61] and wiretapping.[62] Police departments and their political supporters argued that these new techniques and technologies were necessary to deal with emerging threats.[63] They supported giving police officers and their supervisors broad discretion to determine when and how to use these techniques.[64] The results were entirely predictable: excess and abuse.[65] Some beat cops became little more than bullies[66] and extortionists.[67] Some investigators became kidnappers and torturers.[68] Even officers and departments acting with the best of intentions could not resist the logic of practical necessity or the adrenaline of the pursuit. In the process, the very existence of police forces became a threat to the people's sense of security in their persons, houses, papers, and effects.[69] Something had to be done.

Through the late nineteenth and early twentieth centuries, the political branches proved largely incapable of responding to new threats posed by the emergence and expansion of professional, paramilitary police forces.[70] In many ways, they made things worse. Most spectacular was Prohibition, which led to an explosion of law enforcement agencies, personnel, and powers.[71] Prohibition further impelled the pursuit of new surveillance strategies, including wiretapping and large-scale information aggregation.

By constitutional design, responsibility for protecting the security of the people from the threat of law enforcement excesses fell to the judiciary.[72] The Supreme Court responded by reshaping the world of Fourth and Fifth Amendment remedies.[73] Foremost among these efforts were the *Miranda* prophylaxis, the warrant requirement, and the exclusionary rule. The Court's path to adopting each of these measures has much to teach us about constitutional remedies and therefore the role of the Fourth Amendment in our age of surveillance.

The Miranda Prophylaxis

After lying fallow for the better part of a century, the Fourth Amendment made its first significant appearance in the annals of Supreme Court decisions in 1886. In a case called *Boyd v. United States*, the Court confronted a statute, "adopted at a period of great national excitement, when the powers of the government were subjected to a severe strain to protect the national existence," that gave law enforcement officers investigating cases of tax avoidance broad powers to seize and search private records.[74] The Court struck the statute down out of concern that these powers infringed upon both the people's right to be secure from unreasonable search and seizure under the Fourth Amendment and the Fifth Amendment rights of individuals not to be compelled to bear witness against themselves.[75]

Boyd marks an important moment in Fourth Amendment history. It represents the first in what would be a long and continuing line of cases wrestling with new and emerging threats to the security of the people posed by the ever-expanding reach of new law enforcement regimes. It also shows the Court struggling to locate the best constitutional resources to meet those threats. Specifically, the Court in *Boyd* appears to be caught deciding between the Fourth Amendment's protections against unreasonable searches and seizures and the Fifth Amendment's prohibition on compelled self-incrimination. In the end, it decided not to decide, grounding its decision at the intersection between these protections. As Justice Joseph Bradley described the Court's reasoning:

> Breaking into a house and opening boxes and drawers are circumstances of aggravation, but any forcible and compulsory extortion of a man's own testimony or of his private papers to be used as evidence to convict him of crime or to forfeit his goods is within the condemnation of that judgment. In this regard, the Fourth and Fifth Amendments run almost into each other.[76]

In the years after *Boyd*, the Court continued to draw on both the Fourth and the Fifth Amendments to elaborate constitutional remedies designed to preserve basic rights in the face of threats posed by the paramilitary police forces and professional officers. Among the most important of these is the Court's decision in *Miranda v. Arizona*.[77]

The constitutional remedy established by *Miranda* is familiar to any consumer of televised police procedurals. Under *Miranda*, any person who is arrested or otherwise taken into police custody must be told that she has the right to remain silent, to have an attorney present during interrogation, to have an attorney appointed if she does not have an attorney or cannot afford one, and to be apprised of these rights prior to any interrogation.[78]

Although the *Miranda* warnings are grounded in the Fifth Amendment's prohibition on compelled self-incrimination rather than the Fourth Amendment's protections against unreasonable searches and seizures, *Miranda* represents the Supreme Court's most forceful defense of constitutional remedies and its clearest explanation of the requirements that must be met before courts can establish and enforce constitutional remedies. Crucially, *Miranda* was decided during the height of an era when the Supreme Court was responding to a range of law enforcement excesses and working to develop effective constitutional remedies.[79]

None of the rights described in the *Miranda* warnings appear in the text or history of the Fifth Amendment. When it was ratified in 1791, the Fifth Amendment prohibition on compelled self-incrimination was understood as a trial right.[80] It prohibited a criminal defendant from being forced to take the stand at his own trial or to otherwise give sworn testimony against himself. There is no evidence in the text or history of the Fifth Amendment suggesting constraints on extrajudicial interrogations, much less a general right to remain silent or to have an attorney present during police questioning. The rights set forth in *Miranda* are, instead, created by the Court in its role as final guardian and protector of Fifth Amendment rights.[81] This does not undermine the constitutional status of *Miranda*. Quite to the contrary, as the Court has made clear, these rights are constitutional and cannot be abrogated by legislative or executive action absent an equally effective and enforceable alternative remedy.[82]

The Court's primary justification for the *Miranda* prophylaxis was the changing nature of law enforcement in the nineteenth and twentieth centuries. As we have seen, professional police forces did not exist in 1791 America.[83] As a consequence, there were no police investigations and interrogations. Instead, private citizens investigated criminal offenses and witnesses were questioned under oath in open court by grand juries or magistrates.[84] Experiences in England and Europe with the Star Chamber and religious and political inquisitions provided ample demonstrations of opportunities to abuse procedural and substantive rights in these forums.[85] The Fifth Amendment responded to those known dangers by constitutionalizing the rule *nemo tenetur se ipsum accusare* ("no man is bound to accuse himself"), which was well established as a matter of English common law by the late eighteenth century.[86] By its text, and according to then contemporary understandings, the Fifth Amendment did not and could not say anything about custodial interrogations conducted by professional police officers. That is because neither the practice nor the practitioners existed in eighteenth-century America.

The law enforcement landscape had changed dramatically by the early 1900s.[87] Professional paramilitary police forces had become the norm.[88] Police officers led criminal investigations.[89] Investigations routinely included interrogations of suspects in police custody by officers with special training and extensive experience.[90] Either in the form of written and signed statements, or through the testimony of interrogating officers, statements given during police interrogations became a common source of evidence at trial.[91] As a consequence of these changes, concerns about compelled self-accusation migrated from the historically familiar territory of courtrooms to the dark backrooms of police stations where officers routinely used means and methods that can only be characterized as torture, including extended isolation, sleep deprivation, severe beatings, whipping, hanging, and threats of castration.[92]

By the early twentieth century, violence and intimidation were familiar features of custodial police interrogations.[93] According to the famous Wickersham report, commissioned by President Herbert Hoover and submitted to Congress in 1931, "police violence and the 'third degree' flourished" in the early decades of the twentieth century.[94] Despite these widespread abuses, the political branches took little or no action.[95] So, it fell to the courts to impose constitutional constraints.

Starting in 1936, with a case called *Brown v. Mississippi*,[96] the Supreme Court began to exercise supervisory authority over custodial interrogations by applying the due process clauses of the Fifth and Fourteenth Amendments, which provide that no person shall be deprived "of life, liberty, or property without due process of law."[97] In *Brown* and its progeny, the Court held that "involuntary" confessions, along with any investigative fruits of those confessions, must be excluded at trial.[98] By bringing interrogations within the compass of the Constitution, and by enforcing exclusion as a remedial measure when officers violated constitutional rights, the Court hoped to deter officers from the use of coercive techniques and intimidation during interrogations. Unfortunately, that experiment largely failed.

The use of coercive techniques during custodial interrogations was still widespread in the mid-twentieth century.[99] *Brown* and its progeny had achieved some success in deterring the use of extreme physical violence, but other forms of coercion still flourished. Lower court cases, training manuals, and unapologetic self-reporting by officers documented the ubiquitous use of threats, sleep deprivation, humiliation, psychological manipulation, and trickery during questioning.[100] Police investigators also made a habit of continuing interrogations after subjects stated their desires to remain silent or asked for attorneys.[101] It appeared that law enforcement was complying with the letter of *Brown*, but had missed the spiritual message. They adjusted their practices only as much as was necessary "to avoid a charge of duress that [could] be technically substantiated."[102]

Confronted with widespread use of custodial interrogations dominated by professional police interrogators, the Supreme Court could not ignore the obvious: that the Fifth Amendment prohibition on compelled self-incrimination was being circumnavigated on a daily basis in police stations around the country.[103] What was barred in the courtroom had simply migrated to the backrooms of police stations. The only reasonable response, according to the Court, was to extend the Fifth Amendment into the interrogation room[104] by imposing prospective remedial measures sufficient to "dispel the compulsion inherent in custodial surroundings."[105] The Court's reasoning to that conclusion is both illuminating and instructive in the context of our present effort to understand constitutional remedies.

The *Miranda* Court denied that extending the Fifth Amendment outside the courtroom marked any "innovation in [the Court's] jurisprudence."[106] Rather, the Court characterized its holding as "an explication of basic rights enshrined in the Constitution."[107] It nevertheless adverted to Chief Justice John Marshall's frequently cited 1821 command that the Constitution must be read and applied in order that it shall "approach immortality as nearly as human institutions can approach it."[108] For the *Miranda* Court, this required not only extending the reach of the Fifth Amendment, but also imposing prospective remedies capable of curbing "broad ... mischief"[109] and adapting to "what may be."[110] Absent such measures, the Court worried that the rights themselves would be little more than "impotent and lifeless formulas ... declared in words [but] lost in reality"[111] through the operation of "subtle encroachments on individual liberty."[112]

As the Supreme Court noted in *Miranda*, "subtle encroachments" on Fifth Amendment rights, occasioned by the rise of professional police forces and their expanding reliance on custodial interrogations, had reached a tipping point by the first half of the twentieth century.[113] These "deviations from legal modes of procedure"[114] were not caused by widespread malice or malfeasance. To the contrary, the Court regarded temptations to escalate questioning with undue pressure, browbeating, psychological trickery, and even violence, as inherent to the enterprise of custodial interrogations.[115] Even where officers were able to recognize and resist the temptation to use force and violence, the fact that interrogations were conducted behind closed doors and away from the public eye by trained police agents produced an "inherently compelling atmosphere" that "worked to undermine the individual's will to resist and to compel him to speak where he would not otherwise do so freely."[116] In the Court's view, the Fifth Amendment mandated measures sufficient to address and curb these "overzealous police practices."[117]

As final guardians of constitutional rights, it was the Court's duty to "insure that what was proclaimed in the Constitution [did] not become but a 'form of mere words' in the hands of government officials."[118] The result was the Miranda prophylaxis featuring the familiar Miranda warnings.[119]

There are several characteristics of the Miranda prophylaxis that are important to highlight in the context of our efforts to understand constitutional remedies. First, the *Miranda* Court regarded the warnings as an effective measure that was closely tailored to meet specific constitutional concerns.[120] As the Court pointed out, apprising a defendant of his rights is a "threshold requirement for an intelligent decision as to [their] exercise."[121] It also "overcome[s] the inherent pressures of the interrogation atmosphere."[122] "Further, the warning will show the individual that his interrogators are prepared to recognize his privilege should he choose to exercise it."[123] Informing a suspect of the consequences of choosing to speak would provide "assurance of real understanding and intelligent exercise of the privilege."[124] Finally, "the right to have counsel assure[s] that the individual's right to choose between silence and speech remains unfettered throughout the interrogation process."[125]

Second, the Court regarded the warnings as relatively easy to enforce in a reliable, predictable, and regular manner. The alternative considered and rejected by the Court was a totality of the circumstances test, which would have required courts to determine, based on the facts in any given case, whether the suspect was aware of his rights and made a knowing, intelligent, and voluntary decision to give a statement.[126] As the Court noted, rules based on these kinds of fact-intensive inquiries are difficult to apply consistently.[127] They also offer very little guidance to law enforcement officers.[128] By contrast, "the expedient of giving an adequate warning as to the availability of the privilege is ... simple ... [and] clear-cut,"[129] offering officers in the field "concrete constitutional guidelines."[130] The warnings were easier for courts to enforce than complicated, variable, fact-intensive, and, ultimately, subjective assessments of defendants' "knowledge ... age, education, intelligence, or prior contact with authorities," which often reduce to little "more than speculation."[131]

Third, the Court regarded the prophylaxis as parsimonious in that it struck a conservative balance between the constitutional rights of suspects and the legitimate interests of law enforcement by doing what was necessary to guarantee those rights, but no more.[132] On this point, the *Miranda* Court described the warnings as "absolute prerequisites" and "indispensable" to preserving Fifth Amendment rights.[133] By contrast, the Court thought that the burdens imposed on law enforcement were minimal, preserving ample opportunity to pursue voluntary confessions.[134] By way of evidence, the *Miranda* Court cited the experience of the Federal Bureau of Investigation, which had

> compiled an exemplary record of effective law enforcement while advising any suspect or arrested person, at the outset of an interview, that he is not required to make a statement, that any statement may be used against him in court, that the individual may obtain the services of an attorney of his own choice, and, more recently, that he has a right to free counsel if he is unable to pay.[135]

To further emphasize the parsimonious nature of its interventions, the *Miranda* Court left open the door to "other fully effective means" that might be "devised to inform accused persons of their right of silence and to assure a continuous opportunity to exercise it."[136] As the Court noted a generation later, that invitation remains open.[137]

To be sure, there was and continues to be considerable debate about the wisdom of *Miranda* and the overall effectiveness of the constitutional remedies prescribed by the *Miranda* Court. In the Court's view, however, the *Miranda* warnings have not interfered much with interrogations.[138] To the contrary, officers have simply adapted, often by using the warnings to establish rapport and trust with suspects.[139] The Court's views on *Miranda* are not free from controversy, however.[140] Some critics of *Miranda*, most prominently Paul Cassell, have argued that *Miranda* has demonstrably reduced the ability of law enforcement to clear cases.[141] Fortunately, we can afford to set these debates aside for the moment. What matters for our purposes is the model provided by *Miranda* for how the Court develops, justifies, and applies constitutional remedies.

The Court's reasoning in *Miranda* provides valuable insights into the concept of constitutional remedies by describing a framework for their development and enforcement. In *Miranda*, the Court takes note of broad changes in the nature of state power, the terms of engagement between citizens and state officials, and relationships between law enforcement regimes and citizens.[142] Principal among these were the advent of professional police forces engaged in investigating and prosecuting crime, their use of custodial interrogations designed to secure incriminating statements, and a pattern of abuses. In the Court's view, these developments posed a general and pervasive threat to rights against compelled self-incrimination. According to the Court, the only way to resolve those constitutional concerns was to implement a prospective remedy that would be effective in vindicating constitutional concerns, readily enforceable by executive agents and courts, and parsimonious with respect to their impact on law enforcement's efforts to combat crime. According to the Supreme Court, the *Miranda* prophylaxis meets these requirements and is therefore a constitutional remedy to which each of us has a right under the Fifth Amendment. As the next sections show, there is a parallel story to be told about the Fourth Amendment warrant requirement and the Fourth Amendment exclusionary rule.

The Warrant Requirement

In its most robust form, the warrant requirement holds that "searches conducted outside the judicial process, without prior approval by judge or magistrate, are *per se* unreasonable subject only to a few specifically established and well delineated exceptions."[143] In truth, however, the warrant requirement is much more nuanced.[144] Searches of homes and other highly protected areas generally require prior judicial approval in the form of warrants,[145] but there are many situations where prior judicial review is not required. For example, searches of cars,[146] searches of persons and their property secondary to lawful arrests,[147] and frisks do not require warrants or prior judicial approval. There are even circumstances where searches of homes do not require warrants. For example, prior judicial approval is not required for searches of homes conducted in the throes of an emergency.[148] Searches conducted to effectuate "special needs," such as environmental regulations[149] and to evaluate health and safety, generally do not require warrants.[150]

Given all these "exceptions," many wonder whether it makes much sense to talk about a warrant *requirement*.[151] After all, it is really only nonemergency searches of homes and similar highly protected areas that require warrants, and, even then, only if the purpose of the search is to gather evidence of criminal activity rather than to advance an administrative or regulatory scheme. Some of these concerns surfaced in *Riley v. California*, which was argued before the Supreme Court in April 2014.[152] During oral arguments in that case, Justices Scalia, Kennedy, Alito, and Sotomayor all asked whether it makes sense to talk about a warrant requirement given all its modifications and exceptions, which, together, liberate law enforcement from any obligation to secure a warrant or prior judicial approval in the vast majority of cases.[153]

In addition to these practical concerns, many critics on and off the Court argue that there are no constitutional grounds for the warrant requirement.[154] The most compelling of these attacks come from originalists, who complain that the warrant requirement has no foundation in either the text or history of the Fourth Amendment.[155] These critics are particularly dubious about the proposition that the warrant requirement can be derived from the warrant clause.[156] Warrants offered immunity from liability in trespass, which negated the primary means of holding government agents accountable for their search activities under the common law.[157] And, as we have seen, the Fourth Amendment was inspired in part by criticism of general warrants and writs of assistance. Far from expressing a preference for warrants, there seems to be a good argument that the warrant clause reflected an effort to limit the availability and scope of warrants rather than establishing a constitutional preference for warranted searches.

The Supreme Court first endorsed a warrant requirement in *Agnello v. United States*, decided in 1925.[158] Writing for the Court in that case, Justice Pierce Butler did not offer a textual or historical foundation for the warrant requirement. Rather, he suggested that "it has always been assumed that one's house cannot lawfully be searched without a search warrant, except as an incident to a lawful arrest therein."[159] It does not appear that this assumption met with much challenge or controversy at the time. As a consequence, most proponents have simply assumed the constitutional status of the warrant requirement for the better part of a century.[160] Both the case law and the academic literature are therefore virtually devoid of robust textual, historical, or practical justifications of the warrant requirement, much less coherent explanations of its various exceptions.[161] The result is a rather dimly lit area of constitutional law. With the benefit of our discussions of constitutional remedies in Chapter 4, we are in a position to cast some light.

There is nothing in the text or history of the Constitution that suggests a warrant requirement. In this regard, originalist critics are absolutely right. That does not mean, however, that the warrant requirement is not constitutional. As we have seen, the reasonableness clause secures the right of the people to prospective remedies that provide effective, enforceable, and parsimonious means for guaranteeing their security against threats of unreasonable search and seizure. The warrant requirement – inclusive of its limits and "exceptions" – is one such remedy.

The warrant requirement is not derived from the warrant clause. The warrant requirement is, instead, a constitutional remedy crafted by courts exercising authority granted to them by the reasonableness clause and its imperative command that the "the right of the people to be secure ... shall not be violated." In this regard, the warrant requirement shares a close kinship with the *Miranda* warnings. Like the *Miranda* warnings, the warrant requirement became a feature of the Supreme Court's jurisprudence in the early years of the twentieth century as it struggled to guarantee the security of the people against threats posed by the rise of professional, paramilitary police forces. Also like the *Miranda* warnings, the Supreme Court has defended the warrant requirement as an effective, enforceable, and parsimonious means of addressing this evolving threat. On this basic point, at least, the leading originalist of his generation seems to have agreed.

More than any other judge or scholar, Justice Antonin Scalia was responsible for raising originalism to its present status. Justice Scalia frequently applied originalist methods in justifying his opinions[162] and when condemning opinions written by his colleagues that indulged alternative methods, including living constitutionalism.[163] He wrote extensively about originalism as an academic as well.[164] Justice Scalia's commitment to originalism often put him at the vanguard of the Court when it came to enforcing and extending Fourth Amendment rights – particularly where new technologies were concerned. For example, he wrote the majority opinions in *United States v. Jones*, the 2012 case where the Court held that installing a tracking device on a car is a search governed by the Fourth Amendment,[165] and *Kyllo v. United States*, the 2003 case where the Court held that law enforcement officers must obtain a warrant before using infrared detection devices to "explore details of the home."[166] Given this legacy, it is particularly noteworthy that Justice Scalia believed that the warrant requirement derived from the reasonableness clause, not the warrant clause.[167] Thus, whether one is an originalist, or more inclined to view the Constitution as a living document that evolves to address contemporary challenges, the most promising path for understanding the warrant requirement runs through the reasonableness clause.[168]

Like the *Miranda* warnings, the warrant requirement emerged during an era when society and the courts were struggling to come to terms with new threats posed by the rise of professional, paramilitary police forces.

Unlike the *Miranda* prophylaxis, however, there is no signal case establishing the force and foundation of the warrant requirement. The warrant requirement instead evolved through a line of cases that started in 1886 with *Boyd v. United States*[169] and continues through *Riley v. California*, decided in 2014.

Despite the absence of a defining precedent case – a *Miranda* for the warrant requirement – a clear pattern emerges when we examine these cases as a whole. This pattern is familiar in light of our discussion of *Miranda*. In its warrant requirement cases, the Court routinely notes emerging threats to the security of the people against unreasonable searches and seizures posed by the expansion of professional police forces and aggressive police tactics. The Court cites the dangers of granting law enforcement officers unfettered discretion to engage in searches and seizures. The Court emphasizes the inherent flexibility of the Fourth Amendment's prohibition on unreasonable searches and seizures. The Court then identifies warrants as particularly effective means for guaranteeing that security by limiting the discretion of police officers, interposing courts between citizens and law enforcement, and providing means for holding officers and agencies accountable. The Court also addresses enforceability concerns, pointing out the relative ease of managing a warrant regime and the clear guidance afforded by categorical rules. Finally, the Court tailors the warrant requirement in order to preserve a parsimonious balance between citizen interests and the needs of law enforcement. In some cases, this tailoring leads the Court to enforce an absolute, unyielding warrant requirement. In others, the Court concludes that prior judicial approval is unnecessary, unwieldy, or unduly sacrifices legitimate law enforcement goals. Whatever the result, the Court's explicit goal in all its warrant requirement cases is to craft an overall remedial structure that provides general assurances to each of us and all of us that we are not subject to search or seizure at the whim of law enforcement. That remedial structure, inclusive of all its "exceptions," is what we call the warrant requirement.

The Role of Emerging Threats in the Court's Development of the Warrant Requirement

The warrant requirement emerged during the early twentieth century as professional law enforcement agencies tasked with preventing, detecting, and investigating crime first became features of modern American life. In its early warrant requirement cases, the Court was quite clear that these new agencies and the changing enterprise of crime control raised serious concerns for the security of the people against unreasonable searches and seizures. For example, in *Weeks v. United States*, decided in 1914, the Court identified the "tendency of those who execute the criminal laws of the country to obtain conviction by means of unlawful seizures."[170] A few years later, in *Go-Bart Importing Company v. United States*, Justice Butler highlighted the fact that "present conditions" reinforced the Court's "duty of vigilance" in "effective enforcement" of the Fourth Amendment, "lest there shall be an impairment of the rights for the protection of which it was adopted."[171] Justice Jackson offered a vivid account of those conditions in *United States v. Johnson*, decided by the Court in 1948, describing law enforcement as a "competitive enterprise" in which "zealous officers" are engaged in "ferreting out crime."[172] As Justice Robert Jackson later warned, officers engaged in that competitive enterprise naturally "will push the limit" absent some form of judicial restraint.[173] Leaving the decision whether to search wholly in the hands of those officers would, therefore, "reduce the Amendment to a nullity, and leave the people's homes secure only in the discretion of police officers."[174]

Concerns about unrestrained law enforcement discretion have played a particularly prominent role in the Court's assessments of threats against the right of the people to be secure from unreasonable searches and seizures. For example, in *Boyd*, the Court struck down a tax collection statute because it afforded too much latitude to enforcement agents.[175] Worries about grants of unfettered discretion to law enforcement agents expanded with the growth of the "competitive enterprise" through the early twentieth century. Thus, Justice Jackson, writing for the Court in *Johnson*, warned that leaving decisions whether to search a home solely to the discretion of law enforcement in the first instance would pose "a grave concern, not only to the individual, but to a society which chooses to dwell in reasonable security and freedom from surveillance."[176] As law enforcement added electronic surveillance capacities to its arsenal, the dangers inherent in broad grants of discretion multiplied. This was a point emphasized by the Court in *Berger v. New York*, decided in 1967. There, the Court struck down as unconstitutional a state statute licensing law enforcement's use of electronic eavesdropping devices because the statute failed to limit officers' discretion, thereby permitting "general searches by electronic devices, the truly offensive character of which was first condemned in *Entick v. Carrington* and which were then known as 'general warrants.' "[177]

In more recent warrant requirement cases, the Supreme Court has continued to cite the dangers of expanding law enforcement institutions and their evolving capacities. For example, in *Kyllo v. United States*, decided in 2001, the Court was asked whether the use of a heat detection device to monitor otherwise invisible thermal emanations from a home constituted a Fourth Amendment search.[178] That device allowed officers to "see" the high-powered lamps Mr. Kyllo was using to grow marijuana in his house by gathering infrared radiation that emanated from the outside walls of the structure. On appeal, Kyllo argued that the use of a heat detection device to gather information about the interior of his home required a warrant. Writing for the Court, Justice Scalia agreed. Notably, there is nothing in the text or history of the Fourth Amendment addressing the use of heat detection devices. Furthermore, both the devices and the physics upon which they operate were unknown to those who wrote and read the Fourth Amendment in 1791.[179] As Justice Scalia pointed out, however, eighteenth-century imaginations do not limit the reach of the Fourth Amendment. What matters is the nature of the threats posed by new and emerging technologies to the security of the people against unreasonable searches and seizures if decisions about deployment and use are left solely to the unfettered discretion of law enforcement. Thus, Justice Scalia concluded for the Court that it must not "permit police technology to erode the privacy guaranteed by the Fourth Amendment."[180] Foremost among these guarantees, he continued, is "the right of a man to retreat into his own home and there be free from unreasonable governmental intrusion."[181]

Justice Scalia concluded that granting law enforcement unfettered access to heat detection technology would pose a general threat to the security of the people in their homes, particularly given the indiscriminate nature of heat detection. After all, these devices can detect not only evidence of crimes but also evidence of purely innocent activities, such as when "the lady of the house takes her daily sauna and bath." It is hard to imagine anything more unsettling or disruptive to the domestic sanctity of the home and its inherent intimacy than the possibility that law enforcement is watching us when we bathe![182] It therefore fell to the Court to combat this threat by fashioning a remedy sufficient to preserve the security of the people against threats posed by unfettered access to heat detection devices and "more sophisticated systems that are already in use or in development."[183] The *Kyllo* Court settled on a warrant requirement as the best means to guarantee the security of the people against threats of unreasonable searches using heat detection devices.[184]

In *United States v. Jones*, decided in 2012, the Supreme Court reiterated concerns about threats to the security of the people against unreasonable searches and seizures posed by grants of unfettered discretion for law enforcement to use contemporary surveillance technologies. *Jones* asked the Court to determine whether long-term tracking using GPS-enabled devices should be subject to Fourth Amendment constraints. Although the majority opinion written by Justice Scalia did not need to inquire past installation of the device, a majority of the justices expressed deep concerns regarding new surveillance technologies and their impact on the right of the people to be secure against unreasonable searches and seizures. For example, writing for himself and Justices Ginsburg, Breyer, and Kagan, Justice Alito argued that law enforcement's recently acquired abilities to conduct long-term GPS tracking threaten collective expectations of privacy.[185]

Writing for herself in *Jones*, Justice Sotomayor specified the source of these concerns. She pointed out that law enforcement can, or soon will be able to, monitor our movements "by enlisting factory- or owner-installed vehicle tracking devices or GPS-enables smartphones."[186] In her view, the possibility that government agents can collect this kind of "precise, comprehensive record of a person's public movements" and then "store such records and efficiently mine them for information years into the future" while "evad[ing] the ordinary checks that constrain abusive law enforcement practices: limited police resources and community hostility" means that each of us and all of us can rightly worry that law enforcement is or may be watching.[187] "Awareness that the Government may be watching chills associational and expressive freedoms," she warned.[188] "The net result," she concluded, "is that GPS monitoring – by making available at a relatively low cost such a substantial quantum of intimate information about any person whom the Government, in its unfettered discretion, chooses to track – may alter the relationship between citizen and government in a way that is inimical to democratic society."[189]

Although she wrote only for herself in *Jones*, the Court adopted as its own many of Justice Sotomayor's concerns in *Riley v. California*, which was decided in 2014. Writing for a majority of eight justices in that case, Chief Justice Roberts cited Justice Sotomayor's concurring opinion in *Jones* to emphasize constitutional concerns raised by law enforcement's emerging capacities to engage in the kinds of precise tracking that may reveal intimate details about citizens' lives.[190]

As these cases show, law enforcement continues to evolve, expanding its search and surveillance capacities along the way. For perfectly understandable reasons, law enforcement seeks unfettered discretion to avail itself of these new capacities. For equally understandable reasons, granting that unfettered discretion raises serious concerns for the security of the people against unreasonable searches and seizures. For over one hundred and thirty years, since *Boyd* was decided in 1886, the Court has expressed repeatedly concerns about these developments, asking whether and how the Fourth Amendment might provide some security for the people against these new and emerging threats. Time and again, it has found ample authority to construct prospective remedies in an effort to vindicate the imperative command that the right of the people to be secure against unreasonable searches and seizures shall not be violated.

The Court's Reliance on the Reasonableness Clause in Its Warrant Requirement Cases

Faced with threats to the security of the people posed by expanding law enforcement agencies and discretionary law enforcement actions, the Court repeatedly cites the Fourth Amendment's guarantee against threats of unreasonable searches and seizures as grounds for enforcing and adapting constitutional remedies, including the warrant requirement. Here again, the story starts in 1886 with *Boyd*, where the Court opined that

> The principles laid down in [Entick v. Carrington] affect the very essence of constitutional liberty and security. They reach farther than the concrete form of the case then before the court, with its adventitious circumstances; they apply to all invasions on the part of the government and its employees of the sanctity of a man's home and the privacies of life. It is not the breaking of his doors, and the rummaging of his drawers, that constitutes the essence of the offence; but it is the invasion of his indefeasible right of personal security, personal liberty and private property, where that right has never been forfeited by his conviction of some public offence, – it is the invasion of this sacred right which underlies and constitutes the essence of Lord Camden's judgment.[191]

As the Court would later emphasize, "The Fourth Amendment thus gives concrete expression to a right of the people which is basic to a free society" by "safeguard[ing] the privacy and security of individuals against arbitrary invasions by governmental officials."[192]

In order to preserve these fundamental freedoms in the face of new challenges, the Court has "repeatedly decided that [the Fourth Amendment] should receive a liberal construction, so as to prevent stealthy encroachment upon or 'gradual depreciation' of the rights secured by them, by imperceptible practice of courts or by well intentioned, but mistakenly overzealous, executive officers."[193] In its warrant requirement cases, the Supreme Court maintains that the source of this flexibility is in the reasonableness clause, which "is general and forbids every search that is unreasonable,"[194] and "is construed liberally to safeguard the right of privacy."[195] This does not mean that the Fourth Amendment is a free-flying balloon, untethered from its original moorings. Quite to the contrary, as the Court pointed out in *Carroll v. United States*, "The Fourth Amendment is to be construed in the light of what was deemed an unreasonable search and seizure when it was adopted."[196] That is to say, courts must interpret the Fourth Amendment in a "manner which will conserve public interests as well as the interests and rights of individual citizens."[197] Thus, courts applying the Fourth Amendment must be careful not to mistake originalism for historicism. To do so would render the Fourth Amendment little more than an anachronism, "too stingy," in the words of Professor Anthony Amsterdam, "to preserve the kind of open society to which we are committed and in which the amendment is supposed to function."[198] The *Carroll* Court therefore had no difficulty in applying Fourth Amendment standards of reasonableness to searches of automobiles despite the fact that car searches were well beyond the experiences or imaginations of eighteenth-century Americans.

The Supreme Court is also quite clear in its warrant requirement cases that final responsibility for guaranteeing the security of the people against threats of unreasonable searches and seizures lies with the courts. As several founding-era commentators pointed out, it is tempting for courts to bow to claims of executive necessity, particularly in times of national emergency,[199] but courts are constitutionally bound to defend the Fourth Amendment even in the face of such claims. So, too, are they bound to condemn violations, no matter how small. After all, as the Court pointed out in *Boyd*, "illegitimate and unconstitutional practices get their first footing in that way, namely, by silent approaches and slight deviations from legal modes of procedure."[200] Writing for the Court in *Weeks v. United States*, Justice William Day picked up this theme, concluding that the use of unlawful searches to secure convictions "should find no sanction in the judgments of the courts, which are charged at all times with the support of the Constitution, and to which people of all conditions have a right to appeal for the maintenance of such fundamental rights."[201] Justice Sotomayor recently reiterated the critical role of courts as final guarantors of the people's security in *United States v. Jones*, where she questioned "the appropriateness of entrusting to the Executive, in the absence of any oversight from a coordinate branch, a tool so amenable to misuse, especially in light of the Fourth Amendment's goal to curb arbitrary exercises of police power to and prevent 'a too permeating police surveillance.' "[202]

The Court Holds that the Warrant Requirement Is Effective, Enforceable, and Parsimonious

Having recognized the need to set limits on the discretionary authority of government agents, the authority provided to courts by the reasonableness clause of the Fourth Amendment, and the courts' constitutional role, the Supreme Court repeatedly returns to the warrant requirement as the most effective, enforceable, and parsimonious means for guaranteeing the security of the people against unreasonable searches and seizures. In so doing it has maintained time and again that the warrant requirement is no mere "formality . . . but a fundamental rule that has long been recognized as basic to the privacy of every home in America."[203]

Importantly, the Court has never claimed to ground the warrant requirement in the warrant clause. Rather, the Court describes the warrant requirement as a prospective remedy grounded in the reasonableness clause.[204] There is, of course, a close linkage between the warrant requirement and the warrant clause. It is not one of implication however. It is, instead, a matter of modeling. Our founders did not mandate warrants, but they understood the prospective remedial power of warrants and the warrant process.[205] So too did twentieth-century courts.[206] It is no surprise, then, that the Supreme Court would draw on this wisdom and experience when fashioning a constitutional response to new and emerging threats posed by professional police forces.

The Court has left little doubt that it regards the warrant requirement as an effective means of guaranteeing our collective security against unreasonable government intrusions.[207] As the Court pointed out in *United States v. Lefkowitz*, "Security against unlawful searches is more likely to be attained by resort to search warrants than by reliance upon the caution and sagacity of petty officers while acting under the excitement that attends the capture of persons accused of crime."[208] Justice Marshall Harlan, II, would later emphasize this point in *United States v. White*, where he pointed out that "Interposition of a warrant requirement is designed not to shield 'wrongdoers,' but to secure a measure of privacy and a sense of personal security throughout our society."[209] The warrant requirement achieves this goal by limiting the discretion of law enforcement officers and by interposing courts between officers and citizens.[210] In this regard, the warrant requirement is a tailored means for meeting a specific kind of threat against the security of the people.

As we have seen, one of the primary concerns cited by the Supreme Court in its warrant requirement cases is the threat to the security of the people against unreasonable searches and seizures posed by grants of unfettered discretion to law enforcement. The warrant requirement directly targets that discretion[211] by mandating that the decision as to "When the right of privacy must reasonably yield to the right of search is, as a rule, to be decided by a judicial officer, not by a policeman or government enforcement agent."[212] As the Court put the point in *Weeks v. United States*, the "effect of the Fourth Amendment is to put the courts of the United States and federal officials, in the exercise of their power and authority, under limitations and restraints as to the exercise of such power and authority, and to forever secure the people, their persons, houses, papers, and effects, against all unreasonable searches and seizures under the guise of law."[213] The Court emphasized that point again a few years later in *United States v. Lefkowitz*, where Justice Butler explained that "Security against unlawful searches is more likely to be attained by resort to search warrants than by reliance upon the caution and sagacity of petty officers while acting under the excitement that attends the capture of persons accused of crime."[214] More recently still, Chief Justice Roberts, writing for the Court in *Riley v. California*, emphasized that allowing "individual officers" too much discretion to decide whether to search "in an ad hoc, case-by-case fashion" fails to protect Fourth Amendment rights and also fails to provide the clear guidance and public reassurance secured by "categorical rules" such as the warrant requirement.[215]

In addition to limiting law enforcement discretion, the warrant requirement is effective in guaranteeing the security of the people because it "serves to insure that the deliberate, impartial judgment of a judicial officer will be interposed between the citizen and the police."[216] As Justice Jackson explained in *United States v. Johnson*, "Its protection consists in requiring that those inferences be drawn by a neutral and detached magistrate, instead of being judged by the officer engaged in the often competitive enterprise of ferreting out crime."[217] It therefore guarantees that the decision whether to search or not will be made by a detached arbiter exercising neutral judgment rather than an invested officer caught up in the adrenaline of the chase.[218] The warrant requirement also forces officers to identify, organize, and externalize their reasons for wanting to conduct a search. This process of deliberation and public reason-giving effects a powerful regulatory force on agents and action.[219] It not only reduces the likelihood that law enforcement interests will overwhelm citizen privacy interests; recent studies have shown that it also dramatically reduces error rates[220] while providing invaluable reassurance to the people that their rights are not subject to the whim of overzealous officers charged with ferreting out crime.[221] Finally, by interposing courts between citizens and law enforcement, the warrant requirement slows things down and imposes upon officers a duty of deliberation and care that is easy to forget in the heat of the chase.[222]

In addition to being effective, the warrant requirement is easy to administer and enforce. It starts with a simple rule: searches of homes or other protected areas are presumed to be unreasonable in the absence of a warrant.[223] By contrast, searches of areas not regarded as on par with homes, including automobiles, do not face this presumption. Even where the presumption applies, it can be overcome by showing consent or emergency.[224] If the presumption cannot be overcome, then the evidence seized, along with all investigative fruits, will be excluded from the prosecutor's case-in-chief.[225] On the other hand, searches conducted under the auspices of a warrant are presumed to be reasonable.[226] That presumption goes so far as excusing officers who act on warrants that are deficient in some way, so long as they do so in "good faith."[227]

It is quite common for courts and scholars to refer to searches of cars, consent searches, and emergency searches as "exceptions" to the warrant requirement. Although understandable, that choice of language is misleading. It gives rise to considerable practical skepticism about the warrant requirement, which even supporters regard as too riddled with "exceptions" to deserve the title "requirement." By taking seriously the nature of the warrant requirement as a constitutional remedy we can resolve, or at least quiet somewhat, many of these worries. That is because "exceptions" to the warrant requirement are not truly exceptions at all but simply different classes of cases subject to different categorical treatment under the warrant requirement's overall remedial structure. In other words, the "exceptions" are part of the rule.

To appreciate this point, it is worth taking a closer look at how the warrant requirement functions as an overall remedial structure. The first point to recognize is that all searches are subject to judicial review. The principal distinction between searches of highly protected areas, such as homes, and searches of lesser protected areas, such as cars, is with regard to the timing of that review. For home searches, the warrant requirement demands that judicial review come prior to the search. For searches of cars, consent searches, and emergency searches, the warrant requirement means that judicial review can be reserved until after the fact, usually in the context of a suppression hearing.

These are important clarifications in the present context. As the Supreme Court reiterated in *Riley v. California*, the principal advantage of the warrant requirement from the perspective of enforceability is that it constructs and maintains clear categories.[228] As a prospective remedial structure, the warrant requirement draws clear lines for courts and officers so they will know which searches require prior judicial approval and which do not. Regardless of which category it might fall into, the final decision as to whether a search is reasonable is reserved always for a judicial officer.

One might rightly wonder why the warrant requirement recognizes different rules for different categories of searches. After all, there is no doubt that prior judicial review is a more effective means of preserving the security of the people than review after the fact. If that is right, then why not just require prior judicial review for all searches? The answer is to be found in the requirement that constitutional remedies strike a parsimonious balance between competing interests. Although a blanket requirement for prior judicial review surely would provide the greatest protections for Fourth Amendment interests, the Court's warrant requirement jurisprudence is quite clear that it would strike the wrong balance by imposing excessive limitations on law enforcement, sacrificing too much in terms of its ability to detect, prevent, and prosecute crime.

Mindful of these concerns, the Supreme Court has been careful to tailor the warrant requirement in order to strike a parsimonious balance between the people's right to be secure from unreasonable searches and seizures and the people's interests in safety and security from crime.[229] In doing so, the Court starts with the proposition that the warrant process is not particularly burdensome. For example, in *Berger v. New York*, the Court found that "While the requirements of the Fourth Amendment are not inflexible, or obtusely unyielding to the legitimate needs of law enforcement, it is not asking too much that officers be required to comply with the basic command of the Fourth Amendment before the innermost secrets of one's home or office are invaded."[230] If anything, the burdens of securing a warrant have lightened over the years. Most jurisdictions allow officers to apply for warrants over the telephone. Officers in many jurisdictions can even apply for warrants via e-mail. With judges now carrying portable electronic devices, officers can get a decision in a matter of minutes.[231]

This is not to suggest that requiring advanced judicial approval before conducting a search is costless. As Chief Justice Roberts recognized in *Riley*, it has "an impact on the ability to combat crimes."[232] There is therefore no doubt that "Privacy comes at a cost."[233] That cost is not optional, however. It is a set constraint on our political system imposed by the Fourth Amendment itself.[234] The Supreme Court has, nevertheless, sought to limit the impact of that cost by elaborating two important warrant requirement rules. The first excuses officers from seeking a warrant if a party with lawful authority over the place or item to be searched consents to that search. In these circumstances, the Court has held, the fact that officers sought and secured consent serves to vindicate Fourth Amendment rights. The second excuses officers from the presumption of unreasonableness that might attach to a warrantless search of a home if that search is conducted in exigent circumstances. In these cases, the Court has held that concerns about the safety of officers,[235] the safety of citizens,[236] or the risk that evidence might be destroyed while officers attempt to secure a warrant[237] allow officers to forgo prior judicial approval in favor of judicial review after the fact.[238]

As the Court concluded in *Riley*, these two "exceptions" provide ample room for officers to deal with most situations where securing a warrant would truly compromise their efforts to control crime.[239] On the other hand, emergency searches are, in the Court's view, sufficiently rare that they do not cast a very long shadow in terms of compromising the right of the people to be secure against threats of unreasonable search. There is good reason to think that the Court might be wrong about that, but we can set those issues aside for now. What is important in the present context is the fact that the Court engages in a balancing of interests when elaborating the various rules comprising the warrant requirement in order to achieve some degree of parsimoniousness in the overall remedial structure.

That same balancing is on display in cases where the Supreme Court has held that some kinds of searches do not require prior judicial approval.[240] The prime example is car searches. There is no doubt that citizens harbor significant privacy interests in their cars. It is also true that, were officers permitted to search cars at their whim, beyond the reach of judicial review, then the security of the people against unreasonable searches and seizures would be at severe risk. But cars are not like homes. They are mobile, which means that any evidence they contain is at risk of being lost or destroyed.[241] Cars and drivers are also subject to a host of regulatory regimes, which require licensing and regular inspections.[242] Finally, the passenger areas of most cars are essentially open to public view.[243]

Citing a combination of these factors, the Court has held that requiring prior judicial approval before officers are allowed to search a car would strike the wrong balance between the privacy interests of citizens and the people's interests in effective law enforcement.[244] It therefore reserves judicial review of car searches for a later hearing, where the officer must show that her search was justified by probable cause to believe that evidence of a specific crime would be found in the areas of the car that were searched. In essence, this is a post hoc warrant process that, in the Court's view, provides reasonable Fourth Amendment guarantees without requiring too much sacrifice from law enforcement. Here again, one might think the Court has struck the wrong balance. We can leave those debates for another day, however. For present purposes, what is important is that it has sought to strike a balance.

The Court continues to tweak the warrant requirement. In recent years, it has set new limits on car searches,[245] removed some limits on emergency searches,[246] and extended the warrant requirement to the use of heat detection devices,[247] searches of cellular phones,[248] and, most likely, to the installation of tracking devices on cars and personal property.[249] In each of these cases, the Court has striven to strike a reasonable balance, preserving the security of the people against threats of unreasonable search and seizure by effective and enforceable means while also limiting the impact of those means on law enforcement.

The warrant requirement is, and always will be, a work in progress. That makes good sense given its status as a constitutional remedy, grounded in the reasonableness clause, and designed to meet emerging threats to the security of the people against unreasonable searches and seizures. Were it rigid by design or otherwise allowed to ossify, then the warrant requirement inevitably would become ineffective, unenforceable, and would also lead to unreasonable sacrifices on the part of law enforcement, citizens, or both.

The Exclusionary Rule

In its simplest form, the exclusionary rule provides that "all evidence obtained by searches and seizures in violation of the Constitution is, by that same authority, inadmissible."[250] The "exclusionary rule reaches not only primary evidence obtained as a direct result of an illegal search or seizure, but also evidence later discovered and found to be derivative of an illegality."[251] This is sometimes referred to as "fruit of the poisonous tree." For example, if officers search a home without a warrant, without consent, and without claim of emergency, then that search is contrary to the Fourth Amendment. If officers discover a bag of heroin during that illegal search, then they may confiscate the drugs, but cannot introduce them as evidence at a subsequent criminal trial to prove that the homeowner possessed narcotics. If chemical analysis of those drugs reveals the presence of a unique compound, leading investigators to the discovery of additional evidence linking the defendant to a broader drug conspiracy, then that additional evidence is fruit of the poisonous tree, and therefore cannot be introduced by the prosecutor as evidence in her case-in-chief against the homeowner.

As Justice Harry Blackmun pointed out in *United States v. Janis*, "debate within the Court on the exclusionary rule has always been a warm one."[252] Debates outside the Court have been equally vigorous. Critics often point to the fact that the text and history of the Fourth Amendment do not even remotely suggest that those who read and wrote the Fourth Amendment in 1791 would have thought that it required the exclusion of illegally seized evidence.[253] Critics also complain that the exclusionary rule provides a windfall to guilty defendants.[254] In the words of Judge (and later Justice) Benjamin Cardozo, "The criminal is to go free because the constable has blundered."[255] Compounding this complaint, critics argue that the exclusionary rule offers no remedy for innocent victims of illegal searches who, by definition, do not possess incriminating evidence, are not prosecuted, and therefore do not have need of an exclusionary rule.[256] Finally, critics complain that the exclusionary rule compromises the pursuit of truth in criminal trials by denying juries access to perfectly reliable evidence.[257]

On the other side of the debate, advocates for the exclusionary rule contend that it is inherent in the Fourth Amendment as a matter of principle. For example, in *Weeks v. United States*, the Supreme Court defended the exclusionary rule as essential to the Fourth Amendment itself. "If letters and private documents can thus be seized and held and used in evidence against a citizen accused of an offense," Justice William Day implored, then "the protection of the 4th Amendment, declaring his right to be secure against such searches and seizures, is of no value, and so far as those thus placed are concerned, might as well be stricken from the Constitution."[258] Reinforcing that view, Justice Holmes, writing for the Court a few years later in *Silverthorne Lumber Company v. United States*, concluded that "The essence of a provision forbidding the acquisition of evidence in a certain way is that not merely evidence so acquired shall not be used before the Court but that it shall not be used at all."[259] The alternative, he wrote, "reduces the Fourth Amendment to a form of words."[260] This is not to imply that exclusionary rule advocates are entirely satisfied with the present state of affairs. That is because, much like the warrant requirement, the exclusionary rule has been modified considerably over the years by a range of "exceptions." Many contemporary defenders worry that these exceptions have all but swallowed the rule, at considerable cost to the Fourth Amendment itself.[261]

The basic contours of these debates should seem familiar. They map quite nicely onto contests about the *Miranda* prophylaxis and the warrant requirement. That is no surprise. Like the *Miranda* warnings and the warrant requirement, the exclusionary rule emerged in the late eighteenth and early nineteenth centuries as a "judicially created remedy"[262] designed to guarantee the people's right to be secure from threats of unreasonable search and seizure. Also like the *Miranda* warnings and the warrant requirement, the Court developed the exclusionary rule in response to threats against the security of the people posed by the emergence of professional, paramilitary law enforcement agencies engaged in the competitive enterprise of detecting and prosecuting crime. Over time, the Court has defended the exclusionary rule as an effective and enforceable means of protecting the security of the people by curbing law enforcement excesses. The Court has tailored the exclusionary rule in order to strike a parsimonious balance among competing interests by preserving its remedial benefits while reducing as much as possible its costs to legitimate law enforcement goals and the truth-seeking functions of criminal trials. As we saw in our discussion of the warrant requirement, the result is a body of rules and "exceptions" comprising an overall remedial structure defined by the criteria of effectiveness, enforceability, and parsimoniousness.

The Role of Emerging Threats in the Court's Development of the Exclusionary Rule

The exclusionary rule is largely an American innovation.[263] It is also relatively new.[264] Justice Joseph Story reported for the Supreme Court in 1822 that he had never heard of such a thing.[265] A criminal defendant seeking to exclude illegally seized evidence from his criminal trial was roundly rebuffed by the Supreme Judicial Court of Massachusetts in 1841.[266] In fact, it was not until a century after the founding that the exclusionary rule made an appearance in the annals of the Supreme Court reporter in *Boyd v. United States*,[267] which also gave birth to the warrant requirement. There, and in its subsequent exclusionary rule cases, the Court cites concerns relating to the rise and expansion of professionalized police forces and the threats they pose to the people's right to be secure against unreasonable searches and seizures.

By the mid-twentieth century those concerns had become more acute. Thus, we see the Court in *Elkins v. United States*, decided in 1960, worrying about "expanding federal criminal jurisdiction" and an invisible epidemic of illegal searches suffered by innocent persons that simply never came to the attention of the courts.[268] The Court goes on in *Elkins* to cite additional evidence that alternative means of addressing this epidemic, such as administrative measures, criminal prosecutions, and private civil actions, had largely "failed to secure compliance with constitutional provisions," with the result that the "innocent suffer with the guilty."[269] In short, all the worries the Court cited in *Miranda* and its warrant requirement jurisprudence appear again as a motivating force in its exclusionary rule cases.

The Court's Reliance on the Reasonableness Clause in Its Exclusionary Rule Cases

From the exclusionary rule's earliest days, the Court has appealed to the broad authority granted by the reasonableness clause to justify exclusion as a constitutional remedy. "Constitutional provisions for the security of person and property," we are told by the Supreme Court in 1927, "are to be liberally construed."[270] "The Fourth Amendment," the Court continues,

> was adopted in view of long misuse of power in the matter of searches and seizures both in England and the colonies, and the assurance against any revival of it, so carefully embodied in the fundamental law, is not to be impaired by judicial sanction of equivocal methods, which, regarded superficially, may seem to escape the challenge of illegality but which, in reality, strike at the substance of the constitutional right.[271]

A few years later, the Court explained that the exclusionary rule is "not the product of a merely meticulous reading of technical language."[272] It is, instead, "the translation into practicality of broad considerations of morality and public well-being,"[273] born of "those great principles established by years of endeavor and suffering which have resulted in their embodiment in the fundamental law of the land."[274]

Despite the fact that it is a judicially created remedy, the Supreme Court has been quite clear that the exclusionary rule is constitutional.[275] Writing for the Court in 2011, Justice Alito explained how the Court drew on the broad authority of the reasonableness clause to fashion the exclusionary rule. "The Fourth Amendment," he wrote in *Davis v. United States*, "protects the 'right of the people to be secure in their persons, houses, papers, and effects, against unreasonable searches and seizures.'"[276] Although the "Amendment says nothing about suppressing evidence obtained in violation of this command," he continued, the exclusionary rule stands as "a prudential doctrine created by this Court to compel respect for the constitutional guaranty."[277] This does not mean that the exclusionary rule is any less constitutional in its nature or dimension. Quite to the contrary, as the Court explained in *Mapp v. Ohio*, the exclusionary rule "is of constitutional origin"[278] and "an essential part of both the Fourth and Fourteenth Amendments."[279] By virtue of its constitutional status, the *Mapp* Court held that the exclusionary rule applies in both state and federal courts.[280] Absent constitutional status, the Court would have no authority to require that state courts enforce the exclusionary rule.[281]

The Court Holds that the Exclusionary Rule Is Effective, Enforceable, and Parsimonious

In its cases establishing and elaborating the exclusionary rule, the Supreme Court has been quite clear that exclusion is not a personal right of the defendant but a collective right of the people "designed to safeguard Fourth Amendment rights generally through its deterrent effect."[282] It should therefore come as no surprise that the usual criteria governing constitutional remedies play an important role in both defending the exclusionary rule as an effective[283] and enforceable means of guaranteeing collective security and in tailoring its scope and application according to the demands of parsimoniousness.[284]

According to the modern Supreme Court, the exclusionary rule gives effect to the Fourth Amendment primarily by deterrence.[285] "Its purpose is to deter," the Court tells us in *Elkins v. United States*, "to compel respect for the constitutional guaranty in the only effectively available way – by removing the incentive to disregard it."[286] In keeping with the collective nature of the Fourth Amendment, the primary target for this deterrence is not the individual officer who may have violated the Fourth Amendment in a particular case – what criminal law theorists sometimes call "specific deterrence." The goal instead is general deterrence, which focuses on police officers as a class, and systemic deterrence, which focuses on law enforcement agencies. The exclusionary rule achieves general deterrence by encouraging all officers to think twice before violating the Fourth Amendment in the first place. The rule achieves systemic deterrence by compromising governmental efforts to prosecute and punish offenders. Threatened with the possibility of exclusion, agencies make every effort to avoid Fourth Amendment violations by training police officers and enforcing internal regulations designed to reduce the likelihood of mistakes while also preserving the status of police officers as a model of lawfulness.[287]

The effectiveness of the exclusionary rule in achieving general and systemic deterrence[288] is beyond speculation. As the Supreme Court noted in *Elkins v. United States* and again in *Mapp v. Ohio*, nothing else works.[289] In the early part of the twentieth century, before the Supreme Court required that state courts apply the exclusionary rule, states experimented with a number of alternatives to the exclusionary rule. Reflecting on those efforts in *Elkins*, the Court reported that "Experience has demonstrated, however, that neither administrative, criminal, nor civil remedies are effective in suppressing lawless searches and seizures."[290] What worked – the only thing that worked – was the threat of exclusion.

Citing the experiences of California, and other states that chose to adopt the exclusionary rule of their own accord, the *Elkins* Court reported that the threat of exclusion had an immediate and dramatic effect on both police practice and working relationships between police and prosecutors.[291] Officers started seeking legal advice from prosecutors before conducting searches. Agencies also started training their officers in an effort to prevent violations. The results in all these experiments were consistent: dramatically reduced Fourth Amendment violations. As the Court noted more recently in *Hudson v. Michigan*, that effect has been sustained, providing us with a well-trained and highly professional police force that is less likely to violate the Fourth Amendment rights of citizens than were their pre-exclusionary rule ancestors.[292]

The exclusionary rule could not be easier to enforce. If law enforcement officers violate the Fourth Amendment, and that violation produces evidence, then that evidence may not be admitted as part of the prosecutor's case-in-chief. For law enforcement officers, the threat of exclusions is therefore clear. The task for courts applying the exclusionary rule in particular cases is somewhat more complicated. That is because the overall remedial structure comprising the exclusionary rule includes a number of "exceptions." For example, if officers conduct a search that violates the Fourth Amendment, but do so in an honest and "good faith" belief that they are obeying constitutional demands, then evidence seized as a result need not be excluded.[293] Similarly, if the government can show that illegally seized evidence would inevitably have been secured by legal means, then the exclusionary may not be required.[294] When determining whether one or more of these exceptions applies in a particular case, courts often need to conduct separate suppression hearings. Although these procedures can be time-consuming, and require courts to weigh competing evidence, the law governing exceptions to the exclusionary rule is relatively categorical. Even if it is sometimes time-consuming, this clarity means that the exclusionary rule remains relatively easy to enforce.

As with the *Miranda* prophylaxis and the warrant requirement, the constitutional status of the exclusionary rule as a remedial measure is conditioned on its parsimoniousness.[295] The Supreme Court's defense of the exclusionary rule on this score starts with the propositions that the exclusionary rule does not impose unreasonable burdens on law enforcement in general[296] and that other remedial measures often have proved insufficient to the task of guaranteeing the security of the people against threats of unreasonable searches and seizures.[297] This does not mean that the exclusionary rule as a remedial structure requires exclusion of evidence in all cases, however. "Real deterrent value is a necessary condition for exclusion," Justice Alito pointed out recently in *Davis v. United States*, "but it is not a sufficient one."[298] Instead, the potential for deterrence must be weighed against the "substantial costs" of exclusion, including the "heavy toll on both the judicial system and society at large" incurred when courts must "ignore reliable, trustworthy evidence bearing on guilt or innocence," the "bottom-line effect" of which, "in many cases, is to suppress the truth and set the criminal loose in the community without punishment."[299] Out of respect for the demands of parsimoniousness, the Court will "swallow this bitter pill when necessary, but only as a last resort."[300] "For exclusion to be appropriate," therefore, "the deterrence benefits of suppression must outweigh the rule's heavy costs."[301]

The Supreme Court does not invite lower courts to engage in this balancing on a case-by-case basis. In order to preserve the effectiveness of the exclusionary rule as a deterrent, and in order to maintain ease of enforceability, the Court has instead created categorical rules describing classes of cases where the exclusionary rule does and does not apply.[302] For example, the Court has held that the exclusionary rule requires suppression of evidence only at criminal trials and not in collateral proceedings such as parole revocation procedures,[303] grand jury hearings,[304] civil tax proceedings,[305] and immigration enforcement actions[306] because officers' primary motivations lie in criminal prosecution and not potential collateral consequences. Suppressing evidence in collateral forums when it has already been suppressed at a criminal trial probably would not result in appreciable additional deterrence,[307] or at least would not provide enough additional deterrence to justify the additional costs.[308] For these same reasons, the exclusionary rule does not apply in circumstances where the discovery of evidence is sufficiently "attenuated" from the primary Fourth Amendment violation, such as when an officer conducts an illegal stop, discovers that there is a warrant for the suspect's arrest, conducts that arrest, and then discovers evidence of a crime on the suspect's person.[309] For similar reasons, the Court has held that exclusion is not required when officers act in a good faith belief that they are not violating the Fourth Amendment,[310] such as when they rely on a warrant that turns out to be defective[311] or on an established appellate court decision that is later overturned.[312] In these cases, officers have shown that they respect the Fourth Amendment and have done everything they reasonably can to avoid committing a violation.[313] Given the availability of true malfeasants, the Court has found that punishing these well-meaning officers would not provide sufficient additional deterrent benefit to justify the additional costs. To the contrary, the Court has argued, it might create frustration in the ranks, leading to an overall increase in Fourth Amendment violations.[314] Finally, the Court has held that only defendants whose personal Fourth Amendment rights were violated may request suppression under the exclusionary rule.[315] That does not make exclusion a personal remedy.[316] The Court's rationale focuses instead on the view that general deterrence can be achieved by allowing those whose rights were personally violated to seek suppression.[317] Allowing parties who have not suffered a direct Fourth Amendment violation to benefit from exclusion does not add enough additional deterrence to justify the additional costs.

Conclusion

In Chapter 4, we saw how the reasonableness clause of the Fourth Amendment provides for constitutional remedies designed to guarantee the security of the people against threats of unreasonable searches and seizures. We also saw how the warrant clause provides a model of this kind of remedial structure by barring general warrants and setting substantive and procedural limitations on more specific warrants. This chapter has reviewed three examples of constitutional remedies created by the Supreme Court. In all of these cases the Court applied a formula of sorts. It first took note of an emerging threat against the security of the people posed by expanding law enforcement presence, zealous efforts by law enforcement officers to detect, prevent, and prosecute crime, and unfettered law enforcement discretion to deploy a means or method of search, whether it be interrogation, physical searches, or the use of infrared scanning devices. In fashioning the *Miranda* warnings, the warrant requirement, and the exclusionary rule, the Court attempted to restore the security of the people by setting prospective constraints on law enforcement officers. In fashioning these remedies, the Court carefully tailored the remedy to the threat in order to ensure effectiveness.

It also paid close attention to considerations of enforceability and administrability. Finally, it tailored each of these remedies in order to ensure a parsimonious balance between protections of constitutional rights and effective crime control. Having met these three criteria, the Court has not hesitated to enforce these remedies as constitutional, thereby making them mandatory for the states and safeguarding them against legislative or executive meddling.

The Court's efforts to elaborate constitutional remedies in response to twentieth-century threats against the security of the people have much to teach us about the role of the Fourth Amendment in the twenty-first century. As we saw in Chapter 1, we live in an age of surveillance where the right of the people to be secure against unreasonable searches and seizures is threatened by new technologies and the excessive use of stops and frisks. The Fourth Amendment is well equipped to address these threats. Specifically, the Fourth Amendment provides for the fashioning and enforcement of constitutional remedies that are effective in meeting contemporary threats, enforceable by courts and law enforcement agencies, and parsimonious with respect to the competing interests at stake. In the next chapter, we will explore exactly what those remedies might look like.

Notes

1. This chapter expands on prior work. *See* David Gray, *Fourth Amendment Remedies as Rights: The Warrant Requirement*, 96 B.U. L. REV. 425 (2016) [hereinafter Gray, *Remedies as Rights*]; David Gray, *A Spectacular Non Sequitur: The Supreme Court's Contemporary Fourth Amendment Exclusionary Rule Jurisprudence*, 50 AM. CRIM. L. REV. 1 (2013) [hereinafter Gray, *A Spectacular Non Sequitur*].
2. Byars v. United States, 273 U.S. 28, 34–35 (1927) ("The Fourth Amendment was adopted in view of long misuse of power in the matter of searches and seizures both in England and the colonies, and the assurance against any revival of it, so carefully embodied in the fundamental law, is not to be impaired by judicial sanction of equivocal methods, which, regarded superficially, may seem to escape the challenge of illegality but which, in reality, strike at the substance of the constitutional right."); Thomas Y. Davies, *Recovering the Original Fourth Amendment*, 98 MICH. L. REV. 547, 576–77 (1999).
3. California v. Acevedo, 500 U.S. 565, 582 (1991) (Scalia, J., concurring) (arguing that the reasonableness clause incorporates common-law constraints on search and seizure, including the prohibition on general warrants and, in certain instances, a warrant requirement). Go-Bart Importing Co. v. United States, 282 U.S. 344, 357 (1931) ("[The warrant clause] prevents the issue of warrants on loose, vague or doubtful bases of fact. It emphasizes the purpose to protect against all general searches. Since before the creation of our government, such searches have been

deemed obnoxious to fundamental principles of liberty. They are denounced in the constitutions or statutes of every State in the Union."); Marron v. United States, 275 U.S. 192, 195 (1927) ("General searches have long been deemed to violate fundamental rights. It is plain that the amendment forbids them."); Davies, *supra* note 2, at 576-77 ("the constitutional texts [the Framers] wrote did not simply seek to provide a post-intrusion remedy or condemn only the actual use of a general warrant; rather, the constitutional tests adopted a preventative strategy by consistently prohibiting even the *issuance* of a too-loose warrant.").

4. Given this historical context, it comes as no surprise that then contemporary state constitutions focused narrowly on prohibiting general warrants. For example, the Virginia Declaration of Rights provided that "general warrants, whereby any officer or messenger may be commanded to search suspected places without evidence of a fact committed, or to seize any person or persons not named, or whose offence is not particularly described and supported by evidence, are grievous and oppressive, and ought not to be granted." VA. CONST., Declaration of Rights § 10 (1776). Similarly, the Massachusetts Bill of Rights guaranteed that "Every subject has a right to be secure from all unreasonable searches, and seizures of his person, his houses, his papers, and all his possessions. All warrants, therefore, are contrary to this right, if the cause or foundation of them be not previously supported by oath or affirmation; and if the order in the warrant to a civil officer, to make search in suspected places, or to arrest one or more suspected persons, or to seize their property, be not accompanied with a special designation of the persons or objects of search, arrest, or seizure: and no warrant ought to be issued but in cases, and with the formalities, prescribed by the laws." MASS. CONST., Bill of Rights, art. XIV (1780). The Vermont, New Hampshire, North Carolina, Maryland, Pennsylvania, and Delaware constitutions similarly focused exclusively on banning general warrants. See VT. CONST., Bill of Rights, art. XII (1786) ("That the people have a right to hold themselves, their houses, papers and possessions, free from search or seizure: and therefore warrants, without oaths or affirmations first made, affording sufficient foundation for them, and whereby any officer or messenger may be commanded or required to search suspected places, or to seize any person or persons, his, her or their property not particularly described, are contrary to that right, and ought not to be granted."); N.H. CONST., Bill of Rights, art. XIX (1784) ("Every subject hath a right to be secure from all unreasonable searches and seizures of his person, his houses, his papers, and all his possessions. All warrants, therefore, are contrary to this right, if the cause or foundation of them be not previously supported by oath, or affirmation; and if the order in the warrant to a civil officer, to make search in suspected places, or to arrest one or more suspected persons, or to seize their property, be not accompanied with a special designation of the persons or objects of search, arrest, or seizure; and no warrant ought to be issued but in cases, and with the formalities prescribed by the laws."); MASS. CONST., Bill of Rights, art. XIV (1780) ("Every subject has a right to be secure from all unreasonable searches, and seizures of his person, his houses, his papers, and all his possessions. All warrants, therefore, are contrary to this right, if the cause or foundation of them be not previously supported by oath or affirmation; and if the order in the warrant to a civil officer, to make search in suspected places, or to arrest one or more suspected persons, or to seize their property, be not accompanied with a special designation of the persons or objects of search, arrest, or seizure: and no warrant ought to be issued

but in cases, and with the formalities, prescribed by the laws."); VA. CONST., Declaration of Rights § 10 (1776) ("That general warrants, whereby any officer or messenger may be commanded to search suspected places without evidence of a fact committed, or to seize any person or persons not named, or whose offence is not particularly described and supported by evidence, are grievous and oppressive, and ought not to be granted."); N.C. CONST., Declaration of Rights, art. XI (1776) ("That general warrants – whereby an officer or messenger may be commanded to search suspected places, without evidence of the fact committed, or to seize any person or persons, not named, whose offences are not particularly described, and supported by evidence – are dangerous to liberty, and ought not to be granted."); MD. CONST., Declaration of Rights, art. XXIII (1776) ("That all warrants, without oath or affirmation, to search suspected places, or to seize any person or property, are grievous and oppressive; and all general warrants to search suspected places, or to apprehend suspected persons, without naming or describing the place, or the person in special, are illegal, and ought not to be granted."); PA. CONST., Declaration of Rights, art. X (1776) ("That the people have a right to hold themselves, their houses, papers, and possessions free from search and seizure, and therefore warrants without oaths or affirmations first made, affording a sufficient foundation for them, and whereby any officer or messenger may be commanded or required to search suspected places, or to seize any person or persons, his or their property, not particularly described, are contrary to that right, and ought not to be granted."); DEL. CONST., Declaration of Rights, art. XVII (1776) ("That all warrants without oath to search suspected places, or to seize any person or his property, are grievous and oppressive; and all general warrants to search suspected places, or to apprehend all persons suspected, without naming or describing the place or any person in special, are illegal and ought not to be granted.").

5. Davies, *supra* note 2, at 589.
6. *Id.* at 658.
7. *Id.* at 589.
8. *Id.* at 658.
9. *See* Wolf v. Colorado, 338 U.S. 25, 28 (1949). *See also* Atwater v. Lago Vista, 532 U.S. 318, 351–53 (2001) (pointing out that Fourth Amendment remedies should only be imposed when courts are faced with evidence of widespread abuse).
10. Constitutional law scholar Mark Graber has argued that general warrants and writs of assistance are symptoms rather than the primary pathogen. In his view, it was the rise of the bureaucratic state in the eighteenth century that posed the true threat. Absent that machinery, general warrants posed no real threat because there was neither motive nor means to exploit them. Mark Graber, *State Capacity to See and the Development of the Fourth Amendment: Time Immemorial to 1900ish*, in CAMBRIDGE HANDBOOK OF SURVEILLANCE LAW (David Gray & Stephen Henderson, eds. forthcoming 2017).
11. Wesley MacNeil Oliver, *The Neglected History of Criminal Procedure*, 62 RUTGERS L. REV. 447, 447–48 (2010); Davies, *supra* note 2, at 620–21; Silas J. Wasserstrom, *The Fourth Amendment's Two Clauses*, 26 AM. CRIM. L. REV. 1389, 1395 (1989); Thomas Y. Davies, *Farther and Farther from the Original Fifth Amendment: The Recharacterization of the Right Against Self-incrimination as a "Trial Right"* in Chavez v. Martinez, 70 TENN. L. REV. 987, 1004 (2003); Carol Steiker, *Second Thoughts About First Principles*, 107 HARV. L. REV. 820, 824 (1994).

12. PRESIDENTIAL COMM'N ON LAW ENFORCEMENT & ADMIN. OF JUSTICE, TASK FORCE ON THE POLICE COMMISSION REPORT, THE POLICE 6 (1967) [hereinafter COMMISSION REPORT].
13. TELFORD TAYLOR, TWO STUDIES IN CONSTITUTIONAL INTERPRETATION 28 (1969); Oliver, *supra* note 11, at 447–48, 454–55; Wasserstrom, *supra* note 11, at 1395.
14. COMMISSION REPORT, *supra* note 12, at 4; VERN FOLLEY, AMERICAN LAW ENFORCEMENT 70 (1980); Davies, *supra* note 2, at 641; Oliver, *supra* note 11, at 451–52, 456. *Cf.* Wasserstrom, *supra* note 11, at 1395 (noting that "The few law enforcement officials that there were – sheriffs, constables, and customs inspectors – had very limited power to search or seize without a warrant.").
15. Oliver, *supra* note 11, at 452–65; Davies, *supra* note 2, at 622.
16. TAYLOR, *supra* note 13, at 24; Oliver, *supra* note 11, at 452–53.
17. TAYLOR, *supra* note 13, at 25; Davies, *supra* note 2, at 623.
18. Oliver, *supra* note 11, at 450–52, 55–56 (indicating that eighteenth-century rules of criminal procedure made it risky for officers to make arrests without warrants, that warrants were generally obtained by victims of crimes, and that constables had little incentive to perform any investigation unless a reward was offered).
19. Oliver, *supra* note 11, at 450–51, 455, 464. See also Crawford v. Washington, 541 U.S. 36, 43 (2004) (pointing out that justices of the peace conducted examinations of witnesses in eighteenth-century England).
20. Akhil Reed Amar, *Fourth Amendment First Principles*, 107 HARV. L. REV. 757, 774–78 (1994). Professor Amar goes on to argue that warrants themselves were regarded as a threat to the security of the people in 1789. On this point, he probably goes too far. See Gouled v. United States, 255 U.S. 298, 308 (1921) ("The wording of the Fourth Amendment implies that search warrants were in familiar use when the Constitution was adopted and, plainly, that when issued 'upon probable cause, supported by oath or affirmation, and particularly describing the place to be searched and the persons or things to be seized,' searches, and seizures made under them, are to be regarded as not unreasonable, and therefore not prohibited by the amendment."); TAYLOR, *supra* note 13, at 41 ("It is perhaps too much to say that [the founders] feared the warrant more than the search . . .").
21. Although this is still nominally true today, most government agents are sued in their professional capacities rather than their personal capacities. Furthermore, most government agencies indemnify their agents against tort actions brought against them on the basis of their conduct in office. As a result, government entities rather than their agents are the practical parties in interest whenever someone sues a government official nowadays.
22. Wilkes v. Wood, (1763) 98 Eng. Rep. 489.
23. This calculation was performed using the Bank of England's inflation calculator, which is available at www.bankofengland.co.uk/education/Pages/resources/inflationtools/calculator/flash/default.aspx.
24. Wilkes v. Halifax, (1769) 19 Howell St. Tr. 1401.
25. TAYLOR, *supra* note 13, at 45; Oliver, *supra* note 11, at 524; Wasserstrom, *supra* note 11, at 1394; Anthony G. Amsterdam, *Perspectives on the Fourth Amendment*, 58 MINN. L. REV. 349, 399 (1974).
26. COMMISSION REPORT, *supra* note 12, at 43; FOLLEY, *supra* note 14, at 43, 59.

27. COMMISSION REPORT, *supra* note 12, at 43. *See also* Crawford v. Washington, 541 U.S. 36, 53 (2004) ("England did not have a professional police force until the 19th century . . ."); FOLLEY, *supra* note 14, at 43, 59.
28. Oliver, *supra* note 11, at 448 ("Modern police departments, charged with aggressively investigating and preventing crime, were created over strenuous objections that their very existence would undermine common-law limits on police conduct.").
29. COMMISSION REPORT, *supra* note 12, at 43; Oliver, *supra* note 11, at 447-48, 450, 455 ("Until the latter half of the nineteenth century, victims and magistrates conducted investigations, not police officers. Victims obtained enough information to satisfy themselves that probable cause existed to seek a warrant. After the suspect's arrest, magistrates, not constables, conducted the interrogation.").
30. DAVID R. JOHNSON, POLICING THE URBAN UNDERWORLD: THE IMPACT OF CRIME ON THE DEVELOPMENT OF THE AMERICAN POLICE 1800-1887, at 9 (1979). *See also* FOLLEY, *supra* note 14, at 68-69; COMMISSION REPORT, *supra* note 12, at 45.
31. FOLLEY, *supra* note 14, at 71; JOHNSON, *supra* note 30, at 9; COMMISSION REPORT, *supra* note 12, at 44. Peel is familiar to criminal law students as the intended target of Daniel M'Naughten, of the eponymous *M'Naughten* standard that remains the predominate test for legal insanity.
32. Metropolitan Police Act of 1829.
33. Then and now, officers of the Metropolitan police are called "bobbies" or "peelers" in reference to Sir Robert Peel's role in establishing the organization. *Sir Robert Peel (1788-1850)*, BBC HIST., www.bbc.co.uk/history/historic_figures/peel_sir_robert.shtml (last visited Apr. 11, 2016).
34. This eventually changed, culminating in the creation of the Criminal Investigation Department under the authority of the Home Secretary in 1878. The investigative unit became a permanent part of the Metropolitan Police Service in 1888 amidst the famous Whitechapel murders credited to Jack the Ripper.
35. JOHNSON, *supra* note 30, at 9.
36. COMMISSION REPORT, *supra* note 12, at 44.
37. JOHNSON, *supra* note 30, at 9; Oliver, *supra* note 11, at 459.
38. COMMISSION REPORT, *supra* note 12, at 45; Oliver, *supra* note 11, at 459.
39. COMMISSION REPORT, *supra* note 12, at 45.
40. *See generally* MICHEL FOUCAULT, DISCIPLINE AND PUNISH 21-28 (1979).
41. Oliver, *supra* note 11, at 448.
42. Colonial obsessions with writs of assistance arose from entanglements between a relatively small number of merchants and customs or tax officials, not common engagements between citizens and police officers. *See* TAYLOR, *supra* note 13, at 35, 44; Oliver, *supra* note 11, at 450, 455-57.
43. FOLLEY, *supra* note 14, at 73, 101-02.
44. *Id.* at 156-57.
45. *See, e.g.*, Oliver, *supra* note 11, at 468-71 (describing how, in the late nineteenth century, the use of clubs by New York Police officers "to punish and intimidate those [they] identified as being part of the 'criminal element' was not only accepted, it was publicly encouraged.").

46. *See, e.g.*, Johnson v. United States, 333 U.S. 10, 13 (1948) ("Entry to defendant's living quarters ... was demanded under color of office. It was granted in submission to authority ...").
47. FOLLEY, *supra* note 14, at 78; Oliver, *supra* note 11, at 459.
48. Oliver, *supra* note 11, at 459, 524.
49. *Id.* at 469-70.
50. *Id.* at 469.
51. THOMAS ROPETTO, AMERICAN POLICE: THE BLUE PARADE 199 (2011).
52. *Id.*; Oliver, *supra* note 11, at 473. This is described in the policing literature as the "command and control" model of police-citizen interactions. *See, e.g.*, Eric Miller, *Role-Based Policing*, 94 CALIF. L. REV. 617, 661-62 (2006); Tom Tyler, *Trust and Law Abidingness: A Proactive Model of Social Regulation*, 81 B.U. L. REV. 361, 363-64 (2001).
53. ROPETTO, *supra* note 51, at 39-40; MARILYNN S. JOHNSON, STREET JUSTICE: A HISTORY OF POLICE VIOLENCE IN NEW YORK CITY 63-69 (2003); EDWIN G. BURROWS & MIKE WALLACE, GOTHAM: A HISTORY OF NEW YORK CITY TO 1898, at 638 (1999); Oliver, *supra* note 11, at 471-73.
54. *See, e.g.*, Sean J. Kealy, *Reexamining the Posse Comitatus Act: Toward a Right to Civil Law Enforcement*, 21 YALE L. & POL'Y REV. 383, 386 (2003) (discussing the inculcation of a "warrior mentality" among police officers).
55. *See Id.*
56. *See Id.*
57. Oliver, *supra* note 11, at 460; Wasserstrom, *supra* note 11, at 1395.
58. FOLLEY, *supra* note 14, at 72.
59. *See* Berger v. New York, 388 U.S. 41, 46-49 (1967).
60. Oliver, *supra* note 11, at 465.
61. Miranda v. Arizona, 384 U.S 436, 446 (1966) (summarizing cases dealing with custodial interrogations in which "the police resorted to physical brutality – beating, hanging, whipping – and to sustained and protracted questioning incommunicado in order to extort confessions.").
62. Olmstead v. United States, 277 U.S. 438 (1928) (Brandeis, J., dissenting) ("As a means of espionage, writs of assistance and general warrants are but puny instruments of tyranny and oppression when compared with wiretapping."); Oliver, *supra* note 11, at 466-68.
63. Oliver, *supra* note 11, at 460-61, 478, 482.
64. *Id.* at 461, 468-69.
65. *See supra* note 53.
66. *See, e.g.*, Oliver, *supra* note 11, at 469-70 (describing how one police captain armed squads of officers with clubs, ordering them to go into tough neighborhoods to beat known gang members).
67. *Id.* at 472-73 (explaining that bribery of police was so prevalent in late nineteenth-century New York that estimated illegal contributions was listed in tourist guidebooks).
68. *Id.* at 460 ("In the early years of the Progressive Era, officers were given a very public mandate to torture suspects in interrogation rooms and inflict unnecessary violence upon suspected criminals on the streets.").
69. Wasserstrom, *supra* note 11, at 1395.

70. *See Boyd*, 116 U.S. at 629; Commission Report, *supra* note 12, at 6, 7; Oliver, *supra* note 11, at 448, 460–61, 478–82; Wasserstrom, *supra* note 11, at 1395.
71. *See generally* Lisa McGirr, The War on Alcohol (2015).
72. *See, e.g.*, Weeks v. United States, 232 U.S. 383, 392 (1914) ("The tendency of those who execute the criminal laws of the country to obtain conviction by means of unlawful seizures and enforced confessions ... should find no sanction in the judgments of the courts, which are charged at all times with the support of the Constitution, and to which people of all conditions have a right to appeal for the maintenance of such fundamental rights.").
73. *See* Oliver, *supra* note 11, at 448.
74. 116 U.S. 616, 620–21 (1886).
75. The Fifth Amendment provides that "No person shall be held to answer for a capital, or otherwise infamous crime, unless on a presentment or indictment of a grand jury, except in cases arising in the land or naval forces, or in the militia, when in actual service in time of war or public danger; nor shall any person be subject for the same offense to be twice put in jeopardy of life or limb; nor shall be compelled in any criminal case to be a witness against himself, nor be deprived of life, liberty, or property, without due process of law; nor shall private property be taken for public use, without just compensation." U.S. Const. amend. VI.
76. *Boyd*, 116 U.S. at 630.
77. Miranda v. Arizona, 384 U.S. 436 (1966).
78. Dickerson v. United States, 530 U.S. 428, 443 (2000); Miranda v. Arizona, 384 U.S. 436, 478–79 (1966).
79. *See infra* Part IV.
80. United States v. Patane, 542 U.S. 630, 641 (2004) ("[T]he nature of the right protected by the Self-Incrimination Clause ... is a fundamental trial right.").
81. *See, e.g., Miranda*, 384 U.S. at 478–79; Escobedo v. Illinois, 378 U.S. 478 (1964).
82. *See Dickerson*, 530 U.S. at 432; *Miranda*, 384 U.S. at 490–91.
83. Oliver, *supra* note 11, at 447–48.
84. *Id.* at 453–56; Davies, *supra* note 2, at 620–24, 640–42.
85. *Miranda*, 384 U.S. at 458–60; Brown v. Walker, 161 U.S. 591, 596–97 (1896).
86. *Brown*, 161 U.S. at 596–97.
87. 384 U.S. at 445–46.
88. Oliver, *supra* note 11, at 447–55.
89. *Id.* at 483.
90. *See Id.* at 483–85.
91. Although these out-of-court statements are considered hearsay under the rules of evidence, the common law has long had an exception for statements against interest made by party opponents, which would allow a prior confession to be admitted at trial. That common-law rule is now enshrined in in the Federal Rules of Evidence and the rules of evidence in every state. *See, e.g.*, Fed. R. Evid. 801(d)(2)(A).
92. *See* Brown v. Mississippi, 297 U.S. 278 (1936).
93. Oliver, *supra* note 11, at 483–85.
94. Nat'l Comm'n on Law Observance and Enforcement, Report on Lawlessness in Law Enforcement 5 (1931).
95. Miranda v. Arizona, 384 U.S. 436, 463 (1966).

96. 297 U.S. 278 (1936).
97. *See, e.g.*, Leyra v. Denno, 347 U.S. 556 (1954); Malinski v. New York, 324 U.S. 401 (1945); Ashcraft v. Tennessee, 322 U.S. 143 (1944); Ward v. Texas, 316 U.S. 547 (1942); Vernon v. Alabama, 313 U.S. 547 (1941); White v. Texas, 310 U.S. 530 (1940); Canty v. Alabama, 309 U.S. 629 (1940); Chambers v. Florida, 309 U.S. 227 (1940).
98. Dickerson v. United States, 530 U.S. 428, 432–34 (2000).
99. *Miranda*, 384 U.S. at 446–47.
100. *Id.* at 448–53.
101. *Id.* at 454. *See also* Spano v. New York, 360 U.S. 315 (1959).
102. *Miranda*, 384 U.S. at 451.
103. *Dickerson*, 530 U.S. at 442; *Miranda*, 384 U.S. at 445, 457–58.
104. *Miranda*, 384 U.S. at 467.
105. *Id.* at 450, 458.
106. *Id.* at 442.
107. *Id.*
108. *Id.* (quoting Cohens v. Virginia, 19 U.S. 387 (1821)).
109. *Id.* at 459–60, 490–91.
110. *Id.* at 443–44.
111. *Id.* (quoting and commenting on Weems v. United States, 217 U.S. 349, 373 (1910), and Silverthorne Lumber Co. v. United States, 251 U.S. 385, 391 (1920)).
112. *Miranda*, 384 U.S. at 459.
113. *Id.* at 458–60. *See also* Brown v. Walker, 161 U.S. 591, 596–97 (1896).
114. *Miranda*, 384 U.S. at 459.
115. *Id.* at 442–43 (quoting and commenting on Brown v. Walker, 161 U.S. at 596–97).
116. Dickerson v. United States, 530 U.S. 428, 428 (2000); *Miranda*, 384 U.S. at 467.
117. *Miranda*, 384 U.S. at 444. *See also Dickerson*, 530 U.S. at 428 ("We concluded [in *Miranda*] that the coercion inherent in custodial interrogation ... heightens the risk that an individual will not be 'accorded his privilege under the Fifth Amendment ...' Accordingly, we laid down 'concrete constitutional guidelines for law enforcement agencies and courts to follow.' ").
118. *Miranda*, 384 U.S. at 444, 479, 480–81 (quoting Silverthorne Lumber Co. v. United States, 251 U.S. 385, 391 (1920)); TAYLOR, *supra* note 13, at 5.
119. *Miranda*, 384 U.S. at 444.
120. *Id.* at 467. Whether the prophylaxis is, in fact, effective is a subject of considerable controversy. For present purposes, we need not enter that debate. All that is necessary is to recognize that the Court believed that the Miranda prophylaxis would be effective and that it regarded effectiveness as essential to the warnings' standing as a constitutional remedy.
121. *Id.* at 468.
122. *Id.*
123. *Id.*
124. *Id.* at 469.
125. *Id.*
126. *Id.* at 468–69.
127. *Id.* at 441–42.
128. *Id.*
129. *Id.* at 468–69.

130. *Id.* at 441–42.
131. *Id.* at 468–69.
132. Here and throughout, I use "parsimoniousness" in the sense philosophers do. For this group, credit for this concept of parsimoniousness goes to Sir William of Ockham, who is most famous for his razor, which held that metaphysical theories should be trimmed and honed in order to avoid assumptions unnecessary to explain described phenomena. For example, Ockham's razor would frown on positing the existence of invisible elves sitting on our shoulders and whispering in our ears to explain cognition.
133. *Miranda*, 384 U.S. at 467–69, 471–72, 473.
134. *Id.* at 477–79, 481.
135. *Id.* at 483–86.
136. *Miranda*, 384 U.S. at 444, 467. *See also* Dickerson v. United States, 530 U.S. 428, 440 (2000) ("Additional support for our conclusion that *Miranda* is constitutionally based is found in the Miranda Court's invitation for legislative action to protect the constitutional right against coerced self-incrimination.").
137. *Dickerson*, 530 U.S. at 440, 443–44.
138. *Id.* at 443–44.
139. In his classic piece of narrative journalism, David Simon describes in compelling detail how officers use *Miranda* warnings to assist them in the interrogation process. *See* DAVID SIMON, HOMICIDE 193–207 (1991).
140. *See, e.g.*, Paul G. Cassell, *All Benefits, No Costs: The Grand Illusion of* Miranda's *Defenders*, 90 NW. U. L. REV. 1084 (1996); Paul G. Cassell, *The Costs of the* Miranda *Mandate: A Lesson in the Dangers of Inflexible, "Prophylactic" Supreme Court Inventions*, 28 ARIZ. ST. L.J. 299 (1996); Stephen Schulhofer, Miranda's *Practical Effect: Substantial Benefits and Vanishingly Small Social Costs*, 90 NW. U. L. REV. 500 (1996); Paul G. Cassell, Miranda's *Social Costs: An Empirical Reassessment*, 90 NW. U. L. REV. 387 (1996); Richard A. Leo, *Inside the Interrogation Room*, 86 J. CRIM. L. & CRIMINOLOGY 266 (1996). The Supreme Court had the opportunity to review and assess much of the evidence deployed in these debates in *Dickerson v. United States*, 530 U.S. 428 (2000), which was argued by one of *Miranda's* fiercest academic critics, Professor Paul Cassell. It ultimately found that *Miranda*, as modified by subsequent decisions, had resulted in modest impact on "legitimate law enforcement," the prophylaxis having "become embedded in routine police practice to the point where the warnings have become part of our national culture." *Id.* at 443.
141. Professor Cassell reasserted his case most recently in Paul G. Cassell & Richard Fowles, *Still Handcuffing the Cops?: A Review of Fifty Years of Empirical Evidence of* Miranda's *Harmful Effects on Law Enforcement*, 97 B.U. L. REV. (forthcoming 2017).
142. *Miranda*, 384 U.S. at 427–28.
143. Katz v. United States, 389 U.S. 347, 357 (1967).
144. Amar, *supra* note 20, at 770. The cases Amar cites, Mincey v. Arizona, 537 U.S. 385 (1978), Coolidge v. New Hampshire, 403 U.S. 443 (1971), and Johnson v. United States, 333 U.S. 10 (1948), entail searches of homes or their constitutional equivalent. The fact that officers intruded upon places traditionally granted the highest degrees of Fourth Amendment protection played a critical role in all these cases. It would therefore be wrong to conclude that any of them relied upon a broad,

general, per se warrant rule. It is true that *Mincey* and *Coolidge* repeat a line of purple prose from *Katz*, 389 U.S. at 357 (1967), reading "searches conducted outside the judicial process, without prior approval by judge or magistrate, are per se unreasonable under the Fourth Amendment." In context, however, that quote looks like a throw-away line from Justice Stewart. In that portion of the opinion, he is responding to the government's argument that its agents could have secured a warrant if they had tried, and, therefore, no prejudice should befall the prosecution simply because the officers did not get a warrant. As Justice Stewart points out, that rule would fail to protect the security of the people. 389 U.S. at 556–57.

145. *See, e.g.*, Camara v. Mun. Ct., 387 U.S. 523, 528–29 (1967); Agnello v. United States, 269 U.S. 20, 32 (1925); TAYLOR, *supra* note 13, at 49; Davies, *supra* note 2, at 601–11.
146. Carroll v. United States, 267 U.S. 132 (1925); California v. Carney, 471 U.S. 386 (1985).
147. Chimel v. California, 395 U.S. 752 (1969).
148. Kentucky v. King, 563 U.S. 452 (2011).
149. Palmieri v. Lynch, 392 F.3d 73 (2d Cir. 2004).
150. Camara v. Municipal Court, 387 U.S. 523 (1967).
151. Amar, *supra* note 20, at 770.
152. Riley v. California, 134 S. Ct. 2473 (2014).
153. *See* Transcript of Oral Argument at 42–43, Riley v. California, 134 S. Ct. 2473 (2014) (No.13-132) (Justices Scalia, Sotomayor, Kennedy, and Alito expressing skepticism). In reaching its holding, the *Riley* Court largely adopted a technology-centered approach to evaluating Fourth Amendment interests in quantitative privacy first described in David Gray & Danielle Citron, *The Right to Quantitative Privacy*, 98 MINN. L. REV. 62, 103–25 (2014).
154. *See, e.g.*, TAYLOR, *supra* note 13, at 23–49; Amar, *supra* note 20, at 761–81.
155. *Id.* at 762–68.
156. Amar, *supra* note 20, at 770–71.
157. *Id.*
158. 269 U.S. 20, 32 (1925).
159. *Id.* The Court later withdrew from the exception identified by Justice Butler in *Agnello. See* Payton v. New York, 445 U.S. 573 (1980) (holding that law enforcement must have an arrest warrant in order to conduct a search incident to arrest of a suspect's home).
160. *Agnello*, 269 U.S. at 23.
161. Amar, *supra* note 20, at 770–71; TAYLOR, *supra* note 13, at 44.
162. *See, e.g.*, District of Columbia v. Heller, 554 U.S. 570 (2008).
163. Roper v. Simmons, 543 U.S. 551, 607 (2005) (Scalia, J., dissenting).
164. ANTONIN SCALIA, A MATTER OF INTERPRETATION (1997).
165. United States v. Jones, 132 S. Ct. 945 (2012).
166. 533 U.S. 27, 40 (2001).
167. California v. Acevedo, 500 U.S. 565, 582 (1982) (Scalia, J., concurring) ("Although the Fourth Amendment does not explicitly impose the requirement of a warrant, it is, of course, textually possible to consider that implicit within the requirement of reasonableness.").
168. *See, e.g.*, Vernonia Sch. Dist. 47J v. Acton, 515 U.S. 646, 653 (1995) ("As the text of the Fourth Amendment indicates, the ultimate measure of the constitutionality of

a governmental search is 'reasonableness'... Where a search is undertaken by law enforcement officials to discover evidence of criminal wrongdoing, this Court has said that reasonableness generally requires the obtaining of a judicial warrant."); *Acevedo*, 500 U.S. at 583–84 (Scalia, J., concurring); *see* Camara v. Mun. Ct., 387 U.S. at 528–29 (1967) ("Though there has been general agreement as to the fundamental purpose of the Fourth Amendment, translation of the abstract prohibition against 'unreasonable searches and seizures' into workable guidelines for the decision of particular cases is a difficult task which has for many years divided the members of this Court. Nevertheless, one governing principle, justified by history and by current experience, has consistently been followed: except in certain carefully defined classes of cases, a search of private property without proper consent is 'unreasonable' unless it has been authorized by a valid search warrant."); Agnello v. United States, 269 U.S. 20, 32 (1925) ("The search of a private dwelling without a warrant is, in itself, unreasonable and abhorrent to our laws.").

169. 116 U.S. 616 (1886). Although *Boyd* does not state explicitly the existence of a warrant requirement, Justice Butler later credits *Boyd*, among other early cases, for ingraining the warrant requirement in Fourth Amendment law. *See Agnello*, 269 U.S. at 33 ("While the question has never been directly decided by this Court, it has always been assumed that one's house cannot lawfully be searched without a search warrant, except as an incident to a lawful arrest therein."). *Boyd*'s role in Fourth Amendment jurisprudence recently was revitalized by Chief Justice Roberts, who cited and quoted from *Boyd* extensively in his majority opinion for the Court in *Riley v. California. See, e.g.*, 134 S. Ct. 2473, 2494–95 (2014).
170. Weeks v. United States, 232 U.S. 383, 391 (1914).
171. Go-Bart Importing Co. v. United States, 282 U.S. 344, 390 (1931).
172. Johnson v. United States, 333 U.S. 10, 13–14 (1948).
173. Brinegar v. United States, 338 U.S. 160, 182 (1949) (Jackson, J., dissenting)
174. *Johnson*, 333 U.S. at 14.
175. Boyd v. United States, 116 U.S. 616, 618 (1886) ("As the question raised upon the order for the production by the claimants of the invoice of the twenty-nine cases of glass, and the proceedings had thereon, is not only an important one in the determination of the present case, but is a very grave question of constitutional law, involving the personal security, and privileges and immunities of the citizen, we will set forth the order at large.").
176. 333 U.S. at 14.
177. Berger v. New York, 388 U.S. 41, 58 (1967).
178. 533 U.S. 27, 31 (2001).
179. This is at least true of the general public. Sophisticates such as Ben Franklin and Thomas Jefferson may have had some familiarity with Émilie du Châtelet's investigations of fire, which predicted emanations beyond the light detected by human eyes. They may also have heard some rumors about John Herschel's work with prisms and thermometers, documenting a temperature change on surfaces that did not have the benefit of visible illumination, which he presented to the Royal Society in 1800. But none of this work predicted the scope and ubiquity of what would come to be known as infrared radiation, much less that human beings emitted invisible but detectable rays. Although there were a few primitive devices

capable of detecting infrared radiation, commercial devices were not available until the 1960s.
180. *Kyllo*, 533 U.S. at 34.
181. *Id.* at 31 (quoting Silverman v. United States, 365 U.S. 505 (1961) (internal quotation marks omitted)).
182. *Id.* at 37–38.
183. *Id.* at 36.
184. *Id.* at 40.
185. 132 S. Ct. 945, 963–64 (2012) (Alito, J., concurring).
186. *Id.* at 955 (Sotomayor, J., concurring).
187. *Id.* at 955–56.
188. *Id.* at 956.
189. *Id.* (internal quotation marks and citation omitted).
190. Riley v. California, 134 S. Ct. 2473, 2490 (2014).
191. Boyd v. United States, 116 U.S. 616, 630 (1886).
192. Camara v. Mun. Ct., 387 U.S. 523, 528 (1967).
193. Gouled v. United States, 255 U.S. 298, 304 (1921). *See also* Weems v. United States, 217 U.S. 349, 373 (1910) ("Time works changes, brings into existence new conditions and purposes. Therefore a principle, to be vital, must be capable of wider application than the mischief which gave it birth. This is peculiarly true of constitutions. They are not ephemeral enactments, designed to meet passing occasions. They are, to use the words of Chief Justice Marshall, 'designed to approach immortality as nearly as human institutions can approach it.' The future is their care, and provision for events of good and bad tendencies of which no prophecy can be made ... Under any other rule, a constitution would indeed be as easy of application as it would be deficient in efficacy and power. Its general principles would have little value, and be converted by precedent into impotent and lifeless formulas. Rights declared in words might be lost in reality."); TAYLOR, *supra* note 13, at 5–6, 12–15.
194. Go-Bart Importing Co. v. United States, 282 U.S. 344, 356–57 (1931).
195. United States v. Lefkowitz, 285 U.S. 452, 464 (1932).
196. Carroll v. United States, 267 U.S. 132, 149 (1925).
197. *Id.*
198. Amsterdam, *supra* note 25, at 402.
199. A MARYLAND FARMER, NO. 1 (1788); 2 THE CANADIAN FREEHOLDER: IN THREE DIALOGUES BETWEEN AN ENGLISHMAN AND A FRENCHMAN SETTLED IN CANADA 243–44 (London, B. White 1779).
200. Boyd v. United States, 116 U.S. 616, 635 (1886).
201. 232 U.S. 383, 391 (1914).
202. 132 S. Ct. 945, 956 (1921) (quoting United States v. Di Re, 332 U.S. 581, 595 (1948)).
203. Berger v. New York, 388 U.S. 41, 53, 63 (1967).
204. Vernonia Sch. Dist. 47J v. Acton, 515 U.S. 646, 653 (1995) ("As the text of the Fourth Amendment indicates, the ultimate measure of the constitutionality of a governmental search is 'reasonableness.' ... Where a search is undertaken by law enforcement officials to discover evidence of criminal wrongdoing, this Court has said that reasonableness generally requires the obtaining of a judicial warrant."); California v. Acevedo, 500 U.S. 565, 583–84 (1991) (Scalia, J., concurring);

see Camara v. Mun. Ct., 387 U.S. at 528-29 (1967) ("Though there has been general agreement as to the fundamental purpose of the Fourth Amendment, translation of the abstract prohibition against 'unreasonable searches and seizures' into workable guidelines for the decision of particular cases is a difficult task which has for many years divided the members of this Court. Nevertheless, one governing principle, justified by history and by current experience, has consistently been followed: except in certain carefully defined classes of cases, a search of private property without proper consent is 'unreasonable' unless it has been authorized by a valid search warrant."); Agnello v. United States, 269 U.S. 20, 32 (1925) ("The search of a private dwelling without a warrant is, in itself, unreasonable and abhorrent to our laws.").

205. TAYLOR, *supra* note 13, at 38-42; Davies, *supra* note 2, at 650-57.
206. Gouled v. United States, 255 U.S. 298, 308 (1921) ("The wording of the Fourth Amendment implies that search warrants[,] ... when issued 'upon probable cause, supported by oath or affirmation, and particularly describing the place to be searched and the persons or things to be seized,' searches, and seizures made under them, are to be regarded as not unreasonable, and therefore not prohibited by the amendment.").
207. Oren Bar-Gill & Barry Friedman, *Taking Warrants Seriously*, 106 NW. U. L. REV. 1609, 1610-11 (2012).
208. 285 U.S. 452, 464 (1932).
209. 401 U.S. 745, 789-90 (1971) (Harlan, J., dissenting).
210. RICHARD LEONE & GREG ANRIG, THE WAR ON OUR FREEDOM: CIVIL LIBERTIES IN AN AGE OF TERRORISM (2003) ("By permitting searches and seizures only if reasonable, and interposing the courts between the privacy of citizens and the potential excesses of executive zeal," these constitutional protections help to protect against " 'dragnets, or general searches, which were anathema to the colonists who rebelled against the British crown.' ").
211. Agnello v. United States, 269 U.S. 20, 33 (1925) ("Belief, however well founded, that an article sought is concealed in a dwelling house furnishes no justification for a search of that place without a warrant. And such searches are held unlawful notwithstanding facts unquestionably showing probable cause.").
212. Johnson v. United States, 333 U.S. 10, 14 (1948).
213. 232 U.S. 383, 391 (1914).
214. 285 U.S. 452, 464 (1932).
215. Riley v. California, 134 S. Ct. 2473, 2490 (2014).
216. Wong Sun v. United States, 371 U.S. 471, 481-82 (1963); Berger v. New York, 388 U.S. 41, 59-60 (1967); Brinegar v. United States, 338 U.S. 160, 182 (1949) ("We must remember, too, that freedom from unreasonable search differs from some of the other rights of the Constitution in that there is no way in which the innocent citizen can invoke advance protection. For example, any effective interference with freedom of the press, or free speech, or religion, usually requires a course of suppressions against which the citizen can and often does go to the court and obtain an injunction. Other rights, such as that to an impartial jury or the aid of counsel, are within the supervisory power of the courts themselves. Such a right as just compensation for the taking of private property may be vindicated after the act in terms of money. But an illegal search and seizure usually is a single incident, perpetrated by surprise, conducted in haste, kept purposely beyond the

court's supervision and limited only by the judgment and moderation of officers whose own interests and records are often at stake in the search. There is no opportunity for injunction or appeal to disinterested intervention. The citizen's choice is quietly to submit to whatever the officers undertake or to resist at risk of arrest or immediate violence.").
217. *Johnson*, 333 U.S. at 13-14. *See also Lefkowitz*, 285 U.S. at 464.
218. *Lefkowitz*, 285 U.S. at 464 ("the informed and deliberate determinations of magistrates empowered to issue warrants as to what searches and seizures are permissible under the Constitution are to be preferred over the hurried action of officers and others who may happen to make arrests.").
219. *See* JÜRGEN HABERMAS, BETWEEN FACTS AND NORMS 107-08 (1996); 1 JÜRGEN HABERMAS, THE THEORY OF COMMUNICATIVE ACTION 8-32 (1984).
220. Max Minzner, *Putting Probability Back Into Probable Cause*, 87 TEX. L. REV. 913, 923-25 (2009).
221. Alexander Reinert, *Public Interest(s) and Fourth Amendment Enforcement*, 2010 U. ILL. L. REV. 1461, 1500; Wasserstrom, *supra* note 11, at 1396.
222. Davies, *supra* note 2, at 576-77, 589, 657; Donald Dripps, *Living with Leon*, 95 YALE L.J. 906, 926-27 (1986).
223. Vernonia Sch. Dist. v. Acton, 515 U.S. 646, 653 (1995).
224. Johnson v. United States, 333 U.S. 10, 13-15 (1948).
225. Silverthorne Lumber Co. v. United States, 251 U.S. 385, 392 (1920).
226. Gouled, 255 U.S. 298, 308 (1921).
227. *See* Gray, *A Spectacular Non Sequitur, supra* note 1, at 29-30. As Bill Stuntz has pointed out, the good faith exception plays an important role in reinforcing the systemic effectiveness of the warrant requirement as a constraint on law enforcement. *See* William Stuntz, *Warrants and Fourth Amendment Remedies*, 77 VA. L. REV. 881, 909 (1991).
228. Riley v. California, 134 S. Ct. 2473, 2491-92 (2014).
229. *Johnson*, 333 U.S. at 14 ("Any assumption that evidence sufficient to support a magistrate's disinterested determination to issue a search warrant will justify the officers in making a search without a warrant would reduce the Amendment to a nullity, and leave the people's homes secure only in the discretion of police officers.").
230. 388 U.S. 41, 63 (1967) (internal alterations, quotation marks, and citation omitted).
231. *Riley*, 134 S. Ct. at 2493.
232. *Id.*
233. *Id.*
234. United States v. Cruikshank, 92 U.S. 542, 549 (1875) ("Citizens are the members of the political community to which they belong. They are the people who compose the community, and who, in their associated capacity, have established or submitted themselves to the dominion of a government for the promotion of their general welfare and the protection of their individual as well as their collective rights. In the formation of a government, the people may confer upon it such powers as they choose. The government, when so formed, may, and when called upon should, exercise all the powers it has for the protection of the rights of its citizens and the people within its jurisdiction, but it can exercise no other.

CONCLUSION 239

The duty of a government to afford protection is limited always by the power it possesses for that purpose.").

235. Maryland v. Buie, 494 U.S. 325 (1990) (holding that the interest in officer safety permitted officers to continue searching a home, via a "protective sweep," after finding and arresting a man for whom they had an arrest warrant).

236. Warden, Md. Penitentiary v. Hayden, 387 U.S. 294, 298-99 (1967) ("The Fourth Amendment does not require police officers to delay in the course of an investigation if to do so would gravely endanger their lives or the lives of others ... The permissible scope of search must, therefore, at the least, be as broad as may reasonably be necessary to prevent the dangers that the suspect at large in the house may resist or escape.").

237. Kentucky v. King, 563 U.S. 452 (2011); Segura v. United States, 468 U.S. 796, 808 (1984) ("[S]ociety's interest in the discovery and protection of incriminating evidence from removal or destruction can supersede, at least for a limited period, a person's possessory interest in property, provided that there is probable cause to believe that that property is associated with criminal activity.").

238. *Riley*, 134 S. Ct. at 2494.

239. *Id.* at 2493.

240. *Johnson*, 333 U.S. at 14-15. *See also* Antonin Scalia, *In Memoriam: Edward H. Levi (1912-2000)*, 67 U. CHI. L. REV. 983, 985 (2000) ("The Fourth Amendment, after all, does not require a warrant; it requires reasonable searches and seizures, and in the intelligence field, reasonableness does not demand the service of a warrant.").

241. Carroll v. United States, 267 U.S. 132 (1925).

242. California v. Carney, 471 U.S. 386 (1985).

243. *Id.*

244. Arizona v. Gant, 556 U.S. 332 (2009); *Carney*, 471 U.S. 386; *Carroll*, 267 U.S. 132, 149.

245. Thornton v. United States, 541 U.S. 615 (2004); *Gant*, 556 U.S. 332.

246. Kentucky v. King, 563 U.S. 452 (2011).

247. Kyllo v. United States, 533 U.S. 27 (2001).

248. Riley v. California, 134 S. Ct. 2473 (2014).

249. Jones v. United States, 132 S. Ct. 945 (2012). *But see* United States v. Katzin, 769 F.3d 163 (3d Cir. 2014) (allowing a good faith exception to the exclusionary rule when police officers attached a GPS device to defendant's vehicle).

250. Mapp v. Ohio, 367 U.S. 643, 655 (1961).

251. Segura v. United States, 468 U.S. 796, 804 (1984).

252. United States v. Janis, 428 U.S. 433, 446 (1976).

253. Amar, *supra* note 20; TAYLOR, *supra* note 13.

254. 8 WIGMORE, EVIDENCE § 2184 (3d ed. 1940) ("Titus, you have been found guilty of conducting a lottery; Flavius, you have confessedly violated the constitution. Titus ought to suffer imprisonment for crime, and Flavius for contempt. But no! We shall let you both go free. We shall not punish Flavius directly, but shall do so by reversing Titus' conviction. This is our way of teaching people like Flavius to behave, and of teaching people like Titus to behave, and incidentally of securing respect for the Constitution. Our way of upholding the Constitution is not to strike at the man who breaks it, but to let off somebody else who broke something else.").

255. People v. Defore, 150 N.E. 585, 587 (N.Y. 1926).
256. *See, e.g.*, Tonja Jacobi, *The Law and Economics of the Exclusionary Rule*, 87 Notre Dame L. Rev. 585, 588, 635–38 (2011).
257. United States v. Calandra, 414 U.S. 338, 349–50 (1974); Bivens v. Six Unknown Named Agents of the Fed. Bureau of Narcotics, 403 U.S. 388, 412 (1971) (Burger, C.J., concurring) (indicting the exclusionary rule as the "rule under which evidence of undoubted reliability and probative value has been suppressed and excluded from criminal cases whenever it was obtained in violation of the Fourth Amendment.").
258. 232 U.S. 383, 393 (1914).
259. Silverthorne Lumber Co. v. United States, 251 U.S. 385, 392 (1920).
260. *Id.*
261. *See, e.g.*, David Gray et al., *The Supreme Court's Contemporary Silver Platter Doctrine*, 91 Tex. L. Rev. 7 (2012).
262. Davis v. United States, 131 S. Ct. 2419, 2427 (2011); United States v. Calandra, 414 U.S. 338, 348 (1974).
263. *See, e.g.*, Wolf v. Colorado, 338 U.S. 5, 29 (1949) (noting that "most of the English-speaking world does not regard as vital" the "exclusion of evidence thus obtained" illegally). A notable exception is the Canadian Charter of Rights and Freedoms, which grants courts authority to exclude evidence seized in violation of the Charter if admitting that evidence "would bring the administration of justice into disrepute." Canada Act, 1982, c. 11 § 24(2) (U.K.).
264. *See* William Heffernan, *The Fourth Amendment Exclusionary Rule as a Constitutional Remedy*, 88 Geo. L.J. 799, 808 (2000); Amar, *supra* note 20, at 785–91; Potter Stewart, *The Road to* Mapp v. Ohio *and Beyond: The Origins, Development and Future of the Exclusionary Rule in Search-and-Seizure Cases*, 83 Colum. L. Rev. 1365, 1372–77 (1983). As Amar points out, the primary common-law remedy for illegal searches was a suit in trespass against the offending officer himself. Amar, *supra* note 20, at 774. Prior provision of a warrant served as an absolute defense against such suits, as did success in finding evidence. *Id.* at 767, 774.
265. Amar, *supra* note 20, at 786–77 (quoting United States v. La Jeune Eugenie, 26 F. Cas. 832, 843–44 (C.C.D. Mass. 1822) (No. 15,551)).
266. Commonwealth v. Dana, 43 Mass. (2 Met.) 329, 337 (1841) ("If the search warrant were illegal, or if the officer serving the warrant exceeded his authority, the party on whose complaint the warrant issued, or the officer, would be responsible for the wrong done; but this is no good reason for excluding the papers seized as evidence, if they were pertinent to the issue, as they unquestionably were. When papers are offered in evidence, the court can take no notice how they were obtained, whether lawfully or unlawfully ...").
267. 116 U.S. 616 (1886).
268. 364 U.S. 206, 211, 217–18 (1960).
269. 364 U.S. at 220 (citing and quoting People v. Cahan, 282 P.2d 905, 911–12, 13 (Cal. 1955)).
270. Byars v. United States, 273 U.S. 28, 32 (1927). *Cf.* Wolf v. Colorado, 338 U.S. 25, 27 (1949) ("Due process of law thus conveys neither formal nor fixed nor narrow requirements. It is the compendious expression for all those rights which the courts must enforce because they are basic to our free society. But basic rights do

not become petrified as of any one time, even though, as a matter of human experience, some may not too rhetorically be called eternal verities. It is of the very nature of a free society to advance in its standards of what is deemed reasonable and right. Representing as it does a living principle, due process is not confined within a permanent catalogue of what may at a given time be deemed the limits or the essentials of fundamental rights.").

271. *Byars*, 273 U.S. at 33–34.
272. Nardone v. United States, 308 U.S. 338, 340 (1939).
273. *Id. See also* Weeks v. United States, 232 U.S. 383, 391–92 (1914): "The effect of the Fourth Amendment is to put the courts of the United States and Federal officials, in the exercise of their power and authority, under limitations and restraints as to the exercise of such power and authority, and to forever secure the people, their persons, houses, papers, and effects, against all unreasonable searches and seizures under the guise of law. This protection reaches all alike, whether accused of crime or not, and the duty of giving to it force and effect is obligatory upon all intrusted under our Federal system with the enforcement of the laws. The tendency of those who execute the criminal laws of the country to obtain conviction by means of unlawful seizures and enforced confessions, the latter often obtained after subjecting accused persons to unwarranted practices destructive of rights secured by the Federal Constitution, should find no sanction in the judgments of the courts, which are charged at all times with the support of the Constitution, and to which people of all conditions have a right to appeal for the maintenance of such fundamental rights."
274. *Weeks*, 232 U.S. at 393.
275. *See, e.g.*, Chapman v. United States, 365 U.S. 610 (1961); Kremen v. United States, 353 U.S. 346 (1957) (per curiam); McDonald v. United States, 335 U.S. 451 (1948); Nathanson v. United States, 290 U.S. 41 (1933); Grau v. United States, 287 U.S. 124 (1932); Taylor v. United States, 286 U.S. 1 (1932); United States v. Berkeness, 275 U.S. 149 (1927); Byars v. United States, 273 U.S. 28 (1927); Amos v. United States, 255 U.S. 313 (1921).
276. Davis v. United States, 131 S. Ct. 2419, 2426 (2011) (internal citations and quotation marks omitted).
277. *Id. See also Id.* at 2423 ("The Fourth Amendment protects the right to be free from 'unreasonable searches and seizures,' but it is silent about how this right is to be enforced. To supplement the bare text, this Court created the exclusionary rule, a deterrent sanction that bars the prosecution from introducing evidence obtained by way of a Fourth Amendment violation."); Pa. Bd. of Prob. & Parole v. Scott, 524 U.S. 357, 363 (1998) ("The exclusionary rule is instead a judicially created means of deterring illegal searches and seizures."); United States v. Calandra, 414 U.S. 338, 348 (1974) ("In sum, the rule is a judicially created remedy designed to safeguard Fourth Amendment rights generally through its deterrent effect, rather than a personal constitutional right of the party aggrieved."); Wong Sun v. United States, 371 U.S. 471, 484 (1963) ("In order to make effective the fundamental constitutional guarantees of sanctity of the home and inviolability of the person, this Court held nearly half a century ago that evidence seized during an unlawful search could not constitute proof against the victim of the search.") (internal citation omitted); Wolf v. Colorado, 338 U.S. 25, 28 (1949) ("In Weeks v. United States, *supra*, this Court held that, in a federal prosecution the Fourth Amendment

barred the use of evidence secured through an illegal search and seizure. This ruling was made for the first time in 1914. It was not derived from the explicit requirements of the Fourth Amendment; it was not based on legislation expressing Congressional policy in the enforcement of the Constitution. The decision was a matter of judicial implication.").

278. Mapp v. Ohio, 367 U.S. 655, 649 (1961) ("But the plain and unequivocal language of *Weeks* – and its later paraphrase in *Wolf* – to the effect that the *Weeks* rule is of constitutional origin ..."). *See also* Byars v. United States, 273 U.S. 28, 29–30 (1927) ("[T]he doctrine [cannot] ... be tolerated under our constitutional system, that evidences of crime discovered by a federal officer in making a search without lawful warrant may be used against the victim of the unlawful search where a timely challenge has been interposed.").

279. *Mapp*, 367 U.S. at 657 ("The exclusionary rule is an essential part of both the Fourth and Fourteenth Amendments."). *See also Id.* at 655 ("In short, the admission of the new constitutional right by *Wolf* could not consistently tolerate denial of its most important constitutional privilege, namely, the exclusion of the evidence which an accused had been forced to give by reason of the unlawful seizure. To hold otherwise is to grant the right but, in reality, to withhold its privilege and enjoyment."); Olmstead v. United States, 277 U. S. 438, 462 (1928) ("The striking outcome of the *Weeks* case and those which followed it was the sweeping declaration that the Fourth Amendment, although not referring to or limiting the use of evidence in courts, really forbade its introduction if obtained by government officers through a violation of the Amendment.").

280. 367 U.S. 643 (1961).

281. *See* Dickerson v. United States, 530 U.S. 428, 438 (2000) ("It is beyond dispute that we do not hold a supervisory power of the courts of the several States. With respect to proceedings in state courts, our authority is limited to enforcing the commands of the United States Constitution.").

282. *Calandra*, 414 U.S. at 348. *See also* Herring v. United States, 555 U.S. 135 (2009) (same).

283. *Herring*, 555 U.S. at 141 ("We have repeatedly rejected the argument that exclusion is a necessary consequence of a Fourth Amendment violation. Instead we have focused on the efficacy of the rule in deterring Fourth Amendment violations in the future.").

284. Davis v. United States, 131 S. Ct. 2419, 2426 (2011) ("Exclusion is 'not a personal constitutional right,' nor is it designed to 'redress the injury' occasioned by an unconstitutional search. The rule's sole purpose, we have repeatedly held, is to deter future Fourth Amendment violations.") (internal citations omitted).

285. *Calandra*, 414 U.S. at 347 ("[T]he rule's prime purpose is to deter future unlawful police conduct and thereby effectuate the guarantee of the Fourth Amendment against unreasonable searches and seizures."); Elkins v. United States, 364 U.S. 206, 217 (1960) ("The rule is calculated to prevent, not to repair. Its purpose is to deter – to compel respect for the constitutional guaranty in the only effectively available way – by removing the incentive to disregard it."). For a critique of this view, see Gray, *A Spectacular Non Sequitur*, *supra* note 1.

286. *Elkins*, 364 U.S. at 217 ("The rule is calculated to prevent, not to repair.").

287. Olmstead v. United States, 277 U.S. 438, 485 (1928) (Brandeis, J., dissenting) ("Our Government is the potent, the omnipresent teacher. For good or for ill, it

teaches the whole people by its example. Crime is contagious. If the Government becomes a lawbreaker, it breeds contempt for the law; it invites every man to become a law unto himself; it invites anarchy. To declare that . . . the end justifies the means . . . would bring terrible retribution."). Justice White later countered that withholding probative evidence and letting the guilty go free might also compromise the public's perceptions of judicial integrity. *See* Stone v. Powell, 428 U.S. 465, 485 (1976). He went a step further in *Illinois v. Gates*, where he wrote "I am content that the interests in judicial integrity run along with rather than counter to the deterrence concept, and that to focus upon the latter is to promote, not denigrate, the former." 462 U.S. 213, 259 n.14 (1983) (White, J., concurring). The evidence appears decidedly neutral. Public regard for police and the courts has stayed pretty stable in the years since the Court started expanding exceptions to the exclusionary rule in the 1970s and 1980s. *See, e.g.*, Greg M. Shaw et al., *The Polls - Trends: Crime, The Police, and Civil Liberties*, 62 PUB. OPINION Q. 405 (1998); Mark Warr, *The Polls - Poll Trends: Public Opinion on Crime and Punishment*, 59 PUB. OPINION Q. 296 (1995). There is, however, some data suggesting a general downward trend in public respect for law enforcement since 1967. *See Id.* at 310.
288. *Id.*
289. 367 U.S. 643, 655 (1961) ("[W]ithout the Weeks rule the assurance against unreasonable federal searches and seizures would be 'a form of words,' valueless and undeserving of mention in a perpetual charter of inestimable human liberties, so too, without that rule the freedom from state invasions of privacy would be so ephemeral and so neatly severed from its conceptual nexus with the freedom from all brutish means of coercing evidence as not to merit this Court's high regard as a freedom 'implicit in the concept of ordered liberty.' "); *Elkins*, 364 U.S. at 220-21 (" 'We have been compelled to reach that conclusion because other remedies have completely failed to secure compliance with the constitutional provisions on the part of police officers with the attendant result that the courts under the old rule have been constantly required to participate in, and in effect condone, the lawless activities of law enforcement officers . . . The innocent suffer with the guilty, and we cannot close our eyes to the effect the rule we adopt will have on the rights of those not before the court.' The chief law enforcement officer of California was quoted as having made this practical evaluation of the *Cahan* decision less than two years later: 'The over-all effects of the *Cahan* decision, particularly in view of the rules now worked out by the Supreme Court, have been excellent. A much greater education is called for on the part of all peace officers of California. As a result, I am confident they will be much better police officers. I think there is more cooperation with the District Attorneys and this will make for better administration of criminal justice.' ") (quoting People v. Cahan, 282 P.2d 905, 911-912, 913 (Cal. 1955)).
290. *Elkins*, 364 U.S. at 220-21.
291. *Id.*; *Mapp*, 367 U.S. at 651-53. *See also* Raymond A. Atkins & Paul H. Rubin, *Effects of Criminal Procedure on Crime Rates: Mapping Out the Consequences of the Exclusionary Rule*, 46 J.L. & ECON. 157 (2003).
292. 547 U.S. 586, 598-99 (2006).

293. *See, e.g.*, Davis v. United States, 131 S. Ct. 2419, 2427–28 (2011); Herring v. United States, 555 U.S. 135, 142 (2009); United States v. Leon, 468 U.S. 897, 909 (1984).
294. Nix v. Williams, 467 U.S. 431, 443 (1984) ("By contrast, the derivative evidence analysis ensures that the prosecution is not put in a worse position simply because of some earlier police error or misconduct. The independent source doctrine allows admission of evidence that has been discovered by means wholly independent of any constitutional violation."); 467 U.S. at 443 ("the interest of society in deterring unlawful police conduct and the public interest in having juries receive all probative evidence of a crime are properly balanced by putting the police in the same, not a worse, position that they would have been in if no police error or misconduct had occurred."); 467 U.S. at 444 ("If the prosecution can establish by a preponderance of the evidence that the information ultimately or inevitably would have been discovered by lawful means – here, the volunteers' search – then the deterrence rationale has so little basis that the evidence should be received.").
295. *See, e.g.*, I.N.S. v. Lopez-Mendoza, 468 U.S. 1032, 1041 (1984) ("Imprecise as the exercise may be, the Court recognized in *Janis* that there is no choice but to weigh the likely social benefits of excluding unlawfully seized evidence against the likely costs. On the benefit side of the balance the prime purpose of the [exclusionary] rule, if not the sole one, `is to deter future unlawful police conduct. On the cost side, there is the loss of often probative evidence and all of the secondary costs that flow from the less accurate or more cumbersome adjudication that therefore occurs." (internal citations and quotation marks omitted); Pa. Bd. of Prob. & Parole v. Scott, 524 U.S. 357, 363 (1998) ("because the rule is prudential rather than constitutionally mandated, we have held it to be applicable only where its deterrence benefits outweigh its substantial social costs." (internal quotation marks omitted)).
296. *Elkins*, 364 U.S. at 218 ("The federal courts themselves have operated under the exclusionary rule of Weeks for almost half a century; yet it has not been suggested either that the Federal Bureau of Investigation has thereby been rendered ineffective, or that the administration of criminal justice in the federal courts has thereby been disrupted.").
297. *See Id.* at 220–21 ("We have been compelled to reach that conclusion because other remedies have completely failed to secure compliance with the constitutional provisions on the part of police officers, with the attendant result that the courts under the old rule have been constantly required to participate in, and in effect condone, the lawless activities of law enforcement officers.").
298. Davis v. United States, 131 S. Ct. 2419, 2427 (2011) (internal citations and quotation marks omitted).
299. *Id.* (internal citations and quotation marks omitted); *Scott*, 524 U.S. at 364 ("Because the exclusionary rule precludes consideration of reliable, probative evidence, it imposes significant costs: It undeniably detracts from the truthfinding process and allows many who would otherwise be incarcerated to escape the consequences of their actions.); United States v. Calandra, 414 U.S. 338, 342–46, 350–51 (1974); United States v. Payner, 447 U.S. 727, 734 (1980) ("The Court has acknowledged that the suppression of probative but tainted evidence exacts a costly toll upon the ability of courts to ascertain the truth in a criminal case."); Rakas v. Illinois, 439 U.S. 128, 137 (1978) ("Each time the exclusionary rule is

applied, it exacts a substantial social cost for the vindication of Fourth Amendment rights. Relevant and reliable evidence is kept from the trier of fact and the search for truth at trial is deflected."); *Nix*, 467 U.S. at 445 ("enormous societal cost of excluding truth in the search for truth in the administration of justice.").

300. *Davis*, 131 S. Ct. at 2427 (internal citations and quotation marks omitted); *Calandra*, 414 U.S. at 351–52; *Nix*, 467 U.S. at 442–43 ("The core rationale consistently advanced by this Court for extending the exclusionary rule to evidence that is the fruit of unlawful police conduct has been that this admittedly drastic and socially costly course is needed to deter police from violations of constitutional and statutory protections.").

301. *Davis*, 131 S. Ct. at 2427. *See also* Herring v. United States, 555 U.S. 135, 141 (2009) ("In addition, the benefits of deterrence must outweigh the costs. We have never suggested that the exclusionary rule must apply in every circumstance in which it might provide marginal deterrence. To the extent that application of the exclusionary rule could provide some incremental deterrent, that possible benefit must be weighed against [its] substantial social costs. The principal cost of applying the rule is, of course, letting guilty and possibly dangerous defendants go free – something that offends basic concepts of the criminal justice system. The rule's costly toll upon truth-seeking and law enforcement objectives presents a high obstacle for those urging its application." (internal citations, quotation marks, and alterations omitted)); *Payner*, 447 U.S. at 734 ("Indeed, the decisions of this Court are replete with denunciations of willfully lawless activities undertaken in the name of law enforcement. But our cases also show that these unexceptional principles do not command the exclusion of evidence in every case of illegality. Instead, they must be weighed against the considerable harm that would flow from indiscriminate application of an exclusionary rule." (internal citations omitted)); People v. DeFore, 150 N.E. 585, 589 (N.Y. 1926) ("The question is whether protection for the individual would not be gained at a disproportionate loss of protection for society. On the one side is the social need that crime shall be repressed. On the other, the social need that law shall not be flouted by the insolence of office. There are dangers in any choice. The rule of the Adams case strikes a balance between opposing interests.").

302. *Scott*, 524 U.S. at 363 ("The exclusionary rule is instead a judicially created means of deterring illegal searches and seizures. As such, the rule does not proscribe the introduction of illegally seized evidence in all proceedings or against all persons, but applies only in contexts where its remedial objectives are thought most efficaciously served. (internal citations and quotation marks omitted); *Payner*, 447 U.S. at 733; *Calandra*, 414 U.S. 338.

303. *Scott*, 524 U.S. at 364 ("Application of the exclusionary rule would both hinder the functioning of state parole systems and alter the traditionally flexible, administrative nature of parole revocation proceedings. The rule would provide only minimal deterrence benefits in this context, because application of the rule in the criminal trial context already provides significant deterrence of unconstitutional searches."); *Id.* at 367–68 ("Because the exclusionary rule precludes consideration of reliable, probative evidence, it imposes significant costs: It undeniably detracts from the truthfinding process and allows many who

would otherwise be incarcerated to escape the consequences of their actions ... The noncriminal parole proceeding falls outside the offending officer's zone of primary interest. Thus, even when the officer knows that the subject of his search is a parolee, the officer will be deterred from violating Fourth Amendment rights by the application of the exclusionary rule to criminal trials." (internal citation and quotation marks omitted)).

304. *Calandra*, 414 U.S. at 349 ("In deciding whether to extend the exclusionary rule to grand jury proceedings, we must weigh the potential injury to the historic role and functions of the grand jury against the potential benefits of the rule as applied in this context. It is evident that this extension of the exclusionary rule would seriously impede the grand jury.").

305. United States v. Janis, 428 U.S. 433, 448 (1976) ("In evaluating the need for a deterrent sanction, one must first identify those who are to be deterred. In this case, it is the state officer who is the primary object of the sanction. It is his conduct that is to be controlled. Two factors suggest that a sanction in addition to those that presently exist is unnecessary. First, the local law enforcement official is already 'punished' by the exclusion of the evidence in the state criminal trial. That, necessarily, is of substantial concern to him. Second, the evidence is also excludable in the federal criminal trial, *Elkins v. United States*, so that the entire criminal enforcement process, which is the concern and duty of these officers, is frustrated." (internal citations omitted)); *Id.* at 454 ("If the exclusionary rule is the 'strong medicine' that its proponents claim it to be, then its use in the situations in which it is now applied (resulting, for example, in this case in frustration of the Los Angeles police officers' good faith duties as enforcers of the criminal laws) must be assumed to be a substantial and efficient deterrent. Assuming this efficacy, the additional marginal deterrence provided by forbidding a different sovereign from using the evidence in a civil proceeding surely does not outweigh the cost to society of extending the rule to that situation. If, on the other hand, the exclusionary rule does not result in appreciable deterrence, then, clearly, its use in the instant situation is unwarranted. Under either assumption, therefore, the extension of the rule is unjustified.").

306. I.N.S. v. Lopez-Mendoza, 468 U.S. 1032, 1046 (1984) ("For the reasons we have discussed, we conclude that application of the rule in INS civil deportation proceedings, as in the circumstances discussed in *Janis*, is unlikely to provide significant, much less substantial, additional deterrence. Important as it is to protect the Fourth Amendment rights of all persons, there is no convincing indication that application of the exclusionary rule in civil deportation proceedings will contribute materially to that end. On the other side of the scale, the social costs of applying the exclusionary rule in deportation proceedings are both unusual and significant. The first cost is one that is unique to continuing violations of the law. Applying the exclusionary rule in proceedings that are intended not to punish past transgressions, but to prevent their continuance or renewal, would require the courts to close their eyes to ongoing violations of the law. This Court has never before accepted costs of this character in applying the exclusionary rule.") (internal citation and quotation marks omitted)).

307. *Calandra*, 414 U.S. at 350 "Against this potential damage to the role and functions of the grand jury, we must weigh the benefits to be derived from this proposed

extension of the exclusionary rule. Suppression of the use of illegally seized evidence against the search victim in a criminal trial is thought to be an important method of effectuating the Fourth Amendment. But it does not follow that the Fourth Amendment requires adoption of every proposal that might deter police misconduct.").

308. *Id.* at 351–52. ("Any incremental deterrent effect which might be achieved by extending the rule to grand jury proceedings is uncertain, at best. Whatever deterrence of police misconduct may result from the exclusion of illegally seized evidence from criminal trials, it is unrealistic to assume that application of the rule to grand jury proceedings would significantly further that goal. Such an extension would deter only police investigation consciously directed toward the discovery of evidence solely for use in a grand jury investigation. The incentive to disregard the requirement of the Fourth Amendment solely to obtain an indictment from a grand jury is substantially negated by the inadmissibility of the illegally seized evidence in a subsequent criminal prosecution of the search victim. For the most part, a prosecutor would be unlikely to request an indictment where a conviction could not be obtained. We therefore decline to embrace a view that would achieve a speculative and undoubtedly minimal advance in the deterrence of police misconduct at the expense of substantially impeding the role of the grand jury.").
309. *See* Utah v. Strieff, 579 U.S. _ (2016).
310. Davis v. United States, 131 S. Ct. 2419, 2427–28 (2011) ("The basic insight of the *Leon* line of cases is that the deterrence benefits of exclusion vary with the culpability of the law enforcement conduct at issue. When the police exhibit deliberate, reckless, or grossly negligent disregard for Fourth Amendment rights, the deterrent value of exclusion is strong and tends to outweigh the resulting costs. But when the police act with an objectively reasonable good faith belief that their conduct is lawful, or when their conduct involves only simple, isolated negligence the deterrence rationale loses much of its force, and exclusion cannot pay its way." (internal citations, quotation marks, and alterations omitted)); Herring v. United States, 555 U.S. 135 (2009); United States v. Leon, 468 U.S. 897, 909 (1984).
311. Groh v. Ramirez, 540 U.S. 551 (2004); Massachusetts v. Sheppard, 468 U.S. 981 (1984).
312. *Davis*, 131 S. Ct. at 2429 ("An officer who conducts a search in reliance on binding appellate precedent does no more than 'ac[t] as a reasonable officer would and should act' under the circumstances. The deterrent effect of exclusion in such a case can only be to discourage the officer from do his duty.").
313. *See* Maryland v. Garrison, 480 U.S. 79 (1987) (describing lengths that officers went to when trying to determine the precise location of a suspect's apartment in a subdivided building and applying the good faith exception when the officers in advertently ended up in the wrong apartment while serving the warrant).
314. Herring v. United States, 555 U.S. 135 (2009). For a critique of this view, see Gray, *Remedies as Rights, supra* note 1, and Gray, *A Spectacular Non Sequitur, supra* note 1.
315. United States v. Calandra, 414 U.S. 338, 348 (1974) ("As with any remedial device, the application of the rule has been restricted to those areas where its remedial objectives are thought most efficaciously served. The balancing process implicit in

this approach is expressed in the contours of the standing requirement. Thus, standing to invoke the exclusionary rule has been confined to situations where the Government seeks to use such evidence to incriminate the victim of the unlawful search.). *See also* United States v. Payner, 447 U.S. 727, 733 (1980); Brown v. United States, 411 U.S. 223 (1973); Alderman v. United States, 394 U. S. 165, 174–75 (1969) ("The deterrent values of preventing he incrimination of those whose rights the police have violated have been considered sufficient to justify the suppression of probative evidence even though the case against the defendant is weakened or destroyed. We adhere to that judgment. But we are not convinced that the additional benefits of extending the exclusionary rule to other defendants would justify further encroachment upon the public interest in prosecuting those accused of crime and having them acquitted or convicted on the basis of all the evidence which exposes the truth."); Wong Sun v. United States, 371 U.S. 471, 488 (1963) ("the more apt question in such a case is whether, granting establishment of the primary illegality, the evidence to which instant objection is made has been come at by exploitation of that illegality or instead by means sufficiently distinguishable to be purged of the primary taint.") (internal quotation marks and citation omitted); Jones v. United States, 362 U. S. 257 (1960).

316. *Herring*, 555 U.S. at 141 ("First, the exclusionary rule is not an individual right and applies only where it results in appreciable deterrence. We have repeatedly rejected the argument that exclusion is a necessary consequence of a Fourth Amendment violation. Instead we have focused on the efficacy of the rule in deterring Fourth Amendment violations in the future.") (internal citations, quotation marks, and alterations omitted).

317. *Calandra*, 414 U.S. at 348 ("This standing rule is premised on a recognition that the need for deterrence, and hence the rationale for excluding the evidence, are strongest where the Government's unlawful conduct would result in imposition of a criminal sanction on the victim of the search.").

6

The Fourth Amendment in an Age of Surveillance

> The natural tendency of Government is toward abuse of power. Men entrusted with power, even those aware of its dangers, tend, particularly when pressured, to slight liberty. Our constitutional system guards against this tendency. It establishes many different checks upon power. It is those wise restraints which keep men free. In the field of intelligence those restraints have too often been ignored.[1]

Professor Renée Hutchins has described the Fourth Amendment as "a wall between a free society and overzealous police action – a line of defense implemented by the framers to protect individuals from the tyranny of the police state."[2] Unfortunately, that wall has been reduced to little more than a façade in the face of new technologies and expanding surveillance programs. The culprit is not the Fourth Amendment itself. It is as stout as it ever was. Neither is it necessarily these new means and methods of search and seizure, which are not inherently unconstitutional. The problem lies instead in the Supreme Court's Fourth Amendment jurisprudence, which fails to set reasonable constitutional constraints on the deployment and use of these means and methods.

Much of the responsibility for our current predicament traces to the Supreme Court's landmark decision in *Katz v. United States*, decided in 1967. When the Fourth Amendment was ratified in 1791, "search" would have been understood as seeking, looking through, examining, trying to find, or "looking into every suspected place."[3] As we saw in Chapter 3, the *Katz* Court abandoned this perfectly straightforward and historically responsible definition of "search" in favor of a far more elusive account based on the idea of reasonable expectations of privacy. Although that shift may have seemed progressive at the time, it has spawned a series of doctrinal rules that have proven to be sources of considerable threat to the right of the people to be secure against unreasonable searches and seizures. Most notorious of these are the public observation doctrine, the third-party doctrine, and rules governing Fourth Amendment standing.

Individually, and in combination, these lines of Supreme Court precedent leave most components of our contemporary surveillance state beyond the reach of effective Fourth Amendment regulation.

The Court made a mistake in *Katz*. Rather than creating out of whole cloth a novel definition of "search," the justices should have focused their attention on the text and history of the Fourth Amendment. Had they taken this path, then they would have recognized a few simple truths. First, they would have preserved a nontechnical definition of "search" that would include examining, trying to find, exploring, looking through, making inquiry, seeking, and trying to find.[4] Had they done so, then the public observation and third-party doctrines would not exist. A search is no less a search if it is conducted in a public space or if it seeks information that has been shared with a third party.

Second, the Court would have preserved the Fourth Amendment's focus on collective interests and the grants of broad and unfettered discretion to search or seize, which threaten those collective interests. Had it done so, then the doctrine of Fourth Amendment standing would look very different. Courts would be less concerned about whether a particular person has been subjected to an unreasonable search, focusing instead on whether a defendant or plaintiff has identified a policy or practice that leaves the people insecure against threats of unreasonable search or seizure and how that threat can be ameliorated.

Third, the Court would have focused on the Fourth Amendment command that the right of the people to be secure against unreasonable searches and seizures shall not be violated. The justices would have recognized that this imperative can only be accomplished by the provision of prospective remedies that set limits on government agents and government actions. They would therefore have been focused on developing and enforcing remedial measures in the mode of the warrant clause, which bans general warrants and sets substantive and procedural limits on targeted warrants, thereby effectively guaranteeing the right of the people to be secure against threats of unreasonable search posed by general warrants and writs of assistance.

The Supreme Court was far more faithful to the text and history of the Fourth Amendment in the decades before *Katz*. In the early twentieth century, the Court exercised its constitutional authority to enforce Fourth Amendment remedies by adopting the warrant requirement and the exclusionary rule. In justifying and defending these measures, the Court explained that these were effective, enforceable, and parsimonious means of guaranteeing the security of the people against threats of unreasonable searches and seizures posed by the emergence of professionalized, paramilitary law enforcement agencies. From an originalist perspective, this was all perfectly sensible.

Although the Court took a wrong turn in *Katz*, we need not continue down that path in the twenty-first century. We should instead go back to basics by taking seriously the text and history of the Fourth Amendment. If we do, then we will find that the question posed by contemporary surveillance technologies is not whether they threaten reasonable expectations of privacy. The question instead is whether leaving these means and methods to the unfettered discretion of law enforcement would threaten the right of the people to be secure against unreasonable searches and seizures. If it would, then the Fourth Amendment demands the imposition of prospective remedies sufficient to restore that security.

This chapter applies the lessons learned in Chapters 4 and 5 to the means and methods discussed in Chapter 1. For each, we will ask whether its deployment and use constitute a search or seizure. We will then examine whether leaving the deployment and use of that means or method to the unfettered discretion of law enforcement agents poses a threat to the right of the people to be secure from unreasonable searches and seizures. If it does, then we will consider potential regulatory frameworks and whether they meet the criteria that govern constitutional remedies: effectiveness, enforceability, and parsimoniousness.

Tracking Technologies

The common public meaning of "search" when the Fourth Amendment was ratified included such activities as "seeking," "trying to find," or "looking into every suspected place."[5] By that definition, tracking clearly constitutes a "search." That is true whether the tracking is conducted using traditional means and methods, such as tailing a suspect, or by using advanced technologies. Both entail "seeking" and "trying to find" a "person." Many modern tracking technologies also involve examining, looking through, or exploring our "effects," such as when government agents gather data from GPS-enabled devices, ping cellular phones with cell site simulators, access cell site location information, or interrogate embedded RFID tags. Of course, the fact that an activity constitutes a "search" does not mean that it is subject to Fourth Amendment regulation. As we have found, the

Fourth Amendment guards only against threats of unreasonable searches and seizures.

As is true of all means and methods of conducting searches, an instance of tracking can be reasonable or unreasonable. Officers may have very good reasons that provide ample justification for them to track someone. For example, they might have solid evidence that provides substantial reason to believe that their target is part of a drug conspiracy. They might then track him to see whether he frequents locations associated with that drug conspiracy. Alternatively, officers might choose to track a citizen for insufficient reasons, for illegitimate reasons, or for no reason at all. For example, investigators may have extremely thin grounds for suspecting someone of criminal activity. Or they might track someone for purely malicious reasons, such as to gather evidence of embarrassing personal peccadilloes.[6] They might choose to track a political dissident in order to identify others who share her views. An officer might also track someone who is particularly attractive out of nothing more than prurient interests. Tracking in any of these cases would be unreasonable by Fourth Amendment standards insofar as it would be "Not agreeable to reason," "Exorbitant; claiming or insisting on more than is fit," or "Greater than is fit; immoderate."[7] All the more so if the officers conducting the tracking operations in these examples were left entirely to their own discretion, free from any form of meaningful accountability.

That a means or method can be used to effectuate both reasonable and unreasonable searches is still not enough to trigger Fourth Amendment regulation. As we saw in Chapters 4 and 5, the fundamental question asked by the reasonableness clause is whether granting law enforcement officers an unlimited license to deploy and use a means or method of conducting searches or seizures would threaten the right of the people to be secure in their persons, houses, papers, or effects against unreasonable searches and seizures. As we have seen, general warrants and writs of assistance failed this test because they threatened the right of everyone to be secure against threats of unreasonable physical searches and seizures. The question, then, is whether granting a similar license for government agents to use tracking technologies would result in similar threats to the right of the people to be secure in their persons and effects against unreasonable searches. To answer this question, we need to focus on the means and methods at issue.

Contemporary tracking technologies allow law enforcement and other government agents to pinpoint our locations at any time, to monitor our movements in real time, and to assemble detailed records of our movements over extended periods of time. These technologies, which include GPS-enabled devices, cell site location information (CSLI), and radio frequency identification (RFID), are relatively inexpensive and highly scalable. In fact, much of the technology is already in place. For example, CSLI technology is already widely deployed as part of the infrastructures maintained by our telephone service providers. Most of us carry around GPS-enabled tracking devices in our smartphones, fitness trainers, and navigation systems, many of which readily leak data about our locations that can be captured by modern surveillance technologies.

Scalability matters because it shows the potential for these technologies to facilitate programs of broad and indiscriminate surveillance. Chief Justice John Roberts highlighted this issue during oral arguments in *United States v. Jones*, the GPS tracking case from 2012. In that case, the Solicitor General argued that tracking a citizen using a GPS-enabled device is not a search and therefore should not be subject to Fourth Amendment regulation. In response, the Chief Justice asked whether the Solicitor General thought "there would also not be a search if you put a GPS device on all of our cars, [and] monitored our movements for a month?"[8] Implicit in the Chief Justice's question is the fact that the government would not have good and sufficient reasons to track all of the justices of the Supreme Court for a month. His question suggested that something will have gone very wrong if the Fourth Amendment cannot guarantee the security of the justices – or anyone else – against unreasonable searches conducted using GPS tracking devices.

By contrast, leaving traditional tracking techniques, such as tailing a suspect on the street, to the unfettered discretion of law enforcement does not raise the concerns highlighted by Chief Justice Roberts in the *Jones* case. Human surveillance methods are both expensive and labor intensive. As Justice Samuel Alito has pointed out, this means that the vast majority of us can be perfectly secure that we are not now subject to human surveillance, probably never have been, and likely never will be.[9] Granting to law enforcement officers unfettered discretion to engage in human surveillance therefore does not threaten the right of the people to be secure against unreasonable searches and seizures. The same is true of the technology at issue in *United States v. Knotts*.[10] Recall that in that case the Supreme Court held that the use of a radio beeper device to assist officers as they tailed a suspect did not raise any Fourth Amendment concerns. Of course, the technology at issue there was very limited.[11] It only provided basic directional information and could not pinpoint the suspect's precise location. The technology also had a very small operational radius, which meant that officers had to stay close by. In short, the beeper used in the *Knotts* case could only be used as part of an active, labor-intensive tailing operation and was therefore incapable of facilitating programs of broad and indiscriminate surveillance. For these reasons, the *Knotts* Court was absolutely right to conclude that use of that radio beeper "raises no constitutional issues which visual surveillance would not also raise."[12]

As compared to more traditional methods, modern tracking technologies like GPS, CSLI, and RFID are relatively inexpensive, highly scalable, and capable of autonomous operation. For these reasons, they are ideally suited to facilitating programs of broad and indiscriminate surveillance. Granting government agents an unlimited license to deploy and use these technologies would therefore leave all of us and each of us to wonder whether we or our possessions are being tracked any time or all the time, for good reasons, for bad reasons, or for no reasons at all. It is hard to imagine a more direct threat to the right of the people to be secure in their persons or effects against unreasonable searches than being forced to live in a state of fear that the government is stalking us wherever we go. It follows that government access to these technologies should be subject to Fourth Amendment regulation. In keeping with precedent and past practice, those remedies must be effective in guaranteeing the security of the people, readily enforceable by agencies and courts, and parsimonious with respect to the legitimate government interests at stake.

Congress and the Supreme Court found themselves in a similar situation in 1967 regarding the regulation of wiretapping technology. In 1928, the Supreme Court held that wiretapping was not subject to Fourth Amendment regulation.[13] By 1967, the Court had changed its mind, all but reversing itself in *Katz v. United States* and *Berger v. New York*.[14] The very next year, Congress passed the Wiretap Act, which governs the interception of "any wire, oral, or electronic communication."[15] The Wiretap Act established a remedial structure modeled on the warrant requirement that limits the deployment and use of wiretapping technologies. It also provides a very useful example of how legislatures or courts might approach the challenges posed by tracking technologies.

Before law enforcement officers can deploy or use wiretapping technologies, the Wiretap Act requires that they first secure a court order.[16] When applying for a wiretap order, officers must show probable cause to believe both that an individual "is committing, has committed, or is about to commit" a serious criminal offense and that the proposed wiretapping surveillance will produce evidence relating to that offense.[17] Officers applying for wiretap orders must also show that they have exhausted other investigative means. Under the Act, wiretap orders must meet all the same particularity requirements dictated by the Fourth Amendment warrant clause. Wiretap orders must be limited in terms of duration. In addition, the Act requires minimization procedures designed to prevent the incidental interception of communications that are unrelated to the investigation. Minimization usually requires that officers monitoring a wiretap assess whether a particular call is related to their investigation and, if unrelated, to either stop listening and recording or, if necessary, erase a recording. Finally, officers conducting wiretapping operations must report back regularly to the court that issued the warrant, which guarantees that officers conducting wiretap operations will remain accountable to an independent arbiter.

The Wiretap Act provides a useful model for us as we think about how to regulate access to tracking technologies. A remedial structure akin to the Wiretap Act would certainly be effective in preserving the right of the people to be secure in their persons and effects against unreasonable searches. Requiring a court order based on probable cause would limit law enforcement discretion. Requiring that officers exhaust other means before using tracking technologies and imposing minimization procedures would eliminate the possibility of broad and indiscriminate surveillance.[18] Requiring that officers report back to courts would provide an additional means of holding them accountable and would set additional constraints on their discretion. In combination, these measures would allow the vast majority of us to live free from fear that we were being subjected to unreasonable tracking. That is precisely what the Fourth Amendment requires.

A remedial structure for tracking technologies based on the Wiretap Act would also be easy to enforce. The Wiretap Act has been in force since 1968. Although it has been subject to modest amendments in the intervening years, law enforcement officers and courts now have almost fifty years of experience working with these requirements. Given that wealth of experience, there is every reason to believe that law enforcement and courts would have no difficulty applying a similar structure governing tracking technologies.

A remedial structure for tracking technologies modeled on the Wiretap Act would also be parsimonious. The principal value of most tracking technologies for law enforcement is in their capacities to advance specific investigations. For example, officers might use a GPS tracking device to monitor the movements of a suspect in a drug conspiracy. As another example, officers investigating a bank robbery might gather CSLI for all the mobile phones in the vicinity of the robbery along with historical CSLI going back several days in an effort to identify potential suspects and witnesses. A remedial structure along the lines of the Wiretap Act would allow officers to use tracking technologies in these kinds of cases. Here again, experience proves the point. Although there is no doubt that the Wiretap Act sets limits on the deployment and use of wiretapping technologies, law enforcement and security agencies have never suggested that it effects an unreasonable compromise between law enforcement interests and citizen interests. It is therefore hard to see how striking the same basic compromise with respect to the regulation of tracking technologies would impose unreasonable sacrifices on law enforcement.

Of course, one might argue that allowing for more expansive uses of tracking technologies could advance government interests in law enforcement and national security. For example, if government agencies knew where everyone was all the time and preserved historical records documenting everyone's movements going back for many years, then that might promote criminal law enforcement or national security in some way. That is all very speculative, of course. More importantly, it is precisely the kind of broad and indiscriminate searching that is the hallmark of a surveillance state. As the Church Committee reported, "A tension between order and liberty is inevitable in any society."[19] The Constitution and the Bill of Rights respond to some of these tensions by imposing firm limits on what can and cannot be done in the pursuit of order. As a constitutional matter, some things are just off limits. In this case, the Fourth Amendment requires that we choose liberty over order when faced with programs of broad and indiscriminate surveillance. It is therefore hard to see how a program such as this could be made to conform to Fourth Amendment demands.

The proposal outlined here could be implemented by executive order, administrative regulation, legislative statute, or judicial doctrine. As the overall success of the Wiretap Act shows, the political branches are well situated to elaborate remedial structures necessary to protect the Fourth Amendment rights of the people. Although courts have final authority to assess the constitutional sufficiency of remedial measures created by the political branches, there are good reasons to prefer that the political branches take the lead. We might therefore hope that Congress, the President, governors, and state legislatures will take the initiative to protect Fourth Amendment rights threatened by tracking technologies. In fact, several state legislatures have done precisely that, passing laws that require state and local law enforcement to secure warrants before deploying or using tracking technologies.[20] Of course, if the political branches fail to act, then it is the solemn office of the courts as final guardians of constitutional rights to step into the breach.

Drones

Drones are a diverse species. They can be the size of hot air balloons or insects. Their gazes can encompass a few square feet or many square miles. They can take direction from human hands or operate autonomously. They can deploy for a few minutes or for weeks at a time. Despite these variations, the drones we are interested in here all share a defining feature: they provide a remote observation post from which to conduct surveillance. That surveillance is usually visual, but drones can also serve as listening posts or platforms for monitoring communications. When they are used to conduct surveillance, drones are engaged in searching by any definition because they seek or try to find people or effects, usually by looking into or examining places.[21]

Like tracking technologies, drones are well suited to both reasonable and unreasonable searches. It all depends on the reasons, circumstances, and whether or not there is some means of holding government agents who conduct drone surveillance accountable for their conduct. Given that drone searches can be reasonable or unreasonable, the next question is whether leaving the decision to deploy and use drones to the unfettered discretion of government agents would threaten the right of the people to be secure against unreasonable searches by facilitating programs of broad and indiscriminate surveillance. Given both how drones function and the fact that drone technology is relatively inexpensive and highly scalable, the answer is "yes."

For the most part, surveillance conducted by drones is indiscriminate by nature. As they hover in the atmosphere, drones exercise no judgment or discernment at all with respect to what they see. That is all the more true for drones carrying cameras that have wide visual horizons. Deployed in an urban center or over a busy roadway, drones can observe thousands of people as they go about their daily business. Although human operators can take direct control over drones, most models are highly automated and many have the ability to operate for long periods of time without any direct human control. Deploying and using drones therefore requires very little investment of limited human resources. Once expensive, drones are now quite cheap and getting cheaper. For a few hundred dollars, any police department or government agency can now outfit itself with a drone.

Individually, and in combination, these features of drone technology make it ideally suited to programs of broad and indiscriminate surveillance. We therefore live in an age when the archetype of surveillance states depicted in science fiction and fantasy – the all-seeing eye in the sky – is an imminent reality. As such, living in a world where we are subjected constantly to the possibility of surveillance by drones would certainly threaten the right of the people to be secure from unreasonable searches. The deployment and use of drone technologies therefore cannot be left to the unfettered discretion of law enforcement and other government agents.

Drone technologies should be subject to Fourth Amendment regulation. Before considering what form these regulations might take, it is important to understand the law enforcement interests served by drones. Like wiretaps and tracking technologies, drones are well suited to individual investigations. For example, they can be used to monitor a suspect or to gather information about areas that are either inaccessible or dangerous. Drones are also appropriate for more situational applications, however. For example, drones can provide a remote observation point for officers charged with protecting people attending large public gatherings. They can also be useful in more mundane circumstances, such as traffic enforcement. Any regulatory framework governing the deployment and use of drones must make reasonable accommodations for both investigative uses and these kinds of situational deployments.

Here again, the Wiretap Act provides a useful model. Requiring a court order before deploying or using a drone would set important limits on law enforcement discretion by ensuring that drones would only be deployed in circumstances where there are good and sufficient reasons to justify their use. The standard by which to measure the sufficiency of those reasons is a bit more complex than it was in the case of tracking technologies, however. For example, in cases where a drone would be used to advance specific criminal investigations, the same probable cause standard used by the Wiretap Act might make good sense. But for situational deployments, such as to monitor security at large public gatherings, a probable cause requirement would be unreasonable. In these kinds of cases, a more fact-based test that weighed law enforcement and security interests against citizen privacy interests would make more sense.

Some version of the exhaustion requirement imposed by the Wiretap Act would provide added protection for Fourth Amendment rights that might otherwise be threatened by drones. In essence, the Wiretap Act's exhaustion requirement asks whether law enforcement officers have a reasonable investigative alternative to intercepting communications. Asking that same question when officers apply for a drone order makes equally good sense. By ensuring that there are no other, less intrusive, or otherwise equally appropriate means available to achieve the investigative, security, or law enforcement goals at stake in a particular case, an exhaustion requirement would provide added protection against over-deployment.

Minimization procedures like those required under the Wiretap Act would play a particularly important role in ensuring that drone deployments do not result to a de facto surveillance state. The primary goal would be to limit incidental observations unrelated to the purpose of a deployment. In order to achieve that goal, courts might consider setting limits on the visual scope of the cameras and other surveillance equipment used, limiting a drone's area of operation, limiting the times of day when a drone can be deployed, and limiting the duration of a deployment. Also important will be rules governing the storage and destruction of information captured during a drone deployment, including pictures and video. Any incidental information should probably be destroyed immediately, but even relevant information needs to have a limited shelf life. This will be particularly important in cases where drones are deployed for situational purposes, such as for security at public events or traffic control. Without a data destruction protocol, these kinds of drone deployments could very quickly morph into large-scale surveillance programs that impact not only Fourth Amendment rights, but also First Amendment interests in free speech and association.

Together, these measures would likely be effective in guaranteeing the right of the people to be secure against threats of unreasonable drone searches. The process of seeking and securing a court order sets limits on law enforcement discretion and ensures that drone searches will be conducted only where there are good and sufficient reasons. Some version of an exhaustion requirement would provide added protections, and thoughtful minimization procedures will ensure that individual deployments do not become too broad or indiscriminate. Finally, requiring officers to report back to the judge who issued their order would guarantee accountability.

There is also good reason to think that a structured process of securing court orders would be an enforceable strategy for regulating the deployment and use of drones. Although different in some of the details, the basic structure is very like the regulatory structure prescribed by the Wiretap Act. Courts and law enforcement agencies have decades of successful experience with the Wiretap Act, which suggests that they will have few difficulties applying a similar structure to drone technologies.

Finally, a structure modeled on the Wiretap Act would be parsimonious in that it would not sacrifice legitimate law enforcement and security interests but would still protect the Fourth Amendment right of the people to live free from fear of unreasonable drone searches. Under the regulatory scheme outlined here, government agents would still have reasonable access to drone technology in situations where the technology can advance legitimate security and law enforcement goals. At the same time, it would effectively ban the use of drones to conduct broad and indiscriminate surveillance.

To meet the demands of parsimoniousness, any remedial structure governing access to drone technologies would probably need to have an emergency exception. There are situations where rapidly developing circumstances make it impossible or unreasonable to get a drone warrant. For example, officers might be in pursuit of an armed suspect when he enters a walled compound. Or they might be responding to a bomb threat. In cases such as these it might be perfectly reasonable to deploy a drone so officers can identify potential dangers and make an informed assessment of their options. They may not have the time to secure a court order, however. In order to accommodate these kinds of emergency situations, any regulatory framework governing drone technologies would need to have a safety valve. On this score both the warrant requirement and the Wiretap Act offer useful guides because both of these regulatory regimes include emergency exceptions.

Cell Site Simulators

Cell site simulators intercept communications between cell phone users and their cellular service providers. They can operate in a purely passive mode, intercepting signals from every phone within their areas of operation. They can also actively engage user devices by emitting signals that cause all cellular phones in the area to respond by attempting to communicate with their respective cell networks. Simulators then intercept those communications.[22] By either means, cell site simulators acquire the unique identifier numbers associated with phones located inside their areas of operation, gather location information associated with those phones, and record basic metadata for any calls made by those devices, including the time of calls, duration of calls, and the telephone numbers of parties to those calls.[23] Cell site simulators also have the capacity to intercept the contents of communications, including voice calls, texts, and internet activity.[24] The Department of Justice and other law enforcement agencies have denied using cell site simulators to intercept content, but the capacity to do so remains.

There is no doubt that cell site simulators engage in searches. That is true by 1791 standards in that these devices allow officers to engage in inquiries, to examine communications, to look into cellular devices, and to seek and pursue users. It is also true by the standards of contemporary Fourth Amendment doctrine. The Supreme Court has long held that we have reasonable expectations of privacy in our private communications.[25] For example, in *Katz v. United States*, the Supreme Court held that eavesdropping on private communications using an electronic listening device constitutes a search for purposes of the Fourth Amendment.[26] The Supreme Court has also held that the Fourth Amendment protects the contents of letters and packages, which are "intended to be kept free from inspection."[27] Finally, eavesdropping on communications carried over traditional telephone lines is a search under the Fourth Amendment.[28] Given these precedents, there can be no doubt that cell site simulators also engage in searches when they are used to gather data contained in cellular phones or to intercept private communications between cellphone users and their service providers.[29]

As is the case with all the technologies discussed in this book, the central question raised by cell site simulators is not whether law enforcement officers should be allowed to use these devices in order to investigate and prosecute crimes. They certainly should. The question instead is whether they should have unfettered discretion to use these devices whenever they like, free of Fourth Amendment constraints. Here, the answer is most certainly "no." Granting this kind of unfettered discretion would pose the same kinds of general threats to the security of the people against unreasonable searches posed by general warrants and writs of assistance.

Although cell site simulators can focus on individual devices, their basic mode of operation is completely indiscriminate. They engage every device within their areas of operation and intercept all communications from those devices, regardless of whether those devices or their users are implicated in or suspected of wrongdoing. As a consequence, leaving the deployment and use of these devices to the unfettered discretion of law enforcement would threaten the right of the people to be secure against unreasonable searches.[30] It would allow officers to deploy and use these devices anywhere they pleased, anytime they pleased, for however long they wanted, and to gather and store information relating to thousands of phones and phone calls, for illegitimate reasons, for insufficient reasons, or for no reason at all. That is the very definition of broad and indiscriminate search.[31]

If the deployment and use of cell site simulators constitute a search, and granting law enforcement unfettered authority to deploy and use these devices threatens the security of the people against unreasonable searches, then the next question is what kind of remedial structure might be effective in restoring that security while also being enforceable and parsimonious with respect to the legitimate law enforcement and national security interests at stake.[32] The Wiretap Act again provides a useful model.

Cell site simulators are, in essence, wiretapping devices that target wireless phones. Given the close analogy to wiretapping, there is every reason to believe that the framework described by the Wiretap Act would also provide an effective, enforceable, and parsimonious means of regulating government access to cell site simulators. The process of applying for court orders would put reasonable limits on law enforcement discretion by requiring them to articulate good and sufficient reasons for conducting a search and by reserving the final decision for a detached and neutral magistrate. By limiting access to cell site simulators to truly exceptional circumstances, an exhaustion requirement would ensure the security of the people against routine surveillance. Minimization procedures would provide yet more assurance by setting limits on where, when, and for how long cell site simulators could be used and also by establishing rules governing the storage and destruction of information, including any incidental information gathered by a cell site simulator. Finally, a regulatory framework based in the Wiretap Act would hold officers accountable by requiring that they report back to the judges who issue these orders.

A regulatory framework modeled on the Wiretap Act would be easy to enforce while also striking a parsimonious balance between the Fourth Amendment rights of the people and the people's interests in effective law enforcement. Experience with the Wiretap Act proves the case. Law enforcement and courts have been working with the Wiretap Act since 1968. They are familiar with its operation, its standards, and its application. That experience has been reduced to administrative guidelines and case law, all of which enhances enforceability. Finally, the Wiretap Act enjoys both the imprimatur of legislative policymaking and the proof of long experience, both of which demonstrate that it has not imposed unreasonable limitations on law enforcement.

Big Data

"Big Data" is the aggregation, storage, and analysis of large quantities of information. The goal may be to spot specific events, to uncover patterns, to explain or predict phenomena, or to provide a resource for investigating past crimes. Thus, "Big Data" does not describe a particular means or technology. It instead describes a methodology that leverages modern information gathering, aggregation, storage, and analysis technologies.

We discussed several Big Data programs in Chapter 1. For example, the National Security Agency's (NSA) telephonic metadata program is a Big Data program. So too are the New York Police Department's Domain Awareness System and the health data aggregation and analysis programs operated by the Department of Health and Human Services under the auspices of the Affordable Care Act. Many more surveillance programs use elements of Big Data. For example, the federal "no fly" list and similar efforts utilize Big Data components to identify potential threats. Emerging biometric systems that use technologies like facial recognition,[33] posture analysis, and behavioral patterning also fall under the umbrella of Big Data. In short, Big Data represents a substantial and growing contribution to our emerging surveillance state. The question, then, is what, if any, limits might the

Fourth Amendment set on the deployment and use of Big Data technologies and methods.

The threshold question is whether Big Data programs engage in searches or seizures. According to definitions of "search" prevailing in 1791, to search is to conduct an "Enquiry by looking into every suspected place," an "Inquiry; examination; [or] act of seeking" a "Quest," or a "pursuit."[34] There is probably no more apt description of Big Data. Big Data conducts inquires by looking into every corner of our lives, gathering every available detail regarding what we do, what we say, where we go, and with whom we associate both on- and off-line. That looking is not merely metaphorical. We are prone these days to talking about data as if it is something ethereal that lives in "clouds" or an alternate universe called cyberspace. Amidst these metaphors it is easy to forget that data has a physical presence and a fixable location on hard drives or servers. Big Data programs look into those places in order to examine, seek, and pursue the objects of their quests. Once the information has been aggregated, Big Data programs continue their process of inquiry by examining vast bodies of data and seeking evidence, patterns, or insights. Without need of reinterpretation, stretched analogy, or tenuous metaphor, we can therefore conclude that Big Data programs engage in searches.

In some cases, Big Data programs may also effect seizures. By 1791 standards, to seize meant to "take possession of," "to lay hold on," "to fasten on," or to assert power over a thing or fix it in one's grasp.[35] By definition, Big Data programs take possession of information. Big Data therefore affects the abilities of subjects to control access to information and the use of that information. This loss of control has consequences for individual liberty, particularly when the information is personal, sensitive, or bound up with freedoms of expression or association. Big Data may therefore implicate many of the same concerns raised by general warrants and writs of assistance in the eighteenth century. For example, Big Data programs may result in limitations on the freedom of movement, such as is the case with "no fly" lists. They may also impact the ability of people to get jobs, secure housing, and access credit. Although these kinds of restraints on freedom fall short of full custodial arrests, they place persons in the grasp of state power and therefore constitute "seizures."

The next question for our Fourth Amendment analysis is whether granting government agents unfettered discretion to deploy and use Big Data programs threatens the Fourth Amendment rights of the people to be secure in their persons, houses, papers, or effects against unreasonable search or seizure by facilitating programs of broad and indiscriminate surveillance. By their very nature, Big Data programs conduct searches that are broad and indiscriminate. After all, the whole point of Big Data is to collect mass quantities of information and then to mine and analyze aggregated data to find the proverbial needle in the haystack or to spot important patterns amidst the noise. Much, if not most, of the data captured by Big Data programs is the haystack that hides the needle or the noise that obscures the pattern. Big Data programs therefore run the very real risk of being "unreasonable" in the sense that they are "exorbitant," demanding "more than is fit," and generally "not agreeable to reason."[36] For example, the NSA's telephony metadata program made no distinctions whatsoever in terms of whose metadata was captured. It instead sought to gather all telephony metadata from every domestic telephone call. The vast majority of the information gathered by the program was associated with perfectly innocent communications between perfectly innocent persons. It was nevertheless gathered and stored on an indiscriminate basis. That certainly seems to be unreasonable in the sense that it is excessive, unnecessary, and ill-fitting.

Big Data programs also run the risk of being unreasonable in that they can lead to conclusions that are wrong or otherwise unjustified by the standards governing the processes of reasoned analysis.[37] Here again, the telephony metadata program provides a useful example. According to the President's Civil Liberties Oversight Board, the NSA's telephony metadata program produced, at most, one apprehension and arrest of a suspected terrorist[38] – a taxicab driver who was convicted of sending funds to a local militia group in Somalia near his ancestral home.[39] It is hard to imagine a standard under which that one marginal success would render reasonable searching data associated with every telephone call in the United States for more than a decade. To cite another example, Big Data programs linked to "no fly" lists and fusion centers produce many false positives, which has resulted in targeting nuns, political activists, and even folks with unfortunate names.[40] Yet, these programs also produce many false negatives, allowing known terrorists such as Richard Reid, the notorious "shoe bomber," to board international flights. Here again, it is hard to see the reasonableness in programs that produce few true positives, many false positives, and substantial numbers of false negatives.

Given their breadth, reach, and frequent unreliability, there can be no doubt that granting government agents unfettered discretion to deploy and use Big Data technologies poses a serious threat to the right of the people to be secure against unreasonable searches and seizures by facilitating surveillance programs that are unreasonably broad and indiscriminate. That does not mean that Big Data programs are inherently unconstitutional, however. Despite their dangers, Big Data programs have the potential to advance legitimate law enforcement and security goals. It does mean, however, that the deployment and use of Big Data cannot be left to the unfettered discretion of law enforcement. We must instead identify prospective remedial measures that will be effective in guaranteeing the right of the people to be secure against unreasonable searches and seizures, enforceable by courts and executive agencies, and parsimonious with respect to the balance among the competing interests at stake.

Unlike tracking technologies, drones, and cell site simulators, a regulatory structure based on the warrant requirement or the Wiretap Act would not provide an effective, enforceable, and parsimonious framework for regulating Big Data surveillance programs. That is due to at least two distinguishing features of these technologies. First, there is simply too much variety among Big Data programs in terms of their goals, scopes, the kinds of data they gather, how the data is stored, and how it is used. It is therefore very unlikely that we will find a one-size-fits-all approach to regulating Big Data. Second, Big Data is not particularly well suited to individual investigations. Its primary value lies instead in spotting patterns and identifying potential threats that might otherwise go unnoticed. To achieve these goals, Big Data programs need to be running in the background, constantly gathering, storing, and analyzing information. It would therefore be unreasonable to require a showing of probable cause before initiating a Big Data program because that would be too late. This is not to suggest that Big Data cannot help solve individual crimes. It surely can. For example, an investigator might query a database to help identify potential suspects. To provide that service, however, the database must be there to query, which means that the data gathering must precede the need.

For at least these reasons, a regulatory structure based on the warrant requirement or the Wiretap Act would be unreasonable in the context of Big Data. Regulating the deployment and use of Big Data requires a more nuanced and flexible approach that can accommodate the particular goals of individual programs while also setting reasonable limitations on their scope, reach, and impact. As we think about the forms these remedies might take, it is useful to consider timing as well.

More specifically, we might imagine enforcing constitutional constraints on Big Data programs at one or some combination of at least eight operational stages:

1. Deployment
2. Data Gathering[41]
3. Data Aggregation
4. Data Storage
5. Data Access[42]
6. Data Analysis
7. Accessing the Results of Data Analysis
8. Uses of Data Analysis.

Let us consider some possible interventions at each of these stages.

Deployment

Before deployment, proponents must offer good and sufficient reasons for using Big Data programs. This will require first identifying the goals of a program. That process alone will exercise disciplinary force on government agents, thus limiting their discretion. It will also provide an important first level of review. If the reasons offered in support of a proposed Big Data program are bad – identifying political dissidents, say – then that program inevitably will result in unreasonable searches. It therefore cannot go forward.

The next step is to measure a proposed program according to its stated goals. The very definition of reasonableness is to be found in the fit between reasons and actions. Actions supported by good and sufficient reasons are reasonable. Actions underwritten by bad or insufficient reasons are not reasonable. Similarly, a program that gathers more data than is fitting given its goals, keeps the information longer than is necessary, or engages in irrelevant analysis exposes the people to threats of unreasonable search and seizure.

Pre-deployment review processes must also identify potential negative consequences, including impacts on constitutional rights and privacy. Modifying the design of a Big Data program to minimize its negative impact will help ensure that the program is "Not immoderate" and does not take more than is its due.[43] There is, of course, always the possibility that the negative impact of a proposed Big Data program on Fourth Amendment rights will outweigh its potential benefits. Where that is the case, the Fourth Amendment would stand as a bar on implementation.

Ideally, pre-deployment reviews of a Big Data program would be open, affording all interested parties the opportunity to be heard. The end goal would be to generate some degree of consensus among stakeholders. Of course, there will be occasions when the utility of a Big Data program for law enforcement or national security purposes depends upon its secrecy. Secrecy and rigorous preliminary review are not mutually exclusive, however. Neither is it impossible to maintain secrecy while also making sure that all interested views are represented. For example, proponents of a Big Data program might seek out trustworthy interest organizations or require nondisclosure agreements as a condition of participation. Alternatively, we might create an independent office outside both the executive and the legislative branches modeled on the Privacy and Civil Liberties Oversight Board[44] that would be charged with identifying and advocating for privacy interests and Fourth Amendment rights as new Big Data proposals emerge or old ones require updating. Finally, we might consider creating a specialized judicial or quasi-judicial body charged with reviewing and approving Big Data programs through an adversarial process. The Foreign Surveillance Intelligence Court created by the Foreign Intelligence Surveillance Act should not be used as a model for such a court. Experience has shown that the combination of ex parte proceedings, the absence of an adversarial process, and secrecy has rendered the Foreign Intelligence Surveillance Court largely ineffective as a means of guaranteeing the security of the people against threats of unreasonable searches and seizures. Any court established to review Big Data Programs would therefore need to avoid these failings by, at the very least, providing some mechanism by which competing views and interests could be vigorously represented by competent advocates.

Data Gathering

Big Data programs should also be subject to constitutional constraints at the information-gathering stage. Here, there are two main concerns. The first relates to what information is gathered and how much. In order to avoid overbreadth and excessive indiscriminateness, Big Data programs should only gather information that is reasonably likely to advance the goals of the program and no more than is reasonably necessary to do the job. The second major concern that should be addressed at the gathering stage is the means by which information is gathered. For example, tracking technologies, drones, and tapping into location data generated by smartphones are all means that raise serious Fourth Amendment concerns. Integrating these data-gathering technologies into a Big Data program does not automatically resolve these concerns. These kinds of means and methods must instead be subjected to careful scrutiny and, if necessary, constrained by remedial measures designed to mitigate their threats to Fourth Amendment rights while also preserving reasonable service to compelling governmental interests advanced by the Big Data program under review.

Data Aggregation

In many ways, data aggregation is the defining feature of Big Data. It is also at the root of Big Data's Fourth Amendment problems. After all, aggregation is often what makes Big Data searches broad and indiscriminate, and therefore what threatens the right of the people to be secure against unreasonable searches and seizures. Also worrisome at the aggregation stage is the possibility that data collected for one purpose will be aggregated into databases meant to service quite different purposes. This may be unreasonable if information gathered for one purpose is a bad fit for another. Finally, aggregation of data from multiple sources may preserve and perpetuate mistakes. As a consequence, simple clerical errors may lead to substantial harm that is hard, if not impossible, to correct. That is because data aggregation, particularly repeated and successive data aggregation, tends to create a degree of uncritical permanence, rendering mistakes impossible to trace and correct.

Legislatures, executives, and courts seeking to set constraints on Big Data programs at the aggregation stage might consider a number of potential remedial measures. The first is simply to limit the scope of aggregation. By requiring some level of critical thought regarding the sources of data, the kinds of data aggregated, the reliability of that data, and by demanding clear links between data sources and the ultimate goals and purposes of a Big Data program, regulatory regimes can go a long way toward guaranteeing reasonableness.

Another potentially important tool for regulating Big Data programs at the aggregation stage is information siloing. Information silos establish or maintain separation between databases, thereby setting limits on the breadth and generality achieved by aggregation. This can be accomplished either by constructing discrete silos into which aggregated data is segregated or by simply leaving data in the custody and control of those who gathered it in the first place. This is one of the strategies adopted by Congress in its efforts to set limits on the National Security Agency's telephony metadata program. Under the terms of the 2015 USA Freedom Act, caller metadata is no longer turned over to the NSA in bulk.[45] That data remains instead with the telephone companies. In order to gain access to this data, the NSA must formulate targeted search queries. This is not to suggest that data silos are a panacea. To the contrary, data silos may be dangerous, as is demonstrated by intelligence failures in the months before the terrorist attacks of September 11, 2001. As with all other potential remedies, the decision whether to silo data, and how, must therefore take into account the potential consequences for crime control and national security.

A third important means for regulating Big Data programs at the aggregation stage is regular review by independent auditors. These kinds of independent, neutral reviews are useful in two ways. First, they force agencies deploying and using Big Data to evaluate their own practices on an ongoing basis because they know they will need to justify themselves to an independent external reviewer. Second, by virtue of their remove, independent auditors are in a better position to assess the reasonableness of particular practices and the overall reasonableness of a Big Data program.

Data Storage

For the most part, information does not simply flow through Big Data programs. It is, instead, captured and stored. The scale of Big Data programs as measured by their storage capacities is truly staggering. For example, the NSA recently built several data storage facilities capable of storing the contents and metadata associated with several years' worth of Americans' phone calls, electronic mail, and internet activity.[46] This kind of storage capacity provides Big Data programs with long memories, allowing government agents to return to the same data, mining and analyzing it again and again into perpetuity.[47]

There is little doubt that this kind of broad and indiscriminate data storage raises serious Fourth Amendment concerns. It is hard to imagine a more general threat to the right of the people to be secure from unreasonable searches and seizures than granting government agents complete and permanent access to every bit and byte of information we have ever generated in our daily comings and goings in both the physical and virtual worlds. The most obvious remedial solution is to impose limits on how long data can be stored.[48] Regular data destruction may also have the salutary effect of increasing the function and reliability of Big Data programs.[49] Older data tends to be less complete and less reliable. Older data may also reflect realities no longer relevant to contemporary threat assessments. Finally, holding on to data forever inevitably increases the size of databases, which may unduly slow, confuse, or muddy analysis. From both a constitutional and a law enforcement point of view, then, regular data destruction is critical to guaranteeing the reasonableness of Big Data programs.

There are no bright lines when it comes to data destruction and certainly no absolute limits on how long data can be stored. Much depends on the goals of a program and the ways aggregated data serves those goals. In some cases, storing data for a year might be unreasonably long. In other cases, requiring the destruction of data at the ten-year mark may unreasonably compromise critical national security or crime control goals. Here again, continuous internal review and independent audits will play an important role. For example, if, upon conducting an audit of a Big Data program used to identify potential connections between current crimes and past crimes, auditors discover that utility falls off dramatically once data is ten years old, then data should be tagged for destruction once it turns ten.

Data Access

The main question for remedial measures at the data access stage is which people, organizations, and algorithms should have access to aggregated data. In general, Big Data programs should be quite jealous in limiting access. Grants of access should be tied to the legitimate goals of the program. Only those who are most likely to advance those goals should have access. By contrast, people, groups, and algorithms seeking access for purposes unrelated to the program should not have access.[50] Likewise, people, groups, and algorithms that pose significant risks to constitutional rights or privacy interests should have very limited access or none at all. By limiting access along these lines, Big Data programs can dramatically reduce threats of unreasonable searches and seizures.

Data Analysis

Data analysis functions of Big Data programs can be accomplished either by á la carte searches or computer algorithms. The main threats to the right of the people to be secure against unreasonable searches at the analysis stage come from overbroad searches, unlimited searches, and mission creep. The dangers of overbreadth are obvious. Searching databases for connections and patterns unrelated to or only tangentially related to the legitimate governmental interests served by a Big Data program is by definition unreasonable. So too is granting unlimited discretion for agents to access and run searches. It would certainly be unreasonable, for example, if officers could use a Big Data program to investigate an estranged spouse.[51] Finally, there is the danger that a Big Data program justified for one purpose may be used for entirely different purposes that were not contemplated in the design of the program or the development of the regulatory control structures that secure constitutional rights. This kind of mission creep not only threatens to expand the scope of a Big Data program; it also increases the dangers of false negatives and false positives, thereby adding to concerns about unreasonableness.

The solution to limiting the scope of Big Data programs at the analysis stage is to tightly control who has access and who has authority to initiate searches of aggregated data. Authority to initiate searches should be limited to a reasonably small number of people. The scope of searches should also be limited. The standards applied will of course vary according to the goals of the program in question and the nature of the data that has been gathered and aggregated. For example, it may be appropriate to allow law enforcement officers to run searches based on demonstrated investigative needs and the approval of a supervisor if the database in question just covers public records, such as criminal histories, driving records, and property records. Alternatively, it might be more appropriate to require a court order, or even a warrant, before allowing officers to query a database that includes medical health records or detailed location data, such as historical cell site location information or location data generated by personal devices.[52]

Regardless of the front-end limits on access to Big Data analysis, reasonableness dictates the use of audit trails or other means of documenting who gains access, their sources of authority, and the nature of the searches they run. This kind of access control is necessary to preserve accountability before and after the fact. Before the fact, these kinds of controls will enforce limits on access. They will also encourage restraint because those accessing the program will know that *they* are under surveillance. After the fact, reliable audit trails will make evaluating program effectiveness easier while also allowing for accountability in cases of mistake, abuse, or malfeasance.

Accessing the Results of Analysis

In addition to setting limits on who can run searches using a Big Data program and why, reasonableness also demands setting limits on who has access to the results of those searches. Simple measures like unique passwords will be essential in limiting access to the results of searches. Internal administrative controls, such as requirements for supervisory authority before accessing the results of Big Data searches will also help in guaranteeing reasonableness. These kinds of limits will be particularly important in the context of background algorithmic searches. These searches are bound to identify specific persons or to uncover personal information suggesting some reason to be suspicious of a particular person. Those suspicions will always require additional investigation, however, and therefore must be treated with appropriate skepticism. Absent some degree of control over who has access to these results, there is an unreasonable risk that perfectly innocent people will be harassed or erroneously identified as threats by officers or agents who receive a flash notice but have no context for evaluating limitations on reliability. For similar reasons, access to the results of targeted database inquiries should be limited to law enforcement personnel with a direct interest in the relevant investigation. Officers and agents outside that circle simply do not have the context to appreciate the significance of search results, which may seriously compromise an ongoing investigation, lead to inappropriate targeting of innocent persons, or both.

Uses of Data Analysis

The final opportunity to set limits on Big Data programs is at the point where someone puts the results to use. Here, the threat of overbreadth comes mainly from using the results of searches conducted for one purpose to advance separate inquiries or investigations. In order to preserve the focus and tight connections between justification and use that render Big Data programs reasonable from a Fourth Amendment point of view, we must also set limits on who can use the results and how. For example, it might be entirely unreasonable to allow the results of a Big Data program designed to detect potential terrorist threats to be used to investigate incidentally discovered tax fraud. Absent these kinds of controls, the threat of mission creep and the potential for abuse is simply too strong, thereby threatening the right of the people to be secure against unreasonable searches.

In the end, the most important restraint on Big Data at this stage may be Big Data itself. As has been suggested at several points in the foregoing discussion, all Big Data programs should be subjected to recursive analysis and regular independent audits to assess their utility and to evaluate their constitutionality. This is bound to be a data-intensive effort, which suggests that the tools of Big Data are likely to play an important role in regulating and controlling Big Data. Where the results of these analyses show that a Big Data program is gathering the wrong kind of data, aggregating too much data, storing data for too long, conducting the wrong kinds of analysis, granting access to the wrong people, or allowing the results to be used for the wrong purposes, then adjustments will need to be made. Although there will be a considerable amount of art involved in fashioning and refashioning these remedial restraints, there should be quite a lot of science as well. Reasonableness, after all, has an important quantitative dimension that complements its inherently qualitative nature. When assessing the reasonableness of any Big Data program it will therefore be necessary to have good data about the program and to subject that data to clear, rigorous analysis.

Who Should Regulate Big Data?

Without exception, final responsibility for assessing the sufficiency of any remedial structure regulating Big Data programs rests with the courts. In our constitutional system, it is the judiciary that has final authority and responsibility to guarantee the security of the people against unreasonable searches and seizures. That does not mean, however, that courts must or should get involved in micro-managing Big Data programs. Neither does it mean that courts should take the lead in fashioning remedial measures. In fact, there are good reasons to think that courts are ill-suited to this kind of detailed policy work.[53] It may therefore be preferable for the political branches to develop their own systems of review and restraint with the goal of vindicating Fourth Amendment rights.

This sort of legislative prefiguring is not unprecedented. As we know, the Supreme Court held in *Olmstead v. United States* that wiretapping telephone landlines was not a search under the Fourth Amendment, leaving the use of that surveillance technology to the unfettered discretion of law enforcement officers.[54] By 1967, the Court's views had begun to shift. As a consequence, it indicated in *Katz vs. United States*[55] and *Berger v. New York*,[56] that it was prepared to overrule *Olmstead*, thereby subjecting wiretapping to Fourth Amendment regulation. The Court never had that chance, however. That is because Congress passed the Wiretap Act in 1968. As a consequence, the Supreme Court has never been called upon to elaborate constitutional remedies regulating wiretapping technology. The invitation is open for Congress to take similar steps governing Big Data and other modern surveillance means and methods. Should the legislature let that opportunity pass by, then the courts will be obligated to step in.

Stop and Frisk

By both eighteenth century[57] and contemporary standards,[58] stops and frisks constitute searches and seizures. Stops entail taking possession of, grasping, and laying hold on a person and his effects.[59] Likewise, frisks constitute searches in that they involve looking into and examining a person and his effects.[60] The next question, then, is whether leaving the power to conduct stops and frisks to the unfettered discretion of law enforcement would threaten the right of the people to be secure against unreasonable searches and seizures. The answer is undoubtedly "yes." It is hard to imagine a closer analogue to general warrants and writs of assistance than granting law enforcement officers broad authority to stop or frisk anyone they please for good reasons, for bad reasons, or for no reason at all without providing any means for holding those officers accountable.

Here, the Supreme Court appears to agree. The Court was quite clear in *Terry v. Ohio*, which announced the stop and frisk rule, that stops and frisks constitute seizures and searches for purposes of the Fourth Amendment.[61] The Court has also subjected stops and frisks to constitutional review, albeit after the fact, and usually in the context of suppression hearings. Thus, any officer conducting a stop or frisk must be prepared to explain herself to a court by pointing to specific and articulable facts giving rise to a reasonable suspicion of criminal wrongdoing or a reasonable suspicion that the suspect possessed a dangerous weapon. If they cannot do that, then any evidence they may have discovered and seized during a stop or frisk will be suppressed at a subsequent trial.

In other words, there is a remedial structure in place governing access to and use of stops and frisks. Unfortunately, this remedial structure has proven to be wholly ineffective in meeting the Fourth Amendment imperative that the right of the people to be secure from unreasonable searches and seizures "shall not be violated."

The fact that present constraints on stops and frisks are constitutionally ineffective is evidenced by the scope of stop and frisk programs, their disproportionate targeting of politically, economically, and socially vulnerable segments of the population, and their low success rates. In Chapter 1 we discovered that contemporary stop and frisk programs subject large segments of "the people" to the daily threat of unreasonable searches and seizures. Residents in urban areas, members of minority groups, and those who exhibit the markers of poverty are particularly likely to be stopped and frisked. At the same time, minority targets of stops and frisks are proportionally less likely to be guilty of a crime as compared to whites who are stopped or frisked. Also vulnerable are residents of neighborhoods designated as "high crime," which often overlap with communities of color, lower socioeconomic standing, or both. For many innocent, law-abiding residents in these communities the threat of being stopped or frisked is a matter of everyday routine. This is a circumstance wholly contrary to the imperative command at the heart of the Fourth Amendment that the right of the people to be secure against unreasonable searches and seizures shall not be violated.

Despite all this activity, stop and frisk programs have incredibly low success rates. For example, in New York, 473,644 of the 532,911 people stopped in 2012 were released without an arrest or issuance of a summons. That is a yield rate of less than 12 percent. Judging by arrests, the success rate was even worse – less than 6 percent. These low success rates look even more unreasonable once we consider the fact that the vast majority of successful stops or frisks lead to arrests or summonses for minor offenses. As another example, the Department of Justice has reported that stops and frisks conducted by the Baltimore City Police Department in 2014 led to arrests in less than 3.7 percent of cases.[62] In short, stop and frisk programs subject large numbers of innocent people to searches and seizures mostly in order to detect relatively minor offenses. That is a circumstance that violates the right of the people to be secure against unreasonable searches and seizures in that the means and methods used are wholly immoderate as measured by the results.

Based on the statistics, at least, it is hard not to see contemporary stop and frisk practices as anything more than a twenty-first-century version of general warrants. There is simply no way to defend as reasonable the fact that stop and frisk programs leave citizens more vulnerable to police than to criminals, that groups comprising less than 30 percent of the population represent fully 85 percent of stops and frisks while groups comprising 62 percent of the population represent less than 10 percent of those subjected to stops and frisks, or that very few stops and frisks lead to arrests for serious crimes. Certainly, there is nothing reasonable about that fact that stop and frisk programs leave the innocent residents of some areas and neighborhoods subject to seizure and search on a routine and sometimes daily basis as they try to go about their lives. That is simply not the world guaranteed to us, to the people, by the Fourth Amendment.

One might respond to these complaints as missing the point. In fact, many defenders of contemporary stop and frisk programs argue that the primary crime control benefit comes not from arrests and criminal prosecutions generated from stops and frisks, but from the deterrent value of a active police presence achieved in part by aggressive stops and frisk policies.[63] The theories of policing underlying these arguments assert that we get considerable bang for our buck by deploying officers as a means of social control.[64] This requires that officers regularly assert their command authority, proactively address all antisocial behaviors, no matter how minor, and exhibit little or no tolerance for minor offenses. Unfortunately, the evidence does not support the conclusion that aggressive stop and frisk programs provide unique service as crime-control measures.[65]

There is some correlative evidence to support the proposition that aggressive stop and frisk programs have aided in efforts to reduce crime. After all, the emergence and expansion of New York's stop and frisk program coincided with a period during which violent crime decreased dramatically in the city.[66] By contrast, when police in Baltimore stepped back from their stop and frisk program in 2015 after protests over the death of Freddie Gray, violent crime spiked, particularly in minority communities and areas designated as "high crime."[67] As the rules of reason tell us, however, correlation is not cause.

On the whole, evidence that aggressive stop and frisk programs along with associated means of social control policing are successful in reducing crime is equivocal, at best.[68] There are a lot of variables at play when trying to identify the factors affecting crime rates. For example, reduced crime rates in New York City during the 1990's and into the 2000's coincided with dramatic reductions in crime nationwide and a sustained period of economic growth. It also coincided with dramatic increases in property prices and an overall economic renaissance in New York City. In Baltimore, the spike in violent crime in 2015 coincided with the controversy and public outcry regarding the perceived lawlessness of the Baltimore City Police. Ironically, then, the increase in violent crimes that year may have been the result of a stop and frisk program that had gone too far for too long rather than the result of short-term retrenchment of aggressive stop and frisk practices. Finally, there is considerable evidence that any benefits in terms of crime control secured by aggressive stop and frisk programs diminish steeply after a certain point. For example, New York's stop and frisk rates increased modestly through the 1990s topping out at a bit over 97,000 in 2002 as the total number of murders dropped from over 2,600 in 1990 to 587 in 2002.[69] The stop and frisk rate then skyrocketed sevenfold from 2002 to 2011, but murders decreased only modestly from 587 to 515.[70] Further complicating the picture is the fact that stops and frisks in New York dropped dramatically from almost 700,000 in 2011 to less than 50,000 in 2014 while the number of murders in the city dropped considerably, from 515 to 333.[71] Over the next two years of the de Blasio administration the number of murders in New York toggled up to 352 in 2015, but then settled back down to 335 in 2016. 2016 also marked a low-water mark for shooting incidents in New York, which fell below 1,000 for the first time since 1993.[72] In light of all this, it is very hard to make the case that aggressive stop and frisk programs lead directly to reductions in crime rates and impossible to make the case that expanding stop and frisk programs toward infinity results in continuing reductions in crime rates toward zero.

Even if it was the case that aggressive stop and frisk programs contributed to crime reduction, it would not settle the constitutional questions raised by these programs.[73] That is because one of the principal functions of the Fourth Amendment from the founding to the present has been to set limits on government authority to conduct searches and seizures. From its inception, the Fourth Amendment has been particularly skeptical of extravagant claims of executive necessity deployed to defend the necessity of government intrusions. Thus, even if it was possible to achieve perfect security from crime by granting law enforcement officers broad and completely unfettered discretion to conduct searches and seizures, that path is barred by the Fourth Amendment.

Even if one could make the case that aggressive stop and frisk programs work, we simply cannot, as a matter of basic constitutional precommitments, sacrifice the right of the people against unreasonable search and seizure in order to achieve those gains. This does not mean that we need to accept high crime rates or to sacrifice stop and frisk as a law enforcement tool. The point, rather, is that we need to set and enforce remedial restraints on stops and frisks that are effective, enforceable, and parsimonious. Present remedial measures demonstrably do not achieve these constitutional goals.

There are at least two features of these failed measures that deserve careful attention: the reasonable suspicion standard and limitations on Fourth Amendment standing. Although the requirement to demonstrate reasonable suspicion of criminal wrongdoing based on specific and articulable facts before engaging in a stop and frisk may have imposed some restraint on officers' discretion in the years immediately following *Terry*, it has all but dissipated at this point. That is because the years between then and now have provided officers with a ready vocabulary of rote platitudes that courts routinely accept as sufficient to show reasonable suspicion. These stock phrases are so well established and reliable that some departments list them in checklist form on official reports. For example, the NYPD's Unified Form 250, which was used to report incidents of stops or frisks during the peak years of its program, invites officers to conduct stops based on "furtive movements," "inappropriate attire," or a "suspicious bulge." These kinds of descriptions of conduct and circumstance are simply too vague and general to impose any real constraints on law enforcement discretion. After all, when we come right down to it, all of us could be accused most of the time of engaging in furtive movements, wearing inappropriate attire, or having a suspicious bulge. Even if none of those stock phrases apply, then we can probably still be accused of not making eye contact with police, making too much eye contact, or being evasive when engaged in a casual interaction with police, all of which courts have endorsed as grounds for finding reasonable suspicion.[74]

The upshot is that a law enforcement officer can easily justify her decision to stop and frisk just about anyone, anytime, whether it is motivated by good reasons, bad reasons, or no real reasons at all. This circumstance is only made worse by the fact that courts afford considerable deference to officers when reviewing incidents of stop and frisk. Rote phrases like "furtive movements" can therefore insulate officers' true reasons and motives from judicial review. In some cases, these motives may be conscious and worthy of condemnation, such as in cases of overt racism. More often, however, the worn vocabulary of reasonable suspicion shields the subconscious, but nonetheless insidious, effects of implicit bias from conscious review. The consequences are in the statistics. Rather than exercising real control over officer discretion, the reasonable suspicion standard promotes background social biases to normative status. That is how we end up with programs that target vulnerable and marginalized groups who have the misfortune of being seen by officers as "suspicious" by virtue of their social status, if only at a subconscious level.

The second feature of post-*Terry* doctrine that has insulated stop and frisk programs from effective remedial constraint is the rule of Fourth Amendment standing. In general, only people who have suffered a personal violation of their Fourth Amendment rights as a result of government action may challenge the constitutionality of that government action. Moreover, except in very limited circumstances, people who claim a violation of their Fourth Amendment rights can only challenge the specific actions that affected them. Thus, courts generally can only review the reasonableness of a particular search or seizure and only when the person actually searched or seized brings the case. Just as importantly, evidence relating to the overall reasonableness of a program is generally irrelevant in the context of a particular challenge. So, too, is evidence relating to racial bias.[75] The only thing that is relevant is whether the facts at hand could have provided a reasonable officer with sufficient grounds to suspect criminal activity or the presence of a weapon. For these reasons, it is very difficult – and bordering on impossible – to challenge a stop and frisk program as a whole or to introduce evidence relating to the effectiveness and function of an overall program in the context of a more specific challenge.[76]

Also important in this context is that most stop and frisk challenges occur in the minority of cases where a stop or frisk results in arrest. Thus, the primary tool for testing the reasonableness of stop and frisk practices is the suppression hearing. The problem with suppression hearings as checks on stops and frisks is that, by definition, only guilty people seek suppression of incriminating evidence. This means that most challenges to stops and frisks are heavily influenced by hindsight bias. Moreover, suppression hearings offer no possibility of relief to the vast majority of citizens who are stopped or frisked because they were innocent, which means that there is no evidence to suppress. There is always the possibility of a civil action, of course, but very few people have the time or resources to sue the police. That is particularly true of those who are members of the vulnerable populations that suffer most at the hands of stop and frisk programs. The damages available in these actions are also quite low unless the victim suffers serious physical injury, reducing further the motivation for citizens to challenge the police. Finally, even in cases where citizens sue police officers and departments alleging that they were subjected to an unreasonable stop or frisk, they remain powerless to attack the policies and procedures behind the events or to seek, much less demand, reform. All they can do most of the time is demand money and angle for negotiated reforms.

As it stands, then, officers effectively are at their discretion to stop or frisk anyone they like, for good reasons, for bad reasons, or for no reasons at all. In the vast majority of cases, they know that their decisions will not be subject to judicial review. That is because the vast majority of cases do not lead to arrest or prosecution and innocent citizens who are stopped, frisked, and released seldom have the means, motive, or opportunity to challenge their treatment in court. Even in cases where officers are subject to review, courts afford them considerable deference, often citing officers' experiences and training as grounds to trust their judgment. As a result, on the rare occasion when an officer is haled into court to explain a particular incident of stop or frisk, she need only deploy a few stock references to "furtive movements," "high crime area," and her "experiences and training" to persuade a court that she acted reasonably.

As a consequence, most stops and frisks are probably not the results of thoughtful, objective assessments of exceptional circumstances. They are, instead, a routine practice used to project power, assert dominance, or vindicate gut feelings, which inevitably incorporate background social biases. We know the results: stop and frisk programs that are overbroad, have shockingly low success rates, impose undue burdens on particular neighborhoods, and tend to target vulnerable populations.

So, what can be done? One option would be to do away with stops and frisks altogether, requiring that officers have probable cause to arrest or to conduct a full investigative search before seizing or searching anyone. Although it should not be off the table entirely, this option probably fails the test of parsimoniousness in that it would involve excessive compromises against public interests in effective crime control. Where, then, might we look for a solution?

The greatest promise for effective, enforceable, and parsimonious restraints on stops and frisks lies not in doing away with the means and method altogether but in identifying the principal gaps in our current regulatory structure that allow it to be deployed on a largely unregulated basis. Foremost among these is the convergence of procedural and doctrinal limitations that make it largely impossible to mount effective challenges against stop and frisk practices at the programmatic level.

Rules on Fourth Amendment standing and the fact intensive, case-by-case approach to assessing Fourth Amendment reasonableness are heavily implicated in the current state of affairs when it comes to stop and frisk programs. These rules allow individual citizens to challenge specific stops or frisks, but largely immunize the programs that produce those events. Furthermore, due to the wide latitude and inherent flexibility afforded by the reasonable suspicion standard, it is very difficult to establish that any particular stop or frisk is unreasonable. As a result, we live in a world where almost every stop and frisk is likely to be deemed reasonable when viewed in isolation. At the same time, when viewed from on high, the programs themselves are clearly unreasonable, but evidence demonstrating programmatic problems is largely irrelevant in the contexts of individual challenges. This means that unreasonable stop and frisk programs are largely immune from effective challenge. As a result, those who are responsible for policy and training have few reasons to alter course. Fortunately, that all changes if we take seriously the role of the Fourth Amendment as a guarantor of collective rights to effective remedies.

Any individual member of the people should have standing to challenge programs, means, or methods that pose a general threat to the security of the people. Just as John Wilkes stood for all Englishman when he challenged the legal status of general warrants, so too can the target of any particular stop or frisk challenge the program authorizing that stop and frisk. Moreover, taking seriously the collective nature of Fourth Amendment rights means that any member of the people, whether or not she has personally been stopped or frisked, has standing to challenge a program, practice, means, or method that poses a general threat to the people as a whole.

If we expand both the scope of challenges to stops and frisk programs and the range of potential challengers, then constitutional litigation will be much more effective. If we take seriously the collective dimension of the Fourth Amendment then the primary target for Fourth Amendment regulations are the means, methods, and programs that threaten the collective security of the people. Moreover, as it stands, the vast majority of individuals who live with the daily threat of unreasonable stops or frisks do not occupy positions of political or economic power in society. By expanding the range of potential plaintiffs, the collective rights reading of the Fourth Amendment opens the door for powerful, experienced organizations such as the NAACP Legal Defense Fund or the American Civil Liberties Union to pursue civil actions challenging stop and frisk programs on behalf of the people as a whole.

Another important contribution of a collective rights reading of the Fourth Amendment is that it opens the door in terms of the kinds of remedies litigants can pursue. For the most part, the only remedies available in individual lawsuits alleging personal violations of constitutional rights are monetary awards. Injunctive relief, in the form of commands to act or refrain from acting, generally is not available in cases challenging individual instances of stop or frisk. Thus, an individual claiming a violation of her Fourth Amendment rights usually cannot demand programmatic reforms or additional, generally applied procedural constraints on police action.[77] By contrast, the whole point of a Fourth Amendment challenge lodged on behalf of the people as a whole would be to demand reform through the provision and enforcement of prospective remedies that target the programmatic use of search and seizure.

There are a number of reasons to think that opening the door to program-level challenges to stop and frisk practices would be effective in guaranteeing the security of the people against unreasonable searches and seizures. Foremost among these is the fact that the focus would be where it belongs: on the means, methods, and practices rather than on the isolated facts of individual cases. Second, it would promote a serious conversation about the underlying causes of unreasonable stop and frisk policies while also giving constitutional teeth to demands for reform. For example, a challenge might reveal that the chain of command uses stop and frisk statistics as indicators of police activity for purposes of pay and promotion, thereby creating incentives for officers to conduct stops or frisks simply to make their numbers.[78] If that were to be made part of the record in the context of a claim brought on behalf of the people, then a court might bar the practice. As another example, if it turned out that the crimes of suspicion underlying a substantial number of stops and frisks were minor offenses, then requiring suspicion of more serious felonies to justify a stop or frisk might produce results that are overall much more reasonable. As a third example, if careful investigation of a stop and frisk program revealed that officers routinely used stops and frisks as part of a broader culture of "warrior policing" to establish their authority and to exert control over citizens, then retraining and efforts designed to change departmental culture might be a very effective way to guarantee future security against unreasonable stops and frisks.

Another means by which opening the door to program-level challenges against stop and frisk practices might be effective in guaranteeing the security of the people against unreasonable searches and seizures lies not in lawsuits themselves but in the threat of lawsuits. As it stands, law enforcement agencies and their civilian colleagues have very few reasons to heed demands for reform of stop and frisk policies. As a general matter, the populations most often targeted by these policies are also those least likely to wield political power. Even when there is enough political pressure to initiate reform, there is no real mechanism for reviewing, assessing, and enforcing those reforms. The history of stop and frisk programs shows the consequences: steady expansion and the loosening of regulatory standards. A serious threat of legal action can change these dynamics considerably.

Armed with the ability to sue for reform, citizens will be able to exercise much more leverage to get law enforcement agencies to the negotiating table. Furthermore, any settlements reached during multi-party negotiations will have much more teeth if parties know that they can bring the matter to court, if necessary. In short, allowing litigants to sue on behalf of the people when it is the right of the people at jeopardy increases the chances of the very outcome we have seen in New York in the wake of their stop and frisk controversy: a collaborative effort to understand the interests at stake and to pursue meaningful reforms.

Few civil rights actions directed against law enforcement agencies end in trials and verdicts. They instead end, as the *Floyd* case in New York ended, with negotiations and consent decrees supervised by special masters that are ultimately enforceable by courts. The threat of civil action provides greater motive for these kinds of serious multi-party negotiations. An example is in order.

In 1971, sixteen members of politically active groups filed a class action suit against the New York City Police Department and its intelligence unit, then called the "Security and Investigation Section." The case was called *Handschu v. Special Services Division*.[79] In their complaint, the plaintiffs alleged that they were targeted by the Department and its officers, which engaged in a pattern of infiltration, coercion, surveillance, and provocation in an effort to suppress their political activities. The case never reached trial. The plaintiffs and defendants instead entered into a negotiated settlement. The centerpiece of that settlement was an elaborate set of guidelines governing the NYPD's intelligence-gathering practices. Pursuant to those guidelines, the NYPD established an internal oversight board that included civilian and police representatives. The guidelines prohibited intelligence gathering against political groups unless there were good grounds to suspect criminal wrongdoing, in which case the NYPD could initiate an investigation, but had to seek approval from the oversight board within thirty days. Likewise, the NYPD was forbidden from using undercover officers to infiltrate political groups unless it had prior approval from the oversight board. The guidelines also had provisions for the retention, destruction, and review of investigative records. After the guidelines were adopted, the lawsuit was suspended but the United States District Court for the Southern District of New York maintained authority to enforce the guidelines, to hear disputes, and to provide a forum for settling those disputes. In other words, the parties reached a mutually agreeable settlement but the sword of Damocles remained above law enforcement's head.

The negotiated settlement in *Handschu* provides a useful model for the sort of litigation outcomes one might expect from civil actions brought against law enforcement agencies to vindicate the right of the people to be secure in their persons and effects against unreasonable stops and frisks. Foremost among these is that the suit, once filed, eventually drew-in all interested parties. It also bound all interested and affected parties, whether they chose to be actively involved in the lawsuit or not. With the benefit of that assurance, the NYPD had every reason to take seriously the process of settling the case.

The capacity to bring a collective action against stop and frisk policies is largely missing under current Fourth Amendment doctrine. Those limitations threaten to make the Fourth Amendment irrelevant in the face of serious challenges to the rights of the people posed by stop and frisk programs. By providing a pathway for these kinds of actions, however, the a collective rights reading of the Fourth Amendment advanced in this book promises to provide substantially more leverage for citizens to challenge stop and frisk policies and practices.

All of this may seem very thin on particulars. That is as it must and should be, however. The pathologies underlying unreasonably broad and intrusive stop and frisk programs vary from program to program and department to department. Designing effective, enforceable, and parsimonious remedies will therefore require a considerable amount of diagnosis and tailoring. Civil actions targeted at the programmatic level provide a unique means for conducting the kinds of careful investigations and honest reviews that are necessary to this process of designing effective remedies.

Conclusion

This chapter has taken some steps toward describing the role of the Fourth Amendment in our age of surveillance. The bulk of these recommendations can best be described as frameworks. For discrete surveillance technologies best suited to individual investigations, such as tracking technologies, drones, and cell site simulators, the warrant requirement and the Wiretap Act seem to provide the most useful frameworks because they limit deployment while still respecting legitimate law enforcement interests. The framework for limiting the use and deployment of Big Data technologies is, by comparison, much more complicated, requiring thoughtful interventions at every stage of implementation and use. The framework for regulating stop and frisk programs is looser still, and organized around expanding the opportunity to more effective challenges in court.

Despite their differences, the remedial frameworks recommended in this chapter share a very important common feature: an emphasis on process. Identifying and implementing remedial measures that can satisfy the criteria of effectiveness, enforceability, and parsimoniousness will require a significant amount of process at the front end. This means opening the door for all interested parties to participate, either directly or through qualified proxies. It also means that interested parties, including government agencies, will need to be thoughtful and clear about their interests and goals. This kind of open approach is the surest path to reasonableness.[80] By committing to a process of reason-giving, this chapter has left considerable work to be done. That is what process is for, however. It has nevertheless offered a number of measures that policy-makers can consider as they engage in the process of formulating prospective remedial constraints on modern means and methods of search and seizure.

Although this chapter has put considerable faith in process as a means of formulating constitutional remedies, this does not mean that latitude is unlimited. There are, ultimately, non-negotiable constitutional rights at issue here, including the right of the people to be secure against unreasonable searches and seizures. Under the Fourth Amendment, that right "shall not be violated." To satisfy this constitutional imperative will require setting constraints on government actors, and may even mean living with certain risks in terms of crime and security threats. That is the price of the Fourth Amendment, but it is a price well worth paying in order to maintain the basic balance between order and liberty that defines our constitutional democracy.[81]

Notes

1. SELECT COMMITTEE TO STUDY GOVERNMENTAL OPERATIONS WITH RESPECT TO INTELLIGENCE ACTIVITIES, FINAL REPORT TOGETHER WITH ADDITIONAL, SUPPLEMENTAL, AND SEPARATE VIEWS, Apr. 26, 1976, 291 (hereinafter "CHURCH COMMITTEE REPORT").
2. Renée McDonald Hutchins, *Tied Up in* Knotts? *GPS Technology and the Fourth Amendment*, 55 UCLA L. Rev. 409, 444 (2007).
3. SAMUEL JOHNSON, DICTIONARY OF THE ENGLISH LANGUAGE (10th ed. 1792).
4. *Id.*
5. *Id.*
6. This danger is not merely a matter of speculation. As the NSA Inspector General reported to Congress in 2013, there were numerous cases of analysts abusing surveillance capacities for personal reasons, such as to target ex-girlfriends. *See* Letter to Senator Charles E. Grassley from NSA Office of the Inspector General, Sept. 11, 2013, http://icontherecord.tumblr.com/post/62457835497/nsa-inspector-generals-letter-to-senator-charles (last visited Apr. 8, 2016).
7. JOHNSON, *supra* note 5.
8. Transcript of Oral Argument at 9–10, United States v. Jones, 132 S. Ct. 945 (2012) (No. 10–1259).
9. United States v. Jones, 132 S.Ct. 945, 963 (2012) ("In the pre-computer age, the greatest protections of privacy were neither constitutional nor statutory, but practical. Traditional surveillance for any extended period of time was difficult and costly and therefore rarely undertaken.").
10. United States v. Knotts, 460 U.S. 276 (1983).
11. *See* David Gray & Danielle Citron, *The Right to Quantitative Privacy*, 98 MINN. L. REV. 62, 132–33 (2013).
12. *Knotts*, 460 U.S. at 285.
13. Olmstead v. United States, 277 U. S. 438 (1928).
14. *See* Katz v. United States, 389 U.S. 347 (1967); Berger v. New York, 388 U.S. 41 (1967).
15. 18 U.S.C. § 2511.
16. 18 U.S.C. § 2518.
17. 18 U.S.C. § 2518 provides that wiretap orders can only be issued in cases involving offenses enumerated in 18 U.S.C. § 2516, which lists twenty categories of quite serious offenses, including murder, terrorism, and major narcotics felonies.
18. In United States v. Karo, 468 U.S. 705 (1984), the Supreme Court held that using a beeper tracking device similar to the one used in *Knotts* to locate a suspect in his

home violated the Fourth Amendment. More recently, a Maryland appellate court held that the Fourth Amendment prohibits the use of a cell site simulator to locate a person in his home. Andrews v. State, 227 Md. App. 350 (Md. Ct. Spec. App. 2016). Based on these precedents, courts granting tracking orders would likely need to incorporate minimization procedures designed to prevent the use of tracking devices to monitor targets in their homes and similar, highly-protected areas.

19. CHURCH COMMITTEE REPORT at 2.
20. *See, e.g.*, The California Electronic Communications Act (2016) (requiring warrants for real-time and historical CSLI); Md. Crim. Proc. Code, § 1–203.1 (2015) (establishing a warrant requirement for real-time CSLI). For maps showing state laws governing tracking technologies, see www.aclu.org/map/cell-phone-location-tracking-laws-state, or https://cdt.org/insight/survey-of-state-location-privacy-legislation/.
21. JOHNSON, *supra* note 5.
22. Department of Justice, *Department of Justice Policy Guidance: Use of Cell-Site Simulator Technology*, 1–2, Sept. 3, 2015 (hereinafter Dept. of Justice Memo), www.justice.gov/opa/file/767321/download.
23. See Harris Corporation, Stingray Product Description, http://files.cloudprivacy.net/Harris_Stingray_product_sheet; Stephanie K. Pell & Christopher Soghoian, *Your Secret Stingray's No Secret Anymore: The Vanishing Government Monopoly Over Cell Phone Surveillance and Its Impact on National Security and Consumer Privacy*, 28 HARV. J.L. & TECH. 1, 11–12 (2014); Dept. of Justice Memo at 1–2.
24. Pell & Soghoian, *supra* note 23, at 11–12.
25. *See* Berger v. New York, 388 U.S. 41, 51 (1967) (" 'conversation' [falls] within the Fourth Amendment's protections, and that the use of electronic devices to capture it [is] a 'search' within the meaning of the Amendment") (internal citation omitted).
26. 389 U.S. 347, 350–53 (1967).
27. Ex Parte *Jackson*, 96 U.S. 727, 733 (1878).
28. *See, Katz*, 389 U.S. at 353.
29. Unlike some contemporary surveillance technologies, cell site simulators cannot avoid Fourth Amendment scrutiny by appealing to post-*Katz* doctrines. Law enforcement agencies and their legal representatives have argued that cell site simulators should not be subject to Fourth Amendment regulation by virtue of the third-party doctrine. *See, e.g.*, Reply Brief of Appellant at *3, Andrews v. State, WL 1254567, 227 Md. App. 350 (Md. Ct. Spec. App. 2016) (hereinafter "*Andrews* App. Br."), 2016 WL 910249. Their argument is that the actual information gathered by cell site simulators is essentially the same information gathered by pen register devices, which telephone companies can attach to traditional telephone lines in order to gather basic telephony metadata. They also point to a case called Smith v. Maryland, 442 U.S. 735 (1979), where the Supreme Court held that Fourth Amendment rights are not implicated if a telephone company uses a pen register device to gather telephony metadata at the request of law enforcement. Unfortunately for government advocates, this argument fails to account for how cell site simulators operate.

Pen register devices are installed and operated by telephone companies. Moreover, they gather information customers voluntarily share with their telephone providers in order to obtain basic telephone services. By contrast, cell site simulators are operated by law enforcement in order to intercept communications between users and their service providers. Although users may voluntarily share this information with their service providers, they certainly do not share it with law enforcement. This distinction is an important under existing Supreme Court doctrine. Indeed, in every case where the Supreme Court has elaborated and applied the third-party doctrine, the third party has acted as a knowing conduit for information sought by the government. *See, e.g.*, United States v. Miller, 425 U.S. 435, 442–43 (1976) (law enforcement subpoenaed records from defendant's bank); Hoffa v. United States, 385 U.S. 293 (1966) (a government informer conveyed the contents of defendant's communications with that informer to law enforcement); Lewis v. United States, 385 U.S. 206 (1966) (an undercover agent conveyed the contents of defendant's communications with that agent to law enforcement); Lopez v. United States, 373 U.S. 427 (1963) (a cooperating witness conveyed the contents of defendant's communications with that witness to law enforcement). *See also* Upshur v. State, 208 Md. App. 383 (2012) (law enforcement subpoenaed subscriber information from defendant's service provider). In none of these cases did the Supreme Court sanction the government's direct interception of communications. *Smith* is no exception.

In Smith v. Maryland, a telephone company, acting at the request of law enforcement, installed a pen register device on its own infrastructure for the purpose of gathering call record information associated with Smith's telephone. 442 U.S. at 737. The company then passed that information to law enforcement. That arrangement, in which the telephone company acted as the conduit for information passed to law enforcement, was essential to the Court's holding in *Smith*. According to the Court, "When [Smith] used his phone, [he] voluntarily conveyed numerical information to the telephone company and 'exposed' that information to its equipment in the ordinary course of business. In doing so, [Smith] assumed the risk that the company would reveal to police the numbers he dialed." 442 U.S. at 744. The Supreme Court neither held nor implied that Smith also assumed the risk that law enforcement would intercept information directly by, say, tapping telephone lines.

In 2014, the Supreme Court reaffirmed the distinction between gathering information through a third-party and gathering information directly. In Riley v. California, law enforcement argued that it was entitled to access directly the call records stored on a suspect's lawfully seized cellular phone because that information revealed nothing more than what would have been gathered by a pen register device. 134 S.Ct. 2473, 2492 (2014). The Court roundly rejected that proposition, pointing out that the use of "a pen register at telephone company premises to identify numbers dialed by a particular caller" is not a search, because it does not violate reasonable expectations or privacy. *Riley*, 134 S.Ct. at 2492. The Court maintained, however, that accessing that same information directly by searching records stored on a phone is a search because it does violate reasonable expectations of privacy. *Id.*

It of course makes sense to distinguish between direct and indirect information gathering within the bounds of the third-party doctrine. Allowing law enforcement to access by direct means information we might choose to share with others would lead to absurdity by reducing the Fourth Amendment to a nullity. After all, communication by definition entails sharing information with at least one other person. If that simple act of sharing opened the door to government surveillance, then the entire concept of reasonable expectations of privacy would be meaningless because government agents would have an unlimited license to intercept, eavesdrop, and snoop by opening our mail, tapping our phones, and reading our electronic mail. After all, in each of these instances we voluntarily transmit information to third parties. *See* Patricia L. Bellia & Susan Freiwald, *Fourth Amendment Protection for Stored E-Mail*, 2008 U. CHI. L. FORUM 121, 153–54 (2008).

A more accurate statement of the third-party doctrine is that we have no Fourth Amendment complaint if a party to our communications shares that information with government agents through lawful means. *See, e.g.,* United States v. Miller, 425 U. S. 435, 443 (1976) ("the Fourth Amendment does not prohibit the obtaining of information revealed to a third party and conveyed by him to Government authorities"). On this formulation of the rule, law enforcement cannot argue that its use of cell site simulators falls within the compass of the third-party doctrine. After all, agents operating these devices do not go to cellular service providers with requests for call information. They instead cut out the middleman by intercepting directly communications between users and their cellular service providers. This is the cellular equivalent of a wiretap. There can therefore be no doubt that it is a search, the third-party doctrine notwithstanding.

In at least one case, government attorneys have argued that the communications intercepted by cell site simulators, which includes device identifiers, locations, and call data, is subject to direct interception because it is less intimate than the contents of our telephonic communications. *See Andrews*, App. Br., at 10. This, too, is unavailing. As the Supreme Court explained in Kyllo v. United States, courts are not in the business of parsing degrees of intimacy in conduct and communications when it comes to evaluating Fourth Amendment interests. 533 U.S. 27, 37–39 (2001). If we have a reasonable expectation of privacy against interception of communications with our cellular service providers, then interception of those communications by law enforcement is a search, regardless of how intimate or non-intimate the contents. *See also Riley*, 134 S.Ct. at 2492–93 (refusing to draw Fourth Amendment distinctions between "smartphones" versus older "flip" phones based on the information each contains). Moreover, as Justice Sotomayor pointed out recently in United States v. Jones, a person's location and contact information can be extremely revealing of very intimate conduct and associations. *See* 132 S.Ct. 945, 955–56 (2012) (Sotomayor, J., concurring). The Court has since cited Justice Sotomayor's views on this point with approval. *See Riley*, 134 S.Ct. at 2490.

30. *See* Osborn v. United States, 385 U.S. 323, 329 n.7 (1966) (The "indiscriminate use [of eavesdropping] devices in law enforcement raises grave constitutional questions under the Fourth and Fifth Amendments, and imposes a heavier responsibility on this Court in its supervision of the fairness of procedures ..."). *See also* Jones, 132 S.Ct. at 946 (Sotomayor, J., concurring) ("I would also consider the appropriateness of entrusting to the Executive, in the absence of any oversight from a coordinate branch, a tool so amenable to misuse, especially in light of the Fourth Amendment's goal to curb arbitrary exercises of police power to and prevent 'a too permeating police surveillance.' ") (internal citation omitted).

31. The degree and scope of the threat posed by cell site simulators is evidenced further by the suggestion, made by some government attorneys, that, if we really want to avoid surveillance by cell site simulators, we should turn off our phones. Andrews,

App. Br. at 13. It is hard to imagine a world more upside down from a Fourth Amendment point of view. The solution to threats of broad and indiscriminate search is not to ask citizens to "live dark and cloistered lives." Palmieri v. Lynch, 392 F.3d 73, 97 (2nd Cir. 2005) (Straub, J., dissenting). "This much withdrawal is not required in order to claim the benefit of the amendment because, if it were, the amendment's benefit would be too stingy to preserve the kind of open society to which we are committed and in which the amendment is supposed to function." Anthony G. Amsterdam, *Perspectives on the Fourth Amendment*, 58 MINN. L. REV. 349, 402 (1974). Moreover, "placing pressure on persons to return to their individual 'private' worlds to seek refuge from government searches and surveillance diminishes the public sphere's security." Thomas M. Crocker, *The Political Fourth Amendment*, 88 WASH. U. L. REV. 303, 369 (2010). The better course, the course demanded by the Fourth Amendment itself, is to limit law enforcement's access to cell site simulators.
32. Amsterdam, *supra* note 31, at 400. ("The guarantee against unreasonable searches and seizures was written and should be read to assure that any and every form of such interference is at least regulated by fundamental law so that it may be restrained within proper bounds.").
33. Clare Garvie, Alvaro Bedoya, & Jonathan Frankle, *The Perpetual Line-Up: Unregulated Police Face Recognition in America*, Oct. 18, 2016, www.perpetuallineup.org/sites/default/files/2016-10/The%20Perpetual%20Line-Up%20-%20Center%20on%20Privacy%20and%20Technology%20at%20Georgetown%20Law.pdf.
34. JOHNSON, *supra* note 5.
35. *Id.*
36. *Id.*
37. *Id.* (defining "reason" as "The power by which man deduces one proposition from another, or proceeds from premises to consequences.").
38. PRIVACY & CIVIL LIBERTIES OVERSIGHT BOARD, REPORT ON THE TELEPHONE RECORDS PROGRAM CONDUCTED UNDER SECTION 215 OF THE USA PATRIOT ACT AND ON THE OPERATIONS OF THE FOREIGN INTELLIGENCE SURVEILLANCE COURT – (2014).
39. Mattathias Schwartz, *The Whole Haystack*, THE NEW YORKER, Jan. 26, 2015.
40. *See* JEFFREY KAHN, MRS. SHIPLEY'S GHOST: THE RIGHT TO TRAVEL AND TERRORIST WATCHLISTS (2013); Danielle Keats Citron & Frank Pasquale, *Network Accountability for the Domestic Intelligence Apparatus*, 62 HASTINGS L.J. 1441, 1462 (2011).
41. CHURCH COMMITTEE REPORT at 1.
42. *Id.*
43. JOHNSON, *supra* note 5.
44. *See* David Medine, *The Privacy and Civil Liberties Oversight Board*, in THE CAMBRIDGE HANDBOOK OF SURVEILLANCE LAW (David Gray & Stephen Henderson, eds. 2017).
45. Although telephone companies are no longer turning over data in bulk, they continue to automatically hand over data that is responsive to an active query.
46. Bamford, *The NSA is Building the Country's Biggest Spy Center*, WIRED, Mar. 15, 2012 www.wired.com/2012/03/ff_nsadatacenter/.
47. *Jones*, 134 U.S. at 955–56 (Sotomayor, concurring).

48. *See* VIKTOR MAYER-SCHÖNBERGER, DELETE: THE VIRTUE OF FORGETTING IN THE DIGITAL AGE (2011).
49. *Id.*
50. For an example of how failure to control access to data can lead to abuse, *see* Avis Thomas-Lester & Toni Lacy, *Chief's Friend Accused of Extortion*, WASH. POST, Nov. 26, 1997, A1.
51. For an example of this kind of abuse, *see* M.L. Elnick, *Cops Tap Database to Harass, Intimidate*, DETROIT FREE PRESS, July 31, 2001.
52. *See, generally*, American Bar Association, which is modeled after the procedure for issuing grand jury subpoenas. *See* ABA STANDARDS FOR CRIMINAL JUSTICE, LAW ENFORCEMENT ACCESS TO THIRD PARTY RECORDS (2013) (outlining a flexible scheme providing different limitations on access for different information held by third parties based on the privacy interests at stake).
53. *Jones*, 132 S.Ct. at 964 (Alito, J., concurring).
54. 277 U.S. 438 (1928).
55. 389 U.S. 347 (1967).
56. 388 U.S. 41 (1967).
57. See Giles Jacob, *Every Man His Own Lawyer* (1768) ("Constables may not lawfully take up night-walkers, on bare suspicion only of their being of ill fame; if they are not found breaking the peace, or doing some unlawful act, &c." (citing Hale, 1736)). *Cf.* Statute of Winchester (1285) ("And henceforth it is commanded that watches be kept as they were accustomed to be formerly, that is to say, from Ascension day to Michaelmas, in each city by six men at each gate, in each borough by twelve men, in each vill in the open country by six men or four according to the number of the inhabitants, and they shall keep watch continually all night from sunset to sunrise. And if any stranger pass by them, let him be arrested until morning: and if nothing suspicious is found he may go free, but if anything suspicious is found let him be handed over to the sheriff forthwith and he shall receive him without making difficulty and keep him safely until he is delivered in due manner.").
58. Terry v. Ohio, 392 U.S. 1 (1968).
59. JOHNSON, *supra* note 5.
60. *Id.*
61. *Terry*, 392 U.S. at 16 ("There is some suggestion in the use of such terms as 'stop' and 'frisk' that such police conduct is outside the purview of the Fourth Amendment because neither action rises to the level of a 'search' or 'seizure' within the meaning of the Constitution. We emphatically reject this notion.").
62. United States Department of Justice, Civil Rights Division, *Investigation of the Baltimore City Police Department*, Aug. 10, 2016, www.justice.gov/opa/file/883366/download.
63. *See., e.g.*, Jeffrey Bellin, *The Inverse Relationship Between the Constitutionality and Effectiveness of New York City Stop and Frisk*, 94 B. U. L. Rev. 1495, 1515–117 (2014) (citing and quoting advocates).
64. *See*, George Kelling & James Q. Wilson, *Broken Windows*, THE ATLANTIC, Mar. 1982, www.theatlantic.com/magazine/archive/1982/03/broken-windows/304465/.
65. *See* Jeffrey Fagan, Tom Tyler, & Tracey Meares, *Street Stops and Police Legitimacy in New York*, *in* COMPARING THE DEMOCRATIC GOVERNANCE OF POLICE INTELLIGENCE: NEW MODELS OF PARTICIPATION AND EXPERTISE IN

THE UNITED STATES AND EUROPE 203 (Jacqueline Ross and Thierry Delpeuch, eds. 2016).
66. Bellin, *supra* note 63.
67. Kevin Rector, *Deadliest Year in Baltimore History Ends with 344 Homicides*, BALT. SUN, Jan. 1, 2016.
68. *See generally*, David Greenberg, *Studying New York City's Crime Decline: Methodological Issues*, 31 JUSTICE QUARTERLY 54 (2014); Bellin, *supra* note 63.
69. www.nyc.gov/html/nypd/downloads/pdf/analysis_and_planning/seven_major_felony_offenses_2000_2014.pdf. The overall numbers of some of the other major felonies decreased somewhat more dramatically. For example, auto theft went down from 26,656 to 8,093.
70. *Id.*
71. www.nyc.gov/html/nypd/downloads/pdf/analysis_and_planning/seven_major_felony_offenses_2000_2014.pdf.
72. Ashley Southall, *Shootings in New York Fell in 2016 to Lowest Level in More Than 20 Years*, N.Y. Times, Jan. 4, 2017, at A21.
73. Bernard Harcourt, *Punitive Preventive Justice: A Critique*, in PREVENTION AND THE LIMITS OF CRIMINAL LAW 252 (Andrew Ashworth, Lucia Zedner, & Patrick Tomlin, eds. 2012).
74. *See, e.g.*, United States v. Arvizu, 534 U.S. 266 (2002).
75. Whren v. United States, 517 U.S. 806 (1996).
76. There are two potential means by which litigants can challenge stop and frisk practices on a programmatic level: class actions and *Monell* claims. Unfortunately, neither has provided a means to raise any serious challenges against stop and frisk programs. In the case of class actions, it is virtually impossible to establish a sufficient shared factual basis among potential class members. Stops and frisks are measured solely by the specific facts surrounding each stop and frisk under current doctrine. These facts are inevitably unique, however. As a consequence, it is virtually impossible to construct a class sufficient to challenge stop and frisk at a programmatic level. Monell claims, named after the Supreme Court's famous decision in Monell v. Department of Social Services of the City of New York, 436 U.S. 658 (1978), allow plaintiffs to seek damages directly against a municipality based on the conduct of its officers if they can show that the officers acted pursuant to an explicit or implicit policy or custom. Monell claims therefore may allow a particular victim of a stop or frisk to challenge departmental policies and practices. This, in fact, was the strategy adopted by the plaintiffs in Floyd v. The City of New York, in which Judge Shira Sheindlin cited statistical evidence of racial bias in the NYPD's stop and frisk program to justify pretty significant injunctive relief. Floyd v. City of New York, 959 F.Supp. 2d 540 (S.D.N.Y. 2013). That decision is, however, an outlier. More tellingly, however, Judge Scheindlin's order was stayed by the Second Circuit, which also cited her for impropriety and assigned the case to another judge. The City later dropped its appeal and instead agreed to submit to the supervision of a special monitor, who reports to Judge Analisa Torres of the United States District Court for the Southern District of New York. Although this is, in many ways, a positive outcome, the fact is that it is more a result of politics than the law. Few commentators doubt that Judge Scheindlin would have been overruled had the City continued with its appeal before the Second Circuit.

There was a mayoral election in the interim, however, during which stop and frisk was a significant issue. Elected in large part on his pledge to reform stop and frisk practices, Mayor Bill de Blasio decided to submit rather than fight.
77. Here, Judge Scheindlin's decision in the *Floyd* case is the exception that proves the rule. Although she did impose sweeping injunctive relief, her order was vacated on appeal. The police department later entered into a consent decree under which they agreed to certain reforms, but it is not at all clear that a court could have imposed those reforms on its own authority.
78. *See* Ryan Devereaux, *NYPD Officers Testify Stop-and-Frisk Policy Driven by Quota System*, THE GUARDIAN, Mar. 22, 2013. For a first-person account of stop and frisk quotas *see* Stop and Frisk: The Police Officer, www.youtube.com/watch?v=tt4O62_VXs4.
79. Handschu v. Special Services Division, 605 F. Supp. 1384, 1388 (1985).
80. This basic framework maps onto the work of philosopher Jürgen Habermas, who has spent his career arguing persuasively for a discursive approach to reason. On his account, the most reasonable answer to any question of ethics, morality, or policy lies in the results of an ideal speech event. As part of that ideal speech event, all interested parties must be afforded and equal opportunity to express their interests and preferences, but must also leave themselves open to persuasion. On Habermas's account, faith to process will lead to a reasonable outcome. *See generally*, JÜRGEN HABERMAS, THE THEORY OF COMMUNICATIVE ACTION: REASON AND THE RATIONALIZATION OF SOCIETY (Thomas McCarty, trans., 1985).
81. *See* United States v. United States District Court, 407 U.S. 297, 314 (1972) ("The price of lawful public dissent must not be a dread of subjection to an unchecked surveillance power.").

CONCLUSION

Our Fourth Amendment Utopia

We started our journey in these pages with dystopian images of worlds, both fictional and real, where pervasive surveillance is deployed as a tool of social control. Let us end on a more hopeful note.

Although the Constitution was born of dystopian fears, it paints an unapologetically positive vision of the world as it can and should be. The goal, after all, is to form a "more perfect Union, establish Justice, insure domestic Tranquility, provide for the common defence, promote the general Welfare, and secure the Blessings of Liberty to ourselves and our Posterity."[1] The Fourth Amendment and the Bill of Rights more generally paint a particularly vivid picture of this utopian ideal. Here we find images of an intellectually and culturally vibrant people for whom ideas, exploration, thought, creation, and expression are essential features of private and public life. We are presented with a world where people are invested in private pursuits of conscience, meaning, and truth and actively engaged in civic life. We see a people free to live, work, and love without fear of unwarranted governmental intrusion and unjust treatment. In short, we are presented with a vision of a world defined by freedom, liberty, and the promise of opportunity.

The giddy prospect of life in this utopian freedom state inspired our founders to shake off the shackles of oppression and establish a new nation. For them then, as for us now, that vision is as much aspiration as it is a promise. The American story is one of pursuing perfection, oftentimes at a bloody cost. That project continues. But, despite the changes and challenges of the last two hundred and thirty years, the same basic utopian vision remains. What we want today, what thrums at the resonant frequency of our American soul, is precisely that which is guaranteed in our founding texts: the liberty to define and pursue our own individual conceptions of the good life and to participate meaningfully as a people in the management of our collective affairs.

The reading of the Fourth Amendment promoted in this book is of a piece with the American utopia described and guaranteed in the

Constitution and the Bill of Rights. By its text, and read in historical context, the Fourth Amendment guarantees a basic degree of security against threats of unreasonable governmental intrusion. That security is important and valuable in its own right, but it is also linked to the Constitution's broader utopian goals. Specifically, the Fourth Amendment secures for each of us and for all of us the space that is necessary to our individual projects of exploration and development – our pursuit of the good life, however defined.[2] The security guaranteed to the people by the Fourth Amendment is also essential to our collective project of self-governance. By erecting a barrier between the people and the government that "shall not be violated," the Fourth Amendment preserves the independence of the governed and maintains space for the operations of civil society that are critical to a functioning democracy.[3]

As our founders understood all too well, strong forces impel human societies toward dystopia.[4] Power carries its own temptations. High office also brings with it heavy responsibilities, which push those in power to pursue more efficient means of effecting control. Left uncontested, these timeless forces bend all governments toward tyranny. In this regard, the rights guaranteed by the Fourth Amendment and the Bill of Rights more generally provide a regulative ideal and a set of crucial checks that direct our political society back toward the light. In reflecting on this role, philosopher Jon Elster has described the Constitution and the Bill of Rights as a set of "precommitments" that bind us as a people against the political temptations of the moment.[5] They are like the mast to which Ulysses lashed himself as he sailed past the Serenum scopuli so he would not succumb to the temptations of the sirens' songs.[6]

The precommitments contained in the Fourth Amendment and the rest of the Bill of Rights are particularly important in times of actual or perceived emergency.[7] As we saw in Chapter 4, eighteenth-century commentators such as the Maryland Farmer[8] and the Canadian Freeholder were skeptical of government agents' fondness for "doctrines of reason of state, and state necessity, and the impossibility of providing for great emergencies and extraordinary cases, without a discretionary power ... to proceed sometimes by uncommon methods not agreeable to the known forms of law."[9] Two centuries later, Justice Brennan echoed these same concerns, noting that "In times of unrest, whether caused by crime or racial conflict or fear of internal subversion, this basic law and the values that it represents may appear unrealistic or 'extravagant' to some. But the values were those of the authors of our fundamental constitutional concepts."[10]

The dangers posed to our constitutional utopia by claims of executive emergency are particularly acute in the context of national security. In an August 1975 appearance on Meet the Press, Senator Frank Church, chair of the Senate Select Committee charged with investigating illegal and unconstitutional actions by intelligence agencies in the 1960s and 1970s, summed up some of the dangers. Asked whether he thought that "the CIA and military intelligence agencies and the FBI" had leveraged claims of executive emergency in the context of the Cold War to justify actions and plans that "threaten the liberty of American citizens," Senator Church offered the following observation:

> In the need to develop a capacity to know what potential enemies are doing, the United States government has perfected a technological capability that enables us to monitor the messages that go through the air. These messages are between ships at sea. They could be between units – military units in the field. We have a very extensive capability of intercepting messages wherever they may be in the airwaves. Now that is necessary and important to the United States as we look abroad at enemies or potential enemies, we must know. At the same time, that capability at any time could be turned around on the American people and no American would have any privacy left. Such is the capability to monitor everything – telephone conversations, telegrams it doesn't matter. There would be no place to hide if this government ever became a tyranny. If a dictator ever took charge in this country, the technological capacity that the intelligence community has given the government could enable it to impose total tyranny and there would be no way to fight back because the most careful effort to combine together in resistance to the government, no matter how privately it was done, is within the reach of the government to know. Such is the capability of this technology. Now, why is this investigation important? I'll tell you why. Because I don't want to see this country ever go across the bridge. I know that the capacity that is there to make tyranny total in America. And we must see to it that this agency and all agencies that possess this technology operate within the law and under proper supervision so that we never cross over that abyss. That's the abyss from which there is no return.[11]

As we did in 1975, we find ourselves now in the midst of perpetual wars against threats both foreign and domestic. The War on Drugs, which traces its roots to Prohibition, has provided a seemingly bottomless well of rhetorical resources justifying the expansion of law enforcement institutions and executive powers on grounds of necessity and emergency. Picking up where the Cold War left off, the War on Terror is the "great emergency" of the twenty-first century, which has been deployed to justify dramatic expansions in our national security apparatus.

Together, the War on Drugs and the War on Terror have ushered in a new age of surveillance in which government authorities have capacities far beyond what Senator Church could have imagined. His fears of tyrannical abuses of power are therefore very much alive for us today. But the possibility of malevolent perversion of the state's security apparatus is not the only concern posed by the technologies, means, and methods that define our age of surveillance. Far more worrisome is the inevitability of benevolent tyranny.

George Orwell's *1984* is a frequent trope in contemporary debates about surveillance and the Fourth Amendment. In most of these conversations, people refer to Big Brother or the ubiquitous network of "telescreens" used to surveil the citizens of Oceana. Less often discussed is the role of perpetual war in *1984*. Oceana was in a constant state of war with either Eurasia or Eastasia. The workings of the Ministries of Truth, Peace, Love, and Plenty were all rationalized and justified by these "great emergencies," which required extraordinary measures. Within the context of these global conflicts, social control was imagined as an act of love. Big Brother pursued submission, conformance, and acquiescence among its citizens because, in the view of the Inner Party, these were the social attitudes that were best for both the state and its subjects. It was therefore with no small amount of tenderness that O'Brien tortured Winston Smith as part of his reeducation – a reeducation that Smith ultimately embraced as his own salvation.

The real threat to our constitutional utopia in an age of surveillance is not the evil overlord. It is the benevolent tyrant who asks us to trade liberty for security while offering us the easy comforts of familiar platitudes and unquestioning trust. As the parable of Winston Smith teaches us, these are tempting offers. At the cusp of these moments, the Bill of Rights generally, and the Fourth Amendment in particular, have at least two very important roles to play.

First, they establish a set of nonnegotiable precommitments. No matter how seductive the sirens' calls of law enforcement necessity or national security emergency, we simply cannot by mere political process agree to policies, practices, or procedures that threaten the right of the people to be secure against unreasonable searches and seizures. That means we cannot grant executive agents unfettered discretion to deploy and use most modern means and methods of search and seizure. As a precommitment, the Fourth Amendment therefore protects us against ourselves, preserving our constitutional utopia against dystopian threats, no matter how benevolent and attractive the messenger.

Second, the Fourth Amendment, along with other rights guaranteed in the Constitution, reminds us who we are as a people. We are a people for whom liberty is a defining good. We are a people who refuse to live under a government that is not of our own creation and under our control. We are a people blessed with and defined by our dual roles as heirs to and caretakers of a unique and noble birthright. In a world where we are invited to simply accept as fact government surveillance, the Fourth Amendment reminds us of our values and our responsibilities. In so doing, it also supplies us with the best answer to the question that started this book:

Why should we care about contemporary government surveillance programs? We should care, we *must* care, because the prospect of life in a surveillance state is anathema to our constitutional character.

This, then, is the most important role of the Fourth Amendment in our age of surveillance. The Fourth Amendment reminds us of the utopian dream that is America. It reminds us what it means to be American. It compels us to action as Americans. To simply acquiesce would be to fail in our sacred obligation to honor the sacrifices of those who came before us and our solemn duty to preserve for our progeny "the blessings of liberty."

Notes

1. U.S. CONST., Pmbl.
2. Boyd v. United States, 116 U.S. 616, 635 (1886) ("At the very core of the Fourth Amendment stands the right of a man to retreat into his own home and there be free from unreasonable governmental intrusion." (quoting Silverman v. United States, 365 U.S. 505 (1961) (internal quotation marks omitted))).
3. Camara v. Municipal Court, 387 U.S. 523, 528 (1967) ("The basic purpose of this Amendment, as recognized in countless decisions of this Court, is to safeguard the privacy and security of individuals against arbitrary invasions by governmental officials. The Fourth Amendment thus gives concrete expression to a right of the people which 'is basic to a free society.' ").
4. Byars v. United States, 273 U.S. 28, 34–35 (1927) ("The Fourth Amendment was adopted in view of long misuse of power in the matter of searches and seizures both in England and the colonies, and the assurance against any revival of it, so carefully embodied in the fundamental law, is not to be impaired by judicial sanction of equivocal methods, which, regarded superficially, may seem to escape the challenge of illegality but which, in reality, strike at the substance of the constitutional right.").
5. JON ELSTER, ULYSSES AND THE SIRENS: STUDIES IN RATIONALITY AND IRRATIONALITY 36–47 (1979).

6. Homer, Odyssey 214-16 (Robert Fitzgerald trans., Anchor Books 1963).
7. United States v. Di Re, 332 U.S. 581, 595 (1948) ("the forefathers, after consulting the lessons of history, designed our Constitution to place obstacles in the way of a too permeating police surveillance, which they seemed to think was a greater danger to a free people than the escape of criminals from punishment.").
8. A Maryland Farmer, no. 1 (1788) ("suppose for instance, that an officer of the United States should force the house, the asylum of a citizen, by virtue of a general warrant, I would ask, are general warrants illegal by the constitution of the United States? Would a court, or even a jury, but juries are no longer to exist, punish a man who acted by express authority, upon the bare recollection of what once was law and right? I fear not, especially in those cases which may strongly interest the passions of government, and in such only have general warrants been used.").
9. The Canadian Freeholder: Dialogue II, 243-44 (1779). *See also* Thomas Y. Davies, *Recovering the Original Fourth Amendment*, 98 Mich. L. Rev. 547, 578-83 (1999) (documenting the founders' concerns with executive discretion).
10. Florida v. Royer, 460 U.S. 491, 513 (1983) (Brennan, J., concurring). *See also* Coolidge v. New Hampshire, 403 U.S. 443, 455 (1971) ("We must not allow our zeal for effective law enforcement to blind us to the peril to our free society that lies in this Court's disregard of the protections afforded by the Fourth Amendment.").
11. Senator Frank Church, The Intelligence Gathering Debate, on Meet the Press, Aug. 18, 1975, www.youtube.com/watch?v=YAG1N4a84Dk.

INDEX

1984. See Orwell, George

Active Liberty, 155
Adams, John, 70, 143, 150
Affordable Care Act, 39, 89, 263
Alito, Samuel, 15, 16, 100, 105, 111, 114, 116, 127, 202, 220, 223, 253
Amazon, 31, 39, 121
American Bar Association
    Standards for Criminal Justice Law Enforcement Access to Third Party Records, 120
American Civil Liberties Union (ACLU), 56, 66, 283
Amsterdam, Anthony, 109, 154, 210
Angry Birds, 24
Angwin, Julia, 108
Anti-Federalists, 69, 123, 169, 170
Apple, 106
Article I, Section 2, 149
Articles of Confederation, 148
AT&T, 44

Balkin, Jack, 121
Baltimore. Maryland, 37, 54, 277
Benson, Egbert, 139
Bentham, Jeremy, 8
Big Brother, 1, 32, 298
Big Data, 38–48, 263–75
Biometric Surveillance, 41, 43
Blackmun, Harry, 217
Blackstone, William, 162
Bloomberg, Michael, 40, 50
Body Politick, 144, 152, 156
Borg, The, 8
boyd, danah, 14
Bradbury, Ray, 1
Bradley, Cornelius Beach, 166
Bradley, Joseph, 73, 157, 196

Brandeis, Louis, 74
Bratton, William, 40
Brave New World, 1, 8
Brennan-Marquez, Kiel, 121
Breyer, Stephen, 15, 100, 155
Brightest Flashlight, 24
Brown, Michael, 54
Bush, George W., 44

California Electronic Communications Act (CalECPA), 288
Canadian Freeholder, The, 169, 296
Canons of Interpretation, 137
    ejusdem generis, 137
    expressio unius est exclusio alterius, 140
    noscitur a sociis, 137, 147, 157
Cardozo, Benjamin, 217
Carter, Jimmy, 3
Cell Site Location Information (CSLI), 26, 251, 272
Cell Site Simulators, 32–38, 261–63
Central Intelligence Agency (CIA), 2, 25, 42, 107, 297
Chicago, Illinois, 40
Chilling Effect of Surveillance, 11, 30, 208
Church Committee (Senate Select Committee to Study Governmental Operations with Respect to Intelligence Activities), 2, 3, 6, 14, 256
Church, Frank, 2, 297
Citron, Danielle Keats, 124
Clarke, Roger, 41
Cohen, Julie, 8
Cold War, 1, 2, 297
Collective vs. Individual Rights, 146–56
CompStat, 40

INDEX

Constitutional Convention, 149
Constitutional Interpretation, 135–39
Constitutional Remedies, 200–1
  Exclusionary Rule, 217–24
  Miranda Warnings, 195–202
  Warrant Requirement, 202–17
Counter-Majoritarian, 136

Data Brokers, 41
Day, William, 218
de Blasio, William, 52
Declaration of Independence, 145, 148
Democracy, 109, 145, 155, 286, 296
  Political Rights, 146, 152, 154–55
  Self-Governance, 8, 146, 152, 157, 296
Department of Defense (DOD), 2, 3, 42
Department of Health and Human Services, 89, 263
Department of Homeland Security, 31, 36–7, 42
Department of Justice (DOJ), 36, 37, 44, 261
Digital Exhaust, 4, 25
Domain Awareness System (DAS), 40, 42, 83, 263
Drones (Unmanned Aerial Vehicles), 30–32, 257–60
Drug Enforcement Administration (DEA), 36

Eavesdropping, 75
Electronic Communications Privacy Act (ECPA), 3, 37, 78
Electronic Privacy Information Center (EPIC), 36
Elf on the Shelf, 10
Elster, Jon, 296
Encryption, 33–5, 106
Entick, John, 142, 156
Environmental Protection Agency (EPA), 31
Ethical Self-Development, 8, 122, 150
Exclusionary Rule, 217–24

Facebook, 13, 25–6
Fahrenheit 451, 1

Federal Bureau of Investigation (FBI), 36, 42, 44, 47, 73, 89, 107, 192, 201, 297
Federal Communications Commission (FCC), 32, 36
Federalists, 69
Fifth Amendment, 196, 199
First Amendment, 11, 30, 120, 208
Foreign Intelligence Surveillance Act (FISA), 3, 24–47
  Section 215, 44–7, 65
  Section 702, 91
Foreign Surveillance Intelligence Court (FISC), 268
Foucault, Michel, 9
Fourteenth Amendment, 198
Fourth Amendment
  Full Text, 15
  History of, 69–71, 123
  Original Meaning, 139–72
  Political Right, 154
  Standing, 89–92, 156
Frederick, William George (George III), 142
Fries, Charles, 167
Fusion Centers, 40, 265

Garner, Eric, 54
General Warrants, 69–71, 73, 125, 140–42, 154, 157, 161–62, 168–69, 190–91, 203, 224, 262, 264, 275, 277, 282
General Warrants Cases, 142, 154, 158
German Democratic Republic (East Germany), 1
Ginsburg, Douglas, 110
Ginsburg, Ruth Bader, 15
Global Positioning System, 15–16, 23, 24–6, 30, 44, 82–4, 100, 104, 110, 114, 116, 127, 134, 208, 251
Google, 4, 11, 25–6, 39–41, 88, 106
Gray, Jr., Freddie, 54, 277
Great Scotland Yard, 193
Guardian, The, 4, 45

Habeas Corpus Act, 142
Hailstorm. *See* Cell Site Simulators

INDEX

Hale, Matthew, 161
Harlan II, John Marshall, 77
Harris Corporation, 34, 36
Harris, Malcolm, 88
Hayden, Michael, 107
Hello Barbie, 41
Hoffa, James, 85
Holmes, Oliver Wendell, 134, 218
Hoofnagle, Christopher, 41
Hoover, Herbert, 198
Hoover, John Edgar, 73
Hu, Margaret, 41
Hunger Games, The, 1
Hutchins, Renée, 249
Huxley, Aldous, 1, 8

Incidental Data Gathering, 38
Information Fiduciaries, 121
Information Sharing Environments (ISE). *See* Fusion Centers
Information Society Project, 121
Intellectual Freedom, 120
Internal Revenue Service (IRS), 36, 90
International Mobile Subscriber Identity (IMSI) Catchers. *See* Cell Site Simulators
Internet of Things, 25, 41, 62
Internet Service Provider (ISP), 88
Inuit, 7
iPhone, 107
iPhone Decryption Controversy (2016), 107

Jackson, Robert, 154, 206
Johnson, Samuel, 144, 147, 157–58, 160, 167

Kagan, Elena, 15, 100
Kahn, Jeffrey, 12
Katz, Charles, 76
Kerr, Orin, 115
KGB (Committee for State Security, USSR), 1

Lavabit, 106, 108
Licensing Press Act, 142
Living Constitutionalism, 135–39
Location Tracking, 23–30, 251–57

Cell Site Tracking, 26
Drone Tracking, 30–2
GPS Tracking, 23
Internet of Things, 25
Metadata Tracking, 24
Radio Frequency Identification (RFID) Tracking, 27–8, 82, 251
Locke, John, 144, 158
Lord Camden. *See* Pratt, Charles
Lord of the Rings, The, 1

MacArthur, Douglass, 167
Madison, James, 139
Marshall, John, 199
Marthews, Alex, 11, 48
Maryland Farmer, The, 169, 296
Mass Surveillance, 1, 41
Massachusetts Bill of Rights, 149
Matrix, The, 1
McCarthy, Joseph, 1
Metropolitan Police Service, 193
Microsoft, 40–1
Millennials, 13
Minority Report, 1, 42
Miranda Prophylaxis/Miranda Warnings, 195–202
Montagu-Dunk, George, 142
Moore, Jr., Barrington, 7
Mosaic Theory, 109–16
  Durational Approach, 116
Murphy, Francis, 75

National Association for the Advancement of Colored People (NAACP), 283
National Security Agency (NSA), 2, 4, 25–6, 33, 36, 42, 44–7, 89, 107, 263, 265, 270
Natural Law, 145
New Hampshire Bills of Rights, 149
New York City Police Department (NYPD), 50, 52, 279, 285
New York Times, 44, 45
New York, New York, 40, 42, 50, 52, 66, 71, 88, 139, 193, 276, 284
New Yorker, The, 12
No-Fly List, 12

Non-Disclosure Agreements, 36
NSA Surveillance
  APSTARS, 44
  BLACKBOOK, 44
  BLARNEY, 43
  Byblos, 43
  CATALYST, 44
  DISHFIRE, 43
  ESCHELON, 42
  EVILOLIVE, 43
  FAIRVIEW, 43
  GHOSTFIRE, 44
  OAKSTAR, 43
  PICES, 43
  PINWALE, 43
  PREFER, 43
  PRISM, 42
  RHINEHART, 43
  Section 215, Telephonic Metadata, 44–47
  SKYNET, 44
  SPITFIRE, 43
  STELLARWIND, 43
  STORMBREW, 43
  TRACFIN, 43
  TUNDRAFREEZE, 43
  UPSTREAM, 43
  VoiceRT, 43
  WELLSPRING, 43
  XKEYSCORE, 42

Occupy Wall Street, 88
Odysseus, 137
Olmstead, Roy, 73
Originalism, 135–39
Orwell, George, 1, 3, 5, 8, 40, 298
Otis, James, 70, 143, 154, 161–63

Pandora, 24
Panopticon, 8
Peel, Robert, 193
Pell, Stephanie, 33
Pennsylvania Declaration of Rights, 149
Plain Language Action and Information Network, 167
Police
  History of, 71, 191–95
  Militarization of, 194

Pratt, Charles, 142
Preamble, 145
Precommitment, 296, 298
Pretextual Stops, 98
Privacy, 6–14
Privacy International, 6
Private Law Enforcement, 192
Prohibition, 195
Public Observation Doctrine, 15, 78–84, 159, 249
  and Tracking, 82
  and Visual Surveillance, 82

Racial Discrimination
  Disparate Impact, 5, 52–5, 276
  Implicit Bias, 54
Radio Frequency Identification (RFID), 27–28, 82, 251
Reasonable Expectation of Privacy Test, 77
Red Scare, The, 1
Regulating Surveillance
  Big Data, 263–75
  Cell Site Simulators, 261–63
  Content-Based Approach, 120–24
  Drones/Unmanned Aerial Vehicles, 257–60
  Durational Approach, 116
  Market Approaches, 106–9
  Minimization, 255, 259, 262
  Mosaic Theory, 109–16
  Stop and Frisk, 275–85
  Technology-Centered Approach, 124
  Tracking Technologies, 251–57
Reid, Richard, 265
Richards, Neil, 120
Right to Quantitative Privacy, 124
Roberts, John, 114, 128, 208, 215, 253
Rumsfeld, Donald, 4

Saint Nicholas (Santa Claus), 10
Scalia, Antonin, 15, 98, 99, 104, 108, 117, 122, 125, 136, 138, 202, 204, 208
Scheindlin, Shira, 293
Second Earl of Halifax. *See* Montagu-Dunk, George

INDEX

Sentelle, David, 112, 117
September 11, 2001, Terrorist Attacks, 44, 50, 270
Seventeenth Amendment, 149
Silent Circle, 106, 108
Simon, David, 24
Slobogin, Christopher, 41, 118
Snowden, Edward, 4, 11, 26, 42
Social Contract, 145
Soghoian, Christopher, 33
Sotomayor, Sonia, 11, 15–16, 29, 100, 104, 111, 202, 208, 211
Soviet Union (USSR), 1
Standing, Article III, 91
Standing, Fourth Amendment, 15, 89–92
Star Chamber, 141, 197
Star Trek, 8
Stasi (Ministerium für Staatssicherheit), 1
Stewart, Potter, 76
Stingrays. *See* Cell Site Simulators
Stop and Frisk, 5, 48–55, 92–99, 275–85
Story, Joseph, 219
Sunby, Scott, 68

Taft, William Howard, 74
Target, 39
Tenth Amendment, 149
Terminator, The, 1
The Reasonableness Clause, 139–44
The Warrant Clause, 139–44
Third Party Doctrine, 15, 84–89, 159, 249
Tolkien, J.R.R., 1

Tor, 106
Torres, Analisa, 52
Total Information Awareness (Terrorism Information Awareness), 3
Townshend Acts, 70
Tracking. *See* Location Tracking
Triggerfish. *See* Cell Site Simulators
Tucker, Catherine, 11, 48
Twitter, 13, 26, 88

USA Freedom Act, 44, 47, 270
USA Patriot Act, 45, 47

Verizon, 44–5

War on Terror, 4, 5, 124, 297
Warrant Requirement, 202–17
Warren, Samuel, 74
Washington Post, The, 4, 45
Watergate, 2
Webster, Noah, 167
Wickersham Report, 198
Wilkes, John, 142, 192, 282
Wire, The, 24
Wiretap Act, 37, 78, 254, 258, 262, 266, 275, 286
Wiretapping, 2, 34–5, 74, 78, 255
Worshipful Company of Stationers and Newspaper Makers, 141
Writs of Assistance, 70, 71, 73, 125, 140, 141, 154, 157, 161, 168, 190–91, 203, 262, 264, 275

Yahoo, 4, 88
Yugoslavia, 1